Treatment Approaches for Alcohol and Drug Dependence

Treatment Approaches for Alcohol and Drug Dependence

An Introductory Guide

Second Edition

Tracey J. Jarvis
Jenny Tebbutt
Richard P. Mattick
Fiona Shand
National Drug and Alcohol Research Centre
University of New South Wales, Australia

Foreword by
Nick Heather
Northumbria University, Newcastle Upon Tyne, UK

JOHN WILEY & SONS, LTD

Other Wiley Editorial Offices

John Wiley & Sons Inc., 111 River Street, Hoboken, NJ 07030, USA

Jossey-Bass, 989 Market Street, San Francisco, CA 94103-1741, USA

Wiley-VCH Verlag GmbH, Boschstr. 12, D-69469 Weinheim, Germany

John Wiley & Sons Australia Ltd, 33 Park Road, Milton, Queensland 4064, Australia

John Wiley & Sons (Asia) Pte Ltd, 2 Clementi Loop #02-01, Jin Xing Distripark, Singapore 129809

John Wiley & Sons Canada Ltd, 22 Worcester Road, Etobicoke, Ontario, Canada M9W 1L1

Wiley also publishes its books in a variety of electronic formats. Some content that appears
in print may not be available in electronic books.

Library of Congress Cataloging-in-Publication Data

Treatment approaches for alcohol and drug dependence : an introductory guide / Tracey
J. Jarvis ... [et al.] ; foreword by Nick Heather. – 2nd ed.
    p. cm.
  Previous ed. cataloged under: Jarvis, Tracey J.
  Includes bibliographical references and index.
  ISBN-13 978-0-470-09039-8 (pbk. : alk. paper)
  ISBN-10 0-470-09039-1 (pbk. : alk. paper)
  1. Substance abuse – Treatment. I. Jarvis, Tracey J.
  RC564.J37 2005
  616.86'06 – dc22

                                                            2004026270

British Library Cataloguing in Publication Data

A catalogue record for this book is available from the British Library

ISBN-13 978-0-470-09039-8 (pbk)
ISBN-10 0-470-09039-1 (pbk)

Project management by Originator, Gt Yarmouth, Norfolk (typeset in 10/12pt Times)
Printed and bound in Great Britain by Antony Rowe Ltd, Chippenham, Wiltshire
This book is printed on acid-free paper responsibly manufactured from sustainable forestry
in which at least two trees are planted for each one used for paper production.

To Our Families

Contents

About the Authors   ix

Practice Sheets and Client Handouts   xi

Foreword by Nick Heather   xiii

How to Read this Book   xv

Acknowledgements   xix

PART I LAYING THE FOUNDATIONS

1 General Counselling Skills   3

2 Assessment   19

3 Motivational Interviewing   45

4 Goal Setting   63

PART II STRATEGIES FOR ACTION

5 Brief and Early Interventions   79

6 Problem-solving Skills   95

7 Drink and Drug Refusal Skills 103

8 Assertiveness Skills 107

 9 Communication Skills   121

10 Cognitive Therapy.   129

11 Relaxation Training.   143

12 Behavioural Self-management.   155

13 Involving Concerned Others.   169

14 Pharmacotherapies   193

PART III MAINTAINING CHANGE

15 Self-help Groups   211

16 Relapse Prevention Training.   221

17 Extended Care   237

PART IV SPECIAL GROUPS AND MANAGEMENT ISSUES

18 Case Management.   243

19 Working with Young People   253

20 Dual Diagnosis.   269

PART V DESIGNING AN INTERVENTION

21 Putting It All Together   291

22 Vignettes   299

Index.   315

About the Authors

Tracey J. Jarvis, Jenny Tebbutt, Dr Richard P. Mattick and Fiona Shand, National Drug and Alcohol Research Centre, University of New South Wales, Sydney, NSW 2052, Australia.

Tracey Jarvis is a clinical psychologist with expertise in the treatment of substance abuse and dependence, post-traumatic stress disorder and other mental health problems. She has developed tertiary level educational materials and is an experienced trainer in the drug and alcohol field. She has also published research articles in scholarly journals and been responsible for a review of treatment outcome research.

Jenny Tebbutt is a clinical psychologist with extensive experience in the forensic field. She has expertise in the complex psychological treatment and case management of court mandated adolescent and adult clients. She has a strong background in drug and alcohol and child abuse research. She has also published articles in scholarly journals.

Richard P. Mattick is the Professor of Drug and Alcohol Studies at the University of New South Wales, Sydney within the Faculty of Medicine where he is the Director of the National Drug and Alcohol Research Centre. He has authored many scientific articles and books. His fields of expertise include the management of opioid and cocaine dependence, the treatment of young people and the application of pharmacotherapies for alcohol and other drug dependence.

Fiona Shand is a senior research officer with the National Drug and Alcohol Research Centre in Sydney, Australia. She has a background in the development of training materials. More recently she managed the development of evidence-based guidelines for the treatment of alcohol dependence for the Australian Government's National Alcohol Strategy. Fiona has also published articles in scientific journals.

Practice Sheets and Client Handouts

A Decisional Balance Sheet 61
Planning for Change 75
Levels of Risk in Drinking Alcohol 94
Six Steps to Successful Problem-solving 100
Problem-solving (example) 101
Problem-solving (Practice Sheet) 102
Bill of Assertive Rights 119
Common Thinking Errors 137
Strategies for Challenging Negative Thoughts 139
Thought-monitoring (example) 140
Thought-monitoring (Practice Sheet) 141
Monitoring Your Muscle Tension 153
Guidelines for Sensible Drinking 164
Tips for Drinking in Moderation 165
Day Diary 166
Number of Standard Drinks and Blood Alcohol Concentration (Men) 167
Number of Standard Drinks and Blood Alcohol Concentration (Women) . . . 168
Catch Your Partner Doing Something Nice 192
Medication Monitoring Card 207
The Twelve Steps of Alcoholics Anonymous 218
The Twelve Steps of Narcotics Anonymous 219
Urges and Cravings Diary 235
Handy Links 268

Foreword

Roughly ten years ago I wrote a Foreword for the first edition of this book and I am delighted to have the opportunity of doing the same for the second edition. By all accounts, the first edition was a great success and has been found invaluable as a recommended text by many drug and alcohol courses around the world. Building on this secure foundation, the authors have added several chapters and generally brought the text up to date to reflect the new knowledge of treatment effectiveness and best practice that has accumulated in the years since the first edition was published.

As this suggests, there have been major advances in the field of treating drug and alcohol problems during the last 10 years, and these are all taken into account in this second edition. For example, there has been an enormous expansion of interest among researchers and practitioners alike in the treatment philosophy and associated skills known as 'motivational interviewing' and this has been reflected in the book, not only in Chapter 3 but also in Chapter 1, *General Counselling Skills*, and indeed throughout the text. A related phenomenon is the burgeoning application of 'brief interventions', especially in the movement to broaden the base of interventions to include the many people who may not be seeking help for a substance-related problem but are risking or actually harming their health and welfare by their use of a psychoactive substance. This is covered in Chapter 5, *Brief and Early Motivation*, where it is made clear that the remit of brief interventions extends beyond alcohol problems to several other substance use disorders.

From a different perspective, we have seen particularly important developments in research and clinical applications of pharmacotherapies for addictive disorders and these form the basis for Chapter 14. While the special substance-related problems of younger members of the community had been well recognised in the early 1990s, they are now of even greater significance, since the increase in these problems around the world shows no signs of abating. This is recognised in the second edition by the allocation of a separate chapter on working with young people (Chapter 19). This list of significant advances in the field could be multiplied; suffice it merely to say that no major development in the drug and alcohol treatment field has failed to have an influence on the second edition.

With regard to the research foundations for the guidance offered in the book, the first edition was based squarely on the findings of a Quality Assurance Project that had been carried out at the *National Drug and Alcohol Research Centre (NDARC)* in Sydney during my time as Director of the centre. This original basis for the book has remained in place—quite properly since this project was a milestone in the history of attempts to summarise evidence relating to treatment effectiveness in the drug and alcohol field, and has had a considerable impact in Australia and internationally. At the same time, the new edition has taken advantage of the many other systematic reviews and meta-analyses of relevant evidence that have appeared in the years since. One particular influence on the present volume has been a review of the evidence on the treatment of alcohol problems commissioned by the Australian government and carried out by staff at NDARC (Shand, Gates, Fawcett & Mattick, 2003a). This in turn led to the production of guidelines for the treatment of alcohol problems, again by NDARC staff (Shand, Gates, Fawcett & Mattick, 2003b).

In case it should be thought that the Australian background to this book would give it a somewhat parochial flavour, nothing could be further from the truth. There was a time in the distant past when Australia did indeed lag considerably behind Europe and North America in its standards of research and practice in the drug and alcohol field. The injection of funding and human resources brought about by the introduction of the *National Drug and Alcohol Strategy* in the mid-1980s, later reformulated as the *National Drug Strategy*, has radically changed this picture. As someone who has lived and worked in both Australia and the UK and has had a close involvement with the drug and alcohol field in the USA and mainland Europe, I can safely say that the quality of research and scholarship in this field in Australia is now on a par with any in the world. One only wishes that the UK, for example, had been as far-sighted as Australia in creating adequately funded research facilities and national strategies to combat both alcohol and illicit drug problems. Thus there is no need to excuse in any way the Australian origins of this book; its relevance is truly international.

It is to be hoped that this edition will prove as useful to trainers and practitioners as its predecessor. There is no reason to think it will not and every reason to expect that it will.

Nick Heather
Newcastle upon Tyne, UK
October, 2004

REFERENCES

Shand, F., Gates, J., Fawcett, J. & Mattick, R. (2003a). *The Treatment of Alcohol Problems: A Review of the Evidence*. Canberra: Commonwealth Department of Health and Ageing.

Shand, F., Gates, J., Fawcett, J. & Mattick, R. (2003b). *Guidelines for the Treatment of Alcohol Problems*. Canberra: Commonwealth Department of Health and Ageing.

How to Read this Book

WHO IS THIS BOOK FOR?

This book is written for people whose work involves assisting clients to change their use of alcohol and/or other drugs. In the text we refer to you as a 'therapist' and the person seeking help as 'your client'. We trust that you will find this book equally useful whether you work in an inpatient unit, therapeutic community or outpatient setting. If you are a student you might also find this book a valuable introduction to a number of new methods or strategies that you might not have seen applied to the field of alcohol and other drugs. For established therapists this book provides guidelines to enable you to further refine your methods and to apply them in systematic ways that are designed to increase their effectiveness.

WHAT IS IN THIS BOOK?

This book provides brief, user-friendly descriptions of specific techniques that have been found to be effective in the treatment of substance abuse problems. We have chosen techniques that were recommended by clinical experts in the Quality Assurance Project and the Guidelines for the Treatment of Alcohol Problems (see *Foreword*). This book explains how to use these techniques to help your clients change their behaviour. In each chapter you will find:

- Information about the recommended use of the technique.
- A description of key concepts underlying the technique.
- An introductory guide to applying the technique and some trouble shooting of any common problems you might encounter.
- A list of detailed resource materials to follow up and, in some cases, a list of self-help material that you can recommend to your client.
- Where appropriate, instruments for assessment.

- Where appropriate, practice exercises and handout sheets for use with your clients. Some of these client resources are also available free online to purchasers of the print version. Visit www.wiley.com/go/treatmentapproaches to access and download these flexible aids to working with your clients. Many are formatted in Word so that you can customise them for your clients.

WHAT IS NOT IN THIS BOOK?

- This book does not provide session-by-session plans for therapy. Instead we provide a guide for using the basic building blocks of therapy.
- Various therapists and researchers have tended to teach the same skills in slightly different ways. We have not described all of these variations in this book and we strongly recommend that you refer to the *Resources List* at the end of each chapter for further information.
- Treatment research literature has not usually been included in the *Resources Lists* (except where it offers practical guidelines).
- Tobacco use is not specifically addressed in this book because it is well covered elsewhere.
- *This book is not designed to teach clinical skills.* To train clinical personnel, there is a need for specialist training courses. This book should not replace such courses although it may be a valuable resource tool for both trainers and students.

HOW DO YOU USE THIS BOOK?

The key to using this book is *flexibility*. For example, Chapter 2, *Assessment* outlines all the areas relevant to assessing clients who misuse alcohol or other drugs. You may choose to adopt this comprehensive assessment procedure or, if your treatment is intended to be brief, focus on one or two specific areas such as your client's drug use or drinking and the physical and personal negative consequences of that behaviour.

The choice of which combination of treatment techniques to use will emerge out of a process of negotiation with your client. The decision will depend both on the goal of the treatment and on any other specific needs of your client that might be revealed during assessment or as therapy progresses. You might, for example, start off by working on problem solving and relapse prevention training and then later add sessions on assertiveness training because it has become clear that your client needs to develop assertiveness skills.

We do not provide any specific guidelines on the length of treatment. Some techniques require a minimum number of sessions to achieve results (such as relaxation training) while the duration of others will depend on careful monitoring over time (such as pharmacotherapies). The length of your treatment intervention will also depend on a number of factors such as the time and resources you have available, your client's needs, and how long it takes for your client to learn to apply new skills to everyday life.

In Chapter 21, *Putting It All Together* we offer some guidelines to help you tailor a suitable therapy programme for your client. Chapter 22, *Vignettes* gives practical examples of how various techniques can be combined to meet your client s needs.

A NOTE ON GENDER

The techniques described in this book are appropriate for both male and female clients. We have therefore simply alternated the gender of the client referred to in each of the chapters.

RESOURCES LIST

The texts that we have used as key resources for this book are:

Hester, R.K. & Miller, W.R. (1995). *Handbook of Alcoholism Treatment Approaches: Effective Alternatives* (2nd edn). Boston: Allyn and Bacon.

Miller, W.R. & Rollnick, S. (2002). *Motivational Interviewing: Preparing People to Change Addictive Behavior* (2nd edn). New York: Guilford Press.

Monti, P.M., Kadden, R.M., Rohsenow, D.J., Cooney, N.L. & Abrams, D.B. (2002). *Treating Alcohol Dependence: A Coping Skills Training Guide* (2nd edn). New York: Guilford Press.

Shand, F., Gates, J., Fawcett, J. & Mattick, R.P. (2003). *Guidelines for the Treatment of Alcohol Problems*. Canberra: Australian Government Department of Health and Ageing.
  —Available at: www.health.gov.au/pubhlth/publicat/document/alcprobguide.pdf

Acknowledgements

We acknowledge the assistance of Meredith Adams, Bob Cherry, Loretta Elkins, Nick Heather, John Howard, Gary Lake, Kaylene Noonan, Katy O'Neill, Justine O'Sullivan, Garth Popple, Alison Bell, T. Sitharthan and Amanda Baker for their assistance with our first edition.

Many thanks to Dr John Howard (Director of Clinical Services, Training and Research, Ted Noffs Foundation, NSW, Australia), Dr Katy O Neil (Clinical Psychologist, Drug, Alcohol and Gambling Service, Hornsby Hospital, NSW, Australia) and Dr Claudia Sannibale (Senior Clinical Psychologist, Drug Health Services, Royal Prince Alfred Hospital, NSW, Australia) for reading and commenting on chapters for the new edition and providing feedback based on their clinical expertise. Their contribution has assisted us to develop the text so that it would be relevant and user-friendly to therapists in this field. We also thank Eva Congreve, Josephina Kim, Dr Judy Sherrington and Dr Wendy Swift for their expert assistance. Many thanks to Emeritus Professor Nick Heather (Northumbria University, Newcastle upon Tyne, UK) for once again agreeing to write our Foreword. This work was partly supported by the Australian Government Department of Health and Ageing.

1

Laying the Foundations

General Counselling Skills

RECOMMENDED USE

When it comes to counselling, there is nothing unique about the field of alcohol and other drugs. The same skills that are effective for general counselling are also effective for counselling people with drug-related problems. Research has shown that treatment for alcohol and other drug problems is more likely to be successful if therapists use empathic counselling skills (Miller, Benefield & Tonigan, 1993). On the other hand, counselling alone is not usually sufficient to change the drug-taking behaviour of most clients. Rather, good counselling skills will enable you to develop a strong working relationship with your client that will support the implementation of specific strategies designed to combat the drinking or drug problem.

GOALS

The counselling process therefore aims:

- To build a trusting relationship where your client can communicate her concerns and describe her behaviours without fear of judgement.
- To encourage your client to see treatment as a mutual enterprise where she makes active decisions and where you value her ideas and support her endeavours. Your client is encouraged to develop a sense of responsibility and self-confidence.
- To reduce your client's fear and distrust of treatment programmes and thereby encourage her to continue attending treatment and follow-up appointments. Not all clients who are assessed will feel ready for treatment. If a client's initial experience of the treatment staff and environment is positive, this may encourage her to return for treatment at some future point in time.

METHOD

The counselling style described here combines the client-centred approach outlined by Egan (2002) with the motivational interviewing style developed by Miller and Rollnick (2002). It is an approach that encourages your client to explore her own concerns through open-ended questions and empathic feedback. It is client-centred because your client defines which issues are important. However, it is not a wholly 'non-directional' approach, because the motivational interviewing style (Chapter 3) selectively emphasises those issues that favour a change in your client's drug-using behaviour.

This approach is quite different from the style of counselling that involves confrontation. We do not recommend that you confront your client or argue with her in order to convince her of the need for change. In fact, confrontation can be quite counterproductive because it increases your client's resistance to change and might even cause her to increase her substance use (Miller *et al.*, 1993). Instead, we suggest that you foster your client's self-confrontation through open-ended questions and selective feedback.

The ideal therapist is someone who:

- Shows empathy and respect for clients.
- Develops a supportive relationship with the client.
- Has an organised approach to each case and takes careful progress notes.
- Is creative and imaginative.
- Shows self-awareness by not imposing personal concerns on clients.
- Has good common sense and social intelligence.
- Is action-oriented.

In drug and alcohol work, there is an increasing focus on the *engagement* of clients in the treatment process. This focus is partly a response to the high number of clients dropping out of drug and alcohol treatment. The more engaged your client is in the treatment process as indicated by her attending and participating in sessions in a meaningful way, the more likely she is to succeed in her goals. Successful engagement depends both on client characteristics and on your ability to develop a strong therapeutic relationship which is perceived as helpful and empathic (Shand, Gates, Fawcett & Mattick, 2003). It is also helpful to discuss your client's expectations about how long she will be in treatment. For example, you might agree to review her progress after a certain number of sessions. Research also suggests that engaging and retaining clients in treatment depends on overcoming any practical barriers (such as the need for transportation or child care) and the inclusion of relapse prevention training in your intervention.

When you and your client decide to terminate counselling, allow time to review your work together, to reflect on her feelings about finishing and to discuss your plan for extended care (Chapter 17, *Extended Care*). Of course, your client might drop out of treatment before *you* think she is ready! If that happens, a follow-up phone call may help to renew contact.

The microskills that will assist you in effective engagement and counselling are described below.

EMPATHY

Empathy is both a counselling value and a communication skill. As a value, it means that you are committed to understanding your client from *her point of view*. It is as if you are standing in the other person's shoes, looking at the world through her eyes and asking 'What is it like to be this person?'

Empathy requires an *attitude of respect* towards your client. As an empathic therapist your role is to help your client to find her own solutions rather than to impose a solution on her. Show your client that you believe in her ability to make effective choices and that you value the time and effort you spend with her. Convey your empathy not only in what you say, but also in your intonation and body language. Be aware of any differences between you and your client in cultural background, age or gender and always check the accuracy of any assumptions you might make about your client's experiences.

Empathy is different from sympathy. If you feel sympathy, you tend to take sides with your client, and this can distort your ability to hear the whole story. For example, when feeling sorry for your client, you might overlook the way in which self-pity is preventing her from taking constructive action. Being empathic does not mean that you always agree with your client's opinion. Rather, it involves accepting her view and being interested in exploring its implications.

THINGS TO AVOID

The key to an empathic approach is to avoid judgemental or evaluative responses. You are trying to understand how it is for the client, not how *it should be*. Some non-empathic approaches can obstruct further understanding of your client's perspective. Miller and Rollnick (2002) refer to these approaches as 'roadblocks'. They include:

- Ordering or commanding.
- Warning or threatening.
- Giving advice or providing solutions.
- Arguing or persuading.
- Moralising.
- Disagreeing, judging or criticising.
- Ridiculing or labelling.
- Interpreting or analysing.
- Reassuring or sympathising.
- Withdrawing, distracting or humouring.

REFLECTIVE LISTENING

As a communication skill, empathy involves sharing your understanding of your client's point of view. One way to do this is by listening reflectively. Listen to what your client says and notice other signs of emotional expression, such as her emphasis on certain words, her facial expressions and body language, and the intensity of her expressed feelings. Try to identify the core messages being expressed and then share them with your client. For example, Egan (2002) suggests a formula that you could use to guide you:

You feel ...   (*add client's expressed feelings*)
Because ...   (*add the experiences and behaviours that give rise to the feelings*)

For example:

CLIENT: 'I don't even see why I have to *be* here! I wouldn't have come except my parents threatened to kick me out of home if I didn't.'

THERAPIST: 'You feel really angry because your parents pressured you to come against your own judgement. You don't want to get kicked out but you don't want to be here either.'

Of course, this formula is only a starting point. If you start every sentence this way, your conversation will seem less than genuine. However, the formula is a useful reminder as you are developing your skills of empathy and reflective listening.

What we *assume* people mean is not necessarily what they *really* mean. Reflective listening enables you to:

- Show your client that you are really listening to her.
- Check whether your understanding of what your client has said is consistent with her intended meaning.
- Feed back your client's stated concerns, thereby strengthening her awareness of her own reasons for change.
- Empower your client to correct inaccurate feedback, while studying herself through your reflection.

Miller and Rollnick (2002) have also suggested that feedback in the form of a statement, rather than a question, is likely to be more effective in encouraging your client to explore. The following example taken from their book shows how exploring one of your client's concerns with reflective listening might encourage your client to identify other concerns:

CLIENT: 'I worry sometimes that I may be drinking too much for my own good.'

THERAPIST: 'You've been drinking quite a bit.'

CLIENT: 'I don't really feel like it's that much. I can drink a lot and not feel it.'

THERAPIST: 'More than most people.'

CLIENT: 'Yes. I can drink most people under the table.'

THERAPIST: 'And that's what worries you.'

CLIENT: 'Well, that and how I feel. The next morning I'm usually in bad shape. I feel ...'

(Miller & Rollnick, 2002, p. 70)

ROLLING WITH RESISTANCE

Resistance is an observable behaviour (such as arguing, interrupting, denying and ignoring) that occurs during treatment and signals that the client is moving away from a particular change. Resistant behaviours are often responses to the content and style of an interaction between a client and her therapist. It is important to avoid evoking or strengthening resistance because the more your client resists the less likely she is to change. That is, resistance allows clients to express well-practised reasons for not changing. There may be a number of reasons clients 'resist'. For example, a client might have low self-esteem and little belief in her ability to change. Alternatively, she might have been coerced into treatment and therefore not yet be ready to consider change.

Miller and Rollnick (2002) have coined the term 'rolling with resistance' to describe non-confrontational methods for dealing with clients' resistance. Most of these involve reflective listening techniques. For example, suppose your client says:

'I don't see why my drinking is such a problem. All my friends drink as much as I do.'

By using some of the methods outlined by Miller and Rollnick (2002), you could respond to this statement in the following ways.

Simple Reflection

Acknowledge your client's resistance in your reflective response. For example:

'You can't see how *your* drinking can be a problem when your friends don't seem to have any problems.'

Amplified Reflection

Couch your feedback in an amplified or exaggerated form to elicit the other side of your client's ambivalence. This should be done in a way that avoids a sarcastic tone. For example:

'If your friends have no problem with their drinking then there's nothing for you to worry about.'

Double-sided Reflection

Acknowledge what your client has said and add the other side of your client's ambivalence. Try to draw on things that your client has said previously.

'I can see how this must be confusing for you. On the one hand you've come in because you're concerned about drinking and how it affects you, and on the other hand, it seems like you're not drinking any more than your friends do.'

Miller and Rollnick (2002) have provided further comprehensive examples and additional techniques in their chapter on *Responding to Resistance*.

OPEN-ENDED QUESTIONS

Ask your client questions that encourage further exploration. Closed questions that require a 'yes' or 'no' response or a one-word answer are useful for getting at specific information. They should be used sparingly, however, because they can turn the therapy session into a fact-finding mission. They discourage further exploration by your client. Try to transform them into open-ended questions. For example:

'Has your drinking changed over time?'

vs.

'How has your drinking changed over time?'

ELABORATING

Use open-ended questions to elaborate on any statements by your client that express concern about her substance use, her intention to make a particular change or her feelings of self-confidence. For example, when she expresses a desire to make a change in her substance use, flesh out the details by asking 'What type of change?', 'When would be a good time?' or 'Can you give me an example?'

REFRAMING

Reframing is a way of acknowledging what your client has said and, at the same time, drawing her attention to a different meaning or interpretation that is likely to support change. For example, past experiences with treatment failure can be re-framed as evidence that your client may not have found the approach most suitable for her. Reframing your client's explanation of tolerance can also be important (see p. 57).

AFFIRMING THE POSITIVES

Show support for your client's efforts during therapy with direct affirmations. For example, you should acknowledge the courage involved in coming to therapy and commend your client for taking that step. Highlight your client's strengths in coping or refraining from drug use. Draw her attention to those positive things that she might have trivialised. If your client seems to be overwhelmed by her problems, use solution-focused questions to identify exceptions to the problem (Chapter 18, *Case Management*).

SUMMARISING

Summary statements help to draw together the material that you have discussed with your client and can be used for many purposes. Show your client that you are actively listening by summarising the issues that she has raised. Use summaries to:

- Highlight important discoveries.
- Prompt a more thorough exploration.
- Give the broader picture when your client seems blocked.
- Provide an opportunity for your client to hear her own stated reasons for change.
- Highlight your client's ambivalence by linking the negatives and positives together in the one statement (e.g., 'On the one hand, you have said that you like drinking because . . . while, on the other hand, you are concerned about . . . So it sounds like you are torn two ways').
- Close a discussion.

CONFIDENCE TO CHANGE

Raising your client's confidence in her ability to change is an intermediate step towards changing her drug use. It is important to foster an optimistic view that change is achievable. Try to ensure that the weekly goals of therapy are within your client's capabilities so that she will experience a sense of mastery. Your own belief that your client can succeed will also strongly influence her expectations. Be aware that there is a power relationship between you as the therapist and your client. The more you control the process, the less confidence you are placing in your client's ability to make appropriate choices and to take responsibility for changing. Empower your client by helping her to make her own choices and congratulating her when she makes progress.

WORKING IN A GROUP

All of the techniques described in this book can be applied in a group situation. In fact, the group setting provides some unique features that enhance some of these techniques. For example, a group of people can generate a greater variety of ideas in a brainstorming exercise (pp. 97–98) than you and your client can alone. In learning communication skills, your client can benefit from practising with, and receiving feedback from, people with different perspectives. Her plans for relapse prevention might also become more refined as she observes what works and what doesn't work for other people. Your client may also benefit from the opportunity for peer support. This is particularly the case if your clients continue their support for each other after treatment.

Some techniques require several sessions of ongoing group practice before the skills are acquired (e.g., relaxation therapy and assertiveness training). Other techniques could be used within an open group where members vary from week to week (e.g., relapse prevention and refusal skills could be applied in an open group). The following section mainly draws on the work of Vanicelli (1982) who has provided specific guidelines for running groups with alcohol-dependent people. We have also drawn from Monti, Kadden, Rohsenow, Cooney and Abrams (2002) on guidelines about group rules.

GROUP COMPOSITION

Groups need to have a common goal. Therefore, a group that includes people working towards abstinence as well as those with a goal of moderation runs the risk of resentment, confusion and a loss of common purpose. It is better to run separate groups for clients with these different goals.

Keep your group down to a size big enough for group interaction but small enough for everyone to be able to participate. Rose (1977), for example, recommended that the ideal size for a group lies between six and nine people. Such a number will also enable you to form sub-groups, which give all group members the chance to try out newly acquired skills.

Finally, in planning your group, give some consideration to the ratio of men to women. Research suggests that women in therapy benefit more from all female groups than from mixed sex groups (Jarvis, 1992). This is particularly true if issues such as sexual abuse or domestic violence are likely to arise in the course of the group discussion.

GROUP RULES

Be quite clear and explicit in defining the group's primary goal and your clients' responsibility in working towards that goal. Tell your clients exactly what you expect of their participation in the group. Your ground rules might state:

- The minimum number of sessions that you wish clients to attend.
- That clients should attend regularly, be on time and give advance notice if they are unable to meet these requirements. Try to prevent early drop-outs from the group by contacting those clients who miss any of the first few sessions and encouraging them to attend the next one.
- That clients should not come to sessions under the influence of alcohol or other drugs. Explain that such behaviour would interfere with their ability to concentrate on the group tasks and might also distract other members of the group. If a client breaks this rule, she will be asked to leave the session and encouraged to come next time, when she is sober.
- That the identities of fellow group members and all the personal issues discussed during group sessions should remain confidential and not be discussed with family members or friends outside the group.

GROUP COMMUNICATION

In the initial session, invite the group to negotiate an agreement about how they intend to communicate with each other. For example, some behaviours encourage an atmosphere of trust and openness (e.g., listening to each other without interruption) while other behaviours might disempower individuals and distract the group from their goals (e.g., dominating, ridiculing, scapegoating or encouraging others to use or drink). Having a few simple rules from the outset will enable you to remind clients when their communication is likely to make others feel uncomfortable. Further discussion about how to address resistance or iatrogenic group processes are given in Chapters 3, *Motivational Interviewing* and 19, *Working with Young People*.

The group is a powerful setting for behavioural change. As noted above, members need to feel that the group is working towards a common goal and that they are supported by others in the group. Encourage this kind of 'togetherness' by reinforcing any comments by clients that show interest, concern or acceptance of other group members or positive statements about the group as a whole. For example, you might say:

'So you agree with X about ...'

Your group may go through a period where people challenge and disagree with you and each other. This is a natural process and, if handled correctly, the group will be able to move forward to a more stable and trusting level. It is important to make a distinction between disagreement that leads to constructive discussion within the group and disagreement that involves hostility. If group members become hostile to each other, they may undermine each other's progress and disrupt the group. Deflect hostile interaction between group members by getting them to tell you about their concerns rather than abusing each other. Emphasise empathy rather than confrontation as a model for the group.

ROLE-PLAY

Role-play is a method of practising the use of a particular skill by rehearsing a situation that is likely to occur in real life. You can role-play situations with your client in individual therapy. However, the ideal setting for role-play is in a group that provides the opportunity for clients to learn from watching each other perform the same skills. When using role-plays, always begin by modelling the skills yourself, giving your clients an example to follow. At the end of each role-play ask the 'player' to say what she thought she did well and what she would have liked to have done differently. Then ask the group for some feedback, emphasising that comments must be constructive and specific, focusing on body language, tone or what was said. After the group have offered their feedback you can then offer your comments, restricting yourself to a couple of positive and critical points. Role-play can be used for groups learning problem solving, drink or drug refusal skills, assertiveness, communication skills and relapse prevention. It may also be useful in couples therapy (see Chapter 13, *Involving Concerned Others*).

TERMINATION

Prepare your group in advance for breaks in the group routine (such as public holidays) and for the time when the group is going to finish. For example, you might want to encourage sub-groups or pairs of clients to exchange phone numbers so that they can support each other's maintenance plans in the absence of group sessions. Further suggestions that you might want to discuss with the group are in Chapter 17, *Extended Care*.

ETHICAL PRACTICE

Ethics are standards of professional behaviour set up to ensure that your client's rights are respected throughout the treatment process. It is the responsibility of all therapists to maintain ethical behaviour in relation to their clients, trainees and colleagues. Ethical behaviour is guided by two principles: being helpful (beneficence) and not doing harm (nonmaleficence).

Your professional group will have a code of ethics to guide you. You can also look at state laws, licensing regulations and the agreed policy and procedures of your treatment programme. Regular supervision with a more experienced colleague is an excellent way of getting support and guidance to help you make competent, ethical decisions. Peer supervision meetings and case conferences also offer opportunities to discuss and clarify ethical matters.

BOUNDARIES

The professional boundary defines the extent and limitations of the relationship with your client. It preserves your client's confidentiality and creates a 'safe space' for your client to reveal and explore personal issues. Boundaries are signified by the temporal and spatial routines of the counselling process: regular appointment times, consistent length of sessions and a dedicated counselling room. Compared with therapists, case managers and residential workers may have less firm routines of time and space (Chapter 18, *Case Management*). In these roles, you can firm the boundaries by ensuring that contact with your client is clearly linked to your professional role.

You will sometimes need to respond to situations where the boundary becomes less defined. These situations may seem ordinary and potentially harmless. For instance, would you accept a gift from your client? Your answer might depend on the context. An inexpensive token of thanks at the last session has a very different meaning from a gift offered by your client at a difficult stage in the counselling process. In the latter case, it would be ethical to politely decline the gift. Explain and discuss the benefits of keeping your relationship professional so that you can both focus on her counselling needs.

Boundaries are breached in two ways. Some breaches are inadvertent or not intentionally exploitative. These are known as boundary crossings. Commonly cited examples are: a goodbye hug initiated by your client at the completion of treatment; non-sexual physical reassurance at times of extreme stress; running a session over time; or selective self-disclosure. Repetitive boundary crossings are potentially harmful because they blur the boundary, thereby increasing the chances of boundary violation.

Boundary violation is a significant and potentially harmful breach where the therapist over-rides the client's rights or actually does harm to the client. Some examples are: affectionate or flirtatious communication; self-disclosure about the therapist's personal problems; engaging the client in illegal activities; breaking confidentiality; or having sex with a client.

PERSONAL FEELINGS IN COUNSELLING

Warm regard, trust and understanding are the basis of the counselling relationship. It is not unusual for your client to feel a degree of attachment towards you. It might even be the first time your client has experienced such an accepting relationship. However, the counselling relationship, by definition, involves unequal power. Your client is in a more exposed and vulnerable situation while you are acting from a position of expertise and relative security. Sometimes you might even have institutional authority over your client.

It is not unusual for these qualities of the counselling relationship to provoke strong emotional feelings. For example, your client might idealise you at times and, at other times, she might appear hostile. Sometimes disturbed clients can split these feelings across different workers (known as 'splitting', p. 284). Rather than taking these reactions personally, use reflective listening to help your client explore their meaning, based on her own life experiences.

You might also have strong personal reactions to your client at times. This can happen when your client's issues resonate with your own personal concerns. It can also happen if you have certain expectations which you want the client to meet. Consider, for example, how you would feel if you found out that your client had frequently lied to you about the extent of her drug use. While it is reasonable to discuss this behaviour and its consequences with your client, including how it impacts on your ability to help her—to what extent would you express your feelings of anger or sense of betrayal? A good rule of thumb is to monitor your own feelings without imposing them on your client. If you are distracted by a strong feeling, mentally put it to one side. Wait until after the session, then talk with your supervisor or deal with it personally.

There is debate about whether therapists should disclose personal things to their clients. In the 12-step approach, self-disclosure regarding one's own recovery is seen as a positive way of sharing and role modelling. However, there is a risk of taking time and attention away from your client's issues and burdening her with knowledge of your own problems.

Self-disclosure can also signal that the relationship is becoming more personal and can open the way for your client to ask further personal questions or seek friendship with you. Exactly where should you draw the line? It is helpful to ask yourself two questions before self-disclosing: (a) how will it benefit the client? and (b) how will it affect your professional boundaries? You should also consider your own privacy. For example, what if you and your client attend the same Alcoholics Anonymous meeting? Would this make it hard for you to get the full benefits of attending the meeting during times of stress or relapse?

DUAL RELATIONSHIPS

A dual relationship occurs when you take on two (or more) different roles, either at the same time or in succession, in relation to your client, your trainee or your colleague. Dual relationships cause boundary confusion because the two relationships have different boundary rules.

As an example, consider the following scenario (taken from Chapman, 1997). What might go wrong?

Scenario
You need some painting done in your office. Your client is unemployed, short of money and under-confident. You are thinking about hiring your client to do the job since it could have therapeutic benefits.

What if your client does a bad painting job? How would this impact on your counselling relationship? What if your client discloses in counselling that she has been drinking heavily? What impact might this have on your trust in her as a painter?

The personal relationship introduces issues that might impact on feelings of trust for either party.

There are many types of dual relationships that could be relevant for your work. Some are described below.

The unexpected encounter   Such encounters are particularly likely in rural settings or close communities. Consider how you might react to some of the following scenarios:

- Your child becomes friendly with your client's child.
- You bump into your client while you are both drinking alcohol at a party.
- A mutual friend introduces your client as his new date.

It is a good idea to address the incident in your next session together. Explore your client's reactions to the incident. Discuss what needs to be done to ensure her confidentiality and to rebuild the boundary in your counselling alliance.

Dual professional relationships   Sometimes you will be required to take on more than one professional role when dealing with your client. Some examples are:

- Acting as both therapist and case manager for your client.
- A client who sees you individually also attends a group therapy programme where you are the facilitator.
- A former client becomes a co-worker.

With dual professional relationships there is the risk of the two roles becoming merged so that it is not clear which role is operating at any particular time. This can lead to a breach in confidentiality (e.g., when information from one context is inadvertently raised in a different context). It can also lead to a merging of the roles so that important work gets neglected (Chapter 18, *Case Management*). If a dual professional role cannot be avoided, make sure you define the boundaries explicitly. You can, for example, use different locations and times to distinguish concurrent roles. You and your client might also discuss the potential risks ahead of time and then debrief any boundary crossings as they occur.

Personal and professional roles   The most common and potentially most harmful dual relationship occurs when you become personally involved with your client. Some examples are entering into business together, forming a friendship or inviting your client to dinner. Williams and Swartz (1998) made a useful distinction between 'being friendly' and being your client's friend. If your client seems socially isolated, the counselling relationship might be her main close contact. Explore what she wants from a friendship and how to access potential friends in her community.

Sexual relationships are the most harmful example of this type of dual relationship. There is no justification for having sexual relations with your client. Given the power dynamics of the therapeutic relationship, any sexual behaviour by therapists towards clients would be exploitative and abusive.

If you feel sexually attracted to your client, consult with your supervisor before seeing her again. The attraction may be a temporary feeling arising from your own personal issues. Sorting this out with the help of your supervisor might reduce the power of the attraction. However, if the feelings persist and you think the risk of acting on them is high, you should refer the client to another therapist. Consult with your supervisor about the best way to frame this referral for your client.

If your client acts in a sexually flirtatious or physically affectionate manner towards you, your response should be therapeutic rather than personal. This requires some degree of sensitivity and tact! You might start by acknowledging that your client's overtures reflect her sense of trust in the relationship. It's a good idea to restate your reasons for staying at a professional level and not betraying this trust. If she responds with embarrassment or anger, take an empathic, non-judgemental approach and allow time for her to express these feelings.

There is some debate about whether personal relationships with former clients are okay and, if so, how long after the end of therapy you should wait. Once you have a personal relationship with your client, her opportunities for receiving follow-up counselling from you are effectively cut off. Being aware that you might have a later relationship with your client could also influence how you do counselling now.

ETHICAL DILEMMAS

Ethical dilemmas occur when two ethical principles clash. The main ethical dilemma you are likely to face in drug and alcohol work is the obligation to notify authorities when you believe your client might harm herself or somebody else. This involves a conflict between the ethics of confidentiality and the legal duty of care to prevent physical harm. It can sometimes also involve a further dilemma in taking away your client's autonomy through involuntary admission to a psychiatric unit to prevent suicidal or homicidal behaviour. These ethical issues are further discussed in the context of dual diagnosis in Chapter 20.

RESOURCES LIST

Alcoholics Anonymous (undated). *AA Guidelines for AA Members Employed in the Alcoholism Field.*
   —A short paper on how to avoid dual relationships that might arise for AA members. Available from G.S.O., Box 459, Grand Central Station, New York, NY 10163. Alternatively, link to 'AA Guidelines' on: www.aa.org

Beck, A.T., Wright, F.D., Newman, C.F. & Liese, B.S. (2001). *Cognitive Therapy of Substance Abuse*. New York: Guilford Press.
—Chapter 4 of this book provides guidelines on how to build a collaborative therapeutic relationship and Chapter 13 discusses crisis intervention with reference to commonly encountered crisis situations.

Chapman, C. (1997). Dual relationships in substance abuse treatment: Ethical implications. *Alcoholism Treatment Quarterly*, **15**(2), 73–79.
—Deals with ethical issues specific to the drug and alcohol field, including therapists in recovery.

Dove, W.R. (1995). Ethics training for the alcohol/drug abuse professional. *Alcoholism Treatment Quarterly*, **12**(4), 19–30.
—Defines ethical dilemmas and describes common examples in the drug and alcohol field.

Edelwich, J. & Brodsky, A. (1984). Sexual dynamics of the client-counselor relationship. *Alcoholism Treatment Quarterly*, **1**(3), 99–117.
—Written from a psychodynamic perspective, this paper gives ethical guidelines on how to prevent the sexual exploitation of clients by counsellors and therapists.

Egan, G. (2001). *Exercises in Helping Skills: A Training Manual to Accompany 'The Skilled Helper'* (7th edn). Pacific Grove, CA: Brooks/Cole.
—A workbook for training empathic skills.

Egan, G. (2002). *The Skilled Helper: A Problem-Management and Opportunity-Development Approach to Helping* (7th edn). Pacific Grove, CA: Brooks/Cole.
—A comprehensive manual on the application of an empathic, client-centred style of counselling.

Jarvis, T.J. (1992). Implications of gender for alcohol treatment research: A quantitative and qualitative review. *British Journal of Addiction*, **87**, 1249–1261.
—A study that compared men and women in treatment and found that, although their success rates are similar, they have different needs that should be addressed in treatment programmes.

Liberman, R. (1970). A behavioral approach to group dynamics. 1: Reinforcement and prompting of cohesiveness in group therapy. *Behavior Therapy*, **1**, 141–175.
—Gives evidence that therapists can modify group cohesiveness by selective reinforcement.

Miller, W., Benefield, R. & Tonigan, J. (1993). Enhancing motivation for change in problem drinking: A controlled comparison of two therapist styles. *Journal of Consulting and Clinical Psychology*, **61**, 455–461.
—This study found that clients had better outcomes if their therapists were empathic rather than confrontational.

Miller, W.R. & Rollnick, S. (2002). *Motivational Interviewing: Preparing People to Change Addictive Behavior* (2nd edn). New York: Guilford Press.
—Strongly recommended as a guide to the motivational interviewing style of counselling. Chapters 5 and 8 give guidelines on how to recognise and respond effectively to your client's resistance.

Monti, P.M., Kadden, R.M., Rohsenow, D.J., Cooney, N.L. & Abrams, D.B. (2002). *Treating Alcohol Dependence: A Coping Skills Training Guide* (2nd edn). New York: Guilford Press.

—Provides brief guidelines on building groups as well as a session-by-session plan for running skills training groups.

Nurses Registration Board of NSW (1999). *Guidelines for Registered Nurses and Enrolled Nurses Regarding the Boundaries of Medical Practice.* Callaghan, New South Wales: The Centre for Nursing Research and Practice Development, Faculty of Nursing, University of Newcastle.
Available at:
http://www.nursesreg.nsw.gov.au/bounds/guidelin.htm#Information
—Although the case examples in this resource are specific to nursing, the resource has interesting models to help make ethical decisions and these are very relevant for drug and alcohol counselling.

Pearson, B. & Piazza, N. (1997). Classification of dual relationships in the helping professions. *Counselor Education and Supervision*, **37**(2), 89–99.
—A detailed discussion of practical approaches to minimise or manage dual relationships.

Rose, S.D. (1977). *Group Therapy: A Behavioral Approach.* Englewood Cliffs, NJ: Prentice-Hall.
—Provides guidelines for running behaviour therapy groups, based on research findings.

Shand, F., Gates, J., Fawcett, J. & Mattick, R.P. (2003). *Guidelines for the Treatment of Alcohol Problems.* Canberra: Australian Government Department of Health and Ageing.
—Presents evidence-based recommendations for client engagement (p. 35) and effective counselling (pp. 99–105).

Vanicelli, M. (1982). Group psychotherapy with alcoholics: Special techniques. *Journal of Studies on Alcohol*, **43**, 17–37.
—Outlines problems that are unique to running groups aimed at achieving abstinence from alcohol, and tips for resolving them.

Walters, S.T., Ogle, R. & Martin, J.E. (2002). Perils and possibilities of group-based motivational interviewing. In: W.R. Miller & S. Rollnick (eds), *Motivational Interviewing: Preparing People for Change* (2nd edn) (pp. 377–390). New York: Guilford Press.
—Discusses the dynamics of using motivational interviewing in a group setting.

Williams, J. & Swartz, M. (1998). Treatment boundaries in the case management relationship: A clinical case and discussion. *Community Mental Health Journal*, **34**(3), 299–311.
—An excellent discussion of professional boundaries with a drug and alcohol case example.

2

Assessment

BASIC GUIDELINES

Assessment is a purposeful process with several functions. Some of these are outlined below.

- Assessment enables you to gather information that will help you to plan and modify treatment goals and strategies.
- The assessment process provides the chance for you and your client to build a rapport. As your client observes your empathy and courtesy, he will be less likely to take a defensive stance about his drinking or drug use.
- Assessment results enable you to give your client feedback that will help him to develop an alternative view of his situation. This is particularly true when you personalise the health effects of his drug or alcohol use (see pp. 55–57).
- Ongoing assessment helps you and your client to monitor his progress towards treatment goals.

Assessment is *not* about filling in endless forms! Acquiring a large amount of data that is unlikely to be useful in treatment is a waste of time. Therefore, you should focus on that information which is most likely to help you tailor treatment to meet your client's needs. Although information about past experiences can help to clarify the influences that have shaped your client's behaviour, feelings and beliefs, your focus should mainly be on the 'here and now', that is your client's present situation.

In addition to identifying current needs or problems, assessment should also aim to identify the resilience, strengths and skills which your client brings to treatment. Acknowledging such strengths can help you to engage your client and to build his self-confidence and motivation for change (see pp. 248–249).

It is also important that you begin to address some of your client's most pressing concerns as soon as possible. If he perceives that little or no progress is being made in the first sessions, his motivation to stay in treatment may reduce and he might even leave. Therefore, the assessment process should be spread over several sessions, allowing time in each session for setting preliminary treatment goals and working towards those goals. As more in-depth assessment occurs, these goals and strategies can then be adjusted.

The assessment procedure, then, ideally takes the form of open-ended, semi-structured interviews where you and your client together compile a narrative history. Assure your client that what he tells you will remain confidential and will be used only for the purposes of planning his treatment. Advise your client from the outset about any exceptions to this agreement of confidentiality, such as any legal and/or ethical obligations to notify about child abuse, imminent suicide risk or a high likelihood of harm to other people. You will need to be familiar with the legal requirements for notification in your local jurisdiction. Issues of notification are further discussed in Chapters 19, *Working with Young People* and 20, *Dual Diagnosis*.

Standardised questionnaires are often a useful addition to the process of assessment, provided they are presented in the context of a relaxed interview. A well-chosen questionnaire (a) helps you to quickly obtain relevant information and (b) allows you to compare your client's results with those of other clients. If you wish to use a standardised assessment interview, there are a number of excellent inventories available. In particular, we strongly recommend the *Comprehensive Drinker Profile* (CDP) (Miller & Marlatt, 1984a) or its brief form, the *Brief Drinker Profile* (BDP) (Miller & Marlatt, 1984b) for use with drinkers, and the *Opiate Treatment Index* (OTI) (Darke, Ward, Hall, Heather & Wodak, 1991) for use with users of other drugs, especially opioids and other injectable drugs. The *Maudsley Addiction Profile* (MAP) (Marsden, Gossop & Stewart, 1998) can also be used with either drinkers or drug users.

The following sections outline the basic areas that should be covered during assessment. *The extent to which you explore each of these areas will depend upon their relevance for your client.* If you work in a setting where you are providing screening for drug and alcohol problems for the purposes of referral or brief intervention, you will not need to do an intensive assessment. Chapter 5, *Brief and Early Interventions* provides guidelines for screening drug and alcohol problems. Similarly, many clients who seek treatment for relatively mild to moderate alcohol- or drug-related problems only require brief intervention (e.g., one to five sessions). For these clients, less comprehensive assessments are also appropriate (see Chapter 5, *Brief and Early Interventions*).

ASSESSMENT OF THE ALCOHOL OR DRUG PROBLEM

THE CLIENT'S REASONS FOR COMING TO SEE YOU

Explore your client's *current* reasons for seeking help, including any specific events that influenced his decision to seek help and what he hopes to achieve by coming to see you. Are his reasons for seeking help self-generated or do they stem from social or legal coercion? If your client does not see his substance use as being a problem (which may be the case with coerced clients), he might benefit from motivational interviewing in the first session (see Chapter 3, *Motivational Interviewing*).

If your client has been coerced into treatment, he might express anger, resentment or feelings of powerlessness. Give him time to talk this through with you. Where possible, acknowledge any choices he has made within the constraints of the coercion, such as his preparedness to talk openly with you. It is also important to clarify how your own counselling role is affected by the coercion. For example, are you required to reveal information to the legal authority responsible for his attendance at counselling? Your client needs to be aware of how independent you are from the people who coerced him.

Trouble shooting

If your client is intoxicated, it is difficult to conduct a reliable assessment. In this case, focus only on developing rapport. Listen to what he wants to say but postpone formal assessment until the second session. Remind him of the importance of being unintoxicated for that next session.

PATTERN AND CONTEXT OF DRINKING OR DRUG USE

Past Use

Exploring the history of your client's substance use will help you to determine the chronicity of his problem. It will also reveal the conditions under which he has been able to abstain or moderate his drinking or drug use, as well as the triggers to heavy substance use. This information will help to guide your selection of treatment goals and will also be particularly useful when planning relapse prevention (see Chapter 16, *Relapse-prevention Training*). A discussion about previous periods of abstinence—however short—can also help to build your client's confidence. As part of this history taking, also ask about your client's previous treatment experiences.

Current Use

You will need to collect a detailed description of your client's current substance use. To do this, you may need to look at three areas of drug use. These are discussed below.

Alcohol use: Ask your client how frequently he drinks. Does he drink daily or have periodic bouts of binge drinking? Find out how much alcohol your client drinks per week, on a typical drinking day and on a heavy drinking day. Your client may feel a little self-conscious about reporting exact amounts. It can be useful to overestimate your client's level of drinking, thereby allowing him to bring the estimate down to the correct level, without feeling embarrassed about admitting the large amount he drinks. An accurate estimate of your client's drinking levels provides a baseline for comparison to later stages in therapy, as well as being one index of his alcohol dependence. Drinking levels are usually measured in 'standard drinks'. These are defined on pp. 80–81. The risks associated with different levels of drinking are described on p. 94.

Ask your client to describe the sequence of events on a typical drinking day. Ask open-ended questions (p. 8) about the events and activities typically associated with drinking. For example, ask about the approximate time when he starts to drink; where and with whom he usually drinks; the period of time spent drinking; the amount and type of alcohol consumed; and when and how he stops drinking.

If you have more time available (about 30 minutes), you might want to use the *Timeline Followback* (TLFB) method to construct a record of your client's drinking over a particular period of time—usually the past three months. Using a calendar and starting with particular events that might help your client to recall his drinking, such as holidays, special occasions and social events, this method can be used to reconstruct your client's pattern of drinking over time. For detailed instructions on how to use it for assessment, consult Sobell and Sobell (1992).

Injecting drug use: There are a range of illicit drugs that can be injected, including amphetamines, opioids and cocaine. Ask your client how often and how much he typically injects. Estimates of how much he usually spends on the drug each week can also help you to estimate the amount he uses if you know the current street value of the drug. This question has the added advantage of providing an opening to ask about your client's source of money, and therefore his social, vocational and criminal activities. When you are asking him about his pattern of injecting drug use, it is important to ask about needle-sharing and other risk-taking behaviours (see pp. 27–28).

Other drug use: The TLFB method can been used to assess your clients use of other drugs, such as cannabis (Budney, Moore, Vandrey & Hughes, 2003). Most injecting drug users are polydrug users because access to their preferred drug is variable. For clients seeking help primarily for alcohol problems, other drug use should also be assessed, especially where drugs are used in conjunction with alcohol.

LEVEL OF DEPENDENCE

An important factor in determining the goals of treatment is the level of your client's dependence on alcohol or drugs (see Chapter 4, *Goal-setting*). Physical dependence will also suggest the need for managed detoxification. People who are physically dependent on alcohol are likely to experience withdrawal symptoms 6–24 hours after the last drink is consumed. For most people, the alcohol withdrawal syndrome is short-lived (about five days), but some experience severe symptoms such as seizures or delirium tremens in the first 2–3 days, depending on their drinking patterns (Shand, Gates, Fawcett & Mattick, 2003). Opioid and psychostimulant withdrawals are not life-threatening but may lead to relapse. Benzodiazepine withdrawal should be tapered because of the risk of seizures. You should liaise with medical personnel to determine the suitability of detoxification at home, inpatient detoxification and medical management of withdrawal. Some guidelines to withdrawal management procedures are given in the *Resources List*.

The elements of the dependence syndrome first described by Edwards and Gross (1976) are outlined below.

(1) *Narrowing of the behavioural repertoire*: A person who is not dependent will vary the amount and type of substance use, depending upon the situation. With increasing dependence, the person will tend to consume or use the same amount each day.

(2) *Salience of drinking or drug use*: With increasing dependence, the substance use will be given greater priority in the person's life, to the detriment of dietary, health, financial and social factors.

(3) *Subjective awareness of compulsion*: The person's subjective experience of dependence is characterised by a loss of control over the substance use, an irresistible impulse to keep using the substance, an inability to stop using at certain times, or constant cravings when not using.

(4) *Increased tolerance*: Heavy use leads to an adaptation to higher amounts of the substance. This is known as tolerance and is evident when amounts that previously had mind-altering effects now produce fewer obvious effects. The dependent person responds to tolerance by using larger amounts in order to achieve the desired effect.

(5) *Repeated withdrawal symptoms*: As dependence increases, the frequency and severity of withdrawal symptoms also increases. For *alcohol* users these may include perspiration, tremor, anxiety, agitation, a rise in body temperature, hallucinations, disorientation and/or nausea; for *opioid* users they may include goosebumps (especially on the chest), perspiration, dilated pupils, runny nose or eyes, excessive yawning, vomiting, diarrhoea or nausea, reported loss of appetite, sneezing, aching or cramped muscles, heart pounding or high blood pressure, feelings of coldness, problems in sleeping, stomach cramps, restlessness, and muscle spasm or twitching. Withdrawal from *psychostimulants*, such as amphetamines and cocaine, can be associated with hunger, extreme fatigue, anxiety, irritability, depression and sleep disturbance. *Benzodiazepine* withdrawal may lead to anxiety reactions and, infrequently, has been known to cause seizures. Withdrawal from *cannabis* can be associated with tension, irritability, decreased appetite, angry or anxious feelings and sleep disturbance.

(6) *Relief from or avoidance of withdrawal symptoms*: The person seeks relief from withdrawal symptoms through further substance use (e.g., morning drinking) or maintains a steady level of substance use in order to avoid withdrawal.

(7) *Post-abstinence reinstatement*: A return to substance use after a period of abstinence will be characterised by a rapid return to the pre-abstinence level of substance use and dependence symptomatology.

These dependence symptoms became the basis for the development of the criteria in standardised diagnostic classifications such as the *Diagnostic and Statistical Manual of Mental Disorders* (DSM) and the *International Classification of Diseases* (ICD). Currently the DSM-IV criteria for substance dependence are, briefly: (1) tolerance, (2) withdrawal, (3) taking the substance more than intended, (4) unsuccessful efforts to cut down or control substance use, (5) a great deal of time spent obtaining the substance or recovering from its effects, (6) important social, occupational or recreational activities given up or reduced because of substance use, and (7) continued use despite knowledge of persistent or recurrent physical or psychological problems made worse by the substance use. There are also criteria outlined in the DSM-IV for diagnosing substance abuse.

As well as asking questions about the signs of dependence, you may wish to use standardised questionnaires to measure dependence. Three commonly used questionnaires are provided at the end of this chapter and described below.

- The *Severity of Alcohol Dependence Questionnaire* (SADQ-C; pp. 38–39) was developed by Stockwell, Sitharthan, McGrath and Lang (1994). The SADQ-C mainly measures the physical aspects of moderate–severe alcohol dependence. Answers to each question are rated on a four-point scale as follows: 0 = almost never, 1 = sometimes, 2 = often, 3 = nearly always. Scores lower than or equal to 20 indicate low dependence, scores between 21 and 30 indicate moderate dependence and scores higher than 30 indicate a high level of dependence.
- The *Short form Alcohol Dependence Data Scale* (SADD; p. 40) was developed by Raistrick, Dunbar and Davidson (1983). The SADD measures the more subjective aspects of early alcohol dependence. Raistrick *et al.* (1983) have recommended that scores of 1 to 9 be considered low dependence, 10 to 19 medium dependence, and 20 or more high dependence, on the basis of a four-point (0–3) rating scale similar to that used in the SADQ-C.
- The *Severity of Opiate Dependence Questionnaire* (SODQ; pp. 41–42) was developed by Sutherland, Edwards, Taylor, Phillips, Gossop and Brady (1986). It is scored in the same way as the SADQ-C.
- The *Severity of Dependence Scale* (SDS; p. 43) was developed by Gossop *et al.* (1995) as a short measure of dependence for use with different types of drugs. The first four questions are scored in the same way as the SADQ-C and question five is also scored on a four-point scale as follows: 0 = not difficult, 1 = quite difficult, 2 = very difficult and 3 = impossible. Cut-off scores for the SDS of 4, 3 and 6 indicate dependence for amphetamine, cannabis and benzodiazepines respectively (Dawe, Loxton, Hides, Kavanagh & Mattick, 2002).

If your client has a high severity of dependence, he is likely to benefit from a longer and more intense form of treatment which not only addresses his drinking or drug problem, but also helps him to deal with other problems associated with his substance use. However, the results from dependence questionnaires should not be used in a rigid way to prejudge the type of intervention you offer your client (Shand *et al.*, 2003). Instead, provide him with personalised feedback based on the results and then explore his reactions and preferences for treatment (see Chapter 3, *Motivational Interviewing*).

BACKGROUND INFORMATION

Information about your client's background will serve three basic purposes. First, it will give you a more complete appreciation of his total life experience and his reasons for seeking help. Second, it is important to evaluate the resources available to your client as he tries to change the substance use. Third, background information will highlight those problems and concerns which are either influencing or being influenced by your client's substance use.

LIFESTYLE AND SOCIAL STABILITY

Both the OTI and the BDP are useful for assessing lifestyle problems that are associated with drug use or drinking. Other useful instruments include the *Alcohol Problems Questionnaire* (APQ) (Drummond, 1990) and the *Addiction Severity Index* (ASI) (McLellan *et al.*, 1992). Keep a balanced approach when assessing your client's problems by also exploring his areas of strength and support. For further information about needs- and strengths-based assessments, see Chapter 18, *Case Management*.

Areas of life that might be relevant to assess would include those listed below.

Vocational and Financial Background

Does your client's vocational background indicate a lack of stability or financial security? Does he have stable accommodation? Has he noticed any changes in work performance over the time he's been drinking or using drugs? Does your client's current occupation bring him in contact with drugs, other drug users or drinkers? How stressful or satisfying is his job? Alternatively, are there features of his workplace that might help him during treatment? How much is his alcohol or other drug use costing him, financially?

Family Background and Social Support

With whom does your client live? Who are the significant people in your client's life? Does he feel supported by his family, friends or partner? Is there any family history of substance use? Do significant others use drugs or drink excessively? Has your client been encouraged to or discouraged from entering treatment? The following areas may need further exploration if they are relevant for your client's family: dependent children, the need for child care while the client attends treatment, child abuse, domestic violence, marital distress and unhappiness within the family home.

If your client's social network is highly supportive of drinking or drug use, he may need assistance in building a more supportive social network (see Chapters 15, *Self-help Groups* and 16, *Relapse-prevention Training*). It can be useful to map out your client's main social contacts, including who is likely to support his endeavours to change and who is likely to influence him to use or drink. The technique of drawing a 'social atom' described in Chapter 19, *Working with Young People* can be adapted for adult clients.

Involvement of Concerned Others in Treatment

If your client is accompanied by family or concerned others when he comes to assessment, find out how they view his drug or alcohol problem. Are there any differences of opinion about the seriousness of the problem? Provide the opportunity for concerned others to ask questions and voice their concerns and expectations about therapy. It is also a good time to help put the substance use into perspective. For instance, changing the substance use will not necessarily resolve all relationship or family problems. Family or relationship therapy is a specialist area and we would strongly suggest that you refer your clients to appropriately trained specialists if they are seeking this kind of intervention.

Nevertheless, your client's progress will certainly be enhanced if he has the support of others. Consider the possibility that your client's family, friends or partner may wish to be directly involved in his treatment. Chapter 13, *Involving Concerned Others* outlines three approaches that you could use to involve your client's partner, family or concerned others in his treatment program.

Coping Skills

The skills training approach we have outlined in this book is based on the assumption that some clients relapse because they lack skills to help them cope with socially demanding or personally stressful situations. Since it is not very useful to provide training in skills that your client already has, you should evaluate your client's strengths and limitations in coping with stress or other intense mood states, communicating with others, refusing alcohol or drugs in response to social pressure and coping with cravings or other triggers to use or drink.

You can gather information about your client's coping skills by asking him what kinds of situations have caused him to relapse and what kinds of situations would make it hard for him to refrain from substance use. Explore any situations where your client has the skills but finds it difficult to apply them. You might want to start with a situational confidence questionnaire, such as those listed in the *Resources List* for Chapter 16, *Relapse-prevention Training*.

Interests and Hobbies

It is helpful to find out what your client's current interests are as well as things that he used to enjoy in the past. You can build on these activities as substitutes for the drinking or drug use and as a way of meeting new friends.

Sexual Problems or Sexual Abuse

Is your client having any problems with his fertility, sexual arousal or sexual responses? For some clients, such problems may be related to their substance use.

Is sexual abuse a relevant issue for your client? A high percentage of women in treatment for drug or alcohol problems have been sexually abused. Although the prevalence is lower among men compared with women, it is still a possibility that you need to be aware of when counselling male clients. Questions about sexual abuse should be framed in a non-threatening way, allowing your client to discuss the experience without fear of rejection. It may help to ask about 'unwanted sexual contact' because your client might not know what you mean by 'sexual abuse'. Avoid probing further if rapport is still weak or if he does not seem ready to disclose. You may need to refer him to an agency specialising in sexual abuse issues. Raising traumatic material without the aid of specialist counselling adds to the risk of relapse, especially if your client has been misusing substances as a form of self-medication. Further guidelines about screening and referral for issues of sexual abuse are given in Chapter 20, *Dual Diagnosis*.

Perpetrators of child sexual abuse are also likely to abuse alcohol or other drugs. You may need to prepare your client for the possibility that official notification of his behaviour is necessary to prevent risk to others.

Legal Problems

Is your client facing any current convictions? Has this resulted in legal coercion into treatment? If so, how does the legal coercion influence his goals and expectations? How often during the last month has he been involved in crime? Has he ever been convicted for drink driving or other crimes that were related to his drinking? When recording this information, be aware that your client's records could be subpoenaed at any time.

Risk-taking Behaviour

Your client's pattern of drug or alcohol use may also place him at risk of a number of other harms. It may be important to assess your client's risk of any of the following:

- Overdose as a result of mixing depressant drugs (e.g., heroin with pills or alcohol) or other toxic reactions as a result of taking drug 'cocktails'.

- Transmission of HIV and other sexually transmitted diseases via unprotected sex as a result of impulsive, intoxicated behaviour.
- Transmission of infections as a result of sharing pipes or stems.
- Dehydration and overheating after using MDMA (Ecstasy) or other designer drugs, as a result of combining them with alcohol or not resting and cooling the body adequately. Alternatively over-hydration can occur as a result of drinking too much water in a short space of time.
- Injury to self or others as a result of driving or using machinery while intoxicated.
- Alcohol- or drug-induced psychological problems, such as anxiety and depression, or drug-induced psychosis (see Chapter 20, *Dual Diagnosis*) as a result of heavy use of amphetamines or cannabis.

Risks associated with injecting drug use include:

- The transmission of infectious diseases such as HIV and forms of hepatitis via the sharing of needles and other injecting equipment.
- Abscesses and collapsed veins due to repeated injections in the same areas of the body, skin popping or injecting solutions that contain particles.
- Embolism due to injecting pills or other solutions that contains particles.
- Bacterial infection from using unclean equipment, not cleaning the injection site or using contaminated water to mix the shot or clean the equipment.

Assess your client's risk-taking behaviour by asking your client about (a) the way he uses and (b) whether he has experienced any harms (such as those above), as a result of his drug or alcohol use. It is especially important to assess the risk of exposure to and transmission of HIV and other infections, particularly with those clients who use injectable drugs. There are two main areas in which such risks may occur:

(1) *Injecting practices*: How often does your client inject drugs? How often does he share needles or other injecting equipment with other users? How often and how effectively does he clean the needles before reusing them?
(2) *Sexual behaviour*: How many sexual partners has your client had in the past month? Does he use condoms when having sexual intercourse? In what situations are condoms not used? How many times has your client had anal sex in the last month?

You should also assess your client's knowledge about which alcohol and/or drug practices are safe and which are risky. Be aware that even if a client has this knowledge, he may continue to behave in an unsafe way. Further information about assisting clients to reduce drug-related harm is given in Chapters 4, *Goal-setting*, 19, *Working with Young People* and 20, *Dual Diagnosis*.

PHYSICAL HEALTH PROBLEMS

Information from a medical check-up is useful for several purposes. First, it can add to your knowledge about your client's level of dependence. Second, you may need to use this information to determine whether your client is eligible for certain treatment techniques (such as pharmacotherapy). It will also assist in the negotiation of appropriate treatment goals (Chapter 4, *Goal Setting*). Finally, personalised feedback of the medical results can help to motivate your client towards change (pp. 55–57).

ALCOHOL-RELATED HEALTH PROBLEMS

People who misuse alcohol are vulnerable to liver dysfunction, pancreatitis and digestive disorders, problems with the heart and blood circulation, poor nutrition and alcohol-related brain damage. Frequent intoxication may lead to accidents and injuries. Excessive drinking during pregnancy may lead to foetal alcohol syndrome (retardation in development of the foetus). For the heavy-drinking client, a medical check-up should include some assessment of his blood pressure, cholesterol levels and liver function. Listed below are some of the enzymes that are important to liver function. A liver function test measures the levels of these enzymes in the blood. Any levels that are raised outside the normal range provide evidence that the person's liver is at risk of serious damage. The enzymes are:

- Aspartate aminotransferase (AST).
- Alanine aminotransferase (ALT).
- Gamma glutamyltransferase (GGT).
- Alkaline phosphate.

Another test that is commonly included in the assessment of physical damage or risk related to heavy drinking is a measurement of the mean corpuscular volume (MCV). This measures the level of red blood cells and an abnormally low MCV can indicate bone marrow toxicity. For each of these tests, the pathologist's report will indicate whether or not your client's level falls within the normal, healthy range. Normal results do not necessarily imply that the person is drinking within safe limits. Special care should be taken to clarify this point when feeding back results (see p. 57). See the *Resources List* for guidelines to the health effects of excessive alcohol consumption.

DRUG-RELATED HEALTH PROBLEMS

Illicit drug users are vulnerable to poor nutrition, dental caries, respiratory illness, menstrual irregularities, skin disease, sexually transmitted diseases and chronic liver disease. Injecting drug users are particularly vulnerable to viral infections such as Hepatitis B and C, and HIV or damaged veins. Drug use during pregnancy may lead to withdrawal symptoms in the newly born child. Smoking cannabis has similar risks to health as smoking nicotine, such as bronchitis and lung disease.

MENTAL HEALTH PROBLEMS

Many people with drug or alcohol problems also suffer from psychiatric distress or disturbed moods. For some people, the substance use began with an attempt by the person to self-medicate depressed or anxious feelings. Alternatively, substance use can lead to depression or anxiety. The person's moods may considerably improve after a period of abstinence. Therefore, you might choose to assess your client's emotional and psychological state *both* at the first contact meeting and several weeks after abstinence or use reduction. It is also important to screen your client for suicide risk. Guidelines for the assessment and management of psychiatric disturbances are provided in Chapter 20, *Dual Diagnosis*, where you will also find resources for screening mental health status.

BRAIN INJURY AND COGNITIVE IMPAIRMENT

There is a high prevalence of cognitive dysfunction among people with alcohol problems, particularly older clients with longer and heavier drinking histories (Lishman, 1997). This is known as alcohol-related brain injury. Some signs of brain injury, such as the severe memory disturbances and confusion associated with Wernicke–Korsakoff's disease are easily detected. In other cases, the impairment is more subtle but might influence the person's capacity for learning new skills during treatment. There is also increasing recognition that cognitive impairment can result from illicit drug use, specifically long-term cannabis use, but also heavy use of amphetamines and possibly MDMA (Ecstasy).

Because alcohol has an immediate effect on general cognitive functioning, assessment for cognitive impairment should be carried out two or three weeks after completion of acute alcohol withdrawal. Be aware that benzodiazepines can also mimic cognitive impairment. Benzodiazepines are often used during alcohol withdrawal and some clients take them longer than intended. Other factors might also influence your client's cognitive functioning at the time of assessment. For example, test-related anxiety can influence how he performs, so try to encourage a relaxed approach. Normal ageing can also bring about memory loss.

Assess your client's ability to recall day-to-day information, such as telephone numbers, appointments, conversations and shopping lists, especially if heavy drinking is a part of the clinical picture. Explore whether he has any difficulties learning new information. For example, he might have difficulty with changes in routine, remembering new locations or learning new procedures at work. Open discussion with your client will assist in determining the extent of memory loss or learning difficulties. The *Mini-Mental State Examination* (MMSE) is an assessment tool that is quick and easy to administer, although its sensitivity to anything more than gross deficits is limited. If you think your client has some cognitive impairment, it is advisable to refer him to a clinical psychologist or neuropsychologist for a more comprehensive assessment. Because any alcohol-related brain injury will be further aggravated by continued drinking or drug use, evidence of impairment will suggest that you focus on the goal of abstinence.

Alcohol and benzodiazepines can also lead to a loss of memory for events that take place while a person is intoxicated. These 'blackouts' may be frequent for clients who are dependent on alcohol but can also be experienced by social drinkers after heavy drinking. Find out from your client if, when and how often blackouts are experienced and whether he views them as a problem. A blackout is a particularly salient example of how alcohol may interfere with your client's personal control. By using motivational interviewing techniques to discuss your client's blackouts, you might heighten his ambivalence about continuing to drink.

Injecting drug use is unlikely to cause brain injury except where a person has overdosed. The possibility that this might have occurred is worth checking out with your client. If he has had an overdose, find out what degree of medical treatment was required and whether your client is aware of any resultant injury.

Details of how to adjust drug and alcohol counselling for clients with cognitive impairment are given in Chapter 20, *Dual Diagnosis* (p. 283). The suitability of residential care for clients with cognitive impairment is discussed in Chapter 21, *Putting It All Together*.

STAGES OF CHANGE

How a person fares in treatment may depend on how ready he is to change the drinking or drug-using behaviour. A useful model for assessing your client's willingness to participate in treatment is the 'stages of change' model (first outlined by Prochaska & DiClemente, 1982). It is not recommended here as a rigid structure in which to pigeon-hole clients. Rather, we see it as a flexible framework to guide you in responding effectively to your client's readiness for change. According to Prochaska, DiClemente and Norcross (1992), there are five stages of change that will require different therapeutic responses. These are discussed below.

A PRE-CONTEMPLATIVE STAGE

During this stage, your client is not considering changing. He believes the positive aspects of drinking or drug use outweigh the costs. He might say: 'I enjoy drinking', or 'I am not interested in stopping drug use', or 'I've tried before and failed'.

People at this stage do not usually attend treatment centres unless they are coerced (e.g., by the legal system or by a relative). They are most likely to be identified by general counsellors or health care workers. If your client is in the pre-contemplative stage, he will probably not respond to action-oriented intervention. It is therefore more appropriate to use careful motivational strategies (pp. 54–55) to provide him with information that will help him to move into contemplation.

A CONTEMPLATIVE STAGE

During this stage, your client becomes more aware of the costs of drinking or using drugs and the benefits of changing, but is ambivalent about changing, may feel trapped and does not act. This ambivalence might be expressed as: 'I'd like to quit using drugs because of the bad things but I think I'd really miss the high.'

At this stage, motivational interviewing could be particularly effective (Chapter 3, *Motivational Interviewing*). It encourages your client to thoroughly explore the pros and cons of drinking or using drugs and might culminate in a firm decision to take action.

A PREPARATION STAGE

During this stage, your client is preparing to take action within the next month and may have already made a previous attempt at changing his behaviour. During this and the next stage, your client begins to believe that the negative consequences of drinking or using drugs outweigh the benefits. He may indicate a preparedness for action by saying: 'I'm ready to try now', or 'I'd like to find out more about how to give up.'

In addition to encouragement, your client will need assistance in setting goals (Chapter 4, *Goal Setting*). This is also the time when you can introduce a menu of strategies for change.

AN ACTION STAGE

During this stage, your client is engaged in active attempts to reduce or stop drinking or using drugs. At this stage, your client will be involved in a treatment plan that may include a combination of those described in this manual (see Chapter 21, *Putting It All Together*).

A MAINTENANCE STAGE

This stage begins when your client changes his drinking or drug-using behaviour and continues as long as he needs to focus on sustaining that change. During this process, a large number of clients will relapse and return to an earlier stage of change. If your client has received training in relapse prevention (Chapter 16) and is supported by a well-planned extended care programme (Chapter 17) he will be better equipped to prevent any slips from developing into full-blown relapses.

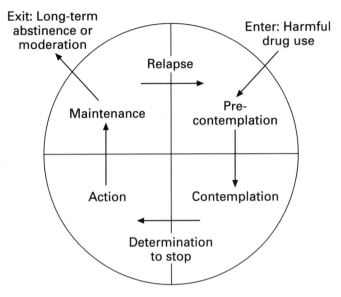

Figure 1. A model of the change process in addictive behaviour
Source: Adapted from Prochaska and Diclemente (1982)

Even in the preparation, action and maintenance stages, your client might continue to have doubts about changing his drinking or drug use. Use motivational interviewing (Chapter 3) whenever your client is struggling with a decision or wants to review his reasons for changing (Shand *et al.*, 2003).

Your client might progress in a linear fashion through these stages. However, this is the exception rather than the rule. Some clients stay at a particular stage for a long time or move back and forth between stages. Your client might relapse several times before he achieves long-term change. Each time this happens, he will gain new information about his behaviour and will be able to apply that information in his next attempt. This cyclical pattern of change is illustrated in Figure 1.

To assess your client's stage of change, simply discuss the issue with him. It might help to ask some specific questions about how much he wants to change. For example, you might ask: 'How interested are you in changing your drinking now?' and 'Do you feel that you *ought* to stop using drugs, or do you really *want* to?' To find out whether your client is prepared to take action for change, you might ask: 'What would you be prepared to do to solve this drinking problem?' and 'How confident are you that you can achieve this?'

If your client feels discouraged at previous unsuccessful attempts to stay abstinent or maintain moderation, you could use Figure 1 to put these attempts into perspective. Explain that each time he has gone around the circle, he has learnt something new that will help him next time. The discussion about preparedness for change can comfortably lead into motivational interviewing.

RESOURCES LIST

ASSESSMENT INSTRUMENTS

Darke, S., Ward, J., Hall, W., Heather, N. & Wodak, A. (1991). *The Opiate Treatment Index (OTI) Manual*, Technical Report Number 11. Sydney: National Drug and Alcohol Research Centre.
—Although mainly designed for assessing opioid users, this scale assesses a whole range of different drugs as well as risk taking and other lifestyle factors. For a copy of the OTI and the accompanying manual, write to the National Drug and Alcohol Research Centre, University of New South Wales, Sydney NSW 2052, Australia.
Also available at: www.med.unsw.edu.au/ndarc

Darke, S., Hall, W., Wodak, A., Heather, N. & Ward, J. (1992). Development and validation of a multi-dimensional instrument for assessing outcome of treatment among opiate users: The opiate treatment index. *British Journal of Addiction*, **87**, 733–742.
—Provides data on the reliability and validity of the Opiate Treatment Index.

Dawe, S., Loxton, N.J., Hides, L., Kavanagh, D.J. & Mattick, R.P. (2002). *Review of Diagnostic Screening Instruments for Alcohol and Other Drug Use and other Psychiatric Disorders* (2nd edn), Canberra: Commonwealth of Australia.
Available at: http://www.health.gov.au/pubhlth/publicat/document/mono48.pdf
—A comprehensive resource providing detailed descriptions of screening and assessment tools for substance abuse and psychiatric disorders.

Drummond, D. (1990). The relationship between alcohol dependence and alcohol-related problems in a clinical population. *British Journal of Addiction*, **85**(3), 357–366.
—Describes the Alcohol Problems Questionnaire (APQ), a valid and reliable measure of alcohol-related problems which is independent of levels of consumption.

Folstein, M.F., Folstein, S.E. & McHugh, P.R. (1975). Mini-mental state. A practical method for grading the cognitive state of patients for the clinician. *Journal of Psychiatric Research*, **12**, 189–198.
—Designed as a simple, quick test of general cognitive functioning.

Gossop, M., Darke, S., Griffiths, P., Hando, J., Powis, B., Hall, W. & Strang, J. (1995). The Severity of Dependence Scale (SDS): Psychometric properties of the SDS in English and Australian samples of heroin, cocaine and amphetamine users. *Addiction*, **90**, 607–614.
Also available at:
www.nelmh.org/downloads/other_info/severity_dependence_scale.pdf
—The SDS focuses on the psychological aspects of dependence, including impaired control of drug use and preoccupations and concerns about use in the past 12 months.

Lezak, M.D. (1995). *Neuropsychological Assessment* (3rd edn). New York: Oxford University Press.
—This classic text describes some tests that can assist you in screening for alcohol-related brain damage, such as: the *Mini Mental State, Rey–Osterrieth Complex Figure Test*, designed to test perceptual organisation and visual memory; *Rey Auditory-Verbal Learning Test (AVLT)*, designed to measure memory recall and recognition; *Trail Making Test (TMT)*, designed to test visual conceptual and visuomotor tracking.

Marsden, J., Gossop, M. & Stewart, D. (1998). *The Maudsley Addiction Profile (MAP): A Brief Instrument for Treatment Outcome Research. Development and User Manual.* London: National Addiction Centre/Institute of Psychiatry.
—Designed for use with drinkers or drug users, this instrument measures substance use, risk-taking behaviour, physical and psychological health and personal and social functioning domains.

McLellan, A.T., Kushner, H., Metzger, D., Peters, R., Smith, I., Grissom, G., Pettinati, H. & Argeriou, M. (1992) The fifth edition of the Addiction Severity Index. *Journal of Substance Abuse Treatment*, **9**, 199–213.
A free copy of the questionnaire is available at: www.tresearch.org
—Assesses the client's drug and alcohol history along with related lifestyle issues.

Miller, W.R. & Marlatt, G.A. (1984a). *Comprehensive Drinker Profile.* Odessa, Florida: Psychological Assessment Resources.
—The original and more comprehensive version of the scale below.

Miller, W.R. & Marlatt, G.A. (1984b). *Brief Drinker Profile.* Odessa, Florida: Psychological Assessment Resources.
—An excellent measure of alcohol consumption and related lifestyle issues.

Raistrick, D., Dunbar, G. & Davidson, R. (1983). Development of a questionnaire to measure alcohol dependence. *British Journal of Addiction*, **78**, 89–95.
—This alternative to the SADQ-C includes items testing for psychological aspects of alcohol dependence such as subjective compulsion to drink, salience of drink-seeking behaviour and narrowing of the drinking repertoire.

Sobell, L. & Sobell, M. (1992). Timeline follow-back: A technique for assessing self-reported alcohol consumption. In: R. Litten & J. Allen (eds), *Measuring Alcohol Consumption.* New Jersey: Humana Press Inc.
The TLFB User's Guide is also available for purchase from the Centre for Addiction and Mental Health, 33 Russell Street, Toronto, Ontario, Canada, M5S 2S1 or at: www.camh.net/publications/clinicaltoolsandassessments.html
—Explains how to reconstruct your client's drinking pattern over the past three months and how to use that information to assess alcohol problems.

Stockwell, T., Murphy, D. & Hodgson, R. (1983). The severity of alcohol dependence questionnaire: Its use, reliability and validity. *British Journal of Addiction*, **78**, 145–155.
—Presents results of test-retest reliability and validity for the SADQ, as well as normative data.

Stockwell, T., Sitharthan, T., McGrath, D. & Lang, E. (1994). The measurement of alcohol dependence and impaired control in community samples. *British Journal of Addiction*, **89**, 167–174.
—Describes the modification of the original SADQ so that it is applicable to drinkers in the community who have not sought treatment.

Sutherland, G., Edwards, G., Taylor, C., Phillips, G., Gossop, M. & Brady, R. (1986). The measurement of opiate dependence. *British Journal of Addiction*, **81**, 485–494.
—Designed to be comparable with the original SADQ, this scale measures physical and affective withdrawal symptoms, withdrawal relief drug-taking and rapidity of reinstatement of symptoms after abstinence.

Wechsler, D. (1997). *Wechsler Adult Intelligence Scale—Third Edition (WAIS-III)*. New York, NY: Harcourt, Brace, Jovanovich.
—A comprehensive IQ test with both performance and verbal scales and 11 subscales which can be used by qualified psychologists for clients from 16 to 89 years old.

Wechsler, D. (2003). *Wechsler Intelligence Scale for Children—Fourth Edition (WISC-IV)*. New York, NY: Harcourt, Brace, Jovanovich.
—A comprehensive IQ test similar to the WAIS-III but designed for assessing clients from 6 to 16 years, 11 months.

Wechsler, D. (1997). *Wechsler Memory Scale—Third Edition (WMS-III)*. New York, NY: Harcourt, Brace, Jovanovich.
—A comprehensive test for assessing short- and long-term memory with adult clients, available to qualified psychologists.

OTHER RESOURCES

Budney, A.J., Moore, B.A., Vandrey, R.G. & Hughes, J.R. (2003). The time course and significance of cannabis withdrawal, *Journal of Abnormal Psychology*, **112**(3), 393–402.
—A research study that describes common symptoms associated with withdrawal from cannabis.

Better Health Good Health Care (2000). *Alcohol and Other Drugs Policy for Nursing Practice in NSW: Clinical Guidelines*. Sydney: NSW Department of Health.
—Includes guidelines for the management of withdrawal syndromes.

DiClemente, C.C. & Marden Velasquez, M. (2002). Motivational interviewing and the stages of change. In: W.R. Miller & S. Rollnick (eds), *Motivational Interviewing: Preparing People to Change Addictive Behavior* (2nd edn). New York: Guilford Press.
—This chapter describes how the 'stages of change' model interlocks with the practice of motivational interviewing.

Edwards, G.E., Marshall, E.J. & Cook, C.C.H. (2003) *The Treatment of Drinking Problems: A Guide for the Helping Professions* (3rd edn). Cambridge, UK: Cambridge University Press.
—Covers the key issues of working with alcohol problems, including guidelines on how to use assessment to plan your client's treatment, with case study examples.

Edwards, G. & Gross, M.M. (1976). Alcohol dependence: Provisional description of a clinical syndrome. *British Medical Journal*, **1**, 1058–1061.
—A detailed description of the symptoms of the alcohol-dependence syndrome and how they are likely to affect your client.

Lishman, W.A. (1997). *Organic Psychiatry: The Psychological Consequences of Cerebral Disorder* (3rd edn). Oxford: Blackwell Scientific Publications.
—An excellent summary of cerebral dysfunction and clinical signs and symptoms thereof.

Miller, W.R. (1995). Increasing motivation for change. In: R.K. Hester & W.R. Miller (eds), *Handbook of Alcoholism Treatment Approaches: Effective Alternatives* (2nd edn) (pp. 89–104). Boston: Allyn and Bacon.
—This chapter includes a brief and practical summary of the 'stages of change' model.

Miller, W.R. & Rollnick, S. (1991). *Motivational Interviewing: Preparing People to Change Addictive Behavior*. New York: Guilford Press.

—Chapter 7 of this first edition gives a brief discussion of the most important areas of assessment, including assessment of motivation.

Shand, F., Gates, J., Fawcett, J. & Mattick, R.P. (2003). *Guidelines for the Treatment of Alcohol Problems*. Canberra: Australian Government Department of Health and Ageing.
—A key resource providing guidelines for the screening and assessment of clients with alcohol problems (pp. 25–56) and the management of alcohol withdrawal (pp. 59–80).

National Health and Medical Research Council (2001). *Australian Alcohol Guidelines: Health Risks and Benefits*. Canberra: NH&MRC.
Available at: www.alcoholguidelines.gov.au
—Gives a detailed summary of the health and psycho-social effects of excessive alcohol consumption.

Prochaska, J.O. & DiClemente, C.C. (1982). Transtheoretical therapy: Toward a more integrative model of change. *Psychotherapy: Theory, Research and Practice*, **19**(3), 276–288.
—One of the first papers to describe the 'stages of change' model.

Prochaska, J.O., DiClemente, C.C. & Norcross, J.C. (1992). In search of how people change: Applications to addictive behaviors. *American Psychologist*, **47**, 1102–1114.
—Describes the theoretical model of 'stages of change' and the processes that are used to progress through these stages. The paper examines relevant research findings and implications for therapy.

Saunders, J., Ward, H. & Novak, H. (1996). *Guide to Home Detoxification*. Sydney: Drug and Alcohol Department, Central Sydney Area Health Service, National Drug Strategy.
—Guidelines for the management of withdrawal syndromes outside the clinical setting.

Severity of Alcohol Dependence Questionnaire—Form C
SADQ-C

NAME _____ AGE _____ SEX _____

Have you drunk any alcohol in the past six months?   YES/NO

If YES, please answer all the following questions about your drinking by circling your most appropriate response.

DURING THE PAST *SIX MONTHS*

1. The day after drinking alcohol, I woke up feeling sweaty.

      ALMOST NEVER   SOMETIMES   OFTEN   NEARLY ALWAYS

2. The day after drinking alcohol, my hands shook first thing in the morning.

      ALMOST NEVER   SOMETIMES   OFTEN   NEARLY ALWAYS

3. The day after drinking alcohol, my whole body shook violently first thing in the morning if I didn't have a drink.

      ALMOST NEVER   SOMETIMES   OFTEN   NEARLY ALWAYS

4. The day after drinking alcohol, I woke up absolutely drenched in sweat.

      ALMOST NEVER   SOMETIMES   OFTEN   NEARLY ALWAYS

5. The day after drinking alcohol, I dreaded waking up in the morning.

      ALMOST NEVER   SOMETIMES   OFTEN   NEARLY ALWAYS

6. The day after drinking alcohol, I was frightened of meeting people first thing in the morning.

      ALMOST NEVER   SOMETIMES   OFTEN   NEARLY ALWAYS

7. The day after drinking alcohol, I felt at the edge of despair when I awoke.

      ALMOST NEVER   SOMETIMES   OFTEN   NEARLY ALWAYS

8. The day after drinking alcohol, I felt very frightened when I awoke.

      ALMOST NEVER   SOMETIMES   OFTEN   NEARLY ALWAYS

9. The day after drinking alcohol, I liked to have an alcoholic drink in the morning.

      ALMOST NEVER   SOMETIMES   OFTEN   NEARLY ALWAYS

10. The day after drinking alcohol, I always gulped my first few alcoholic drinks down as quickly as possible.

      ALMOST NEVER   SOMETIMES   OFTEN   NEARLY ALWAYS

SADQ-C *continued*

___

DURING THE PAST *SIX MONTHS*

11. The day after drinking alcohol, I drank more alcohol in the morning to get rid of the shakes.

    ALMOST NEVER   SOMETIMES   OFTEN   NEARLY ALWAYS

12. The day after drinking alcohol, I had a very strong craving for a drink when I awoke.

    ALMOST NEVER   SOMETIMES   OFTEN   NEARLY ALWAYS

13. I drank more than a quarter of a bottle of spirits in a day (OR 1 bottle of wine OR 7 middies[1] of beer).

    ALMOST NEVER   SOMETIMES   OFTEN   NEARLY ALWAYS

14. I drank more than half a bottle of spirits per day (OR 2 bottles of wine OR 15 middies[1] of beer).

    ALMOST NEVER   SOMETIMES   OFTEN   NEARLY ALWAYS

15. I drank more than one bottle of spirits per day (OR 4 bottles of wine OR 30 middies[1] of beer).

    ALMOST NEVER   SOMETIMES   OFTEN   NEARLY ALWAYS

16. I drank more than two bottles of spirits per day (OR 8 bottles of wine OR 60 middies[1] of beer).

    ALMOST NEVER   SOMETIMES   OFTEN   NEARLY ALWAYS

IMAGINE THE FOLLOWING SITUATION:

(1) You have HARDLY DRUNK ANY ALCOHOL for A FEW WEEKS
(2) You then drink VERY HEAVILY for TWO DAYS

HOW WOULD YOU FEEL THE *MORNING AFTER* THOSE TWO DAYS OF HEAVY DRINKING?

17. I would start to sweat.

    NOT AT ALL   SLIGHTLY   MODERATELY   QUITE A LOT

18. My hands would shake.

    NOT AT ALL   SLIGHTLY   MODERATELY   QUITE A LOT

19. My body would shake.

    NOT AT ALL   SLIGHTLY   MODERATELY   QUITE A LOT

20. I would be craving for a drink

    NOT AT ALL   SLIGHTLY   MODERATELY   QUITE A LOT

Source: Stockwell, T., Sitharthan, T., McGrath, D. & Long, E. (1994). The measurement of alcohol dependence and impaired control in community samples. *British Journal of Addiction*, **89**, 167–174. Reproduced with permission from Blackwell Publishing Ltd.
[1] Middies are equal to one standard drink of beer (see definitions of standard drinks, p. 164).

Short form Alcohol Dependence Data Scale
SADD

The following questions cover a wide range of topics to do with drinking. Please read each question carefully but do not think too much about its exact meaning. Think about your MOST RECENT drinking habits and answer each question by placing a tick (✓) under the MOST APPROPRIATE heading. If you have any difficulties ASK FOR HELP.

	NEVER	SOME-TIMES	OFTEN	NEARLY ALWAYS
1. Do you find dificulty in getting the thought of drink out of your mind?	....	....	....	....
2. Is getting drunk more important than your next meal?	....	....	....	....
3. Do you plan your day around when and where you can drink?	....	....	....	....
4. Do you drink in the morning, afternoon and evening?	....	....	....	....
5. Do you drink for the effect of alcohol without caring what the drink is?	....	....	....	....
6. Do you drink as much as you want irrespective of what you are doing the next day?	....	....	....	....
7. Given that many problems might be caused by alcohol do you still drink too much?	....	....	....	....
8. Do you know that you won't be able to stop drinking once you start?	....	....	....	....
9. Do you try to control your drinking by giving it up completely for days or weeks at a time?	....	....	....	....
10. The morning after a heavy drinking session do you need your first drink to get yourself going?	....	....	....	....
11. The morning after a heavy drinking session do you wake up with a definite shakiness of your hands?	....	....	....	....
12. After a heavy drinking session do you wake up and retch or vomit?	....	....	....	....
13. The morning after a heavy drinking session do go out of your way to avoid people?	....	....	....	....
14. After a heavy drinking session do you see frightening things that later you realise were imaginary?	....	....	....	....
15. Do you go drinking and the next day find you have forgotten what happened the night before?	....	....	....	....

Source: Raistrick, D., Dunbar, G. & Davidson, R. (1983). Development of a questionnaire to measure alcohol dependce. *British Journal of Addiction*, **78**, 89–95. Reproduced with permission from Blackwell Publishing Ltd.

Severity of Opiate Dependence Questionnaire
SODQ-C

NAME _____ AGE _____ SEX _____

First of all, we would like you to recall a recent month when you were using opiates heavily in a way that, for you, was fairly typical of a heavy use period. Please fill in the month and the year.

MONTH _____ YEAR _____

ANSWER EVERY QUESTION BY CIRCLING ONE RESPONSE ONLY

1.   ON WAKING, AND BEFORE MY FIRST DOSE OF OPIATES:

(a) My body aches or feels stiff

NEVER OR   SOMETIMES   OFTEN   ALWAYS OR
ALMOST NEVER   NEARLY ALWAYS

(b) I get stomach cramps

NEVER OR   SOMETIMES   OFTEN   ALWAYS OR
ALMOST NEVER   NEARLY ALWAYS

(c) I feel sick

NEVER OR   SOMETIMES   OFTEN   ALWAYS OR
ALMOST NEVER   NEARLY ALWAYS

(d) I notice my heart pounding

NEVER OR   SOMETIMES   OFTEN   ALWAYS OR
ALMOST NEVER   NEARLY ALWAYS

(e) I have hot and cold flushes

NEVER OR   SOMETIMES   OFTEN   ALWAYS OR
ALMOST NEVER   NEARLY ALWAYS

(f) I feel miserable or depressed

NEVER OR   SOMETIMES   OFTEN   ALWAYS OR
ALMOST NEVER   NEARLY ALWAYS

(g) I feel tense or panicky

NEVER OR   SOMETIMES   OFTEN   ALWAYS OR
ALMOST NEVER   NEARLY ALWAYS

(h) I feel irritable or angry

NEVER OR   SOMETIMES   OFTEN   ALWAYS OR
ALMOST NEVER   NEARLY ALWAYS

(i) I feel restless and unable to relax

NEVER OR   SOMETIMES   OFTEN   ALWAYS OR
ALMOST NEVER   NEARLY ALWAYS

(j) I have a strong craving

NEVER OR   SOMETIMES   OFTEN   ALWAYS OR
ALMOST NEVER   NEARLY ALWAYS

SODQ-C *continued*

ANSWER EVERY QUESTION BY CIRCLING ONE RESPONSE ONLY

2.   PLEASE COMPLETE ALL SECTIONS (a–f) OF THIS QUESTION

(a)   I try to save some opiates to use on waking

| NEVER OR ALMOST NEVER | SOMETIMES | OFTEN | ALWAYS OR NEARLY ALWAYS |

(b)   I like to take my first dose of opiates within two hours of waking up

| NEVER OR ALMOST NEVER | SOMETIMES | OFTEN | ALWAYS OR NEARLY ALWAYS |

(c)   In the morning, I use opiates to stop myself feeling sick

| NEVER OR ALMOST NEVER | SOMETIMES | OFTEN | ALWAYS OR NEARLY ALWAYS |

(d)   The first thing I think of doing when I wake up is to take some opiates

| NEVER OR ALMOST NEVER | SOMETIMES | OFTEN | ALWAYS OR NEARLY ALWAYS |

(e)   When I wake up I take opiates to stop myself aching or feeling stiff

| NEVER OR ALMOST NEVER | SOMETIMES | OFTEN | ALWAYS OR NEARLY ALWAYS |

(f)   The first thing I do after I wake up is to take some opiates

| NEVER OR ALMOST NEVER | SOMETIMES | OFTEN | ALWAYS OR NEARLY ALWAYS |

3.   PLEASE THINK OF YOUR OPIATE USE DURING A TYPICAL PERIOD OF DRUG TAKING FOR THESE QUESTIONS:

(a)   Did you think your opiate use was out of control?

| NEVER OR ALMOST NEVER | SOMETIMES | OFTEN | ALWAYS OR NEARLY ALWAYS |

(b)   Did the prospect of missing a fix (or dose) make you very anxious or worried?

| NEVER OR ALMOST NEVER | SOMETIMES | OFTEN | ALWAYS OR NEARLY ALWAYS |

(c)   Did you worry about your opiate use?

| NEVER OR ALMOST NEVER | SOMETIMES | OFTEN | ALWAYS OR NEARLY ALWAYS |

(d)   Did you wish you could stop?

| NEVER OR ALMOST NEVER | SOMETIMES | OFTEN | ALWAYS OR NEARLY ALWAYS |

(e)   How difficult would you find it to stop or go without?

| NEVER OR ALMOST NEVER | SOMETIMES | OFTEN | ALWAYS OR NEARLY ALWAYS |

Source: Sutherland, G., Edwards, G., Taylor, C., Phillips, G., Gossop, M. & Brady, R. (1986). The measurement of opiate dependence. *British Journal of Addiction*, **81**, 485–494. Reproduced with permission from Blackwell Publishing Ltd.

Severity of Dependence Scale
SDS

The following questions ask about the drug that you mainly use and your experience of that drug in the past 12 months. Please answer each question by circling one response only.

Name of the drug that you mainly use . . . .

In the past 12 months . . .

1. Did you think your use of this drug was out of control?

| NEVER OR | SOMETIMES | OFTEN | ALWAYS OR |
| ALMOST NEVER | | | NEARLY ALWAYS |

2. Did the prospect of missing (a cone, fix or dose) make you anxious or worried?

| NEVER OR | SOMETIMES | OFTEN | ALWAYS OR |
| ALMOST NEVER | | | NEARLY ALWAYS |

3. Did you worry about your use of this drug?

| NEVER OR | SOMETIMES | OFTEN | ALWAYS OR |
| ALMOST NEVER | | | NEARLY ALWAYS |

4. Did you wish you could stop?

| NEVER OR | SOMETIMES | OFTEN | ALWAYS OR |
| ALMOST NEVER | | | NEARLY ALWAYS |

5. How difficult did you find it to stop or go without this drug?

| NOT DIFFICULT | QUITE DIFFICULT | VERY DIFFICULT | IMPOSSIBLE |

Source: Gossop, M., Darke, S., Griffiths, P., Hando, J., Powis, B., Hall, W. & Strang, J. (1995). The Severity of Dependence Scale (SDS): Psychometric properties of the SDS in English and Australian samples of heroin, cocaine and amphetamine users. *Addiction*, **90**, 607–614. Reproduced with permission from Blackwell Publishing Ltd.

3

Motivational Interviewing

RECOMMENDED USE

Motivational interviewing is a style of counselling that can be used throughout the therapeutic process (see Chapter 1, *General Counselling Skills*). It is a valuable approach whenever your client is struggling with decisions about change. However, specific motivational interviewing strategies are thought to be particularly useful during initial sessions with substance users who are 'contemplators' experiencing ambivalence about changing drinking or drug use (see p. 32).

For other clients who are still 'pre-contemplators', motivational interviewing can be used to begin the process of thinking about change. These clients are unlikely to present to a drug and alcohol treatment setting unless coerced by others and are more likely to be seen in primary health care settings. Motivational interviewing is a key technique for use in brief and early interventions (Chapter 5) with both pre-contemplators and contemplators. With clients who present for drug and alcohol counselling because of coercion, a motivational interviewing style is recommended for your initial contact, with the aim of encouraging your client to agree to a further assessment session.

If your client is already highly motivated and ready to change, the use of motivational interviewing strategies early in treatment will not be necessary. You may find it useful, however, to reinforce motivation with such clients by exploring and re-affirming what they hope to achieve by changing.

As motivational interviewing involves a highly individualised approach it is not generally undertaken in group settings. However, methods for enhancing motivation in a group setting are also discussed briefly below.

GOALS

In essence, the goal of motivational interviewing is to have your client talk herself into deciding to change drug use behaviour. However, motivational interviewing emphasises the client's right to choose and to accept the responsibility for the results of her decision.

Motivational interviewing strategies avoid traditional confrontational methods because such 'offensive' tactics (e.g., '*you* have a major *problem*') quite naturally bring out 'defensive' reactions (e.g., '*I don't* have a problem'). Such confrontation is both unhelpful and counter-productive when the aim is to get your client to take the position of being the one who presents the arguments for change!

KEY CONCEPTS

EMPATHY

Empathy is defined in detail in Chapter 1, *General Counselling Skills*. In motivational interviewing the concept is also used to describe the style of listening in which your client's comments are reflected back to her, often in a slightly modified or reframed fashion but always with an attitude of respect and acceptance.

This non-judgemental attitude does not imply that you need to agree with your client's perspective. Rather, your empathic acceptance builds a therapeutic rapport that supports your client's self-esteem and allows her the freedom to explore the possibility of change.

AMBIVALENCE

Ambivalence is a common and natural experience of feeling torn between wanting and not wanting to do something. It is *not* a sign of unwillingness to change or one of denial. In the context of substance use it is the conflict between wanting to continue to drink or use drugs and the desire to cut down or stop. The closer your client is to deciding to change her drug use, the greater these feelings of conflict are likely to be. Ambivalence can be the greatest obstacle to commitment to change and the major reason for people being stuck in long periods of contemplation. The aim in motivational interviewing is to tip the balance of ambivalence in favour of action.

Be aware that your client's motivation is likely to fluctuate throughout the process of change. Even after she has succeeded in changing her alcohol or drug use, she might sometimes experience ambivalent feelings about the effort involved in maintaining those changes.

RESISTANCE

Resistance is a behaviour where your client moves away from considering a particular change, often in reaction to feeling pressured. It is crucial to motivational interviewing that you avoid evoking or strengthening resistance in your client. We strongly recommend that you read the section on resistance in Chapter 1, *General Counselling Skills*.

CHANGE TALK

Miller and Rollnick (2002) draw a contrast between resistant behaviours and other behaviours which signal that your client is moving towards a particular change. They refer to these other behaviours as 'change talk' or 'self-motivational statements'. Change talk includes statements where your client recognises the disadvantages of her current situation, recognises the advantages of changing, expresses optimism about the possibility of change or expresses her intention (or desire) to change.

When these types of statements come from your client they are far more likely to persuade her to change than words spoken by you or any other person. Eliciting and elaborating 'change talk' from your client is one of the aims of motivational interviewing.

SELF-EFFICACY

Self-efficacy is your client's optimistic belief in her own ability to change. The more confident your client is about being able to make a change, the more likely she is to succeed. Self-efficacy is sometimes measured by asking your client to rate her confidence across a range of high-risk situations. Questionnaires of this type are listed in the *Resources List* of Chapter 16, *Relapse-prevention Training*.

METHOD

Fundamental to the successful use of motivational interviewing strategies are a number of client-centred counselling microskills. These include the use of open-ended questions, reflective listening, elaborating, affirmation and summarising. These are discussed in detail in Chapter 1, *General Counselling Skills*.

In motivational interviewing (unlike many non-directive, client-centred approaches) all of these skills are used in a directive way to encourage your client to explore her ambivalence and to consider the possibility of change. For example, open-ended questions are used to evoke and elaborate on your client's concerns about her substance use or her reasons for change. Summary and reflective listening skills are also used in a directive way, when you *selectively* reinforce your client's change talk.

Keep in mind that the directive use of microskills is not aimed at forcing your client into a decision that is contrary to her interests or values. Instead, the aim is to *collaborate* or work in partnership with your client to explore and negotiate the possibility of change. Always be guided by your client's readiness for change, her values, concerns and experiences, and the types of change that she is willing to consider.

There are many and varied approaches to, and interpretations of, motivational interviewing. Common to these different applications of motivational interviewing, however, are a number of key strategies. Some of these strategies with examples are outlined below. These are drawn directly from the work of Miller, Rollnick, Saunders and their colleagues (see the *Resources List*). There are several ways that these strategies can be used or combined. *Not all of these strategies will be appropriate or necessary to use with all clients.*

Rollnick, Heather and Bell (1992) have suggested that when using any of the strategies you should try to begin with open-ended questions and use reflective listening skills to further explore your client's thoughts and feelings. Each strategy can take anywhere between 5 and 15 minutes. They further suggest that you summarise key points before moving on to another strategy. You might also find it useful to use a whiteboard or notebook to record important points. This will help you in summarising and can be a powerful visual tool to help your client weigh up the costs and benefits of her continued use.

EXPLORING THE GOOD THINGS AND THE LESS GOOD THINGS

The aim of this strategy is to let your client explore her thoughts and feelings about her drinking or drug use. It is also often the best way of assessing a client's stage of change. For this strategy to work well it is *essential* that you be non-judgemental and avoid expressing disapproval or surprise about your client's perceptions of what is either 'good' or 'less good' about her drinking or drug use. The four key aspects of this strategy are described below.

The Good Things

Focusing on the 'good things' first has the advantage of building rapport and of providing you with an understanding of the context of your client's drinking or drug use before you look at more negative aspects. Begin by asking an open-ended question such as:

'What are some of the good things about your use of ...'

or

'What do you like about drinking/using ...'

Acknowledge and summarise all the 'good things' about using without over-prolonging this aspect.

The Less Good Things

The aim here is to allow your client (not you!) to identify the less good aspects of her drinking or drug use. A gentle approach will be more likely to encourage an open discussion, so avoid using phrases like 'bad things' or 'problems' unless your client does so. Often your client will raise the 'less good things' as you examine the 'good things'. This will allow you to move on easily to exploring this side of her substance use. Otherwise, after your summary of the 'good things', begin with an open-ended question such as:

'What are some of the less good things about ...'
'What are the things you don't like so much about your use of ...'

Try to find out why your client thinks these are 'less good things'. Remember, be non-judgemental. This exercise provides an opportunity for your client to explore less positive aspects of her drinking or drug use without the threat of having them labelled by others as problematic. Use follow-up questions such as:

'How does this affect you?'

or

'What don't you like about it?'

Prompt for specifics rather than vague reasons because the more that your client can hear herself describe issues in detail the more she will become convinced by them. For example, statements like 'I'm worried about my health' or 'I'm worried about the effect on my relationship' should lead you to ask:

'Can you give me a recent example of that?'
'Can you tell me a bit more about that?'

If your client has some difficulty in listing 'less good things' or if you feel that she has not explored some important areas (e.g., legal, social, financial, work, family, sexual relationships) you may choose to prompt gently for other reasons. However, you should use this tactic sparingly. For example:

'You mentioned feeling tense in social situations. Some people say they have hassles with their family, too. Is that something that happens with you?'

Exploring Concerns

It is *critical* that you don't assume a 'less good thing' will be a problem or concern for your client. For example, your client's arguments with her partner may not be of major concern if she doesn't really care about the relationship. Clients will often be able to identify a number of 'less good' aspects of drinking or drug use that do not necessarily cause them any current concerns. It is therefore important to follow up your client's statements with further open-ended questions so that you can focus in on the less good aspects which *are* of concern, for example:

'How do you feel about that?'
'Is that a problem or concern for you in any way?'

This highlighting and further exploration of *concerns* is the central strategy of motivational interviewing. Less good aspects of drinking or drug use that are of little concern to your client are unlikely to motivate her to change. On the other hand, in recognising her own concerns about drinking or drug use, your client is more likely to feel a need to change. In exploring concerns with your client, your reflections and summaries are particularly important because you reinforce these concerns by repeating them to her.

At all costs, when using this strategy, avoid making comments like 'Don't you think that being in gaol twice is a problem?' It is your client who must define what is of concern to her. Confrontational statements are only likely to produce denial or defensive reactions.

Summarising

After you have talked about both the 'good' and 'less good' things summarise them in your client's words whenever possible. Such a summary might use statements like: 'It seems then, that on the one hand you like ... *and* on the other hand ...' Say 'and ...' rather than 'but ...' as the former better expresses empathy and understanding of the importance of both the positive and negative sides of drinking or drug use for your client.

Try to avoid simply listing all the 'less good' aspects your client may have mentioned. Instead, in summarising the 'less good' side, focus on the issues that your client has indicated are of some *concern* and which seem to make her most uncomfortable. That is, the aim is to help your client to feel that her concerns and worries outweigh the good things about continuing to use drugs. If appropriate, other strategies that can also help to tip the balance in favour of change are detailed below. Make sure that you allow your client time to react to your summary before moving on to another strategy.

Trouble shooting

If your client is persistently showing resistant behaviours, it may be a sign that your method is either too confrontational or your strategies are inappropriate to your client's current stage of change. For example, if your client is not at all ready to consider change she may resist when the possibility of 'less good things' is being raised. Alternatively, she may be able to list a number of 'less good things' but be largely unconcerned by any of them. If you encounter such 'pre-contemplators', you should consider moving to the *Providing Information* strategy described below (pp. 54–55).

With other clients, the best response to resistance is to 'roll with it'. *Never* meet resistance head on by arguing, or by attempting to persuade, warn or confront your client. These responses will backfire severely because they will push your client into an oppositional position where she will vigorously defend her drinking or drug use!

There are a number of different ways to 'roll' with your client's resistance and these are discussed in detail in Chapter 1, *General Counselling Skills*. The underlying principle, however, is to avoid confrontation or argument. Instead, acknowledge and reframe your client's feelings or disagreements so as to allow the interview to continue exploring issues and concerns.

Saunders, Wilkinson and Allsop (1991, pp. 248–85) have also noted that sometimes clients might distance themselves from a 'less good thing'. For example, your client might say 'My doctor said I'd get AIDS if I shared needles.' Explore this response by asking 'But what do *you* think?' Sometimes an answer to that question might indicate that your client is either poorly informed or misinformed about some consequence of her drinking or drug use. Such misconceptions might need to be altered in an objective and non-confrontational way (see the section on *Providing Information*, pp. 54–55).

LIFE SATISFACTION

To help raise issues and concerns, ask your client to think about how she saw herself in the past and what she would like to see for herself in the future. A contrast between her present and past hopes or future aspirations can often create an uncomfortable discrepancy for your client. This discomfort can be a powerful motivating force for change. Rollnick *et al.* (1992) have suggested that this strategy should only be used with clients who are at least already somewhat concerned about their drug or alcohol use.

Looking back

Begin with the following types of question:

'When you were [eighteen] what sorts of things did you think that you'd be doing now?'

You can then explore with your client how her past expectations differ from the current situation by asking questions like:

'How does that differ from what is happening now?'
'How do you feel about that?'
'What effect did your use of ... have on things?'

The aim of these questions is to guide your client to make links between substance use and her goals or aspirations.

Looking forward

Similarly, with regard to the future:

'How would you like things to be different in the future?'
'What's stopping you doing what you'd like to?'
'How does your use of ... affect your life at the moment?'

Such questions often result in expressions of worry and concern about drug or alcohol use and lead your client into talking about a need for behaviour change. Some therapists alternatively ask more direct questions:

'If you choose to carry on drinking what do you think will happen?'

and

'How do you feel about that?'

When you have explored this area, summarise past/future aspirations in relation to the present and highlight the role of substance use. Use your client's own words wherever possible.

Trouble shooting

This strategy can result in your client expressing strong feelings of hopelessness or despair. While acknowledging the distress, focus on the fact that while it is difficult, your client is able to make choices about changing her current behaviour. Also stress that changing substance use behaviour can lead to positive changes in her life and explore the benefits that your client might obtain from changing. Remember, belief in the possibility for change is an important motivator.

SELF vs. USER

Similar to the strategy outlined above, this approach also aims to increase what Saunders *et al.* (1991) have described as the 'psychological squirm' of your client. It allows her to consider the discrepancy between herself as a person vs. herself as a substance user.

You might ask:

'What would your best friend say are your good qualities?'

(This wording of the question is useful with clients suffering low self-esteem.)

'Tell me ... how would you describe the things you like about yourself?'

Explore these attributes using reflective listening statements and further questioning, summarise and then ask:

'And how would you describe you the heroin user/drinker?'

Again, explore these attributes in some detail, summarise, and then ask:

'How do these things fit together?'

Saunders *et al.* (1991) noted that this exercise invites your client to focus on those aspects of herself as a substance user which contradict her values and how she would like to see herself. It is of course crucial that the setting for this examination is empathic and non-judgemental. Conclude the strategy with a summary, highlighting those discrepancies identified by your client.

HELPING WITH DECISION-MAKING

If you have been successful in helping your client to express concerns about a need for change, the next step is to help her resolve to take action to alter the substance use behaviour. This step is crucial because clients can be concerned about their drinking or drug use but still not make a commitment to action. Miller and Rollnick (2002, p. 127) have suggested that some of the following signs might indicate when your client is ready for this step: decreased resistance; less talking about the problem; a more calm and resolved attitude; increased change talk; talking about how life might be after a change; or experimenting with strategies for change.

It is useful to begin this phase of motivational interviewing by summarising and drawing together the threads of the interview. This will involve reviewing your client's own perception of the problem and summing up her ambivalence—including what remains positive or attractive about the problem. You should also restate your client's comments about wanting or intending to change and offer your own assessment of the situation. Emphasise areas of concern you share with your client and include any objective evidence of the presence of risks or problems. The aim of the summary is to draw together as many reasons for change as possible, while at the same time acknowledging your client's mixed feelings about change.

Following the summary, move on to ask one of the following types of key questions:

'Where does this leave you now?'
'What's going to happen now ... where do we go from here?'
'What does this mean about your drinking/drug use?'

If your client states that she wants to give up or reduce substance use it is extremely important that you do not 'take over' at this point and tell her what to do. This would undermine the whole process of motivational interviewing which has encouraged your client to express responsibility and concern for her behaviour. Remember also that her ambivalence has not 'disappeared', rather the balance has simply been tipped towards change. If you are over-eager or push too hard for action, this balance might well be reversed.

It is also important that you support your client's self-efficacy by reviewing her past successes, exploring her personal strengths, and elaborating on any comments she makes about feelings of confidence (p. 47). Another way that this can be done is by offering your client a range of possible treatment options such as those outlined in Chapter 4, *Goal-setting*. This allows your client to select strategies that meet specific personal needs and reinforces her perceived personal choice and control. Provide the information about the options in a neutral manner. You might also describe what other clients have done in similar situations. Emphasise that you will provide support and guidance to your client but that she is the best judge about what will be best for her.

When your client expresses a preference for a particular goal, spend some time examining that goal to see how achievable it is and what its likely consequences will be. Here are some questions (based on the work of Miller & Rollnick, 1991, p. 120; Miller & Rollnick, 2002, p. 134) that will help to transform a vaguely expressed goal into a more complete picture that is relevant for your client's concerns:

'How would your life be different if you achieved this goal?'
'You have said that you think you would like to cut down. How do you think this would work?'
'What can you think of that might go wrong with your plan?'
'What are some of the skills that you have now that might help you to achieve this goal?'

PROVIDING INFORMATION FOR PRE-CONTEMPLATORS

Providing information can be a useful strategy in a number of contexts. It can be used to provoke thinking about change with some clients who are not currently concerned about their drug or alcohol use. It also provides your client with the opportunity to find out more about the effects of her substance use and correct any misconceptions about risks associated with use. For example, in interventions aimed at reducing harm from injecting drug use, users may be at a contemplation stage for sharing injecting equipment but be pre-contemplators with regard to using condoms. In this case, providing information and personalising the risk (see below) can raise your client's awareness of the interconnections between risk behaviours (Baker & Dixon, 1991).

It is often useful to begin by asking clients what *they* know about the risks associated with their substance use. This serves to acknowledge your client's understanding of the hazards, and allows you to identify any misinformation that needs to be clarified. You can then ask your client if she would like to know more. It is often useful to ask permission to give information, in a very low-key fashion, for example:

'I wonder, would it be useful to spend a few minutes looking at this question of what is a safe level of use while you are pregnant ...?'
'Would you be interested in knowing more about the effects of alcohol on the body?'

If your client agrees, refer to 'expert' opinions and provide the information in a neutral, non-judgemental and non-personal way, for example: 'What can happen to people who drink beyond the recommended limit is ...' After providing the information ask your client:

'What do you make of this? How does it tie in with your use of ...'

or

'I wonder, how is this relevant for you?'

These questions are the key motivational aspect of providing information and it is therefore important that you take time to explore the personal implications of the information for your client. However, you should ensure that you are not using the information as evidence to push the client into change; this is *not* the aim of providing information. Rather you are endeavouring to raise doubts and to increase your client's perception of the risks and problems associated with her drug use. If you are successful in doing so, you may wish to continue the interview by further exploring her concerns and their implications for change (see above).

However, remember that motivational interviewing emphasises the client's responsibility and for some clients this will mean the right to make an informed decision to continue her substance use for the present. With such clients it is nevertheless worthwhile recognising that information provided carefully in the present might well have an important impact some time later.

OTHER APPLICATIONS OF MOTIVATIONAL INTERVIEWING

PERSONALISED FEEDBACK OF ASSESSMENT RESULTS

The providing information strategy described above provides a model for feeding back results from assessment for all your clients. In personalised feedback, you provide your client with *both*: (a) objective measures of her situation (such as the severity of dependence, level of HIV risk taking, cognitive performance or results from a liver function test); *and* (b) a simple explanation about what these results might mean and how they compare with population norms or the types of clients generally seen at your agency.

Personalised feedback helps to increase your client's motivation by providing selected information about health at a 'teachable' moment, such as a moment when her concern regarding her own health is heightened. This will be more effective than giving general education about the effects of alcohol and other drugs, because it is harder for your client to dismiss the personally relevant information that you are providing.

Present the feedback in a quiet, non-judgemental manner. Avoid 'scare' tactics. Your aim is to provide her with enough information for her to draw her own conclusions. If you are about to feed back the results of a standardised questionnaire such as the SADQ-C, begin by asking your client what things she noticed about her responses to the questionnaire.

Try to emphasise from the outset that your client will be free to form her own opinion. Miller and Rollnick (2002, p. 150) have suggested that you preface your feedback with a comment that clearly shows your interest in her opinion. For example:

'I don't know what you will make of this result, but ...'

If you have carried out several standardised tests, present the results in a written format, perhaps even with diagrams. Use this written report as an aid to assist you in explaining the details to your client. Tell your client what her score was on a particular test and then explain how her score is compared with other people's. For instance, she might have scored 36 on the SADQ-C. Explain that people with high levels of dependence on alcohol tend to have scores above 30 on the SADQ-C. High levels of dependence are associated with a range of physical responses to alcohol. Describe these responses of tolerance, withdrawal and drinking to avoid withdrawal.

Always follow up feedback of information by seeking your client's response. For example:

'What do you think about this?'
'How does this fit with your expectations?'
'How do you feel about this?'
'Does this surprise you?'

Be aware that information presented in this way may raise strong emotional issues for your client. Your empathy and reflective listening will help her to explore these feelings without becoming defensive.

If appropriate, provide your client with information explaining how a change in substance use can remedy abnormal findings. At the end of the feedback period, summarise the identified problems and risks and your client's reactions to that information. Emphasise any concerns your client expressed and any comments she might have made indicating her need or desire for change. Allow your client the opportunity to react to or modify your summary.

Trouble shooting

Medical results within the normal range should be dealt with carefully. Your client, for example, might interpret a result in the normal range as indicating that her substance use is causing no problems. It is possible to counter this by suggesting that continued use will undermine your client's ability to maintain good health and that the results might have been even better if she were not drinking or using drugs.

For such clients, you might also choose to address in detail the issue of tolerance. For example, a careful reframing of tolerance is particularly effective if your client has observed that she is less affected by alcohol than she used to be. Ask her what she sees as the advantages and disadvantages of this change. Having acknowledged these pros and cons, you might then ask whether she is aware of the physical implications of tolerance. Explain to her that the effects caused by alcohol are often warning signals that she has drunk too much. With increasing tolerance, however, she might not register these warning signals and will continue to drink even though she may have reached a physically harmful level. It might help to draw an analogy with the way in which pain is a kind of warning signal to prevent a person from further damaging their body.

MOTIVATIONAL INTERVENTIONS IN A GROUP SETTING

Within the group setting, a number of motivational interviewing strategies can be used although it is unlikely that they will be as powerful as when used in the individual setting. For example, a consideration of the 'good' and 'less good' things might be brainstormed on a group level with home practice exercises involving each individual client writing down personally relevant issues in a decision matrix. An example of a matrix is found at the end of this chapter. It requires that clients examine the pros and cons of both change and continued drug use. Remember, when setting such a home practice exercise, you should instruct your clients to focus on those positive and negative issues that are really of concern to them. Otherwise they might simply tote up all the pros and cons while remaining emotionally unmoved.

Rolling with resistance in groups can be more difficult than with individual clients, particularly if one client tends to dominate the group with resistant talk. You might pre-empt some difficult behaviours by setting ground rules for communication (see Chapter 1, *General Counselling Skills*). Walters, Ogle and Martin (2002) have also suggested that you counter strong resistance by inviting quieter or more experienced members of the group to give their point of view. You can also provide summaries reflecting on what has been said in the group which particularly emphasise constructive, non-argument comments by group participants. If you wish to read further about how to adapt motivational interviewing in a group setting, see the *Resources List*.

SUMMARY

Miller and Rollnick (2002, pp. 36–41) have outlined and summarised the four broad clinical principles that underlie motivational interviewing. They are:

- Express empathy:
    Acceptance and respect for your client's position facilitates change.
    Skilful reflective listening is fundamental.
    Ambivalence is normal.
- Develop discrepancy:
    A discrepancy between present behaviour and important goals will motivate
        change.
    The client should present the arguments for change.
- Roll with client resistance:
    Avoid arguing for change because arguments are counter-productive and cause
        defensiveness.
    Flow with resistance rather than opposing it.
    Invite your client to consider new perspectives rather than imposing them.
    Actively involve your client in the search for solutions.
    Resistance is a signal to change strategies.
    Statements that a client makes can be reframed slightly to create a new mo-
        mentum towards change.
- Support self-efficacy:
    Your client's belief in her ability to change is a great motivator.
    Your client's self-efficacy is fostered by your belief in her ability to change.
    The client is responsible for choosing and carrying out personal change.
    There is hope in the range of alternative approaches available.

RESOURCES LIST

Baker, A. & Dixon, J. (1991). Motivational interviewing for HIV risk reduction. In: W.R.
    Miller & S. Rollnick (eds). *Motivational Interviewing: Preparing People to Change
    Addictive Behavior* (pp. 293–302). New York: Guilford Press.
    —Applies the stages of change model and motivational interviewing to the goal of harm-
    reduction.

Miller, W.R. (1983). Motivational interviewing with problem drinkers. *Behavioural Psycho-
    therapy*, **11**, 147–172.

—This is the original and still one of the best descriptions of the principles of motivational interviewing.

Miller, W.R. (1985). Motivation for treatment: A review with special emphasis on alcoholism. *Psychological Bulletin*, **98**, 84–107.
—Also excellent background reading in this area.

Miller, W.R. (1995). Increasing motivation for change. In: R.K. Hester & W.R. Miller (eds), *Handbook of Alcoholism Treatment Approaches: Effective Alternatives* (2nd edn) (pp. 89–104). Boston: Allyn and Bacon.
—A brief summary of the approach.

Miller, W.R. & Rollnick, S. (2002). *Motivational Interviewing: Preparing People to Change Addictive Behavior* (2nd edn). New York: Guilford Press.
—We highly recommend this book. It provides an excellent, detailed and up-to-date account of the principles and practices of motivational interviewing, especially Part II, *Practice*. There are also guidelines on how to apply motivational interviewing in various settings and with various client groups.

Miller, W.R. & Rollnick, S. (1991). *Motivational Interviewing: Preparing People to Change Addictive Behavior*. New York: Guilford Press.
—The original edition of the above text from which we drew some examples. This edition also includes a chapter on personalised feedback of assessment information (pp. 89–99).

Miller, W.R., Zweben, A., DiClemente, C.C. & Rychtarik, R.G. (1994). *Motivational Enhancement Therapy Manual: A Clinical Research Guide for Therapists Treating Individuals with Alcohol Abuse and Dependence*. Project MATCH Monograph Series (Volume 2). NIH Pub. No. 94-3723. Rockville, MD: National Institute on Alcohol Abuse and Alcoholism.
To order a copy, go to: www.niaaa.nih.gov/publications/match.htm
—This session-by-session manual, based largely on the material from Miller and Rollnick (1991), was used for Project MATCH.

Rollnick, S., Heather, N. & Bell, A. (1992). Negotiating behaviour change in medical settings: The development of brief motivational interviewing. *Journal of Mental Health*, **1**, 25–37.
—An extremely useful 'how to' article, particularly in the context of medical settings and brief interventions.

Rollnick, S. & Miller, W.R. (1995). What is motivational interviewing? *Behavioural and Cognitive Psychotherapy*, **23**, 325–334.
—A useful discussion of motivational interviewing as a way of interacting with your client.

Saunders, B., Wilkinson C. & Allsop, S. (1991). Motivational intervention with heroin users attending a methadone clinic. In: W.R. Miller & S. Rollnick (eds), *Motivational Interviewing: Preparing People to Change Addictive Behavior* (pp. 279–292). New York: Guilford Press.
—Describes the use of motivational interviewing as counselling component added to a methadone maintenance program.

Velasquez, M., Maurer, G.G., Crouch, C., & DiClemente, C.C. (2001) *Group Treatment for Substance Abuse: A Stages-of-Change Therapy Manual*. New York: Guilford Press.
—A session-by-session manual on how to run groups based on the stages of change model and the principles of motivational interviewing.

Walters, S.T., Ogle, R. & Martin, J.E. (2002). Perils and possibilities of group-based motivational interviewing. In: W.R. Miller & S. Rollnick (eds) *Motivational Interviewing:
Preparing People for Change* (2nd edn) (pp. 377–390). New York: Guilford Press.
—An excellent discussion on how to apply motivational interviewing in a group setting
and how to overcome some common obstacles in groups.

http://motivationalinterview.org/
—A very informative site covering the main clinical principles of motivational interview-
ing. It also provides bibliographies, lists of training videos and opportunities for further
training. Created and maintained by C. Wanger and W. Conners of the Mid-Atlantic
Addiction Technology Transfer Centre in cooperation with the Motivational Interviewing
Network of Trainers (MINT), W.R Miller and S. Rollnick.

PRACTICE SHEET

A DECISIONAL BALANCE SHEET

Here is an example . . .

Continuing to drink without change		Making a change to my drinking	
Pros	**Cons**	**Pros**	**Cons**
Helps me escape	*Could lose my*	*Happier marriage*	*How to cope?*
I like getting high	*marriage*	*Helps money problems*	*Lose my mates*
	Bad example for the	*Time for kids*	*Miss the high.*
	kids	*Improve my health*	
	Spend too much	*Enjoy work more*	
	Wrecking my health		
	Might lose my job		
	Feel awful		

Fill in your pros and cons below. Don't worry if they seem to contradict each other. The important thing is that they show how you see *your situation at the moment*.

Continuing to drink without change		Making a change to my drinking	
Pros	**Cons**	**Pros**	**Cons**

Source: Adapted from Miller & Rollnick (2002).

4

Goal Setting

BASIC GUIDELINES

Goal setting is an important process that applies the information that has been derived from assessment and lays down a mutually agreed plan for the direction of treatment. By explaining the various options in plain language, you can assist your client to make a responsible decision about his own welfare. The ideal style for negotiating treatment goals with your client is motivational interviewing, which was discussed in Chapter 3.

It is also important to prepare your client for the possibility that the strategies and goals he has chosen might not work out as planned. He needs to understand that the treatment process can involve some trial and error in order to identify the plan that fits best with his personal needs. Your goals should therefore provide *concrete* signposts to guide therapy and measure progress over time, *and* be flexible enough to allow adjustment to new information gained during the course of treatment. Ideally your goals should have the following characteristics:

- *Negotiated*: All goals should be negotiated between you and your client. This ensures that (a) your client is committed to the goals since he was instrumental in defining them and (b) the goals also reflect your professional judgement. Do not insist on a particular set of goals against your client's wishes. Attempting to do so will only decrease your client's motivation and retention in treatment.
- *Specific and observable*: Each goal should be defined in concrete behavioural terms so that both you and your client will be able to identify clearly whether that goal has been achieved. For example, 'cutting down gradually' is a vague term that cannot be clearly measured. 'Cutting down by 3 standard drinks a week' can be measured, leaving no doubt about treatment progress. You may find it useful to make a written summary of your client's goals and plans so that you can both measure his progress throughout therapy. An example of a 'Change plan sheet'

based on the work of Miller, Zweben, DiClemente and Rychtarik (1994) is given in the Practice Sheet at the end of this chapter.

- *Broken into short-term targets*: Working towards a large, major goal can be daunting for clients, particularly those who have experienced a sense of failure during past attempts at changing their drug use or drinking. If goals can be broken down into smaller targets, your client can develop a sense of mastery and encouragement as each target is reached. The experience of achievement will help to enhance your client's self-esteem and increase his motivation to continue in the treatment process.

  While it is easy to see how the overall goals of moderation or reduced HIV risk taking can be broken into smaller targets, the application of short-term targets to the goal of abstinence is less obvious since abstinence is usually achieved by immediate cessation of your client's drinking or drug using. Nevertheless, there may be a number of lifestyle changes that are required to help your client maintain abstinence and it will be easier for your client to manage these if they are broken down into prioritised targets.

- *Achievable*: Negotiation should focus on identifying goals that are achievable. Sometimes it may be necessary for you to compromise your expectations about the ideal goal if your client appears to be unable to achieve that goal at this stage. Success with less ambitious goals is preferable to your client experiencing a sense of total failure and dropping out of treatment as a result.

The later parts of this chapter describe goals concerning alcohol, opioid and other drug use. These primary goals should be the focus of your treatment. However, regardless of the type of substance that your client uses, he may also need help to improve his general lifestyle. Some lifestyle issues will need to be addressed before proceeding with treatment. For example, your client may need immediate assistance with arranging detoxification, preventing suicide, finding accommodation, stabilising financial income or finding refuge from a violent family situation. Other issues might be less urgent but if left unaddressed throughout the course of treatment, they could undermine your client's progress towards a change in his drug or alcohol use.

GOALS TO IMPROVE LIFESTYLE

Clients who misuse alcohol and other drugs are also likely to have problems in other areas of their lives. These problems could have preceded and contributed to the drug dependence. For example, a client might be self-medicating to deal with psychological distress such as depression, post-traumatic stress or social phobia. Psychological discomfort or disturbances are very common among drug-using populations but it is not always clear whether the psychological disturbance preceded or resulted from the substance misuse (see further discussion of this issue in Chapter 20, *Dual Diagnosis*). For many clients the substance use will have led to major disruptions in

Table 1: Lifestyle treatment goals

AREA OF CLIENT'S LIFE	INTERVENTION
Family and relationshps	Couples therapy, assistance for family members, working with concerned others, specialist family therapy, parenting skills, childcare assistance, intervention for domestic violence or sexual abuse.
Employment	Vocational assistance, skills-building, training in job interviews, financial aid, incentives to seek alternatives to drug-related crime.
Legal	Legal advice, court liaison.
Housing	Housing assistance, residential care.
Psychological state	Therapy or treatment for psychological problems such as suicidal risk, anxiety, depression, psychosis, antisocial behaviour, post-traumatic stress disorder or brain injury.
Physical health	Medical treatment including detoxification, nutritional assistance, management of illnesses, advice on dental health, respite care, exercise, assistance for pregnant women.
Social functioning	Communication skills training, assertiveness training, building drug-free social support networks (e.g., self-help groups or peer support).

social, legal, psychological and/or financial stability. Your client may have structured his whole lifestyle around access to his favourite substance. These issues are therefore important to consider during the goal-setting process. Some issues can be dealt with in your treatment programme while others may best be addressed via referral to or liaison with specialist agencies, such as mental health, welfare and legal services. If your client has complex problems, a case management approach is an appropriate way to coordinate his care plan (Chapter 18). Potential areas for concern and suggested interventions are summarised in Table 1.

HARM REDUCTION GOALS

The principle of harm reduction is to reduce the damaging effects of substance abuse on individuals, families and society. Harm reduction does not mean that you condone substance use or encourage your client to keeping using or drinking. In fact, abstinence is one strategy of harm reduction—perhaps the ideal strategy. However, many clients may be unable or unwilling to stop drinking or using drugs at the time they present to you. The goal of your intervention then becomes helping your client to stay alive with the minimum of negative long-term effects, until such a time he is able to make more substantial changes to his substance use (Mentha, 2002).

Changes that might result in harm reduction include:

- Changing the way the substance is taken in (known as the 'route of administration'). This might include educating your client about where to get and how best to use clean injecting equipment. Alternatively, it might involve setting the goal of using the substance without injecting (e.g., by smoking, snorting or eating).
- Replacing the harmful drug with a safer and legally available prescribed substance, such as methadone or buprenorphine (see Chapter 14, *Pharmacotherapies*).
- Reducing the frequency, dosage or mix of substances (e.g., by ceasing the use of drug 'cocktails' or by limiting drinking to the weekend).
- Reducing other behaviours that are potentially harmful (e.g., unprotected sex, driving while intoxicated, neglecting self-care, injecting when alone).
- Quitting alcohol or drug use.

There is some overlap between harm reduction strategies and the strategies for dealing with lapses or relapses (pp. 221–236). A client who has chosen a goal of abstinence might still make contingency plans (e.g., by resolving to drink low alcohol beer or to always use new injecting equipment) in order to reduce his risk of harm in case he experiences a (re)lapse.

GOALS CONCERNING ALCOHOL USE

There are three possible goals in the treatment of alcohol problems and these are described in Table 2.

As discussed above, these overall goals can be broken into smaller targets. For example, if the goal is moderation, you might want to begin by eliminating especially risky behaviours such as drinking while driving, heavy drinking binges or drinking in certain contexts. These issues are discussed at length in Chapter 12, *Behavioural Self-management*.

CHOOSING BETWEEN ABSTINENCE AND MODERATION

In addition to your client's personal preference, consider the following guidelines when choosing between abstinence and moderation:

- *Organic damage*: When physical damage has already occurred as a result of drinking, continued drinking is likely to further aggravate such damage. For

Table 2: Alcohol-related treatment goals

GOAL	DESCRIPTION
Abstinence	Client quits drinking.
Moderated drinking	Client moderates drinking to harm-free levels that reduce the risk of physical, personal or social problems that drinking may be causing. These levels are often guided by recommendations from health authorities. For more information, see Chapter 12, *Behavioural Self-management*.
Attenuated/reduced drinking	For some clients, a reduction of drinking will help to reduce the harm to self or family. This is not an ideal goal but may be the only feasible goal for some clients.

example, a client who has liver or bone marrow dysfunction, pancreatitis or peptic ulceration should be encouraged towards abstinence.

- *Organic brain damage or cognitive dysfunction*: Abstinence is the preferred option for brain-damaged clients because continued drinking will aggravate existing cognitive dysfunction. Clients with brain dysfunction can also experience difficulty in learning the coping skills required for a moderated drinking goal.
- *Psychiatric comorbidity*: Abstinence may be the preferred treatment goal if your client has persistent psychiatric disorders such as anxiety, depression or personality disorder. These disorders should be addressed before deciding in favour of moderation.
- *Physical withdrawal*: If withdrawal has been frequent and/or severe (e.g. your client has had delirium tremens), then abstinence may be indicated.
- *Severity of alcohol dependence*: Abstinence is appropriate for clients with a high severity of dependence while less dependent clients may be able to moderate their drinking successfully. The scores from assessment tools such as the *Severity of Alcohol Dependence Questionnaire (SADQ)* and the *Short form Alcohol Dependence Data Questionnaire (SADD)* (see Chapter 2, *Assessment*) can be used as a guide to planning the goals and intensity of treatment. For example, Heather (1995) suggested that clients with low dependence are likely to benefit from a brief intervention with a goal of moderation whereas clients with moderate dependence could benefit from either a brief or intensive intervention aimed at the goal of their preference, and clients with high dependence are more suited to an intensive abstinence-oriented intervention.
- *History of drinking*: If your client has had repeated unsuccessful attempts at moderating his alcohol intake with professional assistance, then he may find the goal of abstinence more achievable. On the other hand, any evidence that your client has been able to control his drinking in some situations favours the moderation goal. In circumstances where a drinker has repeatedly been unable to comply with abstinence, a moderation goal may be worth considering as an

alternative, provided that there is no alcohol-related organic damage that would be aggravated by further drinking.

- *Social support*: If there are people within your client's social network whose usual level of drinking is light to moderate, this could provide a supportive setting for him to learn moderation. If, however, your client has based his social life around the pub scene and other heavy drinkers, the social support network may not be conducive to moderation. This client is more likely to benefit from restructuring his social network around support for abstinence such as is provided by Alcoholics Anonymous (see Chapters 15, *Self-help Groups* and 16, *Relapse-prevention Training*).
- *Partner's preference*: You might also need to consider the preferences of your client's partner and family members. For instance, your client's partner may have specific concerns about any repercussions from his continued drinking. The support provided by your client's partner, family members and friends for the treatment goal is also going to be an important contributor to outcome (see Chapter 13, *Involving Concerned Others*).

These factors are not hard and fast rules but are useful guidelines to discuss with your client during the decision-making process. *The guidelines will help you to arrive at a treatment goal that is attainable, safe and desirable.*

Trouble shooting

Occasionally you and your client might disagree over the suitability of the goal that he has chosen. For instance, despite a high severity of problems associated with drinking, your client might want to aim for a goal of moderation whereas you might feel that abstinence is more appropriate. There are several ways that you could choose to deal with this difference of opinion. The following options have been derived from the work of Miller (1995). You might choose to:

(1) Decline to help your client towards his goal. You might select this option if you feel that it would be unethical for you to support your client's chosen goal. This decision might be best weighed up after considering the possibility of option 2.
(2) Accept your client's chosen goal on a provisional basis or make a compromise. For example, Miller and Page (1991) have described three options that they called 'warm turkey' to contrast them with immediate abstinence or 'cold turkey'. These options are:
  (a) A negotiated period of trial abstinence. For example, if your client wants to try for moderation, suggest that a six-month period of abstinence would be an advantage before an attempt at moderation. The abstinent period provides time-out for your client to recover from the physical effects of the alcohol and to deal with any other problems related to his heavy drinking. Negotiate an agreement to review the treatment goals at the end of this time-out period.

(b) A gradual tapering of consumption down towards abstinence. To achieve this you will need to set realistic, intermediate goals and provide your client with a 'day diary' for self-monitoring his drinking, such as the one provided in Chapter 12, *Behavioural Self-management.*

(c) A period of trial moderation. For example, your client may want to test out whether or not he is able to learn how to drink in moderation. If, despite having appropriate skills training, he has found that moderation is too difficult to achieve, abstinence may then seem a more reasonable goal.

(3) Try to coerce your client to change his goal. You might choose this option if you feel that you are obliged or able to protect your client from an otherwise risky decision. This approach, however, may be counter-productive if your client becomes defensive and uncooperative. It is also likely to undermine the collaboration that you have so far achieved.

Even when you and your client agree from the outset about what the goal is to be, your negotiations should continue throughout the course of treatment as you regularly review your client's progress towards those goals.

GOALS CONCERNING OPIOID AND OTHER DRUG USE

From a harm reduction perspective, the ideal goal is abstinence from drug use. However, where total abstinence is unrealistic, you and your client will need to consider methods for reducing drug use and associated drug-related harm (e.g., HIV risk-taking behaviours). If your client is a polydrug user, treatment should concentrate on the drug that is causing the most problems. When one drug is reinforcing the use of another, however, it may be more effective to focus on both drugs simultaneously.

ABSTINENCE FROM DRUG USE

The most common setting for treatment aimed at a drug-free lifestyle is the therapeutic community. Most clients will have strong preferences about whether or not they wish to pursue drug-free treatment. Empathic counselling and the skills-based approaches outlined in this book are extremely applicable to this setting. As many of these skills are most effectively taught in groups, the structure of therapeutic communities is ideally suited for this training.

As an alternative to drug-free treatment, pharmacotherapies can provide a means of achieving abstinence or a reduction of illicit drug use (see Chapter 14, *Pharmacotherapies*). These interventions can help to stabilise your client's illicit opioid use, with associated reductions in criminal activity and risk of infection with HIV and Hepatitis B and C. For example, Ward, Mattick and Hall (1998) have recommended that a client's suitability for pharmacotherapy should be based not only on his level of dependence but also on the risks associated with his lifestyle and current health.

REDUCTION OF DRUG-RELATED HARM

Harm reduction is especially concerned with reducing the risk of infection with the human immunodeficiency virus (HIV) and other infectious diseases related to drug use and lifestyle, such as hepatitis and other sexually transmitted diseases. The promotion of safer practices in drug use and sexual behaviour should be addressed in all types of settings. It could be a main goal of treatment if your client is likely to continue to use illicit drugs or be included as part of relapse prevention training within drug-free programmes.

To teach your client effectively about harm reduction, you need to be clear about your own goal as a therapist. For instance, if part of your role is to 'police' your client's illicit drug use, your client may fear that talking honestly with you about his drug use is going to have an adverse effect on him within the programme. Ward, Mattick and Hall (1992) have suggested that policing and counselling should be carried out by two different workers, making it possible for you, as the therapist, to take a non-judgemental attitude when negotiating harm reduction goals. It may also help to explain to your client that working towards harm reduction does not mean that you are condoning his continued illicit drug use.

Goals for Reducing Unsafe Injecting Practices

The following continuum of drug using behaviours reads from the least to the most reduction in risk of HIV and hepatitis. You may wish to help your client identify attainable goals using this continuum:

(1) Sharing injection equipment but decontaminating as effectively as possible for HIV and other blood borne diseases.
(2) Only using new, sterile syringes and equipment (including filters, spoons, cookers, ties and alcohol swabs) when preparing and injecting drugs.
(3) Taking illicit drugs without injecting (e.g., by swallowing, snorting or smoking).
(4) Abstinence from illicit drug use.

Goals for reducing other harms associated with injecting might involve educating your client about vein care or addressing risks of overdose by ceasing to use drug cocktails or by not injecting alone. For further details about a wide range of harm reduction strategies, see the *Resources List*.

Goals for Reducing Unsafe Sexual Practices

Sexual practices can also be ranged in a hierarchy from those most likely to permit the transmission of HIV or other diseases if one partner is infected (e.g., unprotected anal intercourse) to those that carry little risk (e.g. mutual masturbation). Safe sex is any sex where semen or pre-cum, blood or vaginal fluid cannot get into the blood-stream of the other person. Of course, you should also encourage your clients to get vaccinated against Hepatitis B.

Safe sex means ...

- Always using condoms and water-based lubricant for penises and sex toys, with vaginal or anal sex.
- Taking special care with condoms in anal sex.
- Cleaning sex toys before reusing (dildos, dolls etc.).
- Using gloves and lubricants in manual sex where there are cuts or sores on the hands.
- Avoiding menstrual blood when engaging in oral sex with women, if the mouth has cuts or sores (dental dams can be used).
- Engaging in self-masturbation, kissing and hugging, frottage (rubbing) or Spanish (between the breasts).
- Having sex with only one partner in an exclusively monogamous relationship after both people have had negative HIV or hepatitis test results and when they do not share fits or injecting equipment.
- Having no sex.

MENU OF STRATEGIES

Once you and your client have agreed upon a treatment goal, you will need to decide on the preferable strategies for achieving that goal. Provide your client with a menu of strategies from which to choose and discuss each one with him to explore its relevance for his situation. Most of the strategies in this book can be used for goals related to alcohol, opioids or other drugs. Your client might want to consider:

- *Refusal skills and assertiveness training*: Helps your client to respond effectively to social pressure about drinking, using drugs or risk-taking behaviour.
- *Other skills training*: Helps your client to enhance his communication skills and ability to solve problems.
- *Cognitive therapy*: Challenges destructive thought processes, enhance self-esteem and deal with strong emotions.
- *Relaxation training*: An alternative way of dealing with anxiety, and a method for managing cravings.
- *Behavioural self-management*: If his goal is to moderate his drinking.
- *Involving concerned others*: For encouragement and practical support.
- *Self-help groups*: For support from people with the same goals.
- *Pharmacotherapies*: To assist in dealing with cravings or reducing drug-related harm.
- *Relapse-prevention training*: To recognise and deal with situations in which he is likely to relapse and establish a lifestyle in support of his goals.

RESOURCES LIST

Hamilton, M., King, T. & Ritter, A. (2004). *Drug Use in Australia: Preventing Harm*, Melbourne, VIC: Oxford University Press.
—Looks at a range of different approaches to harm reduction, against a background of social, cultural and political contexts.

Gowing, L., Proudfoot, H., Henry-Edwards, S. & Teesson, M. (2001). *Evidence Supporting Treatment: The Effectiveness of Interventions for Illicit Drug Use*. Woden, ACT: Australian National Council on Drugs.
Available at:
http://www.ancd.org.au/publications/pdf/rp3_evidence_supporting.pdf
—Reviews the research literature on the treatment of illicit drug problems and makes recommendations regarding appropriate goals and a range of interventions.

Heather, N. & Robertson, I. (1997). *Problem Drinking* (3rd edn). Oxford: Oxford University Press.
—This classic text includes a discussion of the goals of abstinence and moderation and presents evidence supporting the use of skills-based approaches in treatment for alcohol problems.

Heather, N. (1995). Brief intervention strategies. In: R. Hester & W.R. Miller (eds), *Handbook of Alcoholism Treatment Approaches* (pp. 105–122). Boston: Allyn and Bacon.
—Includes suggested guidelines for how alcohol dependence might be used to plan the intensity and goals of treatment.

Inciardi, J.A. & Harrison, L.D. (eds) (2000). *Harm Reduction: National and International Perspectives*. Newbury Park, CA: Sage Publications.
—Describes harm reduction philosophies and programmes from different parts of the world.

Kelly, J.A., St. Lawrence, J.S., Betts, R., Brasfield, T.L. & Hood, H.V. (1990). A skills-training group intervention model to assist persons in reducing risk behaviors for HIV infection. *AIDS Education and Prevention*, **2**(1), 24–35.
—Practical guidelines for helping clients to reduce unsafe sexual practices.

Marlatt, G.A. (2002). *Harm Reduction: Pragmatic Strategies for Managing High-Risk Behaviours*. New York: Guilford Press.
—How to apply harm reduction to addictive behaviours and other high-risk behaviours.

National Health and Medical Research Council (2001). *Australian Alcohol Guidelines: Health Risks and Benefits*. Canberra: NH&MRC.
Available at: www.alcoholguidelines.gov.au
—Gives a detailed summary of the detrimental health effects of excessive alcohol consumption and other alcohol-related harm.

Shand, F., Gates, J., Fawcett, J. & Mattick, R.P. (2003). *Guidelines for the Treatment of Alcohol Problems* (pp. 34–36). Canberra: Australian Government Department of Health and Ageing.
—Provides brief evidence-based guidelines on the link between assessment, engagement and goal setting.

Mentha, H. (2002). *An Introduction to Working with Alcohol and Other Drug Issues* (2nd edn). Melbourne: Eastern Drug and Alcohol Service.
Available at: http://www.edas.org.au/pdf/introdrug2002.pdf
—An excellent brief introduction to the key issues of drug and alcohol therapy.

Miller, W.R. (1995). Increasing motivation for change. In: R.K. Hester & W.R. Miller (eds), *Handbook of Alcoholism Treatment Approaches: Effective Alternatives* (2nd edn) (pp. 89–104). Boston: Allyn and Bacon.
—This chapter includes guidelines on how to clarify goals with your client.

Miller, W.R. & Page, A.C. (1991). Warm turkey: Other routes to abstinence. *Journal of Substance Abuse Treatment*, **8**(4), 227–232.
—Discusses three approaches to achieving abstinence when abrupt quitting is not the preferred option.

Miller, W.R. & Rollnick, S. (2002). *Motivational Interviewing: Preparing People to Change Addictive Behavior* (2nd edn). New York: Guilford Press.
—Guidelines for negotiating goals and plans for action are discussed in Chapter 10: Phase II: Strengthening commitment to change.

Miller, W.R., Zweben, D.S.W., DiClemente, C.C. & Rychtarik, R.G. (1994). *Motivational Enhancement Therapy Manual: A Clinical Research Guide for Therapists Treating Individuals with Alcohol Abuse and Dependence* (Project MATCH Monograph Series, Volume 2). NIH Pub. No. 94-3723. Rockville, MD: National Institute on Alcohol Abuse and Alcoholism.
Order copies at: www.niaaa.nih.gov/publications/match.htm
—'Phase 2' of this session-by-session manual provides a motivational interviewing approach to strengthening commitment and setting goals.

Ward, J., Mattick, R.P., & Hall, W. (1998). *Methadone Maintenance Treatment and Other Opioid Replacement Therapies*. Amsterdam: Harwood Academic Publishers.
—A comprehensive guide to the use of drug substitution in the treatment of opioid dependence, with guidelines on how to use assessment results to plan treatment goals and interventions.

Ward, J., Mattick, R.P. & Hall. W. (1992). *Key Issues in Methadone Maintenance Treatment*. Sydney: New South Wales University Press.
—A summary of methadone maintenance treatment research and clinical issues.

Weingardt, K.R. & Marlatt, G.A. (1998). Sustaining change. In: W. R. Miller & N. Heather (eds), *Treating Addictive Behaviors* (2nd edn) (pp. 337–351). New York: Plenum Press.
—This chapter provides a concise discussion of the basic principles of harm reduction.

HARM REDUCTION RESOURCES

The following booklets are available from the National Drug and Alcohol Research Centre (NDARC), University of New South Wales, Sydney NSW 2052, Australia. Copies can be ordered from: Publications.resources at:
http://ndarc.med.unsw.edu.au/ndarc.nsf

A user's guide to speed
—Harm reduction and tips for quitting or cutting down amphetamine use.

Ecstasy: Facts and Fiction
—Provides information about the short-term and long-term effects of using ecstacy and how to reduce associated risks of harm.

Heroin
—Based on interviews with heroin users, this booklet provides information on heroin, its effects and the risks involved, with particular emphasis on preventing overdose.

Inhalants
—Examines the different types of inhalants available and the risks associated with their use.

Some useful internet sites include:

http://www.aivl.org.au/
—The site for the Australian Injecting and Illicit Drug Users' League (AIVL) which gives information about a range of harm reduction issues related to injecting drug use and has pamphlets and booklets available for purchase.

http://www.adf.org.au/drugstore/pdf/Harm_Minimise_Fact_Sheet.pdf
—Mainly focusing on the risks associated with intoxication, this fact sheet shows young people how to plan for safety at parties (Knox Community Health Service and the Australian Drug Foundation).

http://www.fds.org.au/pdf/FactSheet17a_HM.pdf
—A two page summary of 'Harm Minimisation for the User' with a special section on injecting drugs and what to do in case of overdose (Family Drug Support, Australia).

http://www.harmreduction.org/brochure.html
—For downloading pamphlets on how to reduce harm associated with drug use (Harm Reduction Coalition, USA), such as: 'Getting Off Right: A Safety Manual for Injecting Drug Users'.

http://www.lindesmith.org/reducingharm/
—Practical information about harm reduction, covering a range of drugs and risk behaviours, including club drugs and cannabis (Drug Policy Alliance).

http://www.wrecked.co.uk
—Quizzes about alcohol, aimed at harm reduction (National Health Service, UK).

http://www.ysas.org.au/harm_reduction/safer_injecting.html
—Describes ways to avoid contracting or passing on viral, bacterial and other infections, how to prevent overdose and vein damage, and how to avoid influencing others to take risks (Youth Substance Abuse Service, Australia).

PRACTICE SHEET

PLANNING FOR CHANGE

What changes do you want to make?

What are the most important reasons for wanting to make these changes?

What steps do you plan to take towards making these changes?

How can other people help you make these changes?

People   Possible ways to help

What obstacles might get in the way of your plan?

How will you know that your plan is working?

Source: Adapted from Miller *et al.* (1994).

II

Strategies for Action

5

Brief and Early Interventions

RECOMMENDED USE

Brief and early interventions aim to screen, detect and intervene with clients before substance dependence develops. Brief and early interventions were founded on the principle that by encouraging the large numbers of risky drinkers in the community to cut down their drinking to recommended health limits, there would be an overall reduction in alcohol-related morbidity, mortality and associated social and economic costs for the general community.

There is now a large body of evidence to support the effectiveness of this approach with drinkers and tobacco smokers, and some evidence to support its relevance for cannabis and other drug users. This suggests that the methods might be effective with a range of drug problems or risk-taking behaviour. Since most brief interventions have been developed for alcohol use, this chapter focusses primarily on how to intervene to reduce risky drinking. Where appropriate, we have indicated resources that you might also use with other drugs.

There are two broad classes of brief interventions: early interventions, sometimes known as 'brief, opportunistic interventions' where a client who has not specifically sought help for his alcohol use is nevertheless detected to have risky levels of drinking; and brief interventions that are offered instead of more intensive interventions to clients who have actively sought help for their drinking problems.

Early interventions are typically delivered in primary health care settings and are also applicable to other health care settings. They are usually delivered in a single session of up to 30 minutes. Early or brief interventions of a slightly longer duration are appropriate in certain circumstances, such as when time is available or with clients who are detected to have higher risk drinking or drug use.

Brief interventions over a few sessions (e.g., one to five sessions) are also appropriate in drug and alcohol treatment settings. In this setting, they are most appropriate for clients who want to change their drug or alcohol use and who present with low to moderate dependence and few alcohol- or drug-related problems.

Early and brief interventions for alcohol may be appropriate for either abstinence or moderation goals. In practice they are typically aimed at the goals of moderate or harm-free drinking (Heather, 1995). However, they might also be the treatment of choice for risky drinkers who need to abstain from alcohol for a period of time, for example, because of pregnancy, during breast-feeding or while taking prescribed medication (Babor & Higgins-Biddle, 2001). Brief interventions are most effective for clients without severe dependence or entrenched alcohol-related problems because these clients are more able to change their drinking in response to clear advice from a credible health professional. Nevertheless, your screening process will detect clients with more severe alcohol problems and you should also offer these clients a brief intervention, a follow-up appointment and options for referral, if necessary.

A good proportion of clients who might benefit from a brief intervention are likely to be in a pre-contemplation stage or ambivalent about changing their alcohol or drug use (see *Stages of Change*, pp. 31–33). Therefore, the strategies of motivational interviewing are very important for intervening effectively. We strongly recommend that you read Chapter 3, *Motivational Interviewing* in combination with this chapter. You might also wish to read Chapter 12, *Behavioural Self-management* which is particularly relevant for clients who are ready to change their drinking. Chapter 4, *Goal-setting* is relevant for brief interventions with clients who use drugs other than alcohol because it provides guidelines for identifying harm reduction goals.

GOALS

Brief and early interventions aim:

- to screen for and detect individuals with risky alcohol or drug use;
- to offer clear information and advice to help clients reduce risky levels of drinking or drug use;
- to offer referral for clients with more severe alcohol- or drug-related problems; and
- to follow-up your client's progress and provide additional guidance if needed.

KEY CONCEPTS

STANDARD DRINKS/UNITS

As different drinks contain different amounts of alcohol a standard drink provides a useful way of recording drinking. While the absolute amount of alcohol in a standard drink varies slightly from country to country (Australia = 10 g, UK = 8 g and USA = 14 g) a standard drink generally approximates the size of a typical serving of beer, wine or spirits. The 'Guidelines for Sensible Drinking' (p. 164) show how to measure standard drinks or units for typical alcoholic beverages served in bars in Australia, the UK and the USA.

RISKY DRINKING

Risky drinking refers to levels of alcohol consumption that have been identified by national health authorities as potentially harmful. Australian guidelines for 'Levels of Risk in Drinking Alcohol' are given at the end of this chapter.

METHOD

SETTINGS FOR BRIEF INTERVENTIONS

Brief and early interventions should be conducted routinely in settings where: (a) the number of risky drinkers is likely to be highest; and (b) where the impact of detection and advice to cut down will have the greatest effect. These settings include:

- *General and specialist medical practices*: Because of their role in primary health care and their high rate of contact and credibility with the general public, general and specialist medical practitioners are ideally positioned to detect clients with drug and alcohol problems and offer them advice on low risk levels of consumption.
- *General hospitals*: In general hospitals, there should be procedures to screen for risky alcohol and other drug use among inpatients and outpatients, and procedures for appropriate intervention. At the very least, any general hospital that has dedicated drug and alcohol health workers on site should have routine formal detection procedures put in place. These detection procedures should be followed by brief intervention and referral as necessary. This may include a letter to the referring doctor giving feedback regarding the level of consumption and advising the need for follow-up of the patient.
- *The workplace*: Detection of excessive alcohol consumption should be a part of any routine health evaluation in the workplace. Such screening and brief intervention will increase the health and safety of workers, and limit hazards and accidents occurring in the workplace.
- *Welfare and general counselling services*: Screening in welfare and counselling services offers the opportunity of referral for intervention, and potentially a better outcome for the clients of these services. It is likely in a significant proportion of cases that excessive alcohol or other drug consumption has contributed to the presenting problem.
- *Drug and alcohol treatment services*: For many clients seeking help for drinking or drug use, brief interventions (up to five sessions) are likely to be as effective as a

more intensive intervention (Shand, Gates, Fawcett & Mattick, 2003). In drug and alcohol treatment services, such brief interventions have dual benefits: (a) to efficiently meet the needs of clients with less severe problems; and (b) to make more time available to provide intensive interventions to higher needs clients. Brief interventions aimed at harm reduction may also be more appropriate for court mandated clients who are pre-contemplators and not yet interested in substantially changing their substance use.

SCREENING AND DETECTION

If you or your colleagues work in a primary health care setting, you need to be prepared to actively screen clients in order to detect those who might benefit from an early intervention. There are a number of screening methods, including asking your client about his drinking or drug use, using standard questionnaires or a medical examination for clinical signs of risky drinking or other risk-taking behaviours. Of these methods, direct questions or the use of a questionnaire are the most efficient and cost-effective approaches and these are outlined below.

Asking About Alcohol and Other Drug Use

Although screening for alcohol and drug use is now more common and even routine in some settings, many health care providers are uncomfortable asking their clients such questions. Your routine assessment of health problems that might be caused or worsened by excessive alcohol consumption (such as hypertension, depression, diabetes, sleep disturbance or obesity) will present an opportunity to ask about drinking.

Begin by explaining the relevance of drinking to your client's health concerns. You might use a general statement linking the two, such as: 'With many people we find that drinking can affect their blood pressure'. To help him speak more freely, use language that normalises drinking. For example, you might say: 'Most people like to have a drink. How often would you drink during an average week?' This can be followed by a question about the quantity consumed on each occasion. Sometimes it is better to over-state the amount your client might be drinking as this will allow him to give you a more accurate estimate without embarrassment. For example, if he says that he 'has a few beers most nights', you could ask 'So how much would you drink each night ... say, more than ten beers?'

Another opportunity arises when providing or renewing prescriptions. Because alcohol interacts negatively with some medications, you could introduce its relevance for your client in the following way: 'Because these medications don't work as well (or are dangerous) when they are combined with alcohol, I'd like to ask you a few questions about your drinking.' By asking these questions with confidence but without judgement, you will encourage your client to discuss his drinking more openly.

If your client seems to have health or other problems that might be related to drug abuse, the above approach could also be used to ask about other drug use (e.g., cannabis, opioid, amphetamine or long-term benzodiazepine use). Because some of these drugs are illicit, it is even more important that you take a non-judgmental approach and, if needed, inform your client regarding his rights of confidentiality.

Screening for Risky Drinking

A simple way of identifying your client's pattern of drinking is by compiling a *One-Week Retrospective Diary* (Shakeshaft, Bowman & Sanson-Fisher, 1998). Ask your client what and how much he drank yesterday, the day before, and so on, until you have gone back over the past week. Make sure that you ask about the types of beverages and what containers they came in, so that you can make accurate estimates of the number of standard drinks he consumed. Use the guidelines for 'Levels of Risk in Drinking Alcohol' at the end of this chapter to evaluate your client's risk of alcohol-related harm.

We also recommend that you use the *Alcohol Use Disorders Identification Test (AUDIT)* a brief scale developed for the World Health Organization (Babor, Higgins-Biddle, Saunders, & Montiero, 2001). A copy of the AUDIT is presented on p. 92.

To score the AUDIT, give a score from 0 to 4, for each of the first eight questions. For the last two questions, 'No' scores 0, 'Yes, but not in the last year' scores 2 and 'Yes, during the last year' scores 4. Qualitative information can be gained from looking at the person's response to individual items. Items one to three examine the pattern of alcohol consumption, items four to six look at signs of dependence, and the final four questions, seven to ten, refer to alcohol-related problems the person may be experiencing. AUDIT scores can be used to guide your decisions about what type of brief or early intervention is needed (see *How to Intervene— Primary Health Care Settings*, below).

Other instruments for screening alcohol problems are listed in the *Resources List*. These include instruments for screening during pregnancy.

Screening for Other Drug Problems

You may be able to detect drugs problems by simply asking your client whether he has ever had a problem with drug use. The *Drug Abuse Screening Test (DAST-20)* (Skinner, 1982) can also be used to measure the degree of problems or consequences related to drug abuse in the past 12 months. Shown on p. 93, the DAST-20 takes about five minutes to administer. All 'yes' answers score 1, except for items 4 and 5, where 'no' scores 1. The Dast-20 is a general scale and therefore may not detect problems that are unique to specific types of drugs.

Be aware that your client's response to the questionnaire items might be influenced by his fear of judgement or other negative consequences. You should also be aware that self-administered questionnaires are limited by literacy and memory problems.

HOW TO INTERVENE—PRIMARY HEALTH CARE SETTINGS

The duration of the intervention will depend on several factors. For example, it might be influenced by the amount of time you have available, the severity of alcohol- or drug-related problems, and your client's stage of change. Some interventions might not even involve face-to-face contact. For example, a letter from a GP advising the patient to reduce his prescribed benzodiazepine medication is a form of brief intervention. The section below focusses on face-to-face interventions in primary health care settings and outlines three levels of intervention: (1) brief, simple advice to cut down during a consultation about other health issues; (2) brief educational counselling focussed on limit setting and strategies for change; and (3) offering a referral to clients in need of more intensive interventions.

Simple Advice in One Session

Early or brief opportunistic interventions in primary health care settings often involve simple advice delivered in one session, ranging between 5 and 30 minutes in duration. Simple advice is particularly appropriate if your client has an AUDIT screening test score in the range of 8–15 or if your client scores below 8 but reports drinking levels above the low-risk limits for any one day or the low-risk weekly limits (Babor & Higgins-Biddle, 2001).

The art of giving brief advice is to keep communication with the client direct and simple. At a minimum, after identifying that your client is drinking in a risky way . . .

- give brief feedback regarding the results of the screening;
- provide clear, firm and non-judgmental advice to cut down consumption;
- describe the low-risk levels of consumption (and perhaps offer him the handout 'Guidelines to Sensible Drinking', p. 164); and
- offer him a follow-up appointment.

At follow-up, reassess his drinking levels. If they remain the same, ask him what 'got in the way' of changing his drinking. If necessary, provide further brief counselling or offer him a referral to a drug and alcohol treatment service.

Brief Educational Counselling

Brief educational counselling is a slightly more systematic and focussed intervention involving a longer session. Babor and Higgins-Biddle (2001) have suggested that the use of this approach in primary health care settings is most appropriate for clients with AUDIT scores in the range of 16–19 (indicating an increased risk of alcohol-related harm), clients who present with a mental or physical health problem due to risky drinking or clients who have other alcohol-related problems such as injuries, violence, poor work performance and social or legal problems related to frequent intoxication. Brief educational counselling is also appropriate if your client has not responded to a previous session of simple advice. Of course, the provision of this more extended form of brief intervention will depend on how much time you have available.

The main components of brief educational counselling are:

- Simple advice as described above.
- Further assessment of the extent of your client's alcohol problem (Chapter 2, *Assessment*).
- Personalised feedback based on your assessment of your client's alcohol consumption and the likely negative consequences associated with risky drinking (pp. 55–57).
- Assessment of your client's readiness for change (pp. 31–33). For example, you might ask him: 'How interested are you in changing your drinking?'
- Advice about limit setting and strategies for cutting down (Chapter 12, *Behavioural Self-management*).
- Provision of self-help material (such as the 'Tips for Drinking in Moderation' handout on p. 165, or other self-help material in the *Resources List* at the end of this chapter).
- The offer of a follow-up appointment.

Trouble shooting

If your client does not make any changes after your intervention, he might be at a pre-contemplation stage—content with his current pattern of drinking despite your feedback about the possible negative consequences. Continue to engage him on other health issues and, where appropriate, provide treatment to reduce drinking- or drug-related harm (e.g., by providing thiamine or information about safer injecting practices, pp. 65–66. As future opportunities arise, you might ask him whether he has had any further thoughts about cutting down. Alternatively, if your client seems interested in changing his drinking or using but does not implement a change after a brief intervention, he may have more severe problems requiring a referral for further more intensive assistance.

Offering a Referral

A referral for a more intensive drug and alcohol treatment programme is most appropriate if your client has a score of 20 or more on the AUDIT screening test, severe alcohol dependence, a prior history of alcohol or drug dependence, liver damage, a prior or current serious mental health problem or if he has not been able to achieve his goals after a brief intervention (Babor & Higgins-Biddle, 2001). These clients may need detoxification treatment and will probably need more intensive or longer term treatment, including the methods we have described in other chapters. A score of more than four on the dependence questions in the AUDIT (questions four to six) is an indication of likely dependence. Further information about assessing your clients alcohol dependence is given in Chapter 2, *Assessment* and, for guidelines on how to use dependence measures to determine the goals and intensity of treatment, see p. 67

Introduce the idea of referral by first giving your client personalised feedback about the results of screening and assessment. Make a clear and firm recommendation about the need for further assessment and intervention and be optimistic about the potential benefits of a referral. Provide your client with information about a range of referral options and ask him what he prefers. If you continue to see your client for other matters after making a referral, monitor his progress and provide further encouragement or guidance, if necessary.

Trouble shooting

Your client might be reluctant to agree to a referral because of feelings of shame associated with the idea of being an 'alcoholic' or because he is at a stage of pre-contemplation about changing his drinking. It is important to roll with resistance and to avoid imposing a label or judgement on your client (Chapter 1, *General Counselling Skills*). It might be helpful to give him a range of referral options for his consideration and offer him a follow-up appointment to come back and talk some more about it.

HOW TO INTERVENE—DRUG AND ALCOHOL SETTINGS

For many clients seeking help from a drug and alcohol treatment service, a few sessions of counselling in a non-residential setting will be all that is needed and often all that is wanted. Brief intervention in a drug and alcohol treatment service is particularly appropriate for clients who have low to moderate dependence and few drug- or alcohol-related problems. As well as simple advice and brief educational counselling (see above), brief sessional interventions might also include the following:

- An assessment of your client's alcohol dependence and other areas of functioning (Chapter 2, *Assessment*).
- A more extensive motivational interviewing approach to help your client explore his ambivalence, to elicit his concerns about drinking and to reflect and affirm his change talk (Chapter 3, *Motivational Interviewing*).
- The identification of high-risk situations and an introduction to relapse prevention strategies (Chapter 16, *Relapse Prevention Training*).
- Arrangements for follow-up appointment(s).

Monitor your client's progress over the course of the counselling sessions and help him to make adjustments in response to any high-risk situations that he encounters. Encourage him to plan for all contingencies. For instance, if your client usually drinks in a social context and plans to avoid this by not going out, you might ask a question to test the feasibility of this plan (e.g., 'Perhaps you'll reach a point where you do want to go out, so how could you do that without drinking too much?'). At the same time, it is important to foster self-efficacy by indicating your optimism that your client's goals are achievable.

BRIEF INTERVENTIONS FOR DRUG USE

Scores from the DAST-20 can be used to guide your decisions about interventions for drug use. A score of zero suggests that your client has no evident drug-related problems. In this case, focus on reinforcing your client's healthy lifestyle choices. Scores of 1–5 indicate that your client might benefit from a brief intervention. Use the individual items of the DAST-20 as a starting point for identifying any concerns he has regarding his drug use. Scores of 6–10 indicate the need for a more intensive approach (e.g., a longer intervention with follow-up appointments and the offer of a referral). If your client scores above 10 on the DAST-20, he is very likely to need a referral for drug and alcohol treatment.

The basic principles of brief intervention for drinking problems outlined above might also be applicable when your client has problems with drugs. Start by giving your client personalised feedback about his screening results or drug-related health problems. Invite him to reflect on this information by asking 'What do you make of this?' (p. 56). Depending on the nature of his problems and his stage of change, give your client information about harm reduction (pp. 70–71) and offer him information about how to cut down or quit his drug use. If he seems interested in changing his drug use, talk briefly about what strategies he would use and ask him when he will be ready to make a change. Offer him self-help materials, such as those listed in the *Resources List*. Where appropriate, provide him with a range of options for referral, including the methods described in other chapters of this book. Monitor his progress in follow-up appointments.

SUMMARY OF COMMON ELEMENTS

The common elements of brief intervention are neatly summed in the acronym 'FRAMES', which stands for:

Feedback about the health implications of your client's drinking levels or drug use.
Responsibility for change resides with your client.
Advice to change his drinking or drug use.
Menu of options for change.
Empathy in your counselling style.
Self-efficacy to be enhanced by conveying an optimistic belief that change is possible.

(Derived from Miller & Sanchez, 1993)

RESOURCES LIST

Adamson, S.J. & Sellman, J.D. (2003) A prototype screening instrument for cannabis use
  disorder: The Cannabis Use Disorders Identification Test (CUDIT) in an alcohol
  dependent clinical sample. *Drug and Alcohol Review*, **22**, 309–315.
  Scale is available from: http://adai.washington.edu/instruments/CUDITinfo.htm
  —A modification of the AUDIT to screen for cannabis problems. This paper presents
  evidence for its validity although more research is needed to evaluate its use.

Babor, T.F., Higgins-Biddle, J.C., Saunders, J.B. & Montiero, M.G. (2001). *The Alcohol Use
  Disorders Identification Test: Guidelines for Use in Primary Care* (2nd edn). Geneva:
  World Health Organization.
  Available at: http://www.who.int/substance_abuse/publications/alcohol/en/
  —The latest version of the AUDIT, a validated and widely accepted brief screening
  instrument for use within primary health care settings.

Babor, T.F. & Higgins-Biddle, J.C. (2001). *Brief Intervention for Hazardous and Harmful
  Drinking: A Manual for Use in Primary Care*. Geneva, Switzerland: World Health
  Organization.
  Available at: http://whqlibdoc.who.int/hq/2001/WHO_MSD_MSB_01.6b.pdf
  —A key resource for our chapter, this manual is designed to be used as a companion to
  the AUDIT. It includes information about the health effects of alcohol, guidelines for
  deciding what level of intervention is appropriate, methods of brief intervention and also
  includes self-help material to give to your client.

Baker, A., Kay-Lambkin, F., Lee, N.K., Claire, M. & Jenner, L. (2003). *A Brief Cognitive
  Behavioural Intervention for Regular Amphetamine Users: A Treatment Guide*. Canberra,
  ACT: Australian Government Department of Health and Ageing.
  Available at:
  www.health.gov.au/pubhlth/publicat/document/cognitive_intervention.pdf
  —An excellent four session manual to assist amphetamine users to reduce levels of
  consumption and risk-taking behaviour.

Bien, T., Miller, W. & Tonigan, J. (1993). Brief interventions for alcohol problems: a review.
  Addiction, **88**(3), 315–355.
  —An excellent review of the effectiveness of brief interventions for alcohol problems,
  including a discussion of the 'FRAMES' approach.

Bohn, M.J., Babor, T., & Kranzler, H.R. (1991). Validity of the Drug Abuse Screening Test
  (DAST-10) in inpatient substance abusers. *Problems of Drug Dependence*, **119**, 233–235.
  —A briefer version of the DAST which correlates well with the DAST-20. Copies of the
  DAST-10 and information about its interpretation are available from Harvey A. Skinner,
  Department of Public Health Sciences, University of Toronto.

Dawe, S., Loxton, N.J., Hides, L., Kavanagh, D.J. & Mattick, R.P. (2002). *Review of
  Diagnostic Screening Instruments for Alcohol and Other Drug Use and other Psychiatric
  Disorders* (2nd edn). Canberra: Commonwealth of Australia.
  Available at: http://www.health.gov.au/pubhlth/publicat/document/mono48.pdf
  —A comprehensive resource providing detailed descriptions of screening and assessment
  tools for substance abuse and psychiatric disorders.

Heather, N. (1995). Brief intervention strategies. In: R.K. Hester & W.R. Miller (eds),
  Alcoholism Treatment Approaches: Effective Alternatives (2nd edn) (pp. 105–122).

Boston: Allyn and Bacon.
—An excellent overview of the principles of brief and early interventions applicable for primary health care and drug and alcohol treatment settings, with a review of their effectiveness.

Heather, N., Bowie, A., Ashton, H., McAvoy, B., Spencer, I., Brodie, J. & Giddings, D. (2004). Randomised controlled trial of two brief interventions against long-term benzodiazepine use: Outcome of intervention. *Addiction Research and Theory*, **12**(2), 141–154.
—Showed that short GP consultations or a letter from the GP advising that the patient reduce their use of benzodiazepines resulted in reduced intake of these drugs without adverse consequences.

Martino, S., Grilo, C.M. & Fehon, D.C. (2000). Development of the Drug Abuse Screening Test for Adolescents (DAST-A). *Addictive Behaviors*, **25**(1), 57–70.
—Presents a version of the DAST that has been adapted for younger clients.

Miller, W.R. & Sanchez, V.C. (1993) Motivating young adults for treatment and lifestyle change. In: G. Howard (ed.), *Issues in Alcohol Use and Misuse by Young Adults* (pp. 55–79). Notre Dame, IN: University of Notre Dame Press.
—Describes the common components of effective brief interventions using the acronym 'FRAMES'.

National Health and Medical Research Council (2001). *Australian Alcohol Guidelines: Health Risks and Benefits*. Canberra: NH&MRC.
Available at: www.alcoholguidelines.gov.au
—Describes and explains the definitions of risky and high-risk drinking and the sensible drinking guidelines recommended by the Australian National Health and Medical Research Council.

Rollnick, S., Heather, N. & Bell, A. (1992). Negotiating behaviour change in medical settings: The development of brief motivational interviewing. *Journal of Mental Health*, **1**, 25–37.
—This excellent article demonstrates the application of a motivational interviewing approach to brief and early interventions.

Russell, M., Martier, S., Sokol, R. & Mudar, P. (1994). Screening for pregnancy risk-drinking. *Alcoholism, Clinical and Experimental Research*, **18**, 1156–1161.
—Describes the *T-ACE* and *TWEAK*, two instruments which can be used for screening risky drinking in prenatal clinics.

Sanchez-Craig, M. (1996) *A Therapist's Manual for Secondary Prevention of Alcohol Problems*. Toronto: Addiction Research Foundation.
Available from the Centre for Addiction and Mental Health, 33 Russell Street, Toronto, ON, Canada M5S 2S1 or
http://www.camh.net/publications/substance_use_addiction.html
—A guide to brief and early interventions for dealing with mild to moderate drinking problems, including case examples and assessment tools. This manual can be used in combination with the self-help booklet *DrinkWise* (see below).

Sanchez-Craig, M., Davila, R. & Cooper, G. (1996). A self-help approach for high-risk drinking: Effect of an initial assessment. *Journal of Consulting and Clinical Psychology*, **64**, 694–700.
—This study of two types of brief intervention using an earlier version of *DrinkWise* (see below) discusses the benefits of self-help material when used in brief interventions.

Saunders, J.B., Aasland, O.G., Babor, T.F., de la Fuente, J.R. & Grant, M. (1993). Development of the Alcohol Use Disorders Identification Test (AUDIT). WHO collaborative project on early detection of persons with harmful alcohol consumption. II: *Addiction*, **88**, 791–804.
—Presents research on the use of the earliest version of the AUDIT to screen for alcohol problems.

Shakeshaft, A., Bowman, J. & Sanson-Fisher, R. (1998). Comparison of three methods to assess binge consumption: One-week retrospective drinking diary, AUDIT, and quantity/frequency. *Substance Abuse*, **19**(4), 191–203.
—Describes and compares the use of these three measures with clients of community-based drug and alcohol counsellors.

Shand, F., Gates, J., Fawcett, J. & Mattick, R.P. (2003). *Guidelines for The Treatment of Alcohol Problems* (pp. 91–95). Canberra: Australian Government Department of Health and Ageing.
—Evidence-based recommendations for brief and early interventions.

Skinner, H.A. (1982). The drug abuse screening test. *Addictive Behaviors*, **7**, 363–371.
—This useful instrument for detecting problems associated with drug use comes in three forms, depending on the number of items: the DAST-28, the DAST-20 (shown on p. 93) and the DAST-10.

SELF-HELP MATERIALS

Commonwealth Department of Veterans Affairs (2003). *Changing the mix: A guide to low risk drinking for the veteran community*. Canberra: Commonwealth Department of Veterans Affairs.
Available at: www.therightmix.gov.au
—A well set out and informative self-help manual designed for veterans.

Heather, N., Richmond, R., Webster, I., Wodak, A., Hardie, M. & Polkinghorne, H. (1989). *A Guide to Healthier Drinking: A Self-help Manual*. Sydney: Clarendon Printing.
—This brief and colourful manual is available from the Brief Intervention Unit at the University of New South Wales, Sydney, NSW 2052, Australia.

Mentha, H. (2001). *Getting Out of It: How to Cut Down or Quit Cannabis*. Victoria, Australia: Inner East Community Health Service.
Available at: www.edas.org.au/pdf/cannabis.pdf
—A practical step-by-step guide to cutting down or quitting cannabis.

Miller, W.R. & Munoz, R.F. (2004). *Controlling Your Drinking: Tools to Make Moderation Work for You*. New York: Guilford.
—Very practical and easy-to-follow guide for clients and therapists.

Robertson, I. & Heather, N. (1993). *So, You Want to Cut Down Your Drinking? A Self-help Guide*. Edinburgh: Scottish Health Education Group.
—Another practical and engaging self-help guide to moderation.

Robertson, I. & Heather, N. (1996). *Let's Drink to Your Health!* (2nd edn). Oxford, UK: BPS Blackwell.
—An extremely useful and comprehensive self-help manual.

Robertson, I. & Heather, N. (1987). *Let's Drink to Your Health! A Guide to Safe and Sensible Drinking*. Sydney: Angus & Robertson.
—An adaptation of the first edition of the above reference for readers from Australia or New Zealand.

Sanchez-Craig, M. (1995) *DrinkWise: How to Quit Drinking or Cut Down*. Toronto, ON, Canada: The Centre for Addiction and Mental Health (CAMH).
Formerly entitled 'Saying When', this resources is available from the Centre for Addiction and Mental Health, 33 Russell Street, Toronto, ON, Canada M5S 2S1 or
http://www.camh.net/publications
—*DrinkWise* offers a step-by-step programme to effectively cut down or quit drinking, by teaching people to identify the situations and feelings that trigger heavy drinking.

The Drug and Alcohol Services Council, South Australia (2001). *Women's Drinking Guide*. Adelaide, Australia: The Drug and Alcohol Services Council.
Available from publications and resources at: www.dasc.sa.gov.au
—An engaging self-help manual to help women reduce risky drinking.

BOOKLETS AND INTERNET SITES

The following booklets are available from the National Drug and Alcohol Research Centre (NDARC). Order copies from: Publications.resources at:
http://ndarc.med.unsw.edu.au/ndarc.nsf

A user's guide to speed.
—Harm reduction and tips for quitting or cutting down amphetamine use. *What's the deal on quitting? A do it yourself guide*
—Designed to assist people who wish to quit using cannabis.

Some examples of internet sites that could assist in brief and early interventions are:

http://www.alcoholguidelines.gov.au
—A very interactive site showing guidelines for sensible drinking, defining standard drinks and providing quizzes, resources and helpful contacts.

http://www.therightmix.gov.au
—A very interactive brief intervention site provided by the Australian Government Department of Veterans Affairs. Includes the AUDIT and a readiness to change assessment, and gives feedback on the level of risk for the individual.

http://www.wrecked.co.uk
—Interactive quizzes about alcohol, with a guide to standard drinks (National Health Service, UK).

AUDIT

Please circle the answer that is correct for you

1. How often do you have a drink containing alcohol?

Never   Monthly or less   2–4 times a month   2–3 times a week   4 or more times a week

2. How many drinks containing alcohol do you have on a typical day when you are drinking?

1 or 2   3 or 4   5 or 6   7, 8 or 9   10 or more

3. How often do you have six or more drinks on one occasion?

Never   Less than monthly   Monthly   Weekly   Daily or almost daily

4. How often during the last year have you found that you were not able to stop drinking once you had started?

Never   Less than monthly   Monthly   Weekly   Daily or almost daily

5. How often during the last year have you failed to do what was normally expected from you because of drinking?

Never   Less than monthly   Monthly   Weekly   Daily or almost daily

6. How often during the last year have you needed a first drink in the morning to get yourself going after a heavy drinking session?

Never   Less than monthly   Monthly   Weekly   Daily or almost daily

7. How often during the last year have you had a feeling of guilt or remorse after drinking? .

Never   Less than monthly   Monthly   Weekly   Daily or almost daily

8. How often during the last year have you been unable to remember what happened the night before because you had been drinking?

Never   Less than monthly   Monthly   Weekly   Daily or almost daily

9. Have you or someone else been injured as a result of your drinking?

No   Yes, but not in the last year   Yes, during the last year

10. Has a relative or friend or a doctor or another health care worker been concerned about your drinking or suggested you cut down?

No   Yes, but not in the last year   Yes, during the last year

TOTAL SCORE . . . .

Source: Babor, T.F., Higgins-Biddle, J.C., Saunders, J.B. & Montiero, M.G. (2001). *The Alcohol Use Disorders Identification Test: Guidelines for Use in Primary Care* (2nd edn). Geneva: World Health Organization. Available at: http://www.who.int/substance_abuse/publications/alcohol/en/

Drug Abuse Screening Test
DAST-20

INSTRUCTIONS

The following questions concern information about your potential involvement with drugs not including alcoholic beverages during the past 12 months. Carefully read each statement and decide if your answer is 'Yes' or 'no'. Then circle the appropriate response beside the questions.

In the statements, 'drug abuse' refers to (1) the use of prescribed or over the counter drugs in excess of the directions and (2) any non-medical use of drugs. The various classes of drugs may include: cannabis (e.g., marijuana, hash), solvents, tranquillisers (e.g., Valium), barbiturates, cocaine, stimulants (e.g., speed), hallucinogens (e.g., LSD) or narcotics (e.g., heroin). Remember that the questions do not include alcoholic beverages.

Please answer every question. If you have difficulty with a statement, then choose the response that is mostly right.

1.	Have you used drugs other than those required for medical reasons?	yes	no
2.	Have you abused prescription drugs?	yes	no
3.	Do you abuse more than one drug at a time?	yes	no
4.	Can you get through the week without using drugs?	yes	no
5.	Are you always able to stop using drugs when you want to?	yes	no
6.	Have you had 'blackouts' or 'flashbacks' as a result of drug use?	yes	no
7.	Do you ever feel bad or guilty about your drug use?	yes	no
8.	Does your spouse (or parents) ever complain about your involvement with drugs?	yes	no
9.	Has drug abuse created problems between you and your spouse or your parents?	yes	no
10.	Have you lost friends because of your use of drugs?	yes	no
11.	Have you neglected your family because of your use of drugs?	yes	no
12.	Have you been in trouble at work (or school) because of drug abuse?	yes	no
13.	Have you lost your job because of drug abuse?	yes	no
14.	Have you gotten into fights when under the influence of drugs?	yes	no
15.	Have you engaged in illegal activities in order to obtain drugs?	yes	no
16.	Have you been arrested for possession of illegal drugs?	yes	no
17.	Have you ever experienced withdrawal symptoms (felt sick) when you stopped taking drugs?	yes	no
18.	Have you had medical problems as a result of your drug use (e.g., memory loss, hepatitis, convulsion, bleeding, etc?)	yes	no
19.	Have you gone to anyone for help for a drug problem?	yes	no
20.	Have you been involved in a treatment programme specifically related to drug use?	yes	no

LEVELS OF RISK IN DRINKING ALCOHOL

Risk in the short-term

	Low risk	Risky	High risk
Males	Up to 6 drinks* a day, no more than 3 days a week	7–10 drinks on any day	11+ on any one day
Females	Up to 4 drinks a day, no more than 3 days a week	5–6 drinks on any day	7+ on any one day

Risk in the long-term

	Low risk	Risky	High risk
Males	Up to 4 drinks per average day Up to 28 drinks per week	5–6 drinks per average day 29–42 drinks per week	7+ drinks per average day 43+ drinks per week
Females	Up to 2 drinks per average day Up to 14 drinks per week	3–4 drinks per average day 15–28 drinks per week	5+ drinks per average day 29+ drinks per week

Source: From the National Health and Medical Research Council, Australia (2001).

* Drinks are standard drinks as defined by Australian guidelines, see 'Guidelines for Sensible Drinking', p. 164.

6

Problem-solving Skills

RECOMMENDED USE

Problem-solving training provides your client with a general skill that will enable her to resolve life problems that might threaten her commitment to change her drinking or drug use. It is appropriate for all clients whether they have abstinence, moderation or harm-reduction goals, and for any type of drug problem. Problem-solving can be taught in either a group or an individual setting although learning is probably facilitated by working in a group of two or more clients.

You can probably teach the basics of problem solving in one or two sessions. However, the skill requires practice to be effectively learnt. Therefore, problem-solving strategies should be practised, refined and reinforced over the remaining course of treatment both in session time and with home practice exercises.

GOALS

The goals of problem-solving skills training are to enable your client to:

- Recognise when a problem exists.
- Generate a variety of potential solutions to the problem.
- Select the most appropriate option and generate a plan for enacting it.
- Be able to evaluate the effectiveness of the selected approach.

METHOD

RATIONALE FOR YOUR CLIENT

Monti, Kadden, Rohsenow, Cooney and Abrams (2002) suggested that you should offer the following rationale for your client. Discuss the way in which people are constantly faced with difficult situations as part of daily life. Difficult situations can either be drug- or alcohol-specific (e.g., being in a group where drugs are available) or more general (e.g., conflict at work). They can arise as a result of individual thoughts or feelings (e.g., depressing thoughts or strong desires to use drugs) or in the course of interactions with others (e.g., arguments). Point out that if a person is unable to deal effectively with such situations as they arise they can become problematic. Emphasise that too often we tend simply either to ignore a problem or to respond with the easiest or first impulsive reaction. However, pressure from an unsolved or poorly solved problem can build up and may well trigger a relapse to drug or alcohol use. You might like to get your client to generate some examples from her experience of when unresolved problems have triggered a relapse. You can then explain that effective problem solving involves your client being able to recognise a problem situation and to take some time to work out an effective solution that will be in her own best interest.

BEFORE STARTING

It is probably useful to prepare a brief summary sheet of the strategy of problem solving to give to your client. An example is provided in the first client handout at the end of this chapter. It is also useful, if possible, to have a whiteboard on which to record your client's brainstorming. In addition, your client should be encouraged to write down examples of the problem-solving process so that she can refer to them later.

THE PROCESS OF PROBLEM-SOLVING

There are six stages to effective problem-solving.

(1) Defining *exactly* what the problem is.
(2) Brainstorming options to deal with the problem.
(3) Choosing the best option(s).
(4) Generating a detailed action plan.
(5) Putting the plan into action.
(6) Evaluating the results.

Defining *exactly* what the problem is

If a problem is well defined, it almost solves itself! However, if the problem is understood only in vague terms, it remains almost impossible to solve. This is because it is unclear what *exactly* the problem is. Therefore, try to define the problem in terms of concrete behaviours that your client can modify. It also helps to break it down into specific parts.

For example, a global problem such as 'My life is out of control' is overwhelming. However, that problem might be broken down into the following more specific problems: (a) I'm lonely because I've lost contact with many of my friends; (b) I feel unattractive because I've gained a lot of weight recently; (c) my job is extremely stressful and unsatisfying; and (d) my boyfriend complains that I don't spend enough time with him. These problems can then be prioritised and the problem-solving technique applied to each. You can help your client clarify and/or break down global problems by careful listening and asking a series of questions such as 'What specific sorts of things happen that make you feel that way?' or 'When exactly do you feel that way?'

Have your client select a problem situation. A relatively easy 'high-risk situation' is a good place to start if these have been identified (Chapter 16, *Relapse-prevention Training*). Help her to frame that problem clearly in concrete behavioural terms. If necessary, get her to break it down into manageable sub-problems and help her to decide the order in which these sub-problems will be tackled.

Trouble shooting

For some clients, recognising when a problem exists may be the most difficult part of problem solving! Monti *et al.* (2002) offer a number of clues for helping clients to identify situations where there may be a problem. These include occasions when your client is aware of: (a) unpleasant physical signs (e.g., craving); (b) negative feelings (e.g., depression, frustration, fear, annoyance); (c) negative reactions from other people (e.g., avoidance, criticism); (d) negative reactions to other people (e.g., anger, withdrawal); and (e) not meeting her own expectations of her behaviour (e.g., performance at work, at home or with friends).

You might also help your client to decide whether a problem area is worth focusing on by getting her to consider how comfortably she could continue to live with the problem and what the consequences would be if the problem were not resolved.

Brainstorming Options to Deal with the Problem

Brainstorming is a technique for generating ideas. There are several rules that help this technique to work.

- *No criticism allowed.* Criticism stifles creativity. The options will be evaluated at a later stage.
- Be as wild, woolly and adventurous as possible—any idea is acceptable. The freer your client is the greater the chance that she might hit on a good novel solution.
- Quantity of ideas is important. The more alternatives there are, the more likely a useful alternative will emerge. Often the best ideas come later in the brainstorming process.
- Think about solutions that have worked before. An old solution might have to be updated and changed but it can provide a good starting point. Ideas can also be combined or added to in the search for a solution. Your client could ask others for suggestions of what has worked for them in similar situations. She should also be

encouraged to think about what she might suggest to a friend facing the same problem.

Brainstorming can work particularly well in a group setting and is often helped if you can start the process by suggesting several options among which are funny or outrageous solutions. Group exercises should involve working on at least one personally relevant problem for each of your clients in turn.

Trouble shooting

Sometimes it can be difficult for a client to brainstorm effective options if she has not defined the problem in terms of a behaviour she can modify (e.g., 'My father bugs me' compared to 'I get annoyed *by my* father and I get sarcastic').

Choosing the Best Option(s)

Begin by deleting any strategies that are obviously impractical. Work through the remaining options by considering the pros and cons of each. The pros and cons can include both the short- and long-term consequences of a choice. Also, get your client to consider what factors might either hinder or help her in putting each option successfully into practice. After weighing up these factors get your client to choose the alternative(s) that she considers to be the most realistic and most likely to be effective.

If you are working with clients in pairs or in larger groups make sure that each client selects their own best solution to a problem. A solution selected by the group may not ultimately be the best or most relevant for the individual concerned.

Generating a Detailed Action Plan

It is important to generate a detailed and concrete plan for putting the selected option into action. This may also involve breaking down the solution into achievable steps. For example, if a solution to a problem was to 'take up a new sport', then the action plan should include deciding what sport, then how to find out where and when to join up and finally setting a date for the first game. In other words the plan should consider the timetable for action along with the 'when, where, how, and with whom', of the selected option.

Putting the Plan into Action

Your client should at least think through, that is mentally rehearse, her plan. In learning problem-solving skills it is also extremely useful, where appropriate, to practise carrying out the plan by using a role-play (as described on p. 12) in session.

Home practice exercises can involve putting the plan into action as it was practised in the session.

Evaluating the Results

Think carefully about whether the selected option resolved the problem totally or only in part. If it was partly or not at all successful, consider whether the action plan needs improving (go back to stage 4) or whether a new strategy is needed (go back to stage 3).

A worked example of problem solving is shown in the second client handout at the end of this chapter, together with a home practice sheet.

RESOURCES LIST

Hawton, K. & Kirk, T. (1989). Problem solving. In: K. Hawton, P.M. Salkovskis, J. Kirk & D.M. Clark (eds), *Cognitive Behaviour for Psychiatric Problems: A Practical Guide* (pp. 406–426). Oxford: Oxford University Press.
—A general guide to problem-solving strategies.

Kadden, R., Carroll, K., Donovan, D., Cooney, N., Monti, P., Abrams, D., Litt, M. & Hester, R. (1995). *Cognitive Behavioral Coping Skills Therapy Manual: A Clinical Research Guide for Therapists Treating Individuals with Alcohol Abuse and Dependence* (Project MATCH Monograph Series, Volume 3). NIH Pub. No. 94-3724. Rockville, MD: National Institute on Alcohol Abuse and Alcoholism.
To order a copy, go to www.niaaa.nih.gov/publications/match.htm
—This session-by-session manual devotes one session to problem-solving, based on guidelines from the book by Monti *et al.* (2002).

Monti, P.M., Kadden, R.M. Rohsenow, D.J., Cooney, N.L. & Abrams, D.B. (2002). *Treating Alcohol Dependence: A Coping Skills Training Guide* (2nd edn) (pp. 99–102). New York: Guilford Press.
—A comprehensive section on problem-solving is provided.

SIX STEPS TO SUCCESSFUL
PROBLEM-SOLVING

(1) **Define exactly what the problem is.**
Make sure the problem is concrete and if necessary broken down into several subproblems.

(2) **Brainstorm options to deal with the problem.**
Remember—no criticism allowed—be adventurous!

(3) **Choose the best option(s) by examining the pros and cons of each potential solution.**
Which solution will work best?

(4) **Generate a detailed action plan.**
Plan the 'when, where, how and with whom' of the selected solution.

(5) **Put the plan into action.**
Role-play or mentally rehearse the plan and then actually carry it out.

(6) **Evaluate the results to see how well the selected solution worked.**
If the solution didn't work go back to stage 3 and try again!

PROBLEM-SOLVING EXAMPLE

Stage 1: My problem is:

I have few friends and it's easy for me to start feeling lonely and depressed—especially in the evenings and on weekends. When I feel lonely, I usually try to drown my sorrows with wine.

Stage 2: Brainstorm possible solutions

Join a club or a class in something that interests me.
Use the internet to chat to people.
Join a singles club.
Join a gym or take up t'ai chi.
Get a dog!
Go out to dance clubs to meet people.
Stop living alone and look for shared accommodation.
Don't dwell on past missed opportunities.

Stage 3: Pros and cons of each solution

Possible solution	Pros	Cons
Go to discos	I like dancing	Risk of drinking
Move house	I'd have company at home I'd meet my flatmate's friends	It'd cost time and money to change accommodation
Join a club or attend a class	Would meet people who share my interests	I'm worried that I won't know what to say or I'll embarrass myself

. . . and the winner is: <u>join a club or attend a class</u>

Stage 4: What's my plan?

<u>How?</u>   To find out what clubs or classes are available locally that might interest me. My interests: cooking, reading, dancing. I've always wanted to try painting.

<u>When?</u>   Find out the information before the next session.

<u>Where?</u>   Look in Saturday's paper. Ring up the local council. Get them to send me details about time, place and price.

<u>With whom?</u>   I'll go to the club or class alone but my therapist will help me practise some conversational skills before my first attendance.

PROBLEM-SOLVING

Stage 1: My problem is:

Stage 2: Brainstorm possible solutions

Stage 3: Pros and cons of each solution

Possible solution	Pros	Cons

. . . and the winner(s) is/are _____

_____

Stage 4: What's my plan?

How?

When?

Where?

With whom?

Stage 5: Carrying out my plan.

Stage 6: How well did it work?

Drink and Drug Refusal Skills

RECOMMENDED USE

All clients face situations where they experience social pressure to drink or use drugs. Drink and drug refusal training teaches clients how to refuse offers with confidence and without making limp excuses! It can be an invaluable tool for helping to prevent relapses for clients with abstinence goals (Chapter 16, *Relapse Prevention Training*). Alternatively, it can be helpful in assisting clients with moderation goals to keep to predetermined limits in the face of temptation to over-drink (Chapter 12, *Behavioural Self-management*). These refusal skills can also be easily adapted to help clients with harm reduction goals avoid risk-taking behaviours such as needle-sharing and unsafe sexual practices.

In short, you should routinely offer this refusal training to clients who indicate a lack of confidence in dealing with social pressure to drink, use drugs and/or engage in risk-taking behaviours. You can teach the skills on an individual basis although a group setting can be particularly effective because clients learn from each other in role-play activities.

GOALS

To teach your client to refuse offers to drink or use drugs in an appropriately assertive way.

METHOD

RATIONALE FOR YOUR CLIENT

Explain to your client that almost everyone, at some time, will be placed in a situation where he is offered drinks or drugs. If your client has chosen to abstain, point out that he will find it impossible to *permanently* avoid all the situations (e.g., restaurants or social functions) where he might be offered a drink or drugs. If your client has chosen moderation as his goal, explain that refusal skills can help him keep to his planned limits.

For all clients, acknowledge that saying 'no thanks' convincingly and confidently can often be difficult and explain that there are a number of strategies that can make saying 'no' easier. These include using appropriate body language, sounding confident and, of course, using direct statements to refuse the offer.

It is also important to stress to your client that there is absolutely no need for him to feel guilty about not drinking or using! In their work, Monti, Kadden, Rohsenow, Cooney and Abrams (2002, p. 65) reminded clients that 'You have a right not to drink'. For clients with drinking problems it is also useful to point out that in many social situations people don't even notice who is or isn't drinking alcohol.

Having covered these important basics with your client you can then go on to teach the key elements of a successful refusal. These are drawn from the section on drink refusal by Monti *et al.* (2002) in their book referenced in the *Resources List*.

BODY LANGUAGE

Explain that feeling unsure or anxious about refusing offers of alcohol or drugs often leads people to slouch or hunch and avoid looking at the other person. Discuss with your client how such body language actually further decreases self-confidence and sends a timid and unconvincing message to the person offering the drink or drug(s). Therefore, one of the first crucial hints for making refusals 'stick' is to *make direct eye contact* with the drink or drug 'pusher'. Standing or sitting straight also helps to create a confident air.

TONE OF VOICE

Again, a shy, uncertain tone will allow room for the other person to question the refusal. Therefore, you should encourage your client to speak in *a firm and unhesitating* manner.

After covering these two 'rules', it might be very useful for you to model examples of 'wrong' and 'right' use of body language and tone of voice by having a client role-play offering you a drink or drug(s). By contrasting a timid with a confident approach you can provide a quite amusing but powerful demonstration of ineffective and effective ways of saying no!

WHAT TO SAY

The following guidelines are based on Monti *et al.* (2002, pp. 65–66):

(1) *Say 'no' first*: Explain to your client that when he hesitates to say 'no' people

doubt that he means it. Therefore 'no thanks' are the best first words to come out of his mouth.

(2) *Suggest an alternative*: After saying 'no' then your client might:
   (a) suggest something else to do (e.g., going for a walk, to a coffee shop, or to the movies instead of going to a pub); and/or
   (b) suggest something else to drink (e.g., coffee, orange juice) or to eat instead.

(3) *Request that the other person stop asking*: If the 'pusher' is being persistent your client should ask him to stop offering drinks or drugs. For example an offer like, 'Oh, go on, for old times sake, be a mate' might be met with 'If you want to be a mate, don't offer me a drink'.

(4) *Change the subject*: After refusing, your client should change the subject in order to avoid getting caught up in a long debate about drinking or drug use. For example: 'No, thanks, I'm not using. It's good to see you, I haven't seen you in ages. What are you doing these days?'

(5) *Avoid excuses and vague answers*: Explain to your client that in most cases it is better to try and avoid using excuses like 'I can't drink at the moment, I'm on antibiotics'. Such excuses can make it difficult to refuse in the future and are not really helpful for strengthening his new resolve to change. Being direct is generally the best course. Often just saying 'No thanks' in a firm fashion will be enough. At other times your client might find it useful to elaborate, for example, 'I don't drink', 'My doctor advised me to quit', 'I am cutting down' or 'I decided to stop using, it wasn't doing me any good'.

After you have explained these principles get your client to describe a number of situations where, in the past, he had problems in refusing drinks or drugs. Choose one and begin by modelling an inappropriate way of responding. Have your client provide feedback about your performance in terms of your body language, tone and what you actually said. Invite him to brainstorm more assertive and appropriate responses. Model the same situation again, this time with an effective response.

You should then ask your client to role-play (p. 12) a situation, either with you or with other clients if you are in a group setting. It will be important to have your client(s) practise being both a 'refuser' and a 'pusher'. Try to cover as wide a range of potential situations as possible but remember not to begin with the very difficult ones!

Trouble shooting

As Monti *et al.* (1989) indicated, there will often be a temptation for clients who are the 'pushers' to get extremely enthusiastic in their task. This can sometimes be quite funny but it may be important to gently remind them that the point of the exercise is to give each other a chance to learn how to respond effectively to realistically (not impossibly!) difficult situations.

Be aware that role-plays about drinking or using can sometimes trigger strong cravings. Allow time for your clients to debrief and identify strategies for coping with any cravings feelings that arise from the role-play. It may be helpful for the participants to move into different chairs for the debriefing, to help them 'get out of the role'. Ask the 'pushers' to say how they are different from the part they played in the role-play. For further ideas about how to debrief role-plays, refer to Chapter 1, *General Counselling Skills*.

RESOURCES LIST

Kadden, R., Carroll, K., Donovan, D., Cooney, N., Monti, P., Abrams, D., Litt, M. & Hester, R. (1995). *Cognitive Behavioral Coping Skills Therapy Manual: A Clinical Research Guide for Therapists Treating Individuals with Alcohol Abuse and Dependence* (Project MATCH Monograph Series, Volume 3). NIH Pub. No. 94-3724. Rockville, MD: National Institute on Alcohol Abuse and Alcoholism.
  To order a copy, go to www.niaaa.nih.gov/publications/match.htm
  —This session-by-session manual devotes one session to drink refusal skills, based on guidelines from the book by Monti *et al.* (2002).

Kelly, J.A., St. Lawrence, J.S., Betts, R., Brasfield, T.L. & Hood, H.V. (1990). A skills-training group intervention model to assist persons in reducing risk behaviors for HIV infection. *AIDS Education and Prevention*, **2**, 24–35.
  —Applies refusal-skills training to the prevention of unsafe sexual practices.

Monti, P.M., Abrams, D.B., Kadden, R.M. & Cooney, N.L. (1889). *Treating Alcohol Dependence: A Coping Skills Training Guide* (pp. 61–63). New York: Guilford Press.

Monti, P.M., Kadden, R.M. Rohsenow, D.J., Cooney, N.L. & (2002). *Treating Alcohol Dependence: A Coping Skills Training Guide* (2nd edn) (pp. 65–66). New York: Guilford Press.
  —We have used the sections on drink refusal skills from these two books as our key resources for this chapter.

8

Assertiveness Skills

RECOMMENDED USE

Assertiveness training is recommended for clients who have particular difficulty in expressing their needs and emotions to others. For many clients, this inability to communicate openly and directly results in feelings of frustration, anger and distress which may contribute to a return to excessive drinking or drug use.

Assertiveness training is equally useful for clients who wish to cut down or abstain from alcohol, other drugs, or risk-taking behaviours. It may be helpful to teach assertiveness in conjunction with drink or drug refusal and/or communication-skills training (Chapters 7 and 9). Assertion skills need to be taught over four or more sessions depending on the pre-existing level of assertiveness of your client(s). Role-play is an essential part of learning assertiveness skills, making group settings ideal for teaching this technique.

GOALS

Assertiveness training does *not* aim to ensure that your client will always 'get what she wants'. Rather, the goals are to enable your client to:

- Recognise when she is being unassertive.
- Develop a variety of ways of dealing appropriately with situations where the usual response is either under-assertive or aggressive.
- Express personal needs, feelings and opinions in a way that she finds satisfactory and which can be clearly understood by others.

KEY CONCEPTS

ASSERTIVENESS

Assertiveness is a method of expressing feelings, needs, wants and opinions, directly and honestly without hostility or rudeness. Being assertive means that, when she chooses to, your client can effectively communicate her view in a way which respects the rights of others.

NON-ASSERTIVENESS

There are several types of non-assertive behaviour of which the two most common are under-assertion and aggression.

Passive Under-assertion

Passive under-assertion is self-denying, inhibited behaviour which allows other people to make decisions or otherwise infringe on your client's rights. Passive clients tend not to let others know what they think or feel. This form of non-assertiveness often leads to feelings of frustration and resentment. For some clients, being under-assertive may result in their bottling up their feelings until they reach a point when they explode aggressively.

Aggression

Aggression is standing up for one's views, but with a disregard for the views or rights of others. Aggression often leads to an escalation of feelings of anger and hostility in your client. Alternately, after an aggressive outburst your client may feel guilty and ashamed of her behaviour. In both cases these strong negative emotions may increase the risk of a relapse to drug use or drinking.

Human Rights

It is important that your client becomes aware that she and others have basic human rights which should be respected in interpersonal situations. These rights, which define the framework for assertiveness, are listed at the end of this chapter.

METHOD

RATIONALE FOR YOUR CLIENT

Begin by introducing the notion of assertiveness to your client. Assertiveness is often referred to as the ability to effectively express positive and negative emotions, thoughts and opinions in everyday situations. It is not a simple skill to master for those who have not practised it. Using the descriptions in the *Key Concepts* (above), outline the advantages of being assertive and the disadvantages of being aggressive or under-assertive. In particular, stress that the non-assertive behaviours can lead to strong negative emotions and that such emotions tend to increase the likelihood of relapse to drinking or using drugs.

Explain to your client that assertiveness training involves learning how not to be 'put down' or taken advantage of by others and so will teach her how to acquire more choice and control over her life. This may in turn help to improve her self-esteem and self-respect. The areas focused on by assertiveness training include giving criticism, handling criticism, making requests and dealing with requests from other people, and giving and receiving compliments.

BEFORE STARTING

There are a number of self-help manuals and books which may provide both you and your client with helpful reading and practical exercises for learning assertiveness skills. Several of these are listed in the *Resources List* at the end of this chapter. No doubt a perusal of your local bookshop's self-help and psychology sections will yield further titles.

THE PROCESS OF ASSERTIVENESS TRAINING

There are a number of stages to teaching appropriate assertiveness. They are:

(1) Defining *exactly* what the problem is.
(2) Discussing non-assertiveness.
(3) Dispelling myths.
(4) Deciding to change non-assertiveness.
(5) Introducing the 'Bill of Rights'.
(6) Putting assertiveness skills into practice.
(7) Handling tricky situations.

Defining exactly what the problem is

In defining what assertiveness is and is not, it is most useful to employ examples from your client's own experiences. Most clients can relatively easily generate situations in which they have been unable to express their feelings clearly and effectively. Have your client identify a number of situations where she was either aggressive or under-assertive. Write these examples down to use for practice exercises in later sessions.

Discussing Non-assertiveness

Get your client to consider how her family members have handled difficult situations and conflict. It is often the case that we learn our way of relating to others from the people we have grown up with. Additionally, through her past relationships your client may have learnt that being assertive brings disapproval or punishment. Openly explore the reasons why your client may have become non-assertive with a view to highlighting the areas where she has the most difficulty, so that you can address these in therapy.

Dispelling myths

It is also common for those who are non-assertive to hold a number of faulty beliefs or myths about being assertive with others. These myths are important for you to address because they may be supporting your client's non-assertiveness.

Individuals will often believe that it is a virtue to be humble 'at all costs' and never to accept compliments. They may also believe that to be a good friend or family member, one has to constantly meet the needs of others and never be prepared to criticise anyone. For these individuals, the notion of expressing unhappiness about something to a friend is seen as a challenge to the friendship rather than as an appropriate way of expressing feelings.

Another common myth believed by non-assertive clients is that others should be able to know how they feel (without being told). Comments like 'He should have understood why I said that' are examples of this myth in action. Your client may often fail to get her needs met because of this mistaken assumption that other people are mind-readers.

Clients may also take on roles or responsibilities, and hold the belief that it is difficult or inappropriate for them to step outside these roles. Such beliefs may prevent your client from challenging a person or situation even though there may be personal costs in not doing so. This frequently happens in the workplace (e.g., where your client may feel uncomfortable about asserting herself in a situation with the boss for fear that this would be construed as rudeness or disrespect). Similarly in family relationships, beliefs about 'the woman's role' might lead your client to feel frustrated and often exhausted, especially if she is attempting to cope with the pressures of her job as well as domestic and childcare responsibilities.

Identifying the beliefs that your client holds about behaviour will further assist you in targeting areas for intervention, and is indeed a part of the intervention. Ask your client whether or not she takes on responsibility or obligations for areas which are not strictly hers. If she does, get her to list situations where she has felt that she is doing things for others which they should take responsibility for.

Deciding to Change Non-assertiveness

It is of course important to establish whether or not your client wishes to become more assertive. Explore with her the pros and cons of changing. For example, the benefits of under-assertiveness may include avoiding conflict and responsibility, maintaining familiar patterns of interacting and an acceptance by others. On the other hand, being under-assertive may decrease your client's satisfaction with social interactions, reduce her influence over decisions made by others and curb her independence. This may in turn reduce her self-respect and the respect that others have for her rights and needs.

Introducing the 'Bill of Rights'

If your client decides that she wants to become more assertive it is time to help her generate a list of her rights in interpersonal situations. This type of list has often been called a 'Bill of Assertive Rights' and typically includes the right to:

- Make mistakes.
- Change one's mind.
- Offer no reasons or excuses for one's behaviour.
- Make one's own decisions.
- Not have to work out solutions for other people's problems.
- Criticise in a constructive and helpful fashion.
- Say 'no' without feeling guilty.
- Tell someone that you do not understand their position or else 'do not care'.
- Not have to depend on others for approval.
- Express feelings and opinions.
- Be listened to by others.
- Disagree with others.
- Have different needs, wants and wishes from other people.

Such a list is included in the client handout at the end of this chapter. It should be tailored to your client's particular situation, and other rights specific to her may be added. Some clients may feel uneasy about a 'Bill of Rights' and it may be worth explaining that these rights also entail some responsibilities. In particular, she will need to respect the same rights for others.

Putting Assertiveness Skills into Practice

To use these assertive rights in a healthy and non-aggressive way requires lots of practice. As a starting point, a number of useful exercises are set out below. It is valuable to work through these (or similar) structured exercises with your client even if they do not directly apply to her. These exercises are equally useful for groups because they cover a wide range of assertiveness skills and situations.

Each of the examples lists an under-assertive, an aggressive and an appropriately assertive response. In some examples the responses are left blank to allow your client to generate possible responses. It is *essential* that your client uses role-play to practise providing appropriately assertive responses. You can help her feel more comfortable with the use of role-play by initially modelling examples of under-assertive, aggressive and assertive responses for her. Your examples can then be discussed and used to guide your client's attempts. For further information about offering your client feedback on her role-play performance, see p. 12.

In learning how to be assertive, your client may need to be trained in some basic communication skills. For example, you may need to teach her how to use I-statements when communicating her feelings and opinions. These skills are discussed in detail in Chapter 9, *Communication Skills*. Your client will also be more effective in her assertiveness if she is direct in her tone of voice, eye contact and body language (Chapter 7, *Drink and Drug Refusal Skills*), avoids anger and unnecessary 'snipes', keeps responses succinct, and respects the rights of the other person.

In Example 1, the assertive speaker begins by 'fogging' (p. 117) to diffuse her mother's criticism. She then goes on to present her own opinion regarding the children. She finishes by using 'I-statements' to say specifically what she finds hurtful and to request a change in her mother's behaviour.

In Example 2, pay special attention to body language, eye contact, and again, the use of 'I-statements'.

In Example 3, emphasise that an assertive response does not obligate the speaker to apologise or offer an excuse when turning down a request. However, this example illustrates that assertiveness can involve offering a constructive alternative suggestion. This may help reinforce the message that it is the request, not the person, that is being rejected.

In Example 4, the request for help would be framed in a direct and non-accusatory way. If the partner persistently ignores this request for help, the 'broken record technique' (p. 116) might be one way for the assertive speaker to ensure that her needs are understood.

Example 1: Dealing with criticism

In this example your sister harshly criticises the way that you deal with your children when they come home from school because you allow them to eat food before dinner. You find this annoying and hurtful and believe you're correct in allowing them to have a snack. What do you say to her?

UNDER-ASSERTIVE: 'Yes, you're probably right. I guess it isn't good for them.'

AGGRESSIVE: 'You should mind your own business! They are not your children.'

ASSERTIVE: 'You may be right, but I find that if I don't give them a snack they become very tired. Besides, they eat their dinner without a problem. If you don't like how I am dealing with the children, I'd prefer it if you would say so without sounding so critical. I find your tone is hurtful.'

Example 2: Dealing with criticism

Your boss criticises you inappropriately in a meeting over something which you have said which he has misunderstood. It was clear that he took you to mean something which you had not intended, but you did not have an opportunity to clarify the situation within the meeting. What do you say later?

UNDER-ASSERTIVE: You say either nothing or 'I apologise' and then try to explain what you had intended.

AGGRESSIVE: You accuse your boss of not understanding what you were talking about, but do not explain what you had been attempting to say in the meeting.

ASSERTIVE: You explain to your boss that you had been attempting to inform the meeting of your views on the situation at hand and you are concerned that he has misunderstood what you were saying. You ask him not to be abrupt with you in a meeting again as you find it offensive.

Example 3: Dealing with requests from other people

A friend of yours whom you think is a very bad driver asks to borrow your new car to go out to an important meeting. You do not wish to lend ther car because you do not feel confident in your friend's driving abilities. What do you say?

UNDER-ASSERTIVE: 'OK! You can borrow the car, but be careful with it.'

AGGRESSIVE: 'You have no right to borrow my car. I wouldn't be so silly as to lend it to you—you're a terrible driver!'

ASSERTIVE: 'Sorry John, I'm not prepared to lend the car to you. However, I'm willing to give you a hand by dropping you to your meeting if I can.'

Very often clients who are non-assertive are too ready to accept criticism and are unable to accept praise. Explain to your client that by acknowledging compliments appropriately she lets others know that what they have said is important. By rejecting or ignoring compliments she will discourage others from offering future compliments—and thereby reduce her own self-esteem and confidence. Being able to both give and accept compliments is therefore an important part of effective assertive communication (see Examples 7 and 8 on p. 115).

When you have finished these exercises review the key areas where a lack of healthy assertiveness causes difficulties for your client. Work with your client's

---

Example 4: Making requests of other people

You have been extremely busy at work. You are having guests to dinner and the house is in a complete mess. Your partner gets home and collapses in front of the television. You need help to clean up the house. What do you do?

UNDER-ASSERTIVE: Say nothing, do it yourself and end up too exhausted to enjoy the company of your friends.

AGGRESSIVE: Say nothing but be angry and hostile all evening and eventually lose your temper over something unrelated to your reason for being angry.

ASSERTIVE: Ask your partner for some help.

Example 5: Making complaints

You have purchased an electric appliance from a department store. Upon using the appliance for the first time you discover that it is faulty and return it to the store. You expect to be given a replacement, but instead you are told that because the box has been opened the appliance will have to be returned to the manufacturer for repair and that will take four weeks. What do you say?

UNDER-ASSERTIVE:

AGGRESSIVE:

ASSERTIVE:

---

personal examples using the same method as you used in the exercises above. Again, make sure that your client practises her assertive responses in the session using role-play. You should also negotiate weekly home practice exercises with your client to encourage her to apply the skills in situations that arise at home or work. The exercises should be challenging but achievable so that they facilitate your client's experience of success in being assertive. Review her progress with these home exercises at the beginning of each session.

You and your client might also particularly focus on areas where assertiveness could be used to reduce your client's risk-taking behaviour or deal with social pressure. For example, she might rehearse how to request that her sexual partner use a condom or how to refuse the offer of a shared needle.

Example 6: Giving criticism

Some workmen at your home have failed to repair a crack in the wall of your house before painting over it. What do you say?

UNDER-ASSERTIVE:

AGGRESSIVE:

ASSERTIVE:

Example 7: Receiving compliments

You have impressed the people you live with by cooking a delicious meal. They praise you for your abilities. What do you say?

NON-ASSERTIVE:

ASSERTIVE:

Example 8: Giving compliments

You wish to praise a friend for help that she gave you in a time of crisis.

NON-ASSERTIVE:

ASSERTIVE:

Handling Tricky Situations

There are a number of situations where being straightforward and direct with people does not bring about the desired result. Despite your client's attempts to explain herself in a reasoned and straightforward way, other people may still behave irrationally. Offer your client the following strategies and role-play them to assist her in handling problem situations.

Strategy 1—the broken record technique: The broken record technique could help your client in situations where somebody is making persistent demands on her or refusing to hear what she is saying. It involves simply repeating the same message over and over, hence the name, 'broken record technique'. By using this method, your client can stick with what she wants to say and avoid being drawn into an argument. This may seem unnatural at first but it can be done in a respectful, non-monotonous way. The following examples show how your client could precede her repeated message with an acknowledgement of the other person's perspective:

'I know that you want to celebrate *but I don't want to drink any alcohol.*'
'I know you are trying to help, *but I feel hurt by your constant criticism.*'

Strategy 2—disarming anger: This strategy is best used when someone is inappropriately aggressive or so angry with your client that reasoned conversation is impossible. Your client may need to actually get the other person's attention if that person is caught up in an angry outburst. She might do this by saying the person's name and making eye contact. She would then say that she can see the other person is angry and that she feels it would be more constructive to talk about the situation once they have calmed down. Of course your client must be prepared to listen to the other person if and when they do calm down!

Strategy 3—dealing with requests: People are often put on the spot by a request and make a hasty, non-assertive decision which they later regret. If your client is often put into this kind of situation instruct her to initially react to requests by saying 'I'm not sure'. This answer allows her to reserve her right to say 'no' or 'yes'. It also gives her more time to decide and, if necessary, a chance to ask for more information. You may need to assist her in role-play to ask assertively for more information. An alternative response to requests that put your client on the spot is 'I will think about it and get back to you'. Your client then has the opportunity to think through the request and perhaps to talk to others about it. If she later decides to agree to the request, she should be direct in saying so and add in conditions if there are any. Assertive responses should not always involve saying 'no'!

Strategy 4—selectively ignoring requests or comments: If another person continues to harp on a subject despite clear messages from your client that she no longer wishes to discuss it, then 'selective ignoring' can be useful. This strategy requires that your client totally ignore the unwelcomed comments while responding to other aspects of the conversation. If your client always fails to respond to a particular topic the other person will eventually give it up. It can be quite difficult to continually ignore comments, especially if they are perceived as unfair or critical. It may be useful to tell your client to say to the individual:

'I've heard what you have to say. I do not agree with it. I'm not willing to discuss it with you further. If you raise it again I will ignore it but I will talk to you about other things.'

Strategy 5—'fogging': Sometimes when faced with unfair criticism it may be useful to be able to 'turn it off' with minimum effort. Your client can do this by simply agreeing with the critic in a vague fashion. She could use phrases such as 'You may be right', or 'I understand that's your point of view', or 'Really!?' It will be helpful to role-play conversations to ensure that your client is comfortable with this method.

Strategy 6—sorting out the issues: Interpersonal conflict often clouds reason and causes issues to become confused. When this happens it may be difficult for your client to be clear about what is a reasonable response on her part. For example, a refusal by your client to do something might lead to a (sometimes wilful or manipulative!) misinterpretation like: 'because you won't do my ironing anymore, it's obvious you no longer care about me ...' It is important that your client is able to sort out facts from interpretations. For example, in response to the above situation she might learn to say something like: 'I do care about you ... its just that I don't want to do your ironing.'

This problem of misinterpretation commonly occurs when a client begins to be assertive. At that time those around her will be surprised or threatened and may feel that the assertiveness is equivalent to rejection. If appropriate, help her to practise and role-play different situations where others might confuse appropriate assertion with rejection.

RESOURCES LIST

Kadden, R., Carroll, K., Donovan, D., Cooney, N., Monti, P., Abrams, D., Litt, M. & Hester, R. (1995). *Cognitive Behavioral Coping Skills Therapy Manual: A Clinical Research Guide for Therapists Treating Individuals with Alcohol Abuse and Dependence* (Project MATCH Monograph Series, Volume 3). NIH Pub. No. 94-3724. Rockville, MD: National Institute on Alcohol Abuse and Alcoholism.
   To order a copy, go to www.niaaa.nih.gov/publications/match.htm
   —This session-by-session manual describes sessions for assertiveness training and receiving criticism, based on guidelines from the book by Monti *et al.* (2002).

Monti, P.M., Kadden, R.M. Rohsenow, D.J., Cooney, N.L. & Abrams, D.B. (2002). *Treating Alcohol Dependence: A Coping Skills Training Guide* (2nd edn). New York: Guilford Press.
   —Provides sessions on Assertiveness (pp. 48–50), Giving and Receiving Positive Feedback (pp. 53–55), Giving Constructive Criticism (pp. 57–61) and Receiving Criticism about Drinking (pp. 61–64).

SELF-HELP BOOKS

The following is a list of self-help books on assertiveness skills (by no means exhaustive). Your client will benefit from having one practical book on the subject and working through its exercises.

Alberti, R.E. & Emmons, M.D. (2001). *Your Perfect Right: Assertiveness and Equality in Your Life and Relationships* (8th edn). San Luis Obispo, CA: Impact Publishers.

Bower, S.A. & Bower, G.H. (1991). *Asserting Yourself: A Practical Guide for Positive Change* (2nd edn). Cambridge, MA: Da Capo Press.

Lindenfield, G. (2001). *Assert Yourself: A Self-help Assertiveness Program for Men and Women*. London: Thorsons.

McClure, J.S. (2003). *Civilized Assertiveness for Women: Communication with Backbone … not Bite*. Denver, CO: Albion Street Press.

Paterson, R.J. (2000). *The Assertiveness Workbook: How to Express Your Ideas and Stand Up for Yourself at Work and in Relationships*. Oakland, CA: New Harbinger.

BILL OF ASSERTIVE RIGHTS

- The right to make mistakes
- The right to change your mind
- The right to offer no reasons or excuses for your behaviour
- The right to make your own decisions
- The right to not have to work out solutions for other people's problems
- The right to criticise in a constructive and helpful fashion
- The right to say 'no' without feeling guilty
- The right to tell someone that you do not understand their position or else 'do not care'
- The right to not have to depend on others for approval
- The right to express feelings and opinions
- The right to be listened to by others
- The right to disagree with others
- The right to have different needs, wants and wishes from other people

Add in your other rights below:

-

-

-

-

9

Communication Skills

RECOMMENDED USE

Communication skills training overlaps with assertiveness training, and the two can be profitably taught together. Communication skills training aims to teach your client how to start and continue conversations, cope with silences, interpret social cues, actively listen to others and comfortably communicate personal feelings, thoughts and opinions. The importance of appropriate communication skills is that they help to reduce your client's feelings of embarrassment and social tension which can lead to a relapse to excessive drinking or drug use.

Communication skills training can be used with those clients who wish either to cut down or to abstain from drinking alcohol or other drug use. It is especially well suited to group settings because different individuals can provide examples to others of good and poor communication patterns. Being able to role-play and model situations is an extremely important aspect of training when using this technique. Communication skills training is also an important aspect of involving concerned others and its use in this context is explained in Chapter 13.

GOALS

The major goals of communication skills training are to enable your client to:

- Initiate conversations and continue these in a comfortable fashion.
- Be sensitive to social cues that provide information about how others are perceiving what he is saying.
- Be able to express important feelings to others.
- Understand the feelings of other people.

KEY CONCEPTS

I-STATEMENTS

An 'I-statement' is a statement that begins with the first person. For example, statements starting with the words 'I feel ...', 'I think ...' or 'I need ...' are all I-statements. By starting speech with an I-statement, your client conveys a direct message about his intentions. He also takes responsibility for his feelings and opinions, without blaming or placing that responsibility on others. This approach therefore allows the listener to respond without defensiveness.

POSITIVE SPECIFIC REQUESTS

O'Farrell (1995) describes positive specific requests as a form of communication in which your client expresses what he wants rather than what he does not want in specific terms and in the form of a request rather than a demand. This kind of communication is clear, non-threatening and leaves matters open to negotiation.

METHOD

RATIONALE FOR YOUR CLIENT

Discuss with your client the way in which people sometimes use alcohol or other drugs to help them feel comfortable or to numb their embarrassment when in conversation or social situations. Ask your client to think of some examples from his own experience where he might have used alcohol or drugs in this way. Explain to your client that the communication skills training will focus on both giving and receiving communication without relying on the effects of substances, and will therefore help to prevent relapse. At first, the skills may not be easy to use but with practice (initially as often as three times a week for 10–15 minutes) they will become more automatic.

Assess your client's current communication skills. You may need to begin by working on methods for initiating and maintaining general conversations. He may also need assistance in expressing personal opinions, feelings and requests. Some techniques concerning giving and receiving compliments or criticism have already been outlined in Chapter 8, *Assertiveness Skills*. You should also focus on developing your client's listening skills and his ability to validate the point of view of others. You might also wish to explore how your client's cognition or self-talk may impede the communication process (see below).

STARTING OR ENTERING A CONVERSATION

To start or enter a conversation your client has to have something to say! Have your client write a list of his areas of interest. Then help him to recognise those topics which may be interesting to others and those which will probably be of limited conversational value.

It may be that your client has few areas in his life that are of general interest. For instance, if his leisure time has completely revolved around drinking at the hotel, he may have few hobbies and might lack general knowledge so that he finds it difficult to contribute to conversations. Encourage him to take the time to learn about events by reading newspapers or books and to develop new hobbies and interests. These new activities will also have the advantage of distracting him from drinking or using drugs!

Before attempting to enter a conversation, your client should listen to what other people are interested in talking about. Stress the importance of staying with topics that are of mutual interest and contrast this with taking over or 'hijacking' a conversation, which is likely to quickly end it, especially if those involved were enjoying the existing topic.

So that your client does not try to 'burst' into conversations, introduce him to the skill of asking others open-ended questions (Chapter 1, *General Counselling Skills*). Use role-play (p. 12) to show how these types of questions encourage discussion. As another useful way of starting or entering conversations, also get him to practise offering small 'titbits' of information. Contrast these strategies with sudden intrusive comments which tend to disrupt the flow of discussion.

Tell your client that many good conversationalists do not talk about significant matters. Enjoyable casual conversation often focuses on the day-to-day aspects of existence, such as the weather, sporting results or what happened at the weekend. As Monti, Kadden, Rohsenow, Cooney and Abrams (2002, p. 51) said, *Small talk is okay!* The idea that conversation can occur on a number of levels may be new to your client if he feels pressured to talk only about things that are important. Emphasise the need to practise conversing on different levels.

KEEPING THE CONVERSATION GOING

Dealing with Silences

Your client may feel that it is his responsibility to keep the conversation going. This sense of obligation might lead him to feel uncomfortable with silences and he might try to cope by talking in monologues. The danger of long monologues is that they tend to dominate the discussion and lose other people's interest. Explain that short silences are natural within conversation when people are thinking about what has been said and what to say next. Use role-play to develop your client's skills and flexibility in altering the topic and direction of conversation and picking up a conversation that has stopped.

Non-verbal Communication

Discuss with your client the importance of non-verbal language in maintaining conversations. Appropriate eye contact, facial expressions and an interesting tone of voice are very important aspects of good communication. Get your client to consider how non-verbal language can sometimes undermine an intended verbal message. For example, a person might *say* that he is interested in what his friend is talking about *but* his lack of eye contact and mumbling voice convey the opposite. Use role-play to enhance your client's awareness of these subtleties of non-verbal communication. Further details on improving non-verbal communication are provided in the Chapter 7, *Drink and Drug Refusal Skills*.

COMMUNICATING PERSONAL INFORMATION

Using I-statements

Discuss how I-statements can make it easier to express personal messages directly and clearly in conversation. For example, you might get your client to compare these two statements:

'Why can't *you* stop criticising me?'
'I feel angry when you find fault with me in front of other people.'

Ask your client how he would feel if he was at the receiving end of either of these statements. Explain that the first statement is likely to generate a defensive answer and lead to further conflict. The second statement conveys a more direct and specific message and leaves room for negotiation.

Montgomery and Evans (1996) have called the second type of statement an X-Y-Z statement because it takes the form: 'When you do X in situation Y, I feel Z.' This kind of specific statement focuses the speaker's comment on a particular behaviour rather than on the entire person. It avoids sidetracks, generalisations and personal insults which can cause a conflict to escalate. Some other examples of X-Y-Z statements (which are also I-statements) include:

'When you borrow my things and don't bring them back, I feel annoyed.'
'I enjoy your company when we go out to the movies.'
'I find it very helpful when you get the kids off to school.'

Notice that the last two examples express positive feelings. Use these examples to demonstrate that I-statements make it easier to express both critical and complimentary feelings towards others. Emphasise the importance of being specific and genuine about what is liked or disliked.

Positive Specific Requests

Introduce the concept of positive specific requests as a way to assist your client to ask for what he needs. They are 'positive' because they state what your client wants rather than what he doesn't want. They are 'specific' because they state what, when and where. They are 'requests' rather than demands because they allow for negotiation. For example, you might get your client to compare these statements:

'If you keep on ignoring me, I won't be around much longer.'
'I would like you to listen to what I say when we talk at dinner time.'

Get your client to write down at least five positive specific requests. If necessary, help him to make them more specific or positive.

ACTIVE LISTENING

Ask your client to listen to something said by you or another client and then repeat that message as accurately as possible. Instruct the listener to repeat both the words and the feelings that were expressed. He should try to do this in a way that is paraphrasing rather than parroting what the other person said. Model this reflective listening approach with specific examples such as: 'What I heard you say was ... Is that right?' The power of these examples will be enhanced if you have incorporated reflective listening as part of your overall counselling style (see pp. 6–7). Explain to your client that reflecting back what has been said in this way will enable him to verify that he has heard the message accurately as well as showing the speaker that he is actively listening. This approach helps to avoid the misunderstandings that happen when one person tries to read another person's mind.

Active listening also involves observing the other person's non-verbal language. As mentioned above, cues such as facial expression, intonation, voice quality and body posture can provide valuable information about how the speaker is feeling.

If you are working with groups, you could use role-plays to build active listening skills. For example, working in pairs, your clients could take turns in listening to each other. The listener could then reflect back to the speaker (or to the larger group) what she heard the speaker say. The speaker could then give feedback about how accurately this reflection matches the speaker's intended message.

VALIDATING THE OTHER PERSON

Validating is perhaps the most difficult communication skill. By validating, the listener not only indicates that the information has been received but also acknowledges or accepts the feelings expressed. This does not mean that the listener has to agree with the speaker's opinion. It means that the listener respects what the other person has said about how he feels rather than insisting that he feel some other way. For example:

'Yes, I can understand how you would feel angry about me being late.'

This validation of the speaker's feelings does not invalidate the listener's perspective. It rests on the underlying assumption that people have the right to think differently, and are prepared to acknowledge that right for each other.

Small group role-plays can help clients to develop their empathy and respect for alternative points of view. For example, clients could role-play three or four different points of view on a particular issue. One client might play a father, for instance, while another plays the mother and a third client plays the child. After a few minutes, ask your clients to swap roles. Continue this process until the participants have experienced all of the different roles. When you debrief this role-play, highlight the concept that different points of views can be equally valid.

SELF-TALK

If your client is having difficulty in communicating, get him to check what he is saying to himself. He may be thinking negatively about how the other person views him or what his or her intentions are. It may often be the cause of his difficulty, and the answer is to change this 'negative self-talk'. For example, your client's attempt to compliment somebody might be impeded by his negative self-talk about being rejected:

'There's not much point. She's probably not interested in me anyway.'

Encourage your client to think of examples of self-talk that would help him, rather than hinder him, in his communication, such as:

'I feel a bit nervous about this but unless I say something, she won't know that I like her.'

Self-talk is also discussed in the section on couples therapy in Chapter 13, *Involving Concerned Others* and in Chapter 10, *Cognitive Therapy*. In particular, Chapter 10 describes how self-talk that leads to drinking or drug using can be effectively challenged.

RESOURCES LIST

Kadden, R., Carroll, K., Donovan, D., Cooney, N., Monti, P., Abrams, D., Litt, M. & Hester, R. (1995). *Cognitive Behavioral Coping Skills Therapy Manual: A Clinical Research Guide for Therapists Treating Individuals with Alcohol Abuse and Dependence* (Project MATCH Monograph Series, Volume 3). NIH Pub. No. 94-3724. Rockville, MD: National Institute on Alcohol Abuse and Alcoholism.
To order a copy, go to www.niaaa.nih.gov/publications/match.htm
—This session-by-session manual describes sessions that deal with starting conversations and non-verbal communication, based on guidelines from the book by Monti *et al.* (2002).

Kotzman, A. (1995). *Listen to Me, Listen to You: Interpersonal Skills Training*. Camberwell, VIC: Australian Council for Educational Resources (ACER).
—A training manual kit for communication skills training.

Montgomery, B. & Evans, L. (1996). *Living and Loving Together: How to Make Your Relationships More Fulfilling*. Ringwood, Australia: Penguin.
—This self-help book about relationships includes a practical guide on communication skills, including I-statements, X-Y-Z statements, validation and self-talk.

Monti, P.M., Kadden, R.M., Rohsenow, D.J., Cooney, N.L. & Abrams, D.B. (2002). *Treating Alcohol Dependence: A Coping Skills Training Guide* (2nd edn). New York: Guilford Press.
—An excellent resource for communication skills training which covers Non-Verbal Communication (pp. 45–48) and Listening Skills (pp. 55–57).

O'Farrell, T. J. (1995). Marital and family therapy. In: R.K. Hester & W.R. Miller (eds), *Handbook of Alcoholism Treatment Approaches: Effective Alternatives* (2nd edn) (pp. 195–220). Boston: Allyn and Bacon.
—Includes a useful section on training in communication skills (p. 205), particularly in the context of relationships.

Tannen, D. (1992). *That's Not What I Meant!: How Conversational Style Makes or Breaks Your Relations with Others*. London: Virago.
—This self-help book explores how misunderstandings occur in communication and the cultural factors that influence conversational style.

10

Cognitive Therapy

RECOMMENDED USE

Cognitive therapy involves teaching your client to identify and challenge thoughts or feelings that may lead to drinking or drug use. This cognitive skill has been shown to be particularly effective when it is taught in combination with other more behavioural coping skills (such as drink and drug refusal and assertiveness training). Cognitive therapy can be taught in either an individual or a group setting.

As well as helping your client to cope more effectively with urges to drink or use, cognitive therapy can also help with other life problems such as low self-esteem, anxiety or depression. More detail on these applications of cognitive therapy are found in the materials listed in the *Resources List*.

Some research suggests that cognitive therapy is not suitable for clients who suffer from alcohol-related brain injury because of its abstract nature. However, this caution might equally apply to clients who are not psychologically minded or whose thinking patterns are rigid or overly intellectualising.

The basic principles of cognitive therapy can probably be communicated in a minimum of two or three hour-long sessions. However, like other skills, cognitive therapy needs to be practised across the *entire* course of treatment in order for your client to be able to use the skills effectively after treatment ends.

GOALS

The goals of cognitive therapy are for your client to be able to:

- Recognise when she is thinking negatively or in a way that could lead to drinking or drug use.
- Interrupt that train of thought.

- Challenge the negative or unproductive thoughts and replace them with more positive or reasonable ones.

KEY CONCEPTS

AUTOMATIC THOUGHTS

The thoughts that lead to bad feelings or urges to drink or use drugs often happen so quickly that your client may be unaware of them occurring. These thoughts are therefore commonly referred to as negative 'automatic' thoughts.

SELF-TALK OR SELF-STATEMENTS

These are other useful terms for describing the thoughts preceding feelings and behaviours. Negative self-talk is the series of thoughts that result in negative feelings or urges and cravings. Positive self-talk or self-statements are those that help to decrease urges, increase self-confidence or change negative feelings.

METHOD

RATIONALE FOR YOUR CLIENT

Explain to your client that thinking influences the way she both feels and behaves. That is, emotions aren't usually caused as a direct result of something happening in the outside world. Rather, the way she feels depends on her *interpretation* of an event or what she 'says to herself' about a particular situation.

You can use a simple example like the effects of dropping a plate to illustrate this point. Some people might respond to this event by thinking things like 'I'm such a useless idiot' or 'I'm totally stupid'. If unchecked, these kinds of thoughts can lead to feelings of anger, frustration or depression. Such feelings often lead to urges to drink or use drugs.

You could also point out that often, as in the example of the broken plate, negative thoughts like 'I'm totally stupid' are unnecessary overreactions to a situation. Because of their undesirable consequences, Monti, Kadden, Rohsenow, Cooney and Abrams (2002) noted that such thoughts are colourfully referred to in Alcoholics Anonymous as 'stinking thinking'!

Explain to your client that the aim of the following sessions will be to help her learn how to catch herself thinking negative or unhelpful thoughts. Having learnt to identify such thoughts she can then learn how to challenge and replace them with more constructive self-talk.

BECOMING AWARE OF NEGATIVE THINKING

The first step is to help your clients learn to identify bad thinking habits. We have chosen the A-B-C model (Ellis & Harper, 1975) as a way of emphasising and clarifying the relationship between thoughts, feelings and behaviours. That is:

| (A)ctivating event | ⇒ | (B)eliefs | ⇒ | (C)onsequent feelings |

For example:

| Losing my keys | ⇒ | 'I'm a bloody idiot' | ⇒ | Angry, irritable |
| Late for child's concert | ⇒ | 'I'm a lousy mother' | ⇒ | Depressed, anxious |

Use this model to generate some exercises for your client. Get her to identify several situations from the recent past where she either experienced strong negative emotions or ended up drinking or using other drugs. Ask her to begin by describing the activating events (A) that 'caused' her feelings. Then spend some time considering what she was telling herself (i.e., what her beliefs (B) were about the situation). Finally, explore the consequences (C) of this self-talk in terms of how it led her to feel bad and/or to drink or use drugs.

Having generated a number of different examples of negative or unproductive self-talk, it can often be useful to introduce your client to the different types of thinking errors derived from the work of Ellis and Harper (1975). Some of these types of thinking errors are described in the first client handout at the end of this chapter. Use this list to classify some of the negative thoughts your client identified in the exercise above. Categorising thoughts using such a list can help clarify what it is about the thoughts that is unproductive or unhelpful.

You should also explain that often such negative thoughts happen so quickly that they almost seem not to have happened at all. For this reason it is often useful to describe them as being 'automatic' thoughts. Often the first sign of trouble your client will detect is a sense that she is beginning to feel bad or is experiencing an urge or craving. These feelings are crucial signals for her to stop and to identify the 'automatic' thoughts that caused her to feel that way. Sometimes anxious clients might find it particularly difficult to recognise when an automatic thought has occurred. In such cases it is useful to suggest that these thoughts commonly precede very strong and prolonged emotional reactions or cravings.

It is essential that your client practises catching her negative automatic thoughts. This is best achieved by using home practice exercises. A thought-monitoring practice sheet is provided at the end of this chapter. At this stage of therapy your client should only be concerned with filling in the first three columns of the sheet. During the week, whenever she starts to feel bad or crave, she should immediately say 'STOP, SLOW DOWN' to herself and then fill in the sheet. Get her to describe the situation leading to the unpleasant feelings and specify what the feelings are. She can rate her feelings on a scale of 0–100 where 1 would indicate a slight feeling and 100 would indicate the most intense feeling possible. Ask her to write down the automatic thoughts or self-statements that are causing her to feel that way. She can also rate the strength of her belief in those thoughts from 0% (don't believe at all) to 100% (completely believe).

CHALLENGING NEGATIVE THINKING

You and your client might notice some common beliefs that underlie her thinking errors. Dryden and Neenan (2003, cited in Ellis & Harper (1975)) have highlighted four beliefs that are based on the self-defeating assumption that the world *has to be* a certain way to be acceptable. By interpreting events through these beliefs, your client will cause herself to experience emotional disturbance out of proportion with the likely consequences of the events and this can result in ineffective action. For example, your client's automatic thinking might stem from a belief in:

- Rigid and absolute demands (e.g., I *must* ... They *have to* ... Life *should* be ...).
- 'Awfulising' beliefs (e.g., It's terrible, a disaster, the end of the world).
- Low frustration tolerance beliefs (e.g., I can't cope. Life is intolerable).
- Depreciation beliefs (e.g., I'm bad. You are bad. Life is bad).

Encourage your client to identify when and how these beliefs are influencing her. You can do this by getting your client to choose a situation from her home practice or an earlier session where an unhelpful or 'automatic' thought was identified. Teach your client to review the automatic thought using four key questions (from Fennell, 1989):

(1) *What is the evidence for and against this way of thinking?* Help your client to sort out the distinction between real events and her interpretations of them. In looking at all the evidence, your client might actually find that there is evidence to contradict her automatic thought!

(2) *What are the advantages/disadvantages of thinking this way?* Many automatic thoughts have *some* advantages for your client—that's why they keep recurring! For example, your client may have an automatic thought that helps her to avoid a difficult situation. However, she should consider whether this advantage is outweighed by disadvantages (e.g., prolonged anxiety, drug use). If the disadvantages outweigh the advantages, it will be worthwhile for your client to try to work out some new ways of thinking.

(3) *Is there a thinking error?* Is the automatic thought an example of one of the categories of thinking errors listed in the client handout? If so, what underlying beliefs does it reflect?

(4) *What alternative ways of thinking about the situation are there?* Have your client brainstorm as many alternative positive thoughts as possible. It might be useful to have your client think about how another person would see things or what she might say to a friend in the same situation.

Some other examples of tips for challenging negative thoughts are presented in the second client handout at the end of this chapter. These examples are based on beliefs that are less extreme, more consistent with reality and likely to result in more positive consequences. Dryden and Neenan (2003) have summarised the following four 'rational' beliefs which can be compared to the self-defeating beliefs outlined above:

- Non-dogmatic preferences (e.g., I prefer things to go my way but I accept that things don't always work out exactly the way I want).
- 'Anti-awfulising' beliefs (e.g., It is bad but not the end of the world).
- High frustration tolerance beliefs (e.g., It is a struggle but I can tolerate it).
- Acceptance beliefs (e.g., I am human. You are human. Life is constantly changing. Mistakes happen. People are free to make choices).

Notice that even with these rational beliefs, your client will still experience emotional distress in response to negative events. The object is *not* to make your client become numb or inappropriately happy! Disappointment, sadness, concern, remorse and anger can be healthy emotional responses that prompt your client to cope with adversity. Cognitive therapy is more concerned with unhealthy emotional reactions that are so consuming that they block your client's ability to cope and increase her risk of having a (re)lapse. For example, if your client's emotional response is despair, depression, anxiety, self-hatred or rage, it is likely that she is not merely responding to the events but is also interpreting the events in terms of self-defeating beliefs.

To foster rational beliefs, encourage your client to write down the positive thoughts that helped her to feel even a little bit better. Stress to her that she should not expect huge changes at first. Rather it will take time and practice for her to become skilled at challenging her negative self-talk.

Encourage your client to practise challenging negative thoughts during the following weeks. Ask her to use the thought-monitoring sheets again, this time also completing the last three columns. Get her to write positive challenges to her automatic thoughts and rate her belief in these challenges (0–100%). After identifying the positive challenges, she can then re-rate her belief in the original automatic thoughts and feelings. The third client handout at the end of this chapter presents a completed example for your client. This home practice exercise will help you and your client to identify the kinds of positive challenges that she finds most useful.

As with other skills in this book, challenging negative thoughts is a life skill that you can model throughout the process of counselling. It is therefore important to notice and address any examples of unhelpful thinking expressed by your client, even when you are discussing other issues.

DEALING WITH STRONG EMOTIONS

As drugs and alcohol often numb or alter the way people experience emotions, your client might experience strong emotional reactions after she stops or reduces her substance use. At first, these emotions might seem alien, frightening or extremely unpleasant. Their intensity might also make it hard for her to identify and challenge any underlying negative thoughts.

Explain to your client that learning to cope with these feelings rather than covering them up with drugs or alcohol is an important step in preventing relapse. The trouble with avoiding the feelings is that this tends to strengthen your client's fear of them. Explain that emotions tend to naturally rise, reach a peak, and then fall in intensity. You could use the analogy of surfing a wave (as applied to cravings and urges in Chapter 16, *Relapse Prevention Training*). When she has strong feelings during a session, encourage her to talk them through rather than withdraw from them.

Your client might be reluctant to discuss strong feelings for fear of becoming overwhelmed or losing control. Discuss this with her and ask whether she would like to work out some strategies beforehand to give her a sense of safety and control. For example, if she signals that she is feeling too uncomfortable, you could take some time-out with a brief relaxation exercise, a period of silence, or by changing the focus of discussion. A non-judgemental approach and reflective listening will also help to defuse some of the intensity of these feelings.

Nevertheless, by staying with the emotion as much as possible and learning to tolerate the experience, your client will gain more confidence and feel less overwhelmed. One way of working with strong emotions suggested by Linehan (1993) is to help your client explore her emotional experience by asking some of the following questions:

- What its like to feel this way?
- What bodily sensations are associated with these feelings?
- What events prompted the feelings?
- What thoughts and interpretations does she have about those events and how do these thoughts affect her feelings?
- What desires and wishes come out of these feelings?
- What urges and actions do the feelings prompt?
- How does she express these feelings in her face and posture?

Linehan (1993) also stressed the importance of communicating to your client that her feelings are valid. This should be done in a genuine way, by finding opportunities to affirm that your client's emotional reaction is an understandable response to the challenges and situations she is facing.

It is sometimes useful to define the gradients of intensity for particular emotions. For example, you might use point rating scales (e.g., 1–100) to highlight different levels of intensity, such as the difference between feeling annoyed and feeling furious. A feeling might be described as 'cool', 'warm' or 'hot'. Drawing faces or using colours are also useful ways of describing feelings when words seem inadequate. By distinguishing the different grades of intensity, your client will learn to identify her early signs of a particular emotion and can then learn to apply adaptive coping strategies before the emotion becomes too intense.

Talk with your client about how to cope with strong emotions between sessions. For example, she could use a diary to express her feelings through words or drawings. The monitoring sheet at the end of this chapter will also help her to explore the relationship between thoughts and feelings. As your client becomes more confident in coping with her strong feelings, she will be more able to apply other strategies, such as challenging her negative thoughts (pp. 132–133), problem solving (Chapter 6), being assertive (Chapter 8) and relaxation therapy (Chapter 11). Of course, these skills will also empower your client to deal with situations where other people express strong emotions!

Trouble shooting

Be aware that strong emotions sometimes relate to unresolved traumatic experiences. If this is relevant for your client, offer her a referral to a specialist trauma therapist. More details on screening and referral for issues of trauma are given in Chapters 2, *Assessment* and 20, *Dual Diagnosis*.

RESOURCES LIST

Beck, A.T., Wright, F.D., Newman, C.F. & Liese, B.S. (2001). *Cognitive Therapy of Substance Abuse*. New York: Guilford Press.
—A comprehensive guide to cognitive therapy with case examples.

Burns, D.D. (1999). *Feeling Good: The New Mood Therapy*. New York: Avon Books.
—Another very useful text in this area.

Ellis, A. and Harper, R. (1975). *A New Guide to Rational Living*. Englewood Cliffs, NJ: Prentice Hall, Inc.
—This is the original description of the use of rational emotive therapy, on which elements of the above approach are based. Other resources for this approach to cognitive therapy are listed at: www.rebt.org
We particularly drew on the following two resources which are available for purchase from the website:
Dryden, W. & Neenan, M. (2003). *The REBT Therapist's Pocket Companion*. New York: Albert Ellis Institute.
Dryden, W. (2003). *The REBT Pocket Companion for Clients*. New York: Albert Ellis Institute.

Fennell, M.J.V. (1989). Depression. In: K. Hawton, P.M Salkovskis, J. Kirk & D.M. Clark (eds), *Cognitive Behaviour Therapy for Psychiatric Problems: A Practical Guide* (pp. 169–234). Oxford: Oxford University Press.
—An excellent, detailed chapter for therapists on the application of cognitive therapy.

Kadden, R., Carroll, K., Donovan, D., Cooney, N., Monti, P., Abrams, D., Litt, M. & Hester, R. (1995). *Cognitive Behavioral Coping Skills Therapy Manual: A Clinical Research Guide for Therapists Treating Individuals with Alcohol Abuse and Dependence*

(Project MATCH Monograph Series, Volume 3). NIH Pub. No. 94-3724. Rockville, MD: National Institute on Alcohol Abuse and Alcoholism.
To order a copy, go to www.niaaa.nih.gov/publications/match.htm
—This session-by-session manual includes a detailed session on dealing with negative moods and depression.

Linehan, M.M. (1993) *Cognitive-Behavioral Treatment of Borderline Personality Disorder*. New York: Guilford Press.
—This advanced text outlines Linehan's 'dialectic therapy' and gives detailed descriptions of the two core strategies: emotional validation and problem solving.

Monti, P.M., Kadden, R.M., Rohsenow, D.J., Cooney, N.L. & Abrams, D.B. (2002). *Treating Alcohol Dependence: A Coping Skills Training Guide* (2nd edn). New York: Guilford Press.
—A major resource for this chapter, this manual has an excellent guide to sessions on Managing Negative Thinking (pp. 108–113) and also covers Anger Management (pp. 104–108).

Tanner, S. & Ball, J. (2000). *Beating the Blues: A Self-help Approach to Overcoming Depression*. Sydney: Doubleday.
—A terrific book for both therapists and clients dealing with depression.

Young, J.E. & Klosko, J.S. (1994). *Reinventing Your Life: How to Break Free from Negative Life Patterns*. New York: Penguin Putnam.
—Another self-help book that shows how to challenge self-defeating patterns of thinking.

COMMON THINKING ERRORS

(1)   All or nothing thinking

Seeing things in black or white categories. For example:

'If I can't be the best it's pointless trying at all.'
'If I don't succeed in this job I'm a total failure.'

(2)   Overgeneralisation

Expecting that because something has gone wrong, it will always do so. For example:

'I relapsed after I stopped five years ago, I'll never be able to stop drinking/using.'

(3)   Mental filter

You see only the negative things and dwell only on them so that it distorts your view of a person or situation.

'I'll never forget the way they let me down that time.'

(4)   Converting positives into negatives

You reject your achievements and other positive experiences by insisting that they 'don't count' for some reason. In this way you can maintain a negative belief that is contradicted by your everyday experience. For example:

'He only gave me that compliment because he knows how bad I feel.'
'I only stayed sober because there wasn't a lot of pressure to drink.'

(5)   Jumping to negative conclusions

Drawing a negative conclusion when there is little or no evidence to support it.

(a)   *Mind reading*. You conclude that someone is reacting negatively to you, and you don't bother to check this out. For example:

'My friend has interrupted me twice. I must be really boring to listen to.'

(b)   The *'Fortune Teller'* error. You anticipate that things will turn out badly, and are convinced that your prediction is an already established fact. These negative expectations can be self-fulfilling. For example:

'They won't like me, so why even try to participate?'
'This relationship is sure to fail.'
'I'll never be able to change my drinking.'

Common Thinking Errors *continued*

(6)   Catastrophising

Exaggerating the impact of events and convincing yourself that if something goes wrong it will be totally unbearable and intolerable. For example:

'If I get a craving, it will be unbearable.'

(7)   Mistaking feelings for facts

Confusing facts with feelings or beliefs. No matter how strong a feeling is—it is not a fact! For example:

'I feel like a failure—therefore I am a failure.'

(8)   Personalising

Blaming yourself for anything unpleasant. You take too much responsibility for other people's feelings and behaviour.

'My partner has come home in a bad mood—it must be something that I have done.'

(9)   Self put-downs

This involves undervaluing yourself and putting yourself down. It can often be the result of an extreme over-reaction to a situation, such as making a mistake. For example:

'I don't deserve any better.'
'I'm weak/stupid/ugly.'
'I'm an idiot.'

(10) Should statements

Using 'shoulds', 'oughts' and 'musts' leads to guilt and sets you up to be disappointed. Directing 'should' statements towards others will make you feel frustrated, angry and resentful. For example:

'I must not get angry.'
'He should always be on time.'

Source: Adapted from Burns (1999), Monti *et al.* (2002) and Tanner & Ball (2000).

STRATEGIES FOR CHALLENGING NEGATIVE THOUGHTS

Decatastrophising

Are you over-reacting? Often events are much less catastrophic than you automatically think. What is really the worst that can happen? How likely is it that the worst could happen? What could you do to manage even if the worst were to happen?

Hopefulness statements

Be kind and encouraging to yourself! Pessimism can be a self-fulfilling prophecy. Try self-statements like 'Even though it's tough, I can handle this situation.' 'I can change, nothing is written in stone.'

Blame the event, not yourself

Everyone makes mistakes sometimes. Mistakes you make in a particular situation are not permanent reflections on you as a person.

Reminding yourself to stay 'on task'

Try to focus on what you need to do. Taking action will make you feel better.

Avoid the 'shoulds' and 'musts'

If you find that your automatic thoughts are full of these types of words then it probably means that you are setting unreasonable demands on yourself or others. Removing these words from your thoughts can allow you (and others) more freedom to be yourself.

Recall good things

Focus on the positive! For example: What other things have gone well recently? What things do you like about yourself? What personal skills do you have that have helped you cope with challenging situations in the past?

Relabelling the distress

Remember, negative thoughts and feelings don't mean you are going to end up drinking. Think of them rather as signals or signposts to use your coping skills to help yourself to feel better.

Encourage yourself

Pat yourself on the back for making positive changes.

Source: Adapted from Monti *et al.* (2002).

EXAMPLE OF A THOUGHT-MONITORING SHEET

Describe SITUATION leading to unpleasant feelings, e.g. 1. Event 2. Daydreams, thoughts or memories	FEELINGS 1. Specify angry, sad, craving, etc. 2. Rate intensity of feelings 1–100	AUTOMATIC THOUGHTS 1. Write automatic thought(s) that preceded feelings 2. Rate belief in automatic thought(s) 0–100% 3. Type of thinking error? e.g., catastrophising	! S T O P !	POSITIVE CHALLENGE 1. Write positive challenge to automatic thought(s) 2. Rate belief in positive challenge 0–100%	OUTCOME THOUGHTS Re-rate belief in automatic thought(s) 0–100%	OUTCOME FEELINGS 1. Specify feelings 2. Rate intensity of feelings 0–100
Had a fight with my partner after I got home late from work	Angry (85) Hopeless (95) Craving (90)	My partner hates me and doesn't trust me and things will never change (100%) There's no point in trying any more – I want a drink (95%) Catastrophising Overgeneralising	! S T O P !	We both had lousy days. As I forgot to phone, my partner was worried about me (40%) This was our first argument since I started treatment and otherwise my partner has been supportive and pleased with how I'm doing (70%) An occasional fight isn't the end of the world – people do get angry from time to time (60%)	Partner hates me? (10%) No point in trying? (30%)	Angry (40) Hopeless (20) Craving (15) Pleasantly surprised by these changes (80)

Source: Adapted from Fennell (1989).

THOUGHT-MONITORING SHEET

Describe SITUATION leading to unpleasant feelings, e.g. 1. Event 2. Daydreams, thoughts or memories	FEELINGS 1. Specify angry, sad, craving, etc. 2. Rate intensity of feelings 1–100	AUTOMATIC THOUGHTS 1. Write automatic thought(s) that preceded feelings 2. Rate belief in automatic thought(s) 0–100% 3. Type of thinking error? e.g., catastrophising	! S T O P ! POSITIVE CHALLENGE 1. Write positive challenge to automatic thought(s) 2. Rate belief in positive challenge 0–100%	OUTCOME THOUGHTS Re-rate belief in automatic thought(s) 0–100%	OUTCOME FEELINGS 1. Specify feelings 2. Rate intensity of feelings 0–100

Remember, ask the questions: (1) What is the evidence for this thought? (2) What are the advantages/disadvantages of thinking this way? (3) Is there a thinking error? (4) What alternatives are there?

11

Relaxation Training

RECOMMENDED USE

Relaxation training involves a range of procedures designed to teach your client how to voluntarily release tension. The tension can be either physical tension in the muscles or psychological or mental tension. Relaxation training will allow your client to recognise tension and achieve deep relaxation during practice. It will also teach him how to relax in everyday situations when stress arises.

Relaxation training is appropriate when your client has reported or displayed some level of tension. It should be used as a component of a broader treatment programme rather than as a treatment by itself. It is suitable for clients aiming for either abstinence or moderation and as part of the treatment for any type of drug problem. You can teach the procedures in either group or individual settings. Group settings may be more economical, provided that any of your clients' individual difficulties in learning the procedures are recognised and addressed.

GOALS

The goals of relaxation training are to enable your client:

- To recognise tension when it exists, either physical or psychological.
- To learn to relax his body in a general, total sense.
- To learn to actively release tension in day-to-day situations in specific muscle groups.
- To use mental imagery or meditative procedures to reduce psychological tension.
- Through this process to learn to cope with high levels of tension that might otherwise increase his risk of relapse to excessive drug or alcohol use.

KEY CONCEPTS

TENSION

Tension is an unpleasant feeling of being on edge, being apprehensive or 'stressed'. If the tension is physical your client might report to you trembling, muscle twitching, shakiness, muscular tension, muscular aches or soreness, restlessness or easy fatigue. Alternatively, it might be psychological tension where your client experiences worry or anxiety.

RELAXATION RESPONSE

According to Benson (2000), each person has a natural response which protects against 'overstress'. This response, which Benson calls the 'relaxation response', decreases the heart rate, lowers metabolism and slows breathing. The elements required to achieve a relaxation response are: (a) a quiet environment; (b) a comfortable position; (c) a passive attitude; and (d) a mental or physical device that promotes tension reduction.

METHOD

RATIONALE FOR YOUR CLIENT

Explain to your client that people have an innate, genetically determined response to threat or stress, known as the flight or fight response. As part of this flight or fight response, the muscles become tense, breathing becomes more rapid and shallow, and the person becomes alert and vigilant for danger. These reactions enable people to deal with threatening situations in an adaptive manner. Normally, the muscles will not remain tense constantly, but will activate and relax according to the situation's needs. Most people will therefore have fluctuating patterns of tension and relaxation over time. However, when a person experiences stress for long periods of time, muscle tension levels can remain high. If this goes on, it can become hard even to recognise the tension, let alone get rid of it.

Inform your client that constant tension might cause him to feel anxious even in ordinary or trivial daily situations. Should his tension get out of hand, it could trigger a relapse to drug or alcohol use. No doubt your client will be able to generate examples from his own experience of psychological or physical tension leading to drug or alcohol use as a way of coping or relaxing. Try to incorporate your client's examples into your rationale. Explain to him that relaxation procedures can be used in tension-provoking situations as a healthier and more effective way of reducing tension than drug or alcohol use.

It is important to point out to your client that effective relaxation training is more than simply thinking of a pleasant scene or relaxing in a non-stressful situation. Although he will begin by learning to relax in relatively unchallenging situations, he will ultimately learn to relax in an efficient manner in the face of real stressors which create a high level of tension. Many people continue relaxation procedures for years after learning the skill. Those who gain the most from these procedures either practise regularly or use the procedures as soon as they notice any increases in tension or anxiety.

BEFORE STARTING

It is important for you as the therapist to understand the nature of relaxation training, so learning the procedures yourself is important (and may provide you with a fringe benefit!).

CONDITIONS FOR TRAINING

It is possible for you to teach basic relaxation procedures to your client in one to three sessions. However, to develop the ability to recognise tension and the skill to release this tension, he will need to practise regularly for up to eight weeks, with your encouragement and supervision. You will need to negotiate an agreement about practice before commencing the exercises. Explain to your client that this practice will help him to achieve really long-lasting effects and will allow him to be able to react to tension with a relaxation response in an easy and reliable fashion. The more he practises, the more he will benefit from the exercises. Try to have some relaxation-training tapes available to assist your client when he practises at home. Play the relaxation tape once with your client and then advise him to practise relaxing to the tape at least once a day, especially in the beginning.

Recommend that your client practises relaxation in a quiet environment which is free of distractions. He may need to find a private room, take the phone off the hook or explain to other household members that he is going to be unavailable for about half an hour. He should also choose a time when he is not mentally preoccupied with other concerns.

Warn your client against practising relaxation in bed because he will probably go to sleep. Explain that sleep is not the same as relaxation because people can be quite tense while they are asleep. One aim of the practice is to learn how to relax while awake. Ideally, your client should practise in a comfortable armchair with good support for his body including his head and shoulders. Practising relaxation in bed is appropriate if your client has had sleeping difficulties and relaxation training is being used to assist him to sleep. Even then, however, it is important that he practises while sitting in a chair as well.

RECOGNISING TENSION

In order to be able to relax, your client needs to learn to identify both the triggers that increase tension and the areas of his body where tension occurs. Have your client consider which day-to-day events cause increased tension. Possible candidates are difficulties in relationships, work or school stress, loud noise, or negative feelings such as boredom, sadness, impatience and anger.

After identifying the triggers that increase tension, ask your client to identify where the tension occurs in his body. In particular, you might ask your client to tell you whether he notices tension in his neck, face, jaw, forehead, arms or legs. The 'tension monitoring sheet' at the end of this chapter will assist you and your client to record these points of tension.

Emphasise that tension can be not only physical but also psychological. Ask your client whether he feels worried and apprehensive. Depending on whether your client experiences physical or psychological tension, you might choose to teach him progressive muscle relaxation or a meditative approach involving mental imagery.

TYPES OF RELAXATION

The following different types of relaxation therapy can be used either separately or in combination. It's a good idea to see what works best for your client and then refine the methods to fit his personal circumstances.

Progressive Muscle Relaxation Procedures

Progressive muscle relaxation involves the active tensing and then relaxing of muscle groups in the body in an orderly and progressive sequence (hence the name). Typically, the individual is required to tense his foot muscles and relax these, then his leg muscles, working upwards through the body and each of the major muscle groups. The aim is to teach your client both to recognise excessive tension by having him produce it deliberately, and to recognise the release of tension and feelings of relaxation.

Meditative Relaxation Procedures

Meditative relaxation procedures involve mental or psychological relaxation techniques. Suggestions of relaxation are combined with focused attention which can have a meditative effect. For example, your client might focus on pleasant imagery. Alternatively, he could focus on silently repeating a word. The word 'relax' is a good one to use for obvious reasons.

Isometric Relaxation Procedures

Isometric relaxation procedures involve one muscle working against another or exerting pressure against an immobile object. While your client might be able to sit quietly in a chair and reduce his tension, this skill may not transfer adequately to everyday situations. For this reason, it is important that your client learns a technique which he can use to help him relax in these everyday situations without others being aware that that is what he is doing. Most of the isometric relaxation exercises do not involve any apparent movement or change in posture and therefore your client can practise them without embarrassment. Other isometric exercises involve some degree of movement and they can be practised when activities such as stretching are not likely to draw attention or be inappropriate.

If using the isometric procedures, encourage your client to practise several times each day so that he becomes skilled in their use. It is especially important that he practises using them when he is in stressful situations. The aim is gradually to train your client to relax in a way that is semi-automatic or without conscious thought.

Important points to remember

When practising any of the different types of relaxation procedures, your client should:

(1) carry out relaxation exercises whenever tension is noticed;
(2) recognise that relaxation is a skilled activity that will improve only with practice; and
(3) avoid tensing his muscles to the point of discomfort or holding the tension for long periods of time.

TRAINING PROCEDURES

Scripts are provided below for the first two types of relaxation procedures. These scripts are for guidance only and the specific details should be changed and expanded to accommodate the personal needs of your client. The whole procedure should take 20 to 30 minutes to complete. Once you have developed a script for your client, you can read it to him in a session and/or make a relaxation tape for him. It is also important to use your client's practice tape in therapy sessions so that there is continuity between therapy and home practice.

Begin with a brief overview of the ideal conditions for the technique. For example you might say:

'I want you to listen to my voice, and to focus on what I am going to say and what I ask you to do. Be sure that you are seated comfortably and that your legs, arms and head are supported. Try to sit in a position where you are able to rest for 30 minutes without pressure points or discomfort developing. If necessary disconnect the telephone, turn off the stove and ask other household members not to interrupt you for 30 minutes. At first, you may find the procedure difficult to master, but with practice it will become easier. Eventually, with daily practice, your natural response to tension will be relaxation. Also be aware that you are in control and if you feel unpleasant sensations, you may stop the exercise.'

Progressive Muscle Relaxation

First, begin by preparing your client for the overall process. For example, you could say:

> 'I am going to guide you through a series of simple exercises which will involve tensing and relaxing groups of muscles in your body in an orderly sequence. Remember, when tensing your muscles it is important not to strain or cause pain but to use only a moderate amount of tension. Your aim is to learn to identify and contrast the feelings of tension and relaxation, so that you can reduce tension later. At the end of the exercises, you will feel more relaxed and this restful feeling should last for some time afterwards.'

Second, guide your client through tensing and relaxing phases for each of the muscle groups you have chosen to work on. For example, you might begin with the feet, then the legs, stomach, arms, hands, neck and head muscles. Get your client to tense and relax each muscle group twice. Notice that the tensing phase is short and sharp, while the relaxing phase allows for a gradual unwinding and time to enjoy the sensations. During the tensing phase, allow your voice to speed up a little and, in contrast, slow your voice down for the relaxation phase. Here are some examples of the phases for the feet and legs which can be modified to apply to any muscle group.

Tensing phase: feet

> 'We will start with your feet in a moment. I will ask you to tense the muscles in your feet by curling the toes either downwards or upwards, and while you are doing this please notice where the tension occurs and how it feels. I will ask you to hold the tension for five seconds. Now, put the tension into your feet and hold that tension for five seconds—one, two, three, four, five.'

Relaxing phase: feet

> 'Now, let that physical tension go and as you do, feel yourself starting to relax in those muscles and more generally. Notice the tension slipping away and the changes in the sensations which you experience. Let all of the tension go. Actively let the tension flow out of your muscles, and notice how they relax, loosen, become slack and unwind. Really focus on those sensations of relaxation in your feet. As you do, feel yourself dropping down in your chair. Your whole body is benefiting from the relaxed sensations. Enjoy these sensations for a few seconds now ... Let any remaining tension go from your feet. You will notice that your feet might be feeling warm. Focus on these pleasant feelings. Allow yourself to focus on the feelings and let other thoughts drift away. When distracting thoughts come to mind, let them go again by bringing your attention back to the feelings in your feet.'

Repeat tensing and relaxing phases.

Tensing phase: legs

'Now, tense the muscles in your legs, and notice where the tension occurs and how it feels. Hold the tension for five seconds—one, two, three, four, five.'

Relaxing phase: legs

'Now, let all the physical tension drain out of your legs. Feel yourself relaxing in those muscles and more generally. Let all of the tension go. Check that your feet are relaxed as well. Feel your legs and feet becoming warm and heavy. Enjoy these sensations for a few seconds now ... Let any remaining tension go from your legs. Allow yourself to focus on the feelings and let other thoughts drift away.'

Repeat tensing and relaxing phases. Then go on to tense and relax other muscle groups.

Meditative Relaxation

In the following example, meditative relaxation combines deep breathing with a focus on the word 'relax'. This meditative approach can be used alone or in combination with any of the other relaxation methods outlined in this chapter.
    Speak slowly and calmly ...

'I am going to guide you through a series of simple exercises which will involve thinking of a word over and over again and letting other thoughts slide by. Your aim is to develop a sense of mental calm, and thereby reduce worrying thoughts and physical tension. Close your eyes and begin by focusing on your breathing. Take a deep breath. Hold it for a couple of seconds. And breathe out. Think of the word "relax". Visualise it and see it floating in your mind. Now as you breathe in, count "one". As you breathe out say the word "relax" in your mind. As you breathe in, count "two". Then say "relax" as you slowly breathe out and really feel the tension and worries leaving you. Again breathe in and count 'three'. Breathe out and say "relax". And with that word "relax", let all the tension in your body drop away. Feel yourself becoming more calm and relaxed. Continue to focus on your breathing and each time you breathe out, say that word "relax" and allow all distracting thoughts to just pass by. Continue to do that now.'

Another approach to meditative relaxation is to combine a simple imaginary scene with deep breathing. The scene described below could be combined with some of the other methods outlined in this chapter, including the meditative approach described above. Alternatively, you could expand the scene to a 30-minute script, using specific details based on what your client sees as a pleasant, relaxing environment. Designing the imaginary scene around your client's preferences is important because a script which is relaxing to one person might provoke anxiety for another person. Here is a short script of an imaginary scene designed to induce relaxed feelings:

> 'Close your eyes and focus on your breathing. Take a deep breath. Hold it for a couple of seconds. And breathe out. Just notice your breathing for a few moments. Imagine that you are somewhere outdoors, in a very pleasant place. A place that feels safe and quiet. Notice your surroundings. The weather is pleasant and warm. The sky is clear and blue. Imagine yourself resting in this place. Notice your breathing. Take slow deep breaths. Hold for a moment and let go. As you let go, feel yourself become more and more relaxed. Imagine yourself looking up at the sky. You see a feather gently floating down. A slight breeze blows it along and it flutters and turns. You can feel the breeze caressing your skin as you watch the feather. Slowly the feather falls. As you watch it coming down, feel yourself sinking deeper and deeper into a relaxed state. Notice your breathing is becoming slower and deeper. Continue to relax as you watch the feather gently floating towards the ground.'

Isometric Relaxation

Training in progressive muscle relaxation will greatly enhance your client's ability to practise isometric relaxation exercises. Before commencing isometric exercises, re-assure your client that the length of time he holds his breath is not critical and that some people find it difficult to hold their breath for very long without feeling distressed. Remind him that he is in control of the exercise and should make adjustments to suit his own needs. Demonstrate the exercises for each muscle group before commencing the procedure and then get your client to try them out. The following is an example of isometric relaxation procedures, using one muscle group and incorporating some aspects of meditative relaxation:

> 'Take a small breath and hold it for a short time—say, to a count of seven. At the same time, pull yourself down into the chair with your hands and hold that tension. At the count of seven, breathe out slowly and silently say the word "relax". As you do this, let go of all the tension in your arms. Just let your hands rest by the side of the chair. Now, for a minute or so, notice your breathing and say "relax" to yourself each time you breathe out. Allow all the tension to leave your body.'

This procedure should be followed for approximately one minute and may be repeated as necessary until your client feels relaxed. You and your client may wish to choose one or more of the following isometric exercises:

(1) Tense all the muscles in the thighs and calves.
(2) Push one muscle group against another. This might involve crossing the legs and pushing down with the upper leg while trying to lift the lower leg.
(3) Place hands under each side of a chair and pull down into the chair.

(4) Place hands behind the head with interlocked fingers. Push forward while pushing the head backwards into the hands (the net effect of which would be no obvious movement).

(5) When standing, straighten legs to tense all the muscles, bending the knees back as far as possible and then releasing the tension.

(6) If travelling on public transport or in a public venue, push against a solid rail or a wall, placing tension in the arms or legs.

Encourage your client to identify muscle groups where tension will typically occur for him and focus on these in the isometric relaxation exercises. For example, if he tends to tense his neck muscles, then exercise (4), where he pushes his head backwards against his interlocked hands, can help to dissipate the tension in his neck.

Trouble shooting

There are a number of difficulties which your client can encounter with relaxation training. Your client for example may initially complain that he cannot relax and that the procedure is not working. Emphasise from the outset that the techniques take time to learn and that the benefits will gradually come with regular practice.

People who have been chronically tense for long periods can also sometimes experience the relaxation sensations as a loss of control and this can be frightening. Warn your client that he may experience unusual sensations at first. Explain that with time these new feelings of relaxation will become familiar and therefore more comfortable to him. Explore your client's reactions immediately after the relaxation exercise. If he indicates that he finds these sensations disturbing, allow some time to discuss his experience. It is also important for you to emphasise and demonstrate that he is in control of the exercise at all times.

Your client may encounter obstacles to practising relaxation, such as insufficient time or a lack of privacy. While helping him to plan a solution to these problems, also remind him of the value of investing time now for greater returns later. Motivational interviewing techniques (Chapter 3) will be useful if your client seems to be making excuses to avoid practising. You can also use problem-solving techniques (Chapter 6) to help him incorporate the exercises into a daily routine. One strategy might be to schedule the exercises into his old drinking or drug-using time-slot so that he is learning to use time more constructively. If he continues to have problems with home practice, ask him to make notes about them at the time of practice and bring them along for discussion.

RESOURCES LIST

Benson, H. (2000). *The Relaxation Response*. New York: Avon.
    —An excellent overview of the effects of relaxation procedures on physiological and psychological parameters.

Clarke, J. C. & Saunders, J. B. (1988). *Alcoholism and Problem Drinking: Theories and Treatments*. Sydney: Pergamon Press.
—Provides an excellent summary of the rationale and method of various relaxation procedures. It is especially useful for trouble-shooting information.

MONITORING YOUR MUSCLE TENSION

Name: . . . .   Date ___/___/____

Over the coming weeks, while you are practising relaxation procedures, use this form to monitor the tension in your body. You will need to do this each day, so make sure that you have enough copies of the form. Before you do your relaxation exercise, indicate the location and intensity of your muscle tension by <u>ticking</u> the appropriate box. After you have finished your relaxation exercise, re-rate your muscle tension by <u>putting a cross</u> in the appropriate box. You can then compare ticks and crosses to monitor the changes you are experiencing as a result of the relaxation procedures. For instance, you might be feeling a medium amount of tension in your neck prior to doing the exercise, so you would tick the box for 'medium'. After the exercise, you might find that your neck tension has reduced and you can put a cross in the 'low' tension box, to reflect this change.

Location of tension	Muscle tension rating			
	High	Medium	Low	Nil
Hands				
Forearms				
Upper arms				
Shoulders				
Neck				
Forehead				
Jaw				
Back				
Upper legs and calves				
Feet				

12

Behavioural Self-management

RECOMMENDED USE

Behavioural self-management training involves a series of strategies such as self-monitoring, setting drinking limits, controlling rates of drinking, drink refusal, identifying problem drinking situations, learning alternative coping skills and self-reward.

Behavioural self-management is intended for those clients who wish to cut down rather than abstain from drinking and who do not have severe problems with, or dependence on, alcohol. Details of guidelines for helping to assess when a moderation goal is appropriate are discussed in Chapter 4, *Goal Setting*. In brief, however, it is stressed that clients choosing moderation should be free from any significant drink-related physical problems or brain damage which would indicate a need to abstain for health reasons. Clients are also more likely to succeed with moderation if they have a drinking history suggesting that they can keep to drinking limits, have no diagnosed psychiatric problems (e.g., depression or personality disorder) and have not shown frequent and/or severe signs of physical withdrawal (e.g., delerium tremens) when they stopped drinking.

If your client's goal is abstinence but her lifestyle has been so heavily involved with alcohol that there is a high likelihood that she will drink again, you might consider introducing the principles of behavioural self-management as a harm reduction strategy. For example, the 'Guidelines for Sensible Drinking' at the end of this chapter could help her to limit the risks to her health in the event of a lapse. Obviously, it is important to avoid promoting the idea of 'safe' drinking if your client has good reasons for choosing abstinence. You would need to stress that these limits are only relevant in cases of lapse or relapse, as a method of harm reduction. Don't use this strategy if you have any doubts about its impact on your client's ability to stay abstinent (Shand, Gates, Fawcett & Mattick, 2003).

Elements of the self-management training approach overlap with many therapeutic techniques dealt with in other chapters of this book. This chapter will cover in most detail those techniques which are useful for moderating drinking and will cross-reference to other chapters where necessary. Behavioural self-management is sometimes combined with pharmacotherapies to assist in managing cravings (Chapter 14) or cue exposure, a method that is briefly described in Chapter 16, *Relapse Prevention Training*.

You can provide behavioural self-management training in either individual or group settings. Researchers using this approach have varied treatment from 6 weeks of 90-minute sessions with individual clients to 8–10 weekly group sessions, each again of approximately 90 minutes.

GOALS

The goal of behavioural self-management is to teach your client specific skills so that she can reduce drinking to stable levels that minimise both the risk of physical ill-health and any other personal or social problems which her drinking might currently cause.

KEY CONCEPTS

GUIDELINES FOR SENSIBLE DRINKING

The 'Guidelines for Sensible Drinking' presented at the end of this chapter are based on measures of standard drinks or units for typical alcoholic beverages served in bars in Australia, the UK and the USA. They are derived from research investigating the levels of drinking that lead to health problems. Standard drinks are explained in more detail in Chapter 5, *Brief and Early Interventions*. You will also find a description of the risks associated with different levels of alcohol consumption in the 'Levels of Risk in Drinking Alcohol' handout on p. 94.

SELF-MONITORING

Self-monitoring is one of the most useful and important aspects of self-management training. It involves daily recording of the amount drunk and the circumstances surrounding drinking. The aim of self-monitoring is to help your client become aware of how much, when, where and why she is drinking. It also provides an important and concrete way to record progress. In the early stages of treatment this information can be extremely useful in helping you and your client to identify those situations that are causing her problems, as well as those drinking situations that are trouble-free. This information can then be used to create drinking rules and to develop strategies for coping with situations in which she is likely to drink more than her set limits. An example of a daily drinking diary is included in the practice sheet at the end of this chapter.

METHOD

RATIONALE FOR YOUR CLIENT

In introducing the self-management approach, emphasise that the aim is to teach your client skills to help her cut down drinking to a harm-free level. The target level of drinking will be decided by your client with your help. Emphasise that learning new drinking habits is difficult and requires considerable patience and effort. Practising the skills and completing any agreed upon homework tasks will therefore be extremely important to making progress. It is also important to be confident in your approach, so tell your client that if she follows the programme there is a very good chance of success. You might, however, also wish to say that moderation is not the best solution for all who try it and that if desired you will also be able to help your client work towards a goal of abstinence.

BEFORE STARTING

It is recommended that before beginning with the specific self-management aspects of this approach, some time should be spent with your client in focusing on and strengthening her resolution to change. On an individual basis this might involve motivational interviewing strategies (Chapter 3). In a group context clients could discuss the pros and cons of drinking, with home practice involving writing down personal reasons for cutting down. Basic educational information, including personalising the health effects of alcohol (pp. 55–57) could also be addressed in early sessions. You might also like to recommend a self-help manual to your client (Chapter 5, *Brief and Early Interventions*).

ELEMENTS OF BEHAVIOURAL SELF-MANAGEMENT

Behavioural self-management training involves the following steps:

(1) Daily self-monitoring.
(2) Setting limits on drinking.
(3) Keeping to set limits.
(4) Identifying troublesome (high-risk) and trouble-free drinking situations and devising strategies to cope with the former.
(5) Maintaining new drinking habits.

Daily Self-monitoring

You will first need to ensure that your client understands what a standard drink or unit is. Explain that, as different drinks contain different amounts of alcohol, a standard drink provides a useful way of recording drinking. Describe how much alcohol a standard drink contains (see p. 164) and show your client the 'Guidelines for Sensible Drinking' at the end of this chapter. It is also important to warn your client that home-poured drinks are often bigger and therefore contain more alcohol. For this reason you might suggest that your client practises pouring standard drinks at home, using a measuring glass.

You can then introduce the notion of 'self-monitoring'. Explain that filling in a 'day diary' will help your client to keep track of her drinking and will act as a good reminder that she is trying to limit drinking. It will also be a good way of learning more about when, where and why she drinks and will be a concrete way for both of you to see how she is progressing over the following weeks. Show your client how to complete a day diary such as the one provided at the end of this chapter. We suggest that your client record the day and date, hours over which she drank, where she was and with whom, what she was doing, how she felt before drinking and what happened (if anything) as a result of drinking. 'What happened' might include either good consequences such as 'met some nice people', or less desirable outcomes such as 'got drunk and angry'. The last columns involve writing down the type of beverage and the amount drunk and then converting that information into standard drinks.

As it might not always be realistic to expect that your client will fill in such details while she is drinking in a public setting, encourage her to complete the diary as *soon as possible* after drinking. It might, however, be very useful to suggest that your client jots down on a small piece of paper, even in tally form, each drink as she consumes it. You should also discuss with her any potential problems or obstacles that might prevent her from filling in the forms. Day diaries should then be reviewed at the beginning of each session throughout treatment, highlighting successes and briefly discussing problems.

Setting Limits on Drinking

It is crucial to the success of behavioural self-management that your client sets realistic and concrete limits to her drinking. These limits should be set at levels that minimise both the risk of physical ill-health and any other social problems which your client's drinking might currently produce. Of course, your client must also be confident that the limits are achievable for her.

You could use the 'Guidelines for Sensible Drinking' provided by the various national health authorities as a basis for setting these limits. These are set out in a table at the end of this chapter and can be used to set either weekly or daily limits. While you might choose to focus on weekly limits, with flexibility in daily levels of drinking, your client should still set a maximum daily limit to avoid binge drinking. In an earlier edition of our book (Jarvis, Tebbutt & Mattick, 1995), we recommended maximum daily limits of 8 drinks for men and 6 drinks for women. Since then, health authorities (National Health and Medical Research Council, 2001) have recommended a maximum daily limit of 6 drinks for men and 4 drinks for women. Although there is no precise way to define binge drinking for a particular individual, it is most important to stress to your client that drinking heavily in a binge pattern should be avoided. You should also encourage your client to have *at least two alcohol-free days* each week and that if she does have a binge drinking episode, this should be followed by a two day break from alcohol, to allow her body to recover.

There are two ways of helping your client to reduce her overall drinking to within responsible limits. The first involves a 'tapering off' approach. Using this method, you would negotiate limits with your client each week, that would be gradually reduced until she reached her final, low-risk goal.

The second, quite different approach (Sanchez-Craig, 1996) involves negotiating with your client for an initial period of abstinence (say, over the first two weeks of treatment) after which she would recommence drinking within set limits. This approach has the advantage of providing a 'time-out' period from all drinking habits. During this period you and your client can focus on monitoring situations in which she is tempted to drink, identify the strategies she has already mastered to cope with urges and temptations, and develop further skills to cope with any situations in which she was not able to successfully abstain (see *Troublesome and Trouble-free Drinking Situations*, below). A period of abstinence will also ensure that your client has recovered from any minor dulling of mental functioning which regular heavy consumption might have caused. After the period of abstinence has been completed, strategies to slow down and limit drinking can be introduced while you continue to identify and solve any new troublesome drinking situations that occur.

Trouble shooting

If your client has not been able to show strong signs of being able to reduce her drinking within six weeks then discuss a goal of abstinence with her and reassess whether other treatment strategies might be of assistance.

Keeping to Set Limits

Provided at the end of this chapter is a list of strategies or 'tips' that your client can use to help her to keep within her drinking limits. Discuss these strategies with your client and encourage her to try them out over the following weeks. Ask her to note on her day diary when a certain strategy has been useful so that she learns to recognise which techniques are most effective for her. Two further strategies are also discussed in more detail below.

Tracking blood alcohol concentrations (BACs): A simple rule to help pace drinking is that of never drinking more than one drink per hour. While this is probably the easiest and most efficient rule to recommend to your client, you might also wish to introduce the notion of BACs using the charts provided at the end of this chapter.

These charts show roughly how many standard drinks can be consumed across different lengths of drinking sessions in order to maintain a level of alcohol in the blood of 0.05% or 0.08%. For example, a woman who is less than 60 kg should not drink more than 3 drinks in 4 hours if she wishes to remain under 0.05%.

Of course, clients should be discouraged from drinking *at all* if they intend to drive or operate any other complex machinery. Drinking before swimming, engaging in water sports or in any other potentially hazardous environment should also be strongly discouraged.

For any prospective drinking session encourage your client to plan both how long she intends to drink for and the maximum BAC she will allow. The charts can then be used as a rough guide to how long each drink should last.

Stress that the charts provide only rough guides because people's bodies deal in different ways with alcohol. For example, the same amount of alcohol has a greater effect: (a) on a light rather than a heavy drinker; (b) on women rather than men (due to lower amounts of water in women's bodies to dilute the alcohol); (c) if drunk quickly (as the rate of drinking exceeds the rate the liver can remove the alcohol); and (d) if drunk on an empty stomach or in a 'bubbly' mixer (as the alcohol gets into the bloodstream more quickly).

Drink refusal: Drink refusal skills are also important for occasions when your client has reached her set limit or is trying to space out her drinks. These skills are essential if your client has difficulty in resisting social and/or peer pressures to drink. Teaching drink refusal involves demonstrating both appropriately assertive and inappropriate ways of refusing offers of drinks. Your client should also have the opportunity to role-play refusing drinks in a variety of situations. Details of drink refusal training are found in Chapter 7.

Troublesome and Trouble-free Drinking Situations

These strategies overlap with aspects of relapse-prevention training and are discussed only briefly here. For more detail refer to Chapter 16.

After a few weeks of self-monitoring, examine your client's day diaries with her and identify troublesome or 'high-risk' drinking occasions. These are situations where drinking to a set limit was difficult to achieve or where drinking resulted in problems. Your client might also generate further examples of these situations from her past experiences. Look for common themes in the troublesome drinking occasions, such as particular drinking friends or places, times of day or certain days of the week, whether your client was hungry or thirsty, how long the drinking sessions lasted or the way she was feeling before starting to drink. For example, your client might find that she always overdrank in the company of certain friends, when she had lots of money with her or when she was angry or upset.

It is important that your client attempts to avoid drinking in these troublesome situations. You may wish, therefore, to use the characteristics of the troublesome occasions to create some drinking rules. In the example above, your client might decide that she: (a) will avoid drinking with the problem friends; (b) limit the amount of money she carries to any drinking session; and (c) not drink when she is angry or upset. The characteristics of the trouble-free drinking situations can also be included in the rules. For example, if your client never has trouble keeping to limits when she has another activity planned for later, one of her drinking rules might state that she will drink only when she has planned something to do afterwards. Encourage your client to write down her drinking rules and keep them in a readily accessible place!

In addition to creating these rules, it will be important to work with your client in generating a range of thoughts and/or behaviours that provide an alternative to drinking in the troublesome situations. For example, if she drinks when angry or upset, work on listing other ways of dealing with those feelings. These might include going for a walk, visiting another friend, applying assertiveness skills (Chapter 8), or challenging thoughts (Chapter 10, *Cognitive Therapy*).

You should also stress to your client the importance of *planning ahead*, that is of considering strategies to help her cope *before* entering a situation where alcohol will be available and where the temptation or pressures to overdrink are strong.

Trouble shooting

In some instances you might find that your client has difficulty in generating alternative thoughts or actions to help her cope with high-risk situations. Under these circumstances you might wish to spend some time teaching problem-solving skills. Details of this procedure are found in Chapter 6. You might also discover that other common themes emerge. For example, your client could be drinking to cope with pressure or anxiety, or drinking as a result of conflict with her spouse. Such themes might indicate that your client would benefit from training in other specific skills such as relaxation, assertiveness or communication skills, or couples therapy. Details of these skills training procedures are given in the relevant chapters in this book.

Maintaining New Drinking Habits

Important aspects of maintaining change involve establishing self-rewards for achieving goals and exploring alternatives to drinking. Encourage your client to reward herself for cutting down her drinking and sticking to her drinking rules. In doing so emphasise that her rewards should be meaningful, planned in advance and given only when a well-defined goal has been met, not given for 'near' successes, and given as soon as possible after they have been earned.

Work with your client in generating the list of rewards that will help her stay on track. Her list could include fun activities or special rewards from her partner. However, it is strongly recommended that your client should avoid using a partner to police her behaviour—especially if goals aren't being met. Another simple self-reward might involve charting weekly progress. This would involve drawing a simple graph on which the total amount drunk each week was plotted.

It is also extremely important that you encourage your client to take up pleasurable activities to replace hours that were once spent drinking. Examples of activities might include taking up a new hobby, family outings, volunteer work, joining a club or a gym, and so on. Help your client to set in place specific and detailed action plans to ensure that she initiates these new activities.

Terminate treatment when your client has reached her goal and is relatively confident that she can cope with potentially high-risk situations. Encourage your client to continue self-monitoring. Make sure that you have discussed ways of coping if she experiences a slip or relapse to heavy drinking. This important aspect of relapse-prevention training is discussed on pp. 228–229. Finally, it is also essential to negotiate arrangements with your client for adequate extended care (Chapter 17). Clients who are unable to maintain moderated drinking should be offered assistance towards achieving an abstinence goal.

RESOURCES LIST

Heather, N., Richmond, R., Webster, I., Wodak, A., Hardie, M., & Polkinghorne, H. (1989). *A Guide to Healthier Drinking*. Kensington, Australia: University of New South Wales, School of Community Medicine and National Drug and Alcohol Research Centre.
—This manual is one example of self-help materials that may be useful to your client as she practices behavioural self-management. More examples are in the *Resources List* of Chapter 5, *Brief and Early Interventions*.

Heather, N. & Robertson, I. (1997). *Problem Drinking* (3rd edn). Oxford, UK: Oxford University Press.
—This is a classic text on the practical applications of social learning theory to problem drinking. It includes a discussion of the goals of abstinence and moderation and presents evidence supporting the use of skills-based approaches in treatment for alcohol problems.

Hester, R.K. (1995). Behavioral self-control training. In: R.K. Hester & W.R. Miller (eds), *Handbook of Alcoholism Treatment Approaches* (2nd edn) (pp. 148–159). Boston: Allyn and Bacon.
—Provides practical guidelines for behavioural self-management as well as research findings regarding its effectiveness.

Jarvis, T.J., Tebbut, J. & Mattick, R.P. (1995) *Treatment Approaches for Alcohol and Drug Dependence: An Introductory Guide* (1st edn) (pp. 148–156) Chichester, UK: Wiley.
—Our first edition provided earlier guidelines for setting limits on alcohol consumption.

Shand, F., Gates, J., Fawcett, J. & Mattick, R.P. (2003). *Guidelines for the Treatment of Alcohol Problems* (pp. 112–114). Canberra, Australia: Australian Government Department of Health and Ageing.
—Evidence-based recommendations for the use of behavioural self-management.

National Health and Medical Research Council (2001). *Australian Alcohol Guidelines*. Canberra, Australia: NH&MRC.
www.alcoholguidelines.gov.au
—Describes and explains definitions of risky and high-risk drinking and the sensible drinking guidelines recommended by the Australian National Health and Medical Research Council.

NHS Scotland (2003) *Alcofacts: A Guide to Sensible Drinking*. Scotland: Health Education Board for Scotland (HEBS).
Available at: http://www.hebs.scot.nhs.uk/services/pubs/pdf/Alcofacts.pdf
—A pamphlet with another set of guidelines to sensible drinking.

Sanchez-Craig, M. (1996). *Therapist's Manual for Secondary Prevention of Alcohol Problems: Procedures for Teaching Moderate Drinking and Abstinence*. Canada: The Centre for Addiction and Mental Health (CAMH).
Can be obtained from the Centre for Addiction and Mental Health, 33 Russell Street, Toronto, ON, Canada M5S 2S1 or at http://www.camh.net/publications
—This therapist's manual details treatment guidelines for clients with moderation or abstinence goals, illustrated with case examples.

The Department of Health UK (2004). *Alcohol Harm Reduction Strategy for England*. London: HMSO.
Full report is available at: http://www.strategy.gov.uk
The Alcohol and Health guidelines can be found at www.dh.gov.uk by searching for the terms 'drinking sensibly'.
—Describes goals and targets for improving the health of people in England, including the most recent guidelines regarding sensible drinking.

Sitharthan, T. & Kavanagh, D.J. (1990). Role of self-efficacy in predicting outcomes from a programme for controlled drinking. *Drug and Alcohol Dependence*, **27**, 87–94.
—Describes the development of a scale to assess your client's confidence in maintaining moderation across a range of situations. Other scales are listed in the *Resources List* of Chapter 16, *Relapse Prevention Training*.

US Departments of Health and Human Services (HHS) and Agriculture (USDA) (2000). *Nutrition and Your Health: Dietary Guidelines for Americans* (5th edn). Washington: USDA.
Available at: http://www.health.gov/dietaryguidelines
—Describes goals and targets for improving the health of Americans, including the most recent guidelines for sensible drinking.

GUIDELINES FOR SENSIBLE DRINKING

Australian Guidelines[a]

For Men

No more than six drinks on any one day (60 g), for risk of harm in the short term.
No more than four standard drinks of alcohol per day (40 g), or 28 standard drinks (280 g) per week for risk of harm in the long term.

For Women

No more than four drinks on any one day (40 g), for risk of harm in the short term.
No more than two standard drinks of alcohol per day (20 g), or 14 standard drinks (140 g) per week for risk of harm in the long term.

Plus one or two alcohol-free days per week to reduce the risk of forming a habit.

What is a drink?

A schooner or stubby of regular beer = 1.5 drinks.
A middie of regular beer = 1 drink.
Halve the alcoholic content by drinking light strength beer.
A 120 ml glass of wine, a 60 ml glass of port/sherry or a 30 ml nip of spirits = 1 drink.

United Kingdom Guidelines[b]

For Men

No more than 3–4 units of alcohol per day.

For Women

No more than 2–3 units of alcohol per day.

Avoid alcohol for 48 hours after an episode of drunkenness to allow the body to recover.

What is a unit?

A pint of ordinary strength lager or a pint of bitter = 2 units.
A pint of strong lager = 3 units.
A point of ordinary strength cider = 2 units.
A 175 ml glass of wine = around 2 units.
A pub measure of spirits = 1 unit.
An alcopop (e.g., Smirnoff Ice, Bacardi Breezer, WKD, Reef) = 1.5 units.

United States Guidelines[c]

For Men

No more than two drinks per day.

For Women

No more than one drink per day.

What is a drink?

12 fluid oz of regular beer = 1 drink.
5 fluid oz of wine = 1 drink.
1.5 fluid oz of 80-proof distilled spirits = 1 drink.

[a] *Source*: National Health and Medical Research Council, Australia (2001).
[b] *Source*: *Alcohol Harm Reduction Strategy for England*, Department of Health, UK (2004). Crown copyright is reproduced with the permission of the Controller of Her Majesty's Stationery Office
[c] *Source*: US Department of Health and Human Services and US Department of Agriculture (2000).

TIPS FOR DRINKING IN MODERATION

- PLAN AHEAD! Decide on the time period over which you will drink and what your limit will be. Then work out how long each drink must last and pace your drinking accordingly. Limit the amount of money you take with you to spend

- AVOID GULPING—take smaller sips and sip more slowly. Count the number of sips you take to finish your glass and then try to increase that on the next drink

- PUT DOWN YOUR GLASS BETWEEN SIPS—if it is in your hand you will drink from it more often

- DON'T REFILL YOUR GLASS UNTIL IT IS EMPTY—and don't let others (friends, waiters) refill it either

- ALTERNATE your drinks—try having an orange juice or a soft drink between alcoholic drinks

- COUNT your drinks

- DRINK LOW ALCOHOL BEVERAGES—try light or low alcohol beers in preference to regular beers

- DILUTE YOUR DRINKS by adding mixers to spirits, soda to wine, etc.

- NEVER DRINK ALCOHOL TO QUENCH YOUR THIRST—try drinking iced water or a soft drink first if you are thirsty

- AVOID SALTY NIBBLES such as crisps and nuts as they increase thirst

- EAT BEFORE DRINKING—this will mean that your drink will take longer to absorb and will have less effect on you. It will also mean that you won't be tempted to drink to stop hunger or simply to fill an empty stomach

- AVOID DRINKING IN 'SHOUTS'—buy your own drinks, explaining that you are trying to cut down. Alternatively, order soft drinks or skip rounds

- SAY 'NO THANKS'

- ORDER SMALLER SIZES of drinks, e.g., drink middies/half pints instead of schooners/pints

- DON'T HAVE YOUR FAVOURITE DRINK—try switching to a less favoured drink (although make sure it isn't a stronger one) to help break the habit, e.g., try a different beer to your usual. Drinking a less favoured drink might also mean you drink it more slowly

PRACTICE SHEET

DAY DIARY

Day, Date Times	Where, with whom, doing what?	Feelings before drinking? Rate strength of craving (0–100)	What did you do (thoughts and actions)?	What happened? Behaviour, feelings, consequences	What did you drink?	Number of standard drinks
Mon 21/3 8pm–10pm	In a restaurant with friends, eating dinner, talking	Anxious, excited Craving (80)	Drank light beer. Recalled reasons for not getting drunk. Went home straight after meal	Stayed sober and had a good time. Felt proud of myself	4 glasses of light beer	2
Sat 26/3 8pm–1pm	At a party with friends, dancing, talking	Feeling left out. Wanting to attract someone but afraid to make the first move Craving (90)	Drank to give myself the courage to join in	Got drunk. Next day, can't remember how I got home. Terrible hangover	375 ml bottle of rum, mixed	$12\frac{1}{2}$

Source: Adapted from Heather et al. (1989).

NUMBER OF STANDARD DRINKS AND BLOOD ALCOHOL CONCENTRATION (BAC)—MEN

Decide on a BAC and find your weight. Read across to the time you would spend drinking. This tells you how many standard drinks it takes, on average, to reach the BAC you chose, in that time. Amounts above 8 drinks have been omitted from the chart because this would be binge drinking*.

		TIME SPENT DRINKING				
BAC	WEIGHT	One hour	Two hours	Three hours	Four hours	Five hours
0.05%	Less than 70 kg (<11 st)	2	3	4	$4\frac{1}{2}$	5
Cheerful & relaxed. Poor judgement, increased risk of accidents	70–80 kg (11–12 st 8 lbs)	$2\frac{1}{2}$	4	5	$5\frac{1}{2}$	6
	More than 80 kg (>12 st 8 lbs)	3	$4\frac{1}{2}$	$5\frac{1}{2}$	$5\frac{1}{2}$	6
0.08%	Less than 70 kg (<11 st)	$3\frac{1}{2}$	4	5	$5\frac{1}{2}$	$6\frac{1}{2}$
Warmth, well being. Less self-control. Slow reactions, impaired driving	70–80 kg (11–12 st 8 lbs)	4	5	6	$6\frac{1}{2}$	$7\frac{1}{2}$
	More than 80 kg (>12 st 8 lbs)	5	6	7	$7\frac{1}{2}$	8
0.12%	Less than 70 kg (<11 st)	$5\frac{1}{2}$	6	$6\frac{1}{2}$	7	$7\frac{1}{2}$
Talkative, excited, emotional. Uninhibited, impulsive	70–80 kg (11–12 st 8 lbs)	6	7	8	—	—
	More than 80 kg (>12 st 8 lbs)	$7\frac{1}{2}$	—	—	—	—

Source: Adapted from Heather *et al.* (1989).

* Binge drinking as defined here is based on higher estimates than other sources.

NUMBER OF STANDARD DRINKS AND BLOOD ALCOHOL CONCENTRATION (BAC)—WOMEN

Decide on a BAC and find your weight. Read across the time you would spend drinking. This tells you how many standard drinks it takes, on average, to reach the BAC you chose, in that time. Amounts above 8 drinks have been omitted from the chart because this would be binge drinking*.

TIME SPENT DRINKING

BAC	WEIGHT	One hour	Two hours	Three hours	Four hours	Five hours
0.05%	Less than 60 kg (<9 st 6 lbs)	$1\frac{1}{2}$	2	$2\frac{1}{2}$	3	$3\frac{1}{2}$
Cheerful & relaxed. Poor judgement, increased risk of accidents	60–70 kg (9 st 6 lbs–11 st)	2	$2\frac{1}{2}$	$3\frac{1}{2}$	4	$4\frac{1}{2}$
	More than 70 kg (>11 st)	$2\frac{1}{2}$	3	4	5	$5\frac{1}{2}$
0.08%	Less than 60 kg (9 st 6 lbs)	$2\frac{1}{2}$	3	$3\frac{1}{2}$	$3\frac{1}{2}$	4
Warmth, well being. Less self-control. Slow reactions, impaired driving	60–70 kg (9 st 6 lbs–11 st)	3	$3\frac{1}{2}$	$4\frac{1}{2}$	$4\frac{1}{2}$	$5\frac{1}{2}$
	More than 70 kg (>11 st)	$3\frac{1}{2}$	$4\frac{1}{2}$	$5\frac{1}{2}$	$5\frac{1}{2}$	6
0.12%	Less than 60 kg (<9 st 6 lbs)	$3\frac{1}{2}$	4	$4\frac{1}{2}$	$4\frac{1}{2}$	5
Talkative, excited, emotional. Uninhibited, impulsive	60–70 kg (9 st 6 lbs–11 lbs)	$4\frac{1}{2}$	5	$5\frac{1}{2}$	$5\frac{1}{2}$	—
	More than 70 kg (>11 st)	5	6	—	—	—

Source: Adapted from Heather *et al.* (1989).

* Binge drinking as defined here is based on higher estimates than other sources.

13

Involving Concerned Others

BASIC GUIDELINES

Substance abuse is not just a problem for your client. As it increases in severity its impact is felt by members of your client's family and friendship network. These people are often instrumental in encouraging him to seek help. They are also likely to play a crucial role in giving him support during and after treatment. Therefore, involving concerned others in your client's treatment will often be an essential part of your role.

There are numerous approaches to family and couples therapy, reflecting the different models of families and substance abuse. The model presented in this chapter is the behavioural model, based on the principle that family members can reward abstinence or moderation and that clients from happier families with better communication have a lower risk of relapse (Rotunda & O'Farrell, 1997). We have chosen this model because the research supports its effectiveness and it is consistent with other methods in this book.

The methods outlined below are designed specifically to address the substance abuse and assist concerned others to support your client's treatment goals. Although they are designed to improve family communication, they are *not* aimed at solving entrenched relationship problems or counteracting violence. If your assessment indicates that your client's family is in need of professional help or that the children are in need of counselling, arrange for a referral to appropriate specialists. Be prepared to offer information about services that can assist when someone's safety is at risk because of violence or abuse.

It may also be less appropriate to use these methods with families from non-western backgrounds. For example, your intervention will be ineffective if it advocates a style of parenting that is not consistent with the family's cultural values. See the *Resources List* for further guidance on how to address cultural issues in counselling.

You and your client might choose to adapt these methods to involve people other than his family. Copello *et al.* (2002) suggested that the ideal people to involve would be people who agree with your client's treatment goals, are readily available to him (especially at times of high risk of relapse) and are willing to offer positive support but also prepared to be firm in encouraging him to continue working towards his treatment goal.

This chapter includes three examples of involving concerned others. The first example describes how to work with couples to support a change in drinking behaviour. The second example shows how to respond when someone seeks help because of a partner's drinking. In the third example, we describe a way of meeting with families to enhance support for a young person's change in substance use. Although these guidelines will give you the basic principles that you need for working with couples or families, we strongly recommend that you expand your skills and understanding through further training and self-education. The *Resources List* provides some suggestions for further reading in this area.

KEY CONCEPTS

POSITIVE INTERACTIONS

Increasing the number of positive interactions between partners or family members will greatly strengthen the relationship as each person experiences direct benefits from being in the company of the other. This chapter outlines two techniques to increase positive interactions: (a) *shared rewarding activities* where the partners or family members negotiate and plan some leisure activities that they can enjoy together without drug use or drinking; and (b) *catch your partner doing something nice* where a couple increase their awareness of the benefits of their relationship.

TIME-OUT

Escalating conflict can be interrupted by taking 'time-out'. The conversation is then postponed until everybody feels calmer or the circumstances are more favourable for a non-aggressive resolution of the conflict.

REFRAMING

Reframing is a technique of cognitive therapy that can be used in couples therapy and family meetings. It is a way of responding to interactions that are negative, defensive, blaming, critical, angry or invalidating. Such interactions tend to disrupt effective communication and may even cause people to drop out of treatment.

A reframe presents a convincing alternative view that highlights the positive concerns family members have for each other. For example, a parent's critical comments about her child might be reframed as worry for the young person's safety. Similarly, a young person's angry fighting might be reframed as a way of trying to connect with a parent. By reframing, you shift the focus from negative emotions, such as anger and hurt, to the positive emotions of caring and concern. It also helps to defuse explosive interactions and models a more constructive approach to communication.

Obviously, sometimes people can make comments that seem to be deliberately hostile, belligerent, intimidating, belittling or aggressive. If you find it hard to reframe a comment because there seems to be a lack of positive concern for the other person, you might point out to the speaker that this form of expression can cause people to become defensive and less inclined to work together. Explain that the only way to get clear and honest communication is for everyone to feel safe from being verbally attacked. It might also be helpful to introduce the concept of 'I-statements' as a non-aggressive form of communication (Chapter 9, *Communication Skills*).

EXAMPLE 1: COUPLES THERAPY

This section describes how to use couples therapy when your client has a drinking problem. The approach aims to enhance the couple's communication in a way that will *support changes in your client's drinking*. The methods presented here are derived from the work of O'Farrell (1995) and from Montgomery and Evans (1996).

Couples therapy is only appropriate when there is agreement between you, your client and your client's partner that the partner's involvement would be beneficial. Since couples therapy aimed at changing problem drinking requires that the partners are able to work together, it is appropriate when the couples are living together or willing to be reconciled for the duration of therapy, do not currently have a psychotic disorder or another severe drug dependence, and where there is an absence of family violence that has caused serious injury or is potentially life threatening (O'Farrell, 1995). Couples therapy can be particularly effective when the couple have sought help after a crisis which has threatened the stability of their relationship.

Therapy with couples can be conducted either with individual couples or in group settings of up to four couples. In the group setting, two therapists are required. Groups provide individual couples with the opportunity to share their experiences and learn from the problems and solutions raised by others.

GOALS

The overall goal is to improve the couple's relationship in ways that will strengthen the capacity and commitment to achieve and sustain a change in drinking. This goal can be broken into several steps:

• To change alcohol-related interactional patterns and develop interactions that support the change in drinking behaviour.

- To help the couple confront and resolve relationship conflicts without your client resorting to drinking.
- To mend rifts in the relationship that have been aggravated as a result of the alcohol abuse.
- To help the couple develop shared activities that are rewarding and do not involve alcohol or other drugs.

METHOD

For the purposes of this section, the term 'drinker' refers to the person who has alcohol problems and the term 'partner' refers to that person's husband, wife or partner. It is important to keep in mind that both partners are your clients. Avoid the temptation to side with one or the other partner when a conflict arises. Ideally, once you have commenced couples therapy, you should only be seeing the drinker in the presence of his partner so that your relationship is with them as a couple rather than with one partner in particular.

Couples therapy emphasises interactions between people. It is very important to *avoid blame* when conducting this therapy. In particular, your client's partner should *not* be made to feel guilty or responsible for your client's drinking. The therapy should also emphasise that the *drinking* is the problem, rather than the drinker. Always focus on the behaviour as the problem on which the partners work together.

Structure each session with an explicit agenda. For example, start by reviewing the events of the past week, including any drinking episodes and the home practice exercises from the previous session. Then introduce and explore further strategies and set new practice exercises. You should initially focus on changing the drinking behaviour, using the techniques discussed in other chapters of this book. Encourage the partner to participate in the negotiation of treatment goals. The couple will need to decide how they are going to change their lifestyle so that the drinker is not exposed to high-risk situations during the first few weeks of therapy. Once initial change in the drinking behaviour has been achieved, concentrate on improving the quality of the couple's communication. This includes training them in methods to deal effectively with conflict and to increase their positive interactions. During the last few sessions, work with the couple in developing relapse-prevention strategies (Chapter 16).

ASSESSMENT

Before proceeding to therapy, you will need to establish that both partners want to try couples therapy and that their relationship is stable enough to allow them to work together. Along with your usual assessment of the drinker's alcohol problems (Chapter 2), briefly assess the partner's drinking pattern in case she also has alcohol-related problems or dependence. Include a brief individual interview with the partner to identify any concerns that she is reluctant to express in the presence of the drinker. An impending crisis in the relationship such as a legal, vocational or financial crisis, warrants immediate attention. Couples therapy should not proceed until this situation has been stabilised. You should also screen for domestic violence and, where appropriate, identify strategies for ensuring safety and make appropriate referrals (Punukollu, 2003).

You might also wish to include in the assessment a structured self-completion questionnaire to help each partner identify areas of satisfaction or dissatisfaction with their relationship (*Resources List*). Encourage the couple to discuss which areas need change in order to (a) help the drinker to stay away from alcohol and (b) help increase satisfaction in their relationship.

Trouble shooting

Couples therapy will be made more complicated if your assessment reveals that the partner also has a drinking problem. Murray and Hobbs (1977) developed a method to help partners who drink excessively together and reinforce each other's drinking. The method was designed for couples aiming at moderation and has not been tested with an abstinence goal.

If you wish to use this method, you should begin by getting the couple to agree on specific drinking limits (Chapter 12, *Behavioural Self-management*). Encourage them to think of previous situations where they reinforced each other's excessive drinking. Explain that one way to avoid this mutual reinforcement is to drink together only when they are staying within the limits. If one partner decides to breach the limits, he should remove himself from his partner's presence and consume his drink in relative isolation (e.g., in the bathroom or in a corner of the bedroom). In this way, he avoids tempting his partner to lapse and his own excessive drinking is not rewarded by his partner's company. You should use this method in conjunction with the other strategies discussed in this section.

DEALING WITH CONFLICT

Explain to the couple that conflict itself is not a bad thing because it reminds us that we are different individuals with different needs. The problem with conflict is that it can escalate to a point where things that are said or done in anger can cause damage to the relationship that cannot easily be repaired. Conflict might also increase the chances of relapse by placing additional stress on the drinker.

Rotunda and O'Farrell (1997) have suggested that you invite the couple to make three commitments which provide a framework for the therapy: (1) not to threaten divorce or separation during the course of the therapy; (2) to only discuss drinking-related past conflicts in the supportive context of therapy and not outside the sessions; and (3) to carry out homework exercises between sessions so that they can practice behaviour that will promote good feelings in the relationship.

Decreasing Alcohol-related Arguments

Discuss whether the couple ever experience conflict about drinking. For example, they might argue about incidents in the past where the drinker has had alcohol-related problems. Conflicts can also be about future situations where the partner fears that the drinker is going to relapse. Explore each partner's perspective about the meaning of this conflict. For example, if the partner brings up the past, the drinker might feel defensive at what he sees as 'nagging'. However, it is important to identify the partner's good intentions. She is probably trying to motivate her partner to change, or to protect their relationship by warning him about the dangers of drinking. Reframing the conflict in this way conveys your empathy for the partner's concerns and opens the way for the suggestion that these arguments might not be the most effective method for preventing her partner's relapse.

Get the couple to brainstorm (pp. 97–98) other ways for the partner to express her concerns and for the drinker to respond without defensiveness. One idea is to specify a particular period of time, each day, during which the drinker will reiterate his commitment to the treatment goal and will listen to his partner's queries or concerns. The partner should agree not to raise past incidents or future events beyond the activities of that particular day. Both partners should agree from the outset to listen to each other without interruption and to finish on a positive note. It would be helpful to role-play (p. 12) such a conversation during therapy.

Time-out

Time-out methods may help the couple to deal with conflict as it arises. The key to effective time-out is the ability to recognise that the conflict is escalating. Encourage the couple to think about how their physical arousal increases as the conflict escalates. Encourage each person to try to identify a point at which it is possible to walk away from the argument easily and compare this to later stages of the conflict when that person feels less in control and more compelled to continue arguing. It is useful to get the partners to identify the kind of negative self-talk (see below) that might contribute to this escalation.

Once the couple can identify that there are early stages of the conflict in which they both feel more in control, introduce the concept of 'time-out'. This is where either one of the partners might say 'I feel uncomfortable, I would like time-out for 15 minutes'. Each partner might go into a separate room and breathe deeply until he/she feels more calm. They should wait until they both feel safe to resume the discussion at a less antagonistic level.

Time-out also provides the opportunity for either partner to request a more appropriate time for dealing with the conflict. For example, one partner might say 'I feel unhappy about discussing this right now. How do you feel about waiting until after we've finished dinner to talk about this?' Explain to the couple that if one partner just leaves an argument without making a time-out statement, this might be interpreted by the other person as an aggressive action. Emphasise the importance of keeping communication avenues open all the time.

When both partners feel that they have been able to express their feelings adequately, this clears the way for a practical resolution to the situation that produced the conflict. You can help the couple to achieve this by teaching them problem-solving skills (Chapter 6). Because the solution could require change in the behaviour of one or both partners, you will also need to help the couple to develop effective negotiation skills. You might need to devote some sessions to role-play communication skills such as positive specific requests (p. 122) and validation (pp. 125–126).

Time-out agreements could be most helpful in dealing with negative interactions that escalate quickly towards the threat of violence. If violence has been a problem for the couple, it is important to negotiate a commitment from the violent partner not to hit or threaten the other person. This would involve monitoring personal levels of arousal and agreeing to take time-out to calm down before violence becomes a possibility. This agreement would also include a plan for the non-violent partner to leave home and stay at some designated place for a specified amount of time if threat of violence occurs, thereby imposing an extended period of time-out.

Trouble shooting

Remember that couples therapy for alcohol problems is not designed to resolve ongoing or serious violence. If the couple have problems of this magnitude, appropriate referral is advisable, including practical support for the non-violent partner.

POSITIVE INTERACTIONS

One of the aims of couples therapy is to increase the positive feelings, good will and commitment in the relationship. For the couple whose relationship has repeatedly been damaged by crises associated with the drinking problem, there is a need to repair that relationship through shared positive experiences. In the more stable relationship, the change in drinking behaviour can itself cause some tension and need for readjustment. You can assist them in this process by helping them to increase their positive interactions.

Shared Rewarding Activities

Get each partner to make a separate list of possible activities that the couple might enjoy sharing. These activities will obviously exclude drinking. Encourage the couple to use their imagination to choose things they might have done before as a couple or have always wanted to try. Then use these lists to help the couple to plan their future activities together. They might need help in negotiating conflicts or problems relating to the activities. Help the couple to avoid potential pitfalls that could prevent the activities from getting started, such as waiting until the last minute before planning or getting side-tracked on trivial details.

Encourage the couple to choose one or two activities to do as home practice and then use the next session to discuss the way in which these activities were planned, any difficulties that arose and the experience of each partner when these activities took place. Discuss with the couple how these shared rewarding activities can be continued as an ongoing source of mutual enjoyment at least once a week.

If the couple have problems in their sexual relationship it's a good idea to exclude sexual activity from this exercise to avoid unnecessary pressure on either partner. Sometimes people use alcohol to achieve emotional or sexual intimacy, but alcohol can also cause sexual problems. The *Resources List* provides some self-help books for improving sexual relationships. The couple might benefit from a referral for therapy which is specifically aimed at enhancing their sexual relationship.

Catch Your Partner Doing Something Nice

Ask the couple 'What are some things that your partner does which show that he or she cares about you?' Give each partner a copy of the practice sheet 'Catch Your Partner Doing Something Nice'. This has been adapted from O'Farrell (1995). Ask each of them to record one caring behaviour a day that they have observed their partner performing. Ask them not to show each other their sheets but to save them until the next session.

In the following session, get each of the partners to read out the caring behaviours that they wrote down. Ask them how it felt to be the recipient of the caring behaviour. Introduce the concept of acknowledging the caring behaviour and model an example. This should be an 'I-statement' (p. 122) and should be specific about what the partner did and how the recipient felt. For example, one partner might say 'I liked it when you ...' or 'When you ..., I felt ...'. Draw the couple's attention to the use of eye contact, smiles, a sincere and pleasant voice. Emphasise the importance of focusing on the positive feelings. Note that it is counter-productive to compare this positive experience with previous negative experiences. Get each partner to role-play acknowledging some of the caring behaviours on his/her list.

For home practice, ask the couple to hold a 2–5 minute daily communication session in which each partner acknowledges one pleasing behaviour noticed that day. Use the next session to further practise this skill and discuss any feelings or problems that might have arisen from the home practice. Encourage the couple to continue this practice at home throughout the treatment programme and after treatment.

Pleasing Days

'Pleasing days' are days when one partner tries to do as many pleasing things for the other as possible. Each partner selects a day without announcing it to the other partner. The aim is to focus on learning what is helpful, pleasing and comfortable to each other. The lists compiled on the practice sheet for the previous exercise could be used for inspiration. These exercises might feel a little artificial for some couples.

You may need to explain that this is part of the learning process and once the couple have adjusted to fit these activities into their relationship, they will become more spontaneous.

Self-talk

Self-talk is discussed in Chapter 9, *Communication Skills*. It is relevant to couples therapy because negative self-talk can undermine the couple's positive interactions, particularly when one person negatively interprets the intentions of another. Get the couple to compare the following examples of self-talk:

'Why is he being nice to me? What does he want from me?'
'That was really considerate of him to do that. I will tell him so.'
'The ungrateful so-and-so. She doesn't even notice the good things I do.'
'That's disappointing but I can't expect her to notice every time I do some good things for her. I'll let her know that I felt disappointed when she didn't notice.'

Emphasise the way in which the more constructive self-talk helps to expand the communication between the partners, rather than cutting off that communication. Encourage each partner to monitor his or her own self-talk and notice how it influences the couple's communication. Get the couple to brainstorm some other examples of helpful and unhelpful self-talk.

SUPPORTING MEDICATION

If the drinker has been prescribed medication to help him stay abstinent, he might benefit from reminders and encouragement from his partner to help him keep taking the medication (Chapter 14, *Pharmacotherapies*). This will work provided that it does not aggravate any existing problems in their relationship. Stress that the partner is not responsible for the drinker's medication and that her role is purely one of support. Talk with the couple about how the partner could support the medication without the drinker becoming defensive.

RELAPSE PREVENTION

Introduce the couple to the concepts involved in relapse prevention. Help them to identify high-risk situations and early warning signs of relapse for the drinker. Introduce the concept of a 'relapse drill' (pp. 228–229) and help the couple to devise strategies to minimise the length and consequences of drinking in the event of a lapse. Get the drinker to role-play and cognitively rehearse these strategies and be sure to discuss any doubts that either partner has about the future.

Trouble shooting

If the drinker relapses during therapy, help the couple to address this in the next session. Get the couple to explore what happened before, during and after the drinking and try to highlight the antecedents and consequences of the drinking (Chapter 16, *Relapse Prevention Training*). The drinking might have been a reaction to some extra-marital stress (e.g., work pressures). In this case, encourage both partners to come up with some ideas of how the drinker might handle this stress in the future, without resorting to alcohol.

Drinking could also be a response to recurring, intense conflicts between the partners. In this case, you should explore the chain of events that lead up to and unfold as a result of the conflict. You will also need to identify how the couple have attempted to deal with this and where their coping strategies have broken down. Encourage them to talk about the source of conflict during the therapy session where you can help them to practise time-out (see above), communication skills and problem solving.

EXAMPLE 2: WHEN THE PARTNER PRESENTS ALONE

Sometimes the drinker will be reluctant to come to therapy but the partner will seek help alone. It is very important to reiterate that couples therapy or therapy involving the partner is not about blaming the partner for the drinker's problems. Although you will want to respond to the partner's request for information about how to help reduce the drinker's problems, your primary emphasis should always be on the partner's welfare. If the partner is feeling isolated, it may help to introduce the idea of getting support for the family from Al-Anon or Alateen (pp. 215–216).

Encourage the partner to talk about her personal goals. Sometimes the partner will have suspended the satisfaction of personal needs until the time when the drinker achieves recovery. Empathic counselling can help her to identify her needs and problem-solving techniques might be used to devise strategies for change.

Encouraging the partner to focus more on her own needs will in fact have an impact on the couple's relationship. As the partner becomes less focused on the drinking, the drinker may be forced to take more responsibility. Encourage the partner to take less responsibility for the protection of the drinker from alcohol related consequences. The partner might like to try an experiment where she stops doing certain things which she normally does to ensure the drinker's comfort. For example, she might *refrain from*: (a) keeping missed meals for the drinker; (b) making the drinker comfortable when he has fallen into intoxicated sleep in the lounge room; (c) making excuses to employers for the drinker's absence from work; (d) cleaning up when the drinker has been sick; or (e) apologising to friends for the drinker's antisocial behaviour. Obviously, this list excludes situations where the consequences of drinking are potentially dangerous (e.g., where the drinker has passed out under potentially dangerous circumstances or where there is a risk of drink driving).

Communication skills will also be useful for the partner. Discuss whether she and the drinker ever get caught up in alcohol-related arguments (see above). Discuss how certain ways of communicating may be aimed at protecting the drinker but seem to result in conflict. Self-talk and 'I-statements' are useful concepts to assist the partner to communicate to the drinker how she feels without becoming trapped in a no-win alcohol-related argument. Once again, the emphasis is on encouraging the partner to take responsibility for her own needs and give back the responsibility for the drinking to the drinker.

It is advisable to screen for and assess the risk of domestic violence (Punukollu, 2003). If the partner has experienced physical violence from the drinker, you will need to help devise a strategy for her own protection. For example, the partner might inform the drinker that the next time this occurs, she will call the police. Alternatively, the strategy might be for the partner to leave the home if she is threatened and stay at a designated place for a specified amount of time. Any physical violence should be met with immediate action so that the drinker realises that the partner is serious and will take action to protect herself. You should also link the partner with other services that provide practical assistance and support for her safety.

EXAMPLE 3: MEETING WITH FAMILIES TO ENHANCE SUPPORT

When working with young clients, it is crucial to help your client to develop a reliable support network (Chapter 19). One way to do this is to meet with your client's family. Families can help build the young person's resilience against substance abuse through their encouragement and practical assistance. They might also be able to support the treatment process by encouraging the young person to attend counselling or stay on medication (if appropriate). If he has been living away from the family home, family meetings are an opportunity to begin to rebuild relationships and perhaps even work out agreements for living at home again.

Meeting with families to enhance support is not the same as family therapy. Although the strategies outlined in this section draw on some of the principles of family therapy, they are restricted to helping the family support the young person to change his drug use and stabilise his lifestyle.

Obviously, it is not always possible or advisable to meet with your client's family. Family members might have serious substance abuse problems, your client might have been abused by his family or there may be other significant problems in family relationships that make it hard for him to get support. Although we use the term 'family' in this section, you and your client might choose to seek support from other people in his life who are concerned about him. These people might belong to his extended family, neighbourhood or community. Alternatively, they might be a service provider, such as a teacher, coach, juvenile justice officer or outreach worker.

GOALS

Apart from the usual goals of treatment, there are goals that are specifically related to enhancing family support. Any of the following goals might be relevant:

- Acknowledging what the family has gone through.
- Education for the family about the process of change.
- Rebuilding trust between the young person and his family.
- Building effective communication strategies.
- Supporting and rewarding safe behaviour.
- Setting limits and consequences.
- Coping with urges, lapses and relapses.
- Spending time together.

METHOD

The strategies described in this section overlap with other chapters and sections of this book. For example, many of the key concepts and principles outlined in the other sections of this chapter and in Chapters 9, *Communication Skills* and 16, *Relapse Prevention Training* are especially useful when meeting with families or concerned others. Chapter 19 provides guidelines for assessing and engaging young people in treatment.

Structure each meeting by setting an agenda. This would include a review of recent events and between-session exercises, followed by a new agenda. At the end of each meeting, summarise the strategies and plans you have talked about and make sure that everybody understands what you have agreed upon.

When talking with the family, avoid labelling the young person as 'the problem'. Instead, frame the substance abuse as 'the problem' and focus attention on its impact on everybody including the young person. This deflects attention away from blaming the young person and promotes the treatment as a mutually beneficial enterprise between all participants.

BEFORE STARTING

If you have already been working with the young person and now wish to involve his family, ask him to identify those people whom he would most like to participate.

Take the time to explore what kind of support your client wants from his family or concerned others and his expectations about meeting with them. You might encourage your client to contact the people he has identified as supportive and invite them to a family meeting. Alternatively, he may need your assistance to initiate this contact.

If you meet the family when the young person first comes for help, start to engage them straight away. For example, you might offer them a two-fold approach involving (a) treatment for the young person (Chapter 19) and (b) meetings with the family. You will need to consider whether the best approach will involve two therapists for the two different roles or, if there are staff constraints, one therapist to provide both therapies. If you are carrying out both roles, be aware that the young person is likely to see himself as your primary client and will expect you to preserve the confidentiality of individual sessions. It is important to openly acknowledge this 'special relationship' by explaining to the family that you cannot reveal information from these individual sessions without the young person's permission. The young person might also expect you to advocate on his behalf in family meetings (p. 250). He might want to prepare for, and debrief from, family sessions during your individual counselling. Nevertheless, during family meetings you should build an alliance with all the participants by listening and taking into consideration each person's point of view. While advocacy is sometimes helpful, it is also important to develop your client's communication skills and encourage him to talk directly with his family.

ASSESSING AND ENGAGING THE FAMILY

Families can be at different stages of coping when a young person seeks help for substance abuse (NSW Department of Health, 2003). For example, your client's family might have only recently recognised the extent of the young person's substance abuse and may still be coming to terms with it. Alternatively, they may have been trying all kinds of solutions for some time, and received all kinds of advice— good and bad! Take the time to explore their understanding of the substance abuse and what solutions they have tried.

Some family members may have put all their energy into trying to solve the problem, to the detriment of their own self-care and other family relationships. Despite these efforts, the problems might have escalated over time, with broken promises, negative interactions and difficulties in setting boundaries. The substance abuse may have contributed to other family problems, such as depression, anxiety, conflict and loss of sleep. The family may have begun to lose hope. They might even feel alienated or unsupported by treatment providers and your suggestions for family meetings might be met with skepticism or defensiveness.

As you explore these issues with the family, acknowledge and validate their efforts to find a solution and the difficulties they have encountered. Use reflective listening to talk through any feelings of anger, guilt, fear, frustration and distrust. Reassure the family that these are normal reactions. They might also benefit from receiving supportive self-help material (*Resources List*).

RATIONALE FOR YOUR CLIENTS

In your first meeting with your client and his family, explain that the family meetings are an opportunity to work out ways of supporting the young person as he changes his substance use and builds a more stable lifestyle. If appropriate, reassure the family that family meetings are not about blaming the family. Rather, the purpose is to provide an opportunity to keep them informed and give them an opportunity to voice their own concerns and needs. Explain that you will be working *with* them to help them find their own solutions rather than imposing a fixed solution that might not work with every family.

Allow time in your initial meetings to get to know each person and their relationships with each other. In your first meetings with the family, work out some basic ground rules about communication. Explain that good communication will help to rebuild trust and ensure that everybody understands each other. Emphasise the importance of one person speaking at a time without being interrupted by the others. As you proceed, it might be helpful to explain, model and encourage the use of other effective communication skills, such as I-statements, positive specific requests, active listening and validating the other person (Chapter 9, *Communication Skills*).

TALKING ABOUT CHANGE

If you have already started with the young person, help him to update his family on what the two of you have done so far. Allow time for them to ask you or your client questions about his treatment progress.

Encourage each person (including your client) to express his or her hopes and expectations about what can be achieved in the family meetings. Use reflective listening and summaries to further explore these goals. Emphasise any points of common interest, e.g.:

'I notice that you want your son to go back to school and he says that he wants to train for a job. Sounds like you are both thinking along similar lines, that getting more education is a positive step.'

To effectively support the young person, family participants will need to understand and have some agreement with your client's treatment goals. If there are differences of opinion about the goals regarding substance abuse, explore each person's underlying concerns. For example, your client's parent might disagree with his harm-reduction goals because of strong beliefs that abstinence is the only goal to be contemplated. One way to deal with these disagreements is to explore what each person hopes will be achieved through their preferred goals. Focus on common underlying themes, such as 'safety from harm' or 'a more stable lifestyle' and the importance of helping the young person achieve these long-term goals as well as changing his drug use. You might also use the technique of reframing to diffuse conflict and refocus everyone's attention on their positive concerns for each other. Take the position that they do not have to resolve these differences straight away but that you will all work together to find agreements or compromises over the course of the meetings.

Spend time talking with your client and his family about the nature of behavioural change. Explain that change is not usually a smooth ride to success and sometimes people have lapses or relapses as a normal part of the learning process (p. 221). You might invite members of your client's family to reflect on their own experiences of behavioural change, such as quitting cigarettes or dieting. Their personal examples might be helpful in highlighting key concepts of change, such as lapses.

Some members of the family may express fears about even considering the possibility of lapses or relapses since they believe that such consideration will condone further drug use. Explain to the family that relapse prevention not only means planning ahead but it also means effectively coping with set backs. Just as with any other learning process, mistakes can happen. The young person might experience strong urges to use, and he might even have a lapse or a relapse. You could introduce the 'fire-drill' analogy, explaining that it is important to prevent lapses and relapses but also to have a plan to minimise the harm they cause, in case they occur. This approach is discussed in detail in Chapter 16, *Relapse Prevention Training*.

REBUILDING TRUST AND RESOLVING CONFLICT

Trust is an important issue to address in your work with the family. Although the young person might have made changes to his substance abuse behaviour, his parents or family might have misgivings about trusting him again, particularly if he has deceived or stolen from them. This can sometimes lead to circular and repetitive patterns of interaction as illustrated in Figure 2.

Help the family to move on from this kind of impasse by inviting each person to talk more about their underlying concerns. Reflect points of positive concern and personal needs. For example, the parent might talk about previous disappointments and her wariness about trusting again. She might also speak in terms of wanting to protect her son. The young person might be seeking recognition for changes he has already made and he might feel that his parent is treating him like a child. Affirm both people's concerns as important and invite the family to explore ways to address these concerns.

When talking about the impact of the substance abuse on the family, try to balance problem-focused questions with solution-focused questions (pp. 248–249). This will help you to build on the existing strengths in the family relationships. For example, you might explore the substance abuse from the following two perspectives:

(a) What influence has the substance abuse had on family relationships and the family's ability to support the young person?
(b) What influences have the family and the young person had on the substance abuse?

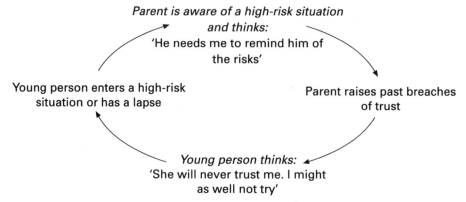

Figure 2: An example of circular patterns of interaction

Draw out the family's strengths by exploring the exceptions to the problem (as described in Chapter 18, *Case Management*, p. 248):

> *To the family*: 'Tell me about a time when you had success in dealing with the substance abuse.'
>
> *To a parent*: 'Tell me about a time when you felt proud of your son.'
>
> *To the young person*: 'Tell me about a time when your family helped you.'

Encourage the family to make specific plans for regular family meetings between sessions. For example, they could set aside a particular time each day, or several times a week, to talk about each other's concerns. Discuss ground rules for these meetings, such as listening to each other without interruption, not bringing up incidents from the past, taking time-out when there is conflict (p. 170) and finishing on a positive note.

SUPPORTING AND REWARDING SAFE BEHAVIOUR

The family meetings should also focus on developing practical strategies to support the young person's endeavours. We have derived the following strategy from Azrin, Donohue, Besalel, Kogan and Acierno (1994) to help families support a new lifestyle for the young person. The strategy was originally designed for young people who live with their families. However, it could be adapted to situations where the young person has regular contact with his family or concerned others.

Begin by inviting everyone to contribute their ideas towards generating two lists: (a) a list of 'safe' situations (where the young person is less likely to use substances); and (b) a list of 'risky' situations (where there is a high risk of substance use). You could build on some of the following suggestions:

(a) *'Safe' situations*: Including activities, places and people that are incompatible with drug and alcohol use. Some safe situations might include coming home early in the evening, attending school, adult supervised recreation, spending time with parents or family, spending time with abstinent friends, doing homework, participating in household chores or seeing his therapist.

(b) *'Risky' situations*: Including activities, places and people that are likely to make it hard for the young person to resist the urge to use drugs or alcohol. Risky activities might include visiting drug-using friends, truanting, or going to places where alcohol and drugs are easily obtained.

Help the family to develop a plan which will promote the young person's participation in safe situations and reduce his involvement in risky situations. This might involve a written schedule of activities for each day comprising a mixture of safe activities and social contacts that the young person would enjoy. Try to find a balance between protecting the young person from risky situations while also giving him some sense of freedom and responsibility. Encourage the family to set regular times across the week for reviewing the progress of the plan and making adjustments.

Using a problem-solving approach (as described in Chapter 6), invite the family to explore and develop strategies for supporting and rewarding the young person's participation in 'safe' situations. Azrin *et al.* (1994) make the following suggestions:

- increased allowance;
- practical assistance (e.g., transportation, use of the family car);
- overnight visits to or by friends on the 'safe' list;
- room privacy;
- special gifts or purchases;
- a later curfew; and
- telephone, stereo or television privileges.

Conflicts about trust sometimes arise in disagreements about what is a 'safe' or 'risky' situation. To promote mutual understanding, ask open-ended questions that get each person thinking about the other's point of view. For example, you might ask:

To the young person:
'If you go into this situation, what do you think your parents will be worried about?'
'How realistic do you think these worries are?'
'What would need to happen to make them less worried?'

To a parent:
'What do you think your son is seeking from this situation?'
'Would you ever consider this situation to be safe and if so, what would need to happen to make it safe?'

The discussion generated by these questions can help your clients to find mutually acceptable solutions. For example, the young person might be allowed to attend a party where alcohol is accessible under agreed conditions (e.g., he makes a relapse-prevention plan, goes with a 'safe' friend and comes home at an agreed time).

SETTING LIMITS AND CONSEQUENCES

Setting limits may be another important strategy to help your client's family to support his treatment goals. For example, your client and his family might negotiate limits around his involvement in unsafe situations. If the family are working out a plan for your client to live at home, they may also want to set limits on his behaviour if he has previously acted in a way that impacted negatively on other family members.

To be effective the limits, and any consequences for breaching the limits, should be stated clearly and applied consistently. They should be developmentally appropriate and acceptable to the young person. This requires a level of commitment from each person which can only really be achieved through consensus. For example, limit setting will not work without the young person's agreement and might even increase his resistance. Make sure that he has the opportunity to express his own opinion on what behaviours should be limited and what consequences should follow, and that his opinion is taken into account in the final plan.

Although consequences need to be somewhat negative to act as a deterrent, they should not be overly harsh. Ideally, they should offer opportunities for learning and family bonding. For example, the young person might agree that the family can impose a more restrictive curfew for a period of time after a relapse. In turn, a parent might agree to spend this time with the young person in a mutually enjoyable activity.

MONITORING AND RESPONDING TO HIGH-RISK SITUATIONS

Your client's family can play an important role in helping the young person to monitor his risk of relapse. Explain the importance of responding effectively to high-risk situations, including urges and lapses. Encourage them to work out an agreed strategy for monitoring that is not overly intrusive but is effective in identifying and responding to high-risk situations. For example, you might want to explore:

- *Self-disclosure*: The ideal method of monitoring is to build trust and set up opportunities for the young person to tell his family when he is experiencing problems. Ask the young person to say what conditions help to make self-disclosure more likely. It might make it easier for him to self-disclose if the family already has a plan for responding to self-disclosed urges, lapses or relapses.
- *Identifying and responding to early warning signs*: Invite the young person and his family to identify behaviours and mood states which seem to be early warning signs that the young person is using or drinking. They might then work out a plan

for responding to these early warning signs by increasing their level of support and communication.

- *Random checking*: Random checking should be framed as a supportive rather than punitive intervention. For example if the young person has truanted in order to use drugs, he and his family might agree that his parent will occasionally call his school to ask about his attendance and progress.

Use the guidelines in Chapter 16, *Relapse Prevention Training* to help the family develop strategies for relapse prevention and recovery from relapse. For example, they might want to help the young person work out a 'relapse drill' which includes seeking help from his parents (pp. 228–229). Instead of viewing lapses and relapses as failures or as bad behaviour, encourage your client's family to look at why they happen and how they can make plans to prevent further lapses or relapses in the future. If the family is willing to take this view, they will be more able to help the young person to quickly refocus on his goals after a lapse or a relapse.

Trouble shooting

If the family has experienced a breakdown in trust, it might be hard for them to respond to lapses and relapses without conflict. The family might view a lapse as a betrayal of their trust. In response to these concerns, explain that it is natural to feel disappointed about lapses. However, they might have noticed that blaming the young person can result in him becoming defensive and thereby discourage him from telling them when he is having problems. Explore ways of talking about lapses and relapses without conflict. Some strategies might include expressing their concerns for each other, using time-out in response to angry feelings (p. 170), using communication skills such as active listening and I-statements (Chapter 9), and working together to build a new relapse-prevention plan (Chapter 16).

SPENDING TIME TOGETHER

The concept of shared rewarding activities (pp. 175–176) is also a good one to talk about in family meetings. Invite the family to explore ways to spend rewarding time together as a family and for individual family members to spend time with the young person. For example, what does he enjoy doing with his father? His mother? His siblings or concerned others? Encourage the family to choose one or two shared activities to do as home practice. Then use the next session to talk about their experiences. Explore any difficulties that arose as well as the good things that happened.

Substance abuse is likely to have affected other relationships within the family, such as the relationship between the young person's parents or between his parents and siblings. Encourage the family to explore how they might strengthen these relationships by spending more time together and improving their communication. If there are significant problems, the family might want to consider a referral for specialist family therapy.

WHEN THE YOUNG PERSON DOES NOT SEEK HELP

If a young person is not yet ready to participate in treatment and his parents or family seek help, you may still be able to draw on some of the strategies described in this section. Obviously, you won't be able to directly negotiate an agreement between the young person and his family. However, you could provide assistance by building communication skills, explaining the principles of relapse prevention and discussing ways to negotiate their own agreements with the young person. You might also adapt some further approaches from the section on *When the Partner Presents Alone* (pp. 178–179).

RESOURCES LIST

GENERAL RESOURCES

Copello, A. & Orford, J. (2002). Editorial: Addiction and the family: Is it time for services to take notice of the evidence? *Addiction*, **97**, 1361–1363.
—Outlines the evidence in favour of several different models for involving concerned others and argues that family involvement should be seen as a routine part of treatment.

Copello, A., Orford, J., Hodgson, R., Tober, G., Barrett, C. & UKATT Research Team (2002). Social behaviour and network therapy: Basic principles and early experiences. *Addictive Behaviors*, **27**, 245–366.
—Describes a new promising approach for building supportive social networks and involving concerned others in treatment. It includes a review of the research and two case examples.

Meyers, R.J., Smith, J.E. & Miller, E.J. (1998). Working through the concerned significant other. In: W.R. Miller & N. Heather (eds), *Treating Addictive Behaviors* (2nd edn) (pp. 149–161). New York: Plenum.
—Describes a method for working with concerned others who present without the drinker or user.

Miller, W.R. (2003). Commentary: A collaborative approach to involving families. *Addiction*, **98**, 5–6.
—Explores four different models of families and substance abuse and argues in favour of a 'collaborative' approach similar to that presented in our chapter.

Monti, P.M., Kadden, R.M. Rohsenow, D.J., Cooney, N.L. & Abrams, D.B. (2002). *Treating Alcohol Dependence: A Coping Skills Training Guide* (2nd edn) (pp. 70–72). New York: Guilford Press.
—Provides a step-by-step approach to help your client develop a social support network.

Sue, D.W. (1990). Culture-specific strategies in counseling: A conceptual framework. Professional Psychology: Research and Practice, **21**(6), 424–433.
—This paper outlines some key issues related to cross-cultural counselling and how to address them.

Punukollu, M. (2003). Domestic violence: Screening made practical. *Journal of Family Practice*, **52**(7), 537–543.

—Gives guidelines on how to screen for domestic violence and how to talk with clients about practical strategies for ensuring safety.

COUPLES THERAPY AND WHEN THE PARTNER PRESENTS ALONE

Kadden, R., Carroll, K., Donovan, D., Cooney, N., Monti, P., Abrams, D., Litt, M. & Hester, R. (1995). *Cognitive Behavioral Coping Skills Therapy Manual: A Clinical Research Guide for Therapists Treating Individuals with Alcohol Abuse and Dependence* (Project MATCH Monograph Series, Volume 3). NIH Pub. No. 94-3724. Rockville, MD: National Institute on Alcohol Abuse and Alcoholism.
To order a copy, go to: www.niaaa.nih.gov/publications/match.htm
—This session-by-session manual provides brief guidelines on couples/family involvement in therapy.

Montgomery, B. & Evans, L. (1996). *Living and Loving Together*. Ringwood, Australia: Penguin.
—An excellent self-help book on improving relationships. It includes chapters on communication and conflict resolution, problem-solving and improving sexual satisfaction.

Murray, R.G. & Hobbs, S.A. (1977). The use of a self-imposed timeout procedure in the modification of excessive alcohol consumption. *Journal of Behavior Therapy and Experimental Psychiatry*, **8**, 377–380.
—Describes in detail a time-out procedure designed to assist couples where both partners wish to reduce their excessive drinking.

O'Farrell, T.J. (1995). Marital and family therapy. In: R.K. Hester & W.R. Miller (eds), *Handbook of Alcoholism Treatment Approaches: Effective Alternatives* (2nd edn) (pp. 195–220). Boston: Allyn and Bacon.
—Comprehensive guidelines for the approach to couples therapy on which this chapter is based. The main focus is on couples and spouses with brief guidelines on family therapy.

O'Farrell, T.J. & Cutter, H.S.G. (1984). Behavioral marital therapy couples groups for male alcoholics and their wives. *Journal of Substance Abuse Treatment*, **1**, 191–204.
—Session-by-session guidelines for a 10-week couples therapy programme.

Rotunda, R.J. & O'Farrell, T.J. (1997) Marital and family therapy of alcohol use disorders: Bridging the gap between research and practice. *Professional Psychology: Research and Practice*, **28**(3), pp. 246–252.
—Very practical description of a behavioural couples therapy programme (Project CALM) involving, couples sessions, couples group sessions, disulfiram and extended care.

Sisson, R.W. & Azrin, N.H. (1986). Family-member involvement to initiate and to promote treatment of problem drinkers. *Journal of Behavior Therapy and Experimental Psychiatry*, **17**, 15–21.
—An approach for assisting partners of problem drinkers when they seek help alone.

The following two scales can be used to assess a couple's satisfaction with their relationship:

Spanier, G.B. (1976). Measuring dyadic adjustment: New scales for assessing the quality of marriage and similar dyads. *Journal of Marriage and the Family*, **38**, 15–28.

—Available for purchase from Multi-Health Systems, North Tonawanda, NY 14120-0950 or at: http://www.mhs.com/

Weiss, R.L. (1980). *The Areas of Change Questionnaire*, Oregon Marital Studies Program, University of Oregon.
—Available for purchase from Dr. Robert L. Weiss, Oregon Marital Assessment Service, 3003 Willamette Street, Suite F, Eugene, OR 97405 USA or at:
http://darkwing.uoregon.edu/~rlweiss/#Assess

There are a wide range of self-help books for promoting sexual intimacy and overcome sexual problems. We have listed a small sample below:

Cage, D. (2004). *On Our Backs Guide to Lesbian Sex*. Los Angeles, CA: Alyson Publications.

Goldstone, S.E. (1999). *The Ins and Outs of Gay Sex*. New York, NY: Dell Publishing.

Heiman, J., LoPiccolo, L. & LoPiccolo, J. (1999). *Becoming Orgasmic: A Sexual and Personal Growth Program for Women*. London: Piatkus Books.

Zilbergeld, B. (1999). *The New Male Sexuality*. New York, NY: Bantam Doubleday Dell Publishing Group.

MEETING WITH FAMILIES TO ENHANCE SUPPORT

Azrin, N.H., Donohue, B., Besalel, V.A., Kogan, E.S. & Acierno, R. (1994). Youth Drug Abuse Treatment: A controlled outcome study. *Journal of Child & Adolescent Substance Abuse*, 3(3), 1–16.
—A research paper which describes and tests the effectiveness of some of the strategies we have outlined, such as 'Supporting and Rewarding Safe Behaviour'.

Mitchell, P., Spooner, C., Copeland, J., Vimpani, G., Toumbourou, J., Howard, J. & Sanson, A. (2001). *The Role of Families in the Development, Identification, Prevention and Treatment of Illicit Drug Problems*. Canberra, ACT: Commonwealth Government.
www.nhmrc.gov.au/publications/pdf/ds8.pdf
—A comprehensive research review, including a review of family therapies and family involvement in treatment.

NSW Department of Health (2003). *Family and Carers Training (FACT) Project: Research report*. North Sydney, NSW: NSW Department of Health.
Available at:
http://www.health.nsw.gov.au/pubs/f/pdf/families_carers_training.pdf
—Guidelines for understanding and addressing the problems and issues faced by families and carers, including working with families from non-English speaking backgrounds.

Szapocznik, J., Hervis, O. & Schwartz, S. (2003). *Brief Strategic Family Therapy for Adolescent Drug Abuse, Therapy Manuals for Drug Abuse: Manual 5*, Bethesda US: National Institute on Drug Abuse, NIH.
Accessible on the Internet:
http://www.drugabuse.gov/TXManuals/bsft/BSFTIndex.html
—Although this manual presents an alternative model of working with families which

requires specialist training, it does offer some practical definitions of relevant techniques such as 'reframing'.

INFORMATION FOR FAMILIES

NSW Department of Health (2004). *Family and Friends Affected by the Drug or Alcohol Use of Someone Close*. North Sydney, NSW: NSW Department of Health.
Available at: `http://www.health.nsw.gov.au/pubs/2004/drugs_families.html`
—A self-help pamphlet for families, developed from the FACT Project research support (see above). The pamphlet provides useful information and supportive tips for family members, as well as contact details for support providers in NSW, Australia.

`http://www.fds.org.au/`
—This site is produced by Family Drug Support (FDS), made up of volunteers with first-hand experience of dealing with a family member's drug dependence. It includes facts sheets, advice and a forum for families.

CATCH YOUR PARTNER DOING SOMETHING NICE!

Here are some examples of pleasing behaviours that you might catch your partner doing.

DAY	DATE	PLEASING BEHAVIOUR
Monday	2/2	Saved my dinner for me when I worked late
Tuesday	3/2	Took the kids for a drive while I had a sleep
Wednesday	4/2	Told me what a good job I did

Using the table below to record one nice thing your partner does for each day of the coming week. Don't show your partner your record until your next therapy session.

Name: _____   Partner's Name: _____

DAY	DATE	PLEASING BEHAVIOUR
Monday		
Tuesday		
Wednesday		
Thursday		
Friday		
Saturday		
Sunday		

Source: Adapted from O'Farrell (1995).

14

Pharmacotherapies

RECOMMENDED USE

Pharmacotherapies will help your client to reduce or quit her alcohol or opioid use. They will also reduce the frequency and severity of relapse and provide your client with time-out from drinking or using, during which she can learn skills to facilitate long-term changes.

If your client is alcohol dependent, either acamprosate or naltrexone can be used to achieve abstinence or to prevent a return to heavy drinking. The effect of these medications is to reduce strong cravings for alcohol. Another medication, disulfiram is also used to achieve abstinence. It acts as a deterrent against further drinking by causing unpleasant side-effects in combination with alcohol.

If your client is opioid dependent, either methadone or buprenorphine can be used to achieve abstinence or reduce her use of heroin and other opioids. These medications are used as 'substitution' treatments because they are legal, longer lasting and less expensive opioids. While they have been used successfully to help clients remain abstinent, many clients may choose to continue to use illicit drugs at reduced levels. Even a reduction in your client's heroin use will assist her to improve her well-being by: decreasing the risks of injecting drug use (e.g., HIV, hepatitis, and vein damage); reducing her involvement in crime; and stabilising her lifestyle.

Pharmacotherapies are appropriate for your client if she is dependent on alcohol or opioids and is willing to take medication on a regular basis. Your role as a therapist is to help your client stay in treatment and take her medication. You can do this by talking through any concerns she has about the medication, helping her to manage the side effects and monitoring her use of the medication. Medication alone is generally not enough for your client to achieve her goals. Help your client prepare for termination of the medication by developing her skills in drink or drug refusal, behavioural self-management and relapse prevention (Chapters 7, 12, and 16).

GOALS

The goals of pharmacological treatment are to:

- assist your client to quit or modify her use of alcohol or illicit opioids (e.g., heroin);
- help your client avoid a relapse to heavy substance use;
- reduce substance-related harm and improve her health, by reducing the risks of HIV, hepatitis and vein damage, reducing involvement in crime and stabilising her lifestyle; and
- provide a period of time-out from alcohol or opioids during which your client can learn skills that will assist her to achieve long-term changes.

KEY CONCEPTS

OPIOIDS

The term 'opioid' refers to a class of drug that includes both synthetic and naturally occurring substances. The term is used throughout this book rather than the term 'opiate' which refers only to naturally occurring opioids. Although we occasionally refer to heroin when discussing opioid dependence, some clients may be dependent on legal opioids, such as morphine, codeine or pethidine. The information in this chapter applies to all opioids of dependence.

SUBSTITUTION OR MAINTENANCE TREATMENT

Substitution or maintenance treatment refers to the use of a long-acting opioid medicine, such as methadone or buprenorphine, to help your client control her use of other opioids on a long-term basis. The treatment can last from several months to several years.

COMPLIANCE

Compliance with medication is usually defined as taking 80 per cent or more of the medication as prescribed. Obviously, if your client keeps taking the medication, she will have better results. She may need your assistance and support in this process.

METHOD

In most countries, these pharmacotherapies can only be prescribed by medical practitioners. Some countries require that they be prescribed as part of a more comprehensive treatment plan in order for your client to receive the medication at a subsidised rate. A successful outcome for your client will require cooperation between you, your client, and her prescribing physician.

RATIONALE FOR YOUR CLIENT

Start by explaining to your client how the medication will help her to achieve lasting changes in her substance use. Explain that long-term habits can take some time and effort to change and that the medication will assist her while she is making these changes. Your client might also use the medication as a daily reminder about why she wants to change. For example, she could remind herself of her goals when she takes the medication (e.g., 'I'm taking this medication so that I can stop drinking, find a job and get back on my feet').

Your client is more likely to keep taking the medication if she is well informed about how it works and how to manage its side effects. Find out what she already knows about the medication and, where appropriate, provide further information. The *Resources List* gives some examples of information that you could give to your client.

MONITORING THE MEDICATION

Encourage your client to set up reminders to help her take her medication. She could take the medication at a regular time each day (e.g., with meals). Alternatively, she could programme reminders into a mobile phone or electronic diary, or place reminder notes on her fridge door, bathroom mirror, or elsewhere at home. You and your client may wish to enlist the support of her family or concerned others to encourage or remind her to take her medication (Chapter 13, *Involving Concerned Others*).

It may also be helpful for your client to keep a daily tally of her medication doses, any incidents of substance use as well as monitoring her cravings and mood states. For example, you might use a monitoring procedure such as the Medication Monitoring Card at the end of this chapter. Invite your client to review the card with you at the beginning of each session in order to explore her experiences and discuss her concerns.

Make sure you follow up any missed appointments with telephone contact. Encourage your client to make another appointment as soon as possible. In the next session, talk about what led her to miss the previous appointment and elicit any reservations she has about treatment.

HELPING YOUR CLIENT STAY ON MEDICATION

The following section draws on the guidelines developed by Teesson *et al.* (2003) for therapy to assist your client to keep taking the medication. Although these guidelines were developed for clients taking naltrexone and acamprosate, the principles are useful for all pharmacotherapies. The guidelines use a combination of motivational interviewing (Chapter 3) to address any ambivalence about the treatment and cognitive therapy (Chapter 10) to help your client challenge negative thinking that might undermine her goals. Teesson *et al.* (2003) suggest that you break your client's therapy into three phases:

(1) Eliciting beliefs about the problem and the treatment.
(2) Exploring ambivalence towards treatment.
(3) Highlighting the need for treatment maintenance and addressing overconfidence.

Eliciting Beliefs

The first phase of therapy follows on from the initial rapport building and assessment. Take some time to review your client's reasons for seeking treatment and what she hopes to achieve. Elicit her beliefs about the extent and nature of her drinking or drug problem and, where appropriate, give her personalised feedback of assessment results (see pp. 55–57). As you explore how the medication will help her to achieve her goals, make the link between continued regular use of the medication and long-lasting changes.

Exploring Your Client's Ambivalence

Your client may be reluctant or ambivalent about taking medication. Common reasons for ambivalence include:

• concerns about the side-effects of the medication;
• ambivalence about changing drinking or drug use;
• misconceptions about the effectiveness of treatment;
• stigma associated with taking medication; and
• a belief that if she misses a dose, she has failed and will relapse.

To encourage your client to talk about her own concerns, raise one or two examples of these concerns and explore their relevance for her. You could take the approach of motivational interviewing (Chapter 3) by asking 'What are some of the things you don't like about taking the medication?' and then 'What are some of the good things about taking the medication?' Use double-sided reflection (Chapter 1, *General Counselling Skills*) to help your client explore both sides of her ambivalence. For example, you might use a double-sided statement:

'You don't like taking the medication because it's a chemical, yet you think it will help you to stop using and improve your health.'
'the headaches are really bothering you, but you are finding it easier to control your drinking.'

Take the time to elaborate on the 'good things' that your client associates with the medication. Use reflective listening to emphasis *her* view of what the good things are and acknowledge any indirect benefits that she mentions, such as getting a job or getting on better with people.

If your client experiences aversive side effects, she may be more inclined to stop the medication or drop out of treatment. Offer her more information (*Resources List*) about the side effects and discuss this information with her. You might emphasise that for most people, the symptoms subside after a couple of weeks. Advise her that it is sometimes difficult to distinguish between prolonged withdrawal symptoms and the effects of the medication. If this is relevant for her, suggest that she keep taking the medication for a couple more weeks, to see if the side effects subside. In the meantime, explore some practical coping strategies, such as taking naltrexone with meals to reduce nausea or using relaxation and massage to manage headaches.

Ask your client what other questions or concerns she has about the medication. She might have practical questions such as 'What do I do if I miss a dose?' or 'Should I keep taking naltrexone even if I've been drinking?' She might also have less clearly defined concerns, such as 'I just don't like the idea of taking medications'. Help her to elaborate these concerns by asking open-ended questions such as 'What is it that you don't like about medication?', or 'What does taking medication say about you?' Your client may believe, for instance, that she should be able to stop drinking or using opioids without any help from medication, and that taking medication is a sign of weakness. Use cognitive therapy to help her challenge these thoughts (Chapter 10). For example, you might ask:

'What evidence is there that taking medication for your health and well-being is a sign of weakness? Could it ever be a sign of strength? If so, how?'
'What are the advantages and disadvantages of thinking about the medication as a weakness?'

As your client continues to use the medication, it is important to reiterate that people who use their medication as prescribed tend to do better than those who don't. However, your client may also need reassurance that if she forgets a dose or has a lapse, it is not a complete failure and that she should seek help rather than giving up the treatment.

Treatment Maintenance

It is important to address any stigma associated with the medication by normalising the process. Reassure her that many people struggle with drinking or drug problems. Stress that alcohol or drug problems are often learned ways of coping and that they need to be replaced with new coping strategies. The medication helps this process by making it easier for her to focus on the tasks of building a new lifestyle and practising new behaviours. Frame the medication as a freely chosen strategy to enhance her quality of life (Kemp, Hayward, Applewaite, Everitt & David, 1996). You might also build on this frame by asking her how she would like things to be different in the future and what role the medication and treatment might play in bringing her closer to these goals.

Encourage your client to focus on relapse-prevention strategies (Chapter 16). Identify any new coping skills she might need to develop in order to maintain the changes. We recommend that you draw on the material from other chapters in this book to provide your client with skills training, according to her needs. You should also help your client to build a supportive social network by encouraging her to go to self-help meetings or exploring other ways of meeting people who do not abuse substances (Chapters 15, *Self-help Groups* and 16, *Relapse Prevention Training*). Take the time to acknowledge and reflect on her achievements as she makes these positive changes.

Once your client has successfully stopped or moderated her drinking or using, she might decide to stop taking the medication. For example, she might be tempted to test herself or she might feel that the medication is no longer necessary. Obviously, this is her responsibility and your role is to assist her to make an informed and measured decision. Invite her to review the role of medication in helping her to achieve her goals and explore what risks there might be if she stops taking it at this time. Encourage your client to consider whether there is any need to continue the medication until her new lifestyle and behaviours are firmly established.

PHARMACOTHERAPIES FOR TREATING ALCOHOL DEPENDENCE

In this section, we discuss three pharmacotherapies for treating alcohol dependence: naltrexone, acamprosate and disulfiram. Each of these medications works in a different way.

The duration of treatment with medication will depend on your client's goals (Chapter 4) and how dependent she is on alcohol. If she has concerns about starting medication, you could suggest that she tries it as a three month experiment, with a review of her options at the end of that period. This will give her a chance to see if the medication helps, what side effects she experiences and what differences abstinence or moderation makes to her life. Some clients choose to stay on medication for a year or longer.

NALTREXONE (REVIA©)

How Naltrexone Works

Naltrexone is an opioid antagonist, which means that it blocks the brain's natural opioids, as well as any externally administered opioids. These natural opioids are involved in pain regulation and producing feelings of reward and pleasure. They are also triggered when a person drinks alcohol. Naltrexone is not used to manage alcohol withdrawal. Rather, it has been shown to reduce cravings for alcohol and is prescribed therapeutically for this purpose, once the acute phase of alcohol withdrawal is over (usually a few days after the last drink).

Unlike disulfiram (described below), naltrexone does not interact with alcohol to make the drinker feel ill. Rather, it seems to reduce the subjective high she experiences when drinking alcohol. Naltrexone has no known withdrawal syndrome so it can be discontinued without ill effects. Your client should continue to take the medication even if she experiences a lapse. Use relapse-prevention strategies to deal with lapses or relapses (Chapter 16).

Dosage

Naltrexone is taken as one 50-mg tablet per day for 3 to 12 months, depending on your client's progress. Some clients start on a smaller daily dose of 25 mg for the first few days in order to reduce side effects.

Contraindications

Naltrexone should not be taken by your client if she is using opioids in any form as it reverses their effects. Clients who are prescribed naltrexone are provided with a card stating that they should not be given opiate-based pain killers in the event of an accident, as they will not be effective.

Naltrexone is not suitable for pregnant or lactating women, or for people with renal impairment, liver failure or active hepatitis. It has not been tested for safety on people less than 18 years of age. It is also not normally recommended for clients taking disulfiram as both medications can affect the liver.

Side Effects

Some people experience side effects during the first few weeks of taking naltrexone. These can include headaches, insomnia, nervousness, anxiety, fatigue, dizziness, nausea or vomiting. Although these unpleasant effects usually only last one or two weeks, your client might need support and practical strategies to help her manage their aversive effects. For example, to minimise nausea, advise her to take the medication with complex carbohydrate foods (such as toast or muffins) and not to take it on any empty stomach. If the side effects persist and are undermining your client's acceptance of the medication, she might want to talk with her prescribing physician about changing the dosage or taking an alternative medication such as acamprosate.

Trouble shooting

Sometimes naltrexone is used to help clients withdraw rapidly from opioids. However, compared with methadone and buprenorphine, it is a less effective treatment for opioid dependence because of high client drop-out rates (Gowing, Proudfoot, Henry-Edwards & Teesson, 2001). It is therefore less likely that your client will be prescribed naltrexone as an ongoing treatment for opioid dependence. However if this is the case, make sure she is aware that naltrexone will reduce her tolerance and thereby increase her risk of overdose if she stops taking it and starts using opioids again.

ACAMPROSATE (CAMPRAL©)

How Acamprosate Works

Acamprosate appears to work by stabilising the neurotransmitters that are disturbed by alcohol consumption and withdrawal (the gamma amino butyric acid (GABA) and glutamate systems), thereby calming any over-activity of the brain's chemical systems. Your client might notice that it helps to 'take the edge' off things while she is learning to abstain from drinking.

Treatment with acamprosate normally starts within a few days of the last drink. Your client should continue to take the medication even if she experiences a lapse. Use relapse-prevention strategies to deal with lapses or relapses (Chapter 16).

Dosage

Acamprosate is taken as two 333-mg tablets, three times a day for people over 60 kg (i.e., 6 tablets per day). Clients under 60 kg can be put on a lower dose, usually four tablets per day in three doses: two, one and one. Since acamprosate is not processed by the liver and leaves the body quickly, it has to be taken repeatedly across the day to keep a steady level in the blood stream.

Contraindications

Acamprosate is not suitable for pregnant or lactating women, or for people with renal impairment. It has not been tested for safety on people less than 18 years of age.

Side Effects

Side effects can include nausea, diarrhoea, bloating or pruritis (a red skin rash). For most clients, these side effects are mild and disappear in a few weeks. A less common side effect may be a change in sex drive.

Choosing Between Naltrexone and Acamprosate

There are advantages and disadvantages to both naltrexone and acamprosate. Both methods are effective for clients who have goals of either abstinence or moderation.

On the other hand, taking acamprosate three times a day can be difficult for clients with memory problems and naltrexone is not suitable for clients with severe liver disease. Other factors to consider are the side effects that your client experiences from the medication.

If your client has not done as well as hoped on a single medication, consider consulting with her and the prescribing doctor about combining acamprosate and naltrexone. There is some evidence to suggest that combining both medications is more effective than taking one alone.

DISULFIRAM (ANTABUSE©)

Disulfiram is not often used as a first-line treatment for alcohol dependence, since it is only effective if your client is supervised daily when she takes the medication. It may be prescribed because the client or prescriber has a preference for it, or because the client has not fared well on naltrexone or acamprosate due to an aversive reaction or ineffective results.

How Disulfiram Works

When alcohol is taken during disulfiram treatment, the disulfiram interferes with alcohol's breakdown in the digestive system. A toxic reaction causes the drinker to experience unpleasant sensations such as skin-flushing, sweating, nausea, vomiting, bad headaches and breathing difficulties. Other effects include thirstiness, coughing spasms, palpitations, dizziness, blurred vision, numbness of the hands and feet, and insomnia. The drinker might also experience uneasiness or fear. These effects can last from 2 to 4 hours. Your client's knowledge of this unpleasant interaction between disulfiram and alcohol acts as a deterrent to further drinking.

Find out what your client understands about the unpleasant effects of drinking while on disulfiram. Her understanding of these effects is as much a deterrent as the drug itself! However, do not try to instill fear in your client as this may interfere with her willingness to take the treatment. Instead emphasise that these effects take away the desirability of drinking and therefore assist her in achieving and maintaining abstinence.

You should advise your client to seek medical attention if she experiences a reaction as a result of intentional or inadvertent alcohol consumption. Warn her to avoid all alcohol-containing preparations that might lead to ingestion of alcohol or absorption through the skin. Some examples are: certain cough syrups, sauces, vinegar, foods prepared with wine, alcohol-based cosmetics such as astringents, perfumes, aftershave lotions and alcoholic back rubs.

Your client must be willing to cooperate with regular supervision of the daily disulfiram dosing because unsupervised treatment is far less effective. If your client has been prescribed disulfiram, talk with her and her prescribing physician about how it will be supervised. Effective supervision often involves meeting two or three times a week in the early stages of treatment, to ensure that your client is taking her prescription and to discuss any problems that have arisen. It can often also involve a third person (e.g., a partner or family member) agreeing to observe your client take her prescription. This is usually negotiated with a written agreement and an understanding that the role of the observer is supportive rather than punitive.

PHARMACOTHERAPIES FOR TREATING OPIOID DEPENDENCE

In this section, we discuss two pharmacotherapies for treating opioid dependence: methadone and buprenorphine. Like heroin, both of these medications are opioids and therefore work by substituting for heroin. In this way, they prevent your client from experiencing withdrawal symptoms and cravings. Methadone and buprenorphine are usually taken at the clinic or pharmacy where the dose is provided.

METHADONE

How Methadone Works

Methadone is a long-acting opioid, which means it works on the brain in a similar way to heroin and so is used as a substitution treatment. When your client takes methadone, it reduces her craving for heroin by preventing her from going into withdrawal.

Methadone is taken orally on a daily basis, usually under the supervision of a nurse, general practitioner or pharmacist. In some places, providers allow clients to collect several days' doses to take home but many providers have a policy against giving takeaway doses in order to prevent the drug from being traded illegally. When this is the case, your client will have to visit a clinic or pharmacy every day and this can create difficulties for your client with day-to-day life, employment and travelling. If this is relevant, use problem-solving approaches (Chapter 6) to help your client work out some practical solutions.

Dosage

The most effective methadone dose usually ranges from 60 mg to 100 mg per day. The starting dose is low (not more than 40 mg) to avoid overdose. The dose is then increased over several days to reach the ideal dose for your client. The aim is to help her feel at ease and to prevent withdrawal symptoms. Once the dose is at the right level, she should not feel sedated or euphoric.

BUPRENORPHINE (SUBUTEX©)

How Buprenorphine Works

Buprenorphine is also a long-acting opioid and is used in a similar way to methadone, as a substitution treatment. It can also be used to help your client withdraw from other opioids. As a withdrawal treatment, buprenorhine helps to reduce your client's withdrawal symptoms and cravings more effectively than combinations of other medications such as benzodiazepines and clonidine.

Dosage

If your client has been prescribed buprenorphine as a substitution treatment, the starting dose is low (2–6 mg per day) and is taken daily under supervision until your client has stabilised her dose. Buprenorphine is taken as a tablet dissolved under the tongue. Once your client has stablised her dose, she may be able to take a higher dose once every 2 or 3 days, rather than taking daily medication. This is increased over a period of weeks to 8–24 mg per day. As with methadone, it is often the case that buprenorphine must be taken under clinical supervision.

Trouble shooting

It is dangerous to mix methadone or buprenorphine with alcohol, benzodiazepines, barbiturates, other opioids (e.g., heroin, morphine, pethidine and codeine) or tricyclic antidepressants (e.g., Tryptanol or Tofranil, see p. 288). If your client is using other drugs, inform her of the potential risks associated with mixing these drugs. Encourage your client to be honest with the clinic regarding her use of other drugs so that she can take her doses safely. Each dosing clinic will have its own policy on how to manage intoxicated clients. If your client is intoxicated, she might not be able to get her dose. This is not to punish your client, but to prevent an overdose due to mixing substances.

If your client has been using heroin or other drugs while on the medication, use motivational interviewing (Chapter 3) to highlight the pros and cons of mixing drugs and review her reasons for being on the medication. Explore any triggers that prompted her to use and put in place relapse-prevention strategies (Chapter 16).

Side Effects of Methadone and Buprenorphine

Common side effects include loss of appetite, nausea and vomiting (this usually stops after a few days), increased sweating, constipation, headache, abdominal cramps, lowered sex drive, skin rashes and itching, and changes to the menstrual cycle. Tooth decay is a side effect of all opioids, since there is less saliva available to protect the teeth. Contrary to common beliefs, there is no sugar in methadone syrup, and methadone is no worse for your client's teeth than heroin.

If your client is concerned about specific side effects, she may want to talk to a medical practitioner, pharmacist or dentist. Some side effects might involve a change in treatment. For example, if she feels drowsy after taking a dose, this might indicate that her dose is too high, or that the dose is interacting with other sedative drugs. Most side effects, however, will settle after the first couple of weeks of treatment and in the meantime, you could help your client to work out some simple solutions. For example, chewing sugarless gum helps prevent tooth decay while constipation can be relieved by drinking more water, taking regular exercise and eating a high fibre diet.

Choosing Between Methadone and Buprenorphine

Buprenorphine is as effective as methadone in treating opioid dependence and has certain advantages (e.g., it is longer lasting). Therefore, once your client is stabilised, she will only need to take the medication every two to three days. Buprenorphine is also a little easier to withdraw from than methadone because the withdrawal symptoms are usually less severe. If both medications are available in your client's local area, the final decision will depend on your client's preferences which, in turn, might be influenced by how effective each medication is for her and what kind of side effects she experiences. Methadone has a stronger, more intoxicating effect than buprenorphine, which makes it attractive to some clients, while others prefer the relatively more clear headed feeling associated with buprenorphine. The price of buprenorphine and methadone varies depending on the jurisdiction in which your client lives and where she gets her medication.

Terminating Substitution Treatment for Opioid Dependence

It may take some time before your client is ready to stop the substitution treatment. If she decides to cease the medication, it is advisable that she slowly reduces her dose over several weeks or months in order to minimise the severity of withdrawal symptoms. The rate of reduction is best worked out in consultation with the pre-scribing physician. For buprenorphine, reducing the dose by 2 mg every one or two weeks generally causes only mild discomfort. If your client experiences strong cravings or increases her use of heroin during this period, she should stop the dose reduction or slow it down. Withdrawal symptoms may not occur until she has reached very low doses of 2 mg or less. At this stage, if your client is taking buprenorphine, she will probably need to return to daily doses until she is ready to stop completely.

Give your client information about what symptoms she might experience as she withdraws from the medication. For example, she might experience sweating, nausea, aches, pains or anxiety. Help her to develop coping strategies such as 'surfing the urge' (Chapter 16, *Relapse Prevention Training*) or relaxation therapy (Chapter 11). It is also a good idea to review her relapse-prevention plans to mini-mise the risk of her using again. Continue to provide her with support beyond the end of her substitution treatment.

RESOURCES LIST

Center for Substance Abuse Treatment (1998). *Naltrexone and Alcoholism Treatment: Treatment Improvement Protocol (TIP)* (Series 28). Rockville, MD: US Department of Health and Human Services.

Available at: http://www.health.org/govpubs/BKD268/
—Recommendations based on a combination of clinical experience and research-based evidence.

Gowing, L., Proudfoot, H., Henry-Edwards, S. & Teesson, M. (2001). *Evidence Supporting Treatment: The Effectiveness of Interventions for Illicit Drug Use*. Woden, ACT: Australian National Council on Drugs.
Available at:
http://www.ancd.org.au/publications/pdf/rp3_evidence_supporting.pdf
—This comprehensive review of treatments provides details and summaries of the research on the use of buprenorphine, methadone, naltrexone and LAAM pharmacotherapies for illicit drug use.

Henry-Edwards, S., Gowing, L., White, J., Ali, R., Bell, J., Brough, R., Lintzeris, N., Ritter, A. & Quigley, A. (2003). *Clinical Guidelines and Procedures for the Use of Methadone in the Maintenance Treatment of Opioid Dependence* (Abbreviated Version). Canberra, Australia: National Expert Advisory Committee on Illicit Drugs.
Available at:
http://www.health.gov.au/pubhlth/publicat/document/methadone_cguide_s.pdf
—A summary of the key areas of methadone treatment.

Jarvis, T.J., Tebbutt, J. & Mattick, R.P. (1995). *Treatment Approaches for Alcohol and Drug Dependence: An Introductory Guide* (1st edn) (pp. 148–156). Chichester, UK: Wiley.
—Chapter 13 of the first edition of our book provided a detailed discussion of how to support clients taking Antabuse (disulfiram) including supervision for taking medication.

Kemp, R., Hayward, P., Applewaite, G., Everitt, B. & David, A. (1996). Compliance therapy in psychotic patients: Randomised controlled trial. *British Medical Journal*, **312**, 345–349.
—Includes a succinct description of 'compliance therapy' used to assist people to keep taking psychiatric medication.

Lintzeris, N., Clark, N., Muhleisen, P., Ritter, A., Ali, R., Bell, J., Gowing, L., Hawkin, L., Henry-Edwards, S., Mattick, R.P., Monheit, B., Newton, I., Quigley, A., Whicker, S. & White, J. (2001). *National Clinical Guidelines and Procedures for the Use of Buprenorphine in the Treatment of Heroin Dependence*. Canberra, Australia: National Expert Advisory Committee on Illicit Drugs.
Available at:
http://www.nationaldrugstrategy.gov.au/pdf/buprenorphine_guide.htm
—This comprehensive document covers all aspects of buprenorphine treatment.

O'Brien, Susannah (2004). *Treatment Options for Heroin and Other Opioid Dependence*. Canberra, ACT: Commonwealth Department of Health and Ageing.
—These guidelines include three booklets: (a) *A Guide for Users*; (b) *A Guide for Families and Carers*; and (c) *A Guide for Frontline Workers*. They are concise user friendly materials providing an overview of the full range of treatment options for opioid dependence including pharmacotherapies.

O'Farrell, T. J. & Bayog, R.D. (1986). Antabuse contracts for married alcoholics and their spouses: A method to maintain Antabuse ingestion and decrease conflict about drinking. *Journal of Substance Abuse Treatment*, **3**, 1–8.
—A detailed guide to helping partners assist in disulfiram supervision.

Shand, F., Gates, J., Fawcett, J. & Mattick, R.P. (2003). *Guidelines for the Treatment of Alcohol Problems* (pp. 130–142). Canberra, Australia: Australian Government Department of Health and Ageing.
—Describes how to use pharmocotherapies as relapse prevention treatment for alcohol problems.

Teesson, M., Sannibale, C., Reid, S., Proudfoot, H., Gournay, K. & Haber, P. (2003). *Manual for Compliance Therapy in Alcohol Pharmacotherapy. NDARC Technical Report No 157.* Sydney: National Drug and Alcohol Research Centre.
—Our section on helping your client to say on medication draws on the methods outlined in this manual. These methods are currently being researched in a controlled study and preliminary results indicate that they may help people stay longer on acamprosate medication (Reid, Teesson, Sannibale, Matsuda & Haber, in prep.).

Ward, J., Mattick, R.P. & Hall, W. (1998). *Methadone Maintenance Treatment and Other Opioid Replacement Therapies.* Amsterdam: Harwood Academic Publishers.
—A comprehensive guide to the use of drug substitution in the treatment of opioid dependence, covering research and clinical issues including dose, duration, ancillary services, medication in pregnancy, reduction of infectious disease and extended care.

INFORMATION FOR YOUR CLIENT

For consumer information about ...
Acamprosate, go to:
    http://www.alphapharm.com.au/alphapharm/public/health/home.jsp
    and type 'campral' into the search field.

Naltrexone, go to: http://www.orphan.com.au/ReViaCMI.pdf

Disulfiram, go to: http://www.orphan.com.au/Antabuse_CMI.html

Lintzeris, N. & Bath, N. (eds) (2000). *Subutex: A Guide to Treatment.* Melbourne, VIC: Turning Point.
Can be ordered at: http://www.aivl.org.au/resources.html
—A guide to buprenorphine for people with opioid dependence who are receiving this medication.

National Drug and Alcohol Treatment Centre (2000). *What You Need to Know About Methadone ... and Other Treatment Options.* Sydney, NSW: NDARC.
Order copies at: Publications.resources at: http://ndarc.med.unsw.edu.au/ndarc.nsf
—Designed for heroin users, this booklet gives detailed information about methadone treatment and also discusses other pharmacotherapies such as naltrexone, buprenorphine and LAAM.

MEDICATION MONITORING CARD

CLIENT HANDOUT

DAY	MONDAY	TUESDAY	WEDNESDAY	THURSDAY	FRIDAY	SATURDAY	SUNDAY
Tablets taken							
Rate your craving (0–100)							
How many drinks of alcohol did you have today (if any)?							
How many times did you use heroin or other opioids today (if any)?							
Describe your overall mood, today							

Source: Adapted from Teesson, Sannibale, Reid, Proudfoot, Gournay & Haber (2003).

III

Maintaining Change

15

Self-help Groups

RECOMMENDED USE

Self-help groups are a widely used source of support for people wanting to stop or reduce their drinking or drug use. Some are abstinence based, such as Alcoholics Anonymous (AA), Narcotics Anonymous (NA) and Smart Recovery®, whilst others such as Moderation Management accept moderated drinking as an appropriate goal for some drinkers. At the time of writing, Moderation Management groups were limited to the USA. Both Smart Recovery® and Moderation Management are based on cognitive–behavioural and relapse-prevention strategies. Their goals and philosophies are quite different to those of AA and NA. For more information on these alternative groups, see the *Resources List*.

The self-help services offered by AA and NA are still the most widely available. Although their 12-step philosophy is sometimes incorporated in drug and alcohol treatment, AA and NA are not considered by their members to be a form of treatment. Rather, they are fellowships of men and women who share the experience of alcohol or drug dependence and want to help each other to stay drug-free.

AA might be suitable if your client has alcohol dependence and chooses abstinence as her treatment goal. Because of the abstinence philosophy of AA, it is counterproductive to recommend them if your client has a goal of moderation. NA may be appropriate if your client is dependent on other drugs, particularly if she is undergoing a drug-free method of treatment. Individual AA/NA groups determine their own guidelines and some groups are happy to accept members who are taking pharmacotherapies such as methadone.

Self-help groups offer your client highly accessible and ongoing social support from others who have had similar experiences. They are particularly helpful as an alternative source of support for drinkers whose social group is heavily involved in drinking (Longabaugh, Wirtz, Zweben & Stout, 1998). However, if your client is unwilling to attend a self-help group, it is still important to encourage her to increase her social support, perhaps through involvement in other groups (e.g., sports, arts, or other special interest groups, see Chapter 16, *Relapse Prevention Training*).

The following chapter outlines the basic principles of AA and recommends the ways in which you might incorporate referral to AA/NA in your treatment plan.

GOALS

Self-help groups in the tradition of AA share the view that dependence on alcohol or drugs results from a person's genetic or constitutional make-up rather than from the qualities of the drug itself. They therefore distinguish 'alcoholics' and 'addicts' from 'social drinkers' or 'experimenters'. True addiction is seen as being an illness that cannot be cured but can be arrested. The 12-step programme is designed to arrest the addiction by assisting the person to stay abstinent one day at a time with the consistent social support provided in meetings. The *primary purpose* of AA is the achievement of day-to-day abstinence from alcohol and to help others with alcohol dependence. The *primary purpose* of NA is to stay drug-free and offer assistance to other drug-dependent people.

KEY CONCEPTS

THE 12 STEPS

The process of recovery defined by AA/NA is based on 12 steps that are presented in two charts at the end of this chapter. The commitment to a drug-free lifestyle requires that your client accepts that she is powerless over her drinking or drug-taking. This first step is the essential foundation on which the remaining steps are built. Your client works through each step at her own pace, with the encouragement and support of her sponsor and other members.

THE 12 TRADITIONS

The 12 traditions outline the philosophy for the organisation within which 12-step groups run. These traditions ensure that the personal ambitions of any AA/NA member or any influence outside AA/NA cannot distract the group from the primary goal, which is to give the 12-step message to other alcohol dependent people. For example, so that they do not become involved in disputes about money, AA and other 12-step groups are totally self-supported via voluntary donations from their membership. Similarly, there is a major emphasis on setting aside personal egos for the common good. This is expressed in tradition 12: 'Anonymity is the spiritual foundation of our traditions, ever reminding us to place principles before personalities.'

MEMBER

Tradition 3 of AA/NA states that 'The only requirement for AA membership is a desire to stop drinking/using.'

OPEN AND CLOSED MEETINGS

Open meetings are available to any interested person, regardless of whether or not she has a drinking problem. The open meeting often involves one or more members telling their stories to the group and the newcomer or visitor is not usually required to speak or identify herself as an 'alcoholic'. In contrast, closed meetings are open only to people wanting to change their drinking behaviour. They are more likely to involve discussions in which everyone is encouraged to contribute.

SPONSOR

Newcomers are assisted in their adjustment to the 12-step group through sponsorship by a longer term member. The sponsor is someone who has achieved ongoing recovery and can therefore serve as a role model for your client and introduce her to the concepts and practices of the 12-step programme. As trust develops, the sponsor may also act as a confidant for your client. According to McCrady and Delaney (1995), the ideal sponsor is someone who is the same gender as the person being sponsored and who can be contacted as often as needed. This accessibility is particularly important in helping the sponsored person to cope effectively with cravings, lapses or relapses.

METHOD

RATIONALE FOR YOUR CLIENT

When introducing your client to 12-step groups, emphasise the value of being able to meet others who have had similar problems and experiences and can therefore give her understanding and support. Stress that this support is available from other members whenever your client needs it. It is ongoing and therefore available for as long and as often as she wants to attend. Make sure your client knows that her attendance at meetings is free and totally voluntary. She should also be aware that what is said during meetings is kept confidential and anonymous. Encourage your client to attend AA/NA meetings at least three times so that she can make an informed decision about whether or not to continue involvement with the group.

   Explain to your client that participation in AA will increase the likelihood that she will stay abstinent. By meeting others who are practising abstinence, she will also increase her confidence in her own ability to do so (Connors, Tonigan & Miller,

2001). Stress the importance of participating regularly and over a period of time so that she can benefit from the long-term support offered by AA. For example, Moos and Moos (2004) found that people who attended two to four AA meetings a week for four months had fewer alcohol problems and better social functioning. They also found that the longer people attended AA, the better the results. Encourage your client to keep a personal journal for recording AA meetings attended, personal reactions, cravings, alcohol-free days and any alcohol consumed.

12-step groups are not just about recovery but they also provide an opportunity for having fun and making friends, without needing to drink or use drugs. People who attend AA/NA come from all walks of life, so your client should be able to meet others with similar interests. It may be a new experience for your client to join a social network that does not involve drinking or using.

BEFORE STARTING

Increase your awareness of the activity of self-help groups in your local area. Most (if not all) of these groups will be based on the 12-step model. The easiest way to find out more about 12-step groups is to attend some of the open meetings. Try to develop some acquaintances with AA/NA hospital or institution committee members and the local general service officers. Be aware that there are AA/NA meetings especially for particular groups, such as women, gay men or lesbians, and for people who are attending for the first time. Being able to contact a variety of people in the self-help network and having awareness of meetings for special interest groups will allow you flexibility when you are advising your client. Besides AA and NA, there are also other kinds of 12-step groups which you might want to investigate, such as Pills Anonymous or Gamblers Anonymous.

You should familiarise yourself with the self-help literature and telephone services. Ensure that pamphlets and booklets produced by AA/NA are available in your clinic for clients to peruse. In particular, both AA and NA provide listings of the days, times, locations and types of meetings being held in your local area. This information will be invaluable in helping your client to plan her first meeting attendance. You can get a copy of the list at a meeting, by telephoning AA/NA, or from your local AA website (*Resources List*). You might also want to give your client a copy of either the NA or AA 12-steps, listed at the end of this chapter.

LINKING AA WITH THERAPY

You might choose to recommend AA/NA to all of your clients (who are aiming for abstinence or a drug-free lifestyle) by highlighting the advantages of social support, accessibility and self-help. AA/NA can easily be incorporated into your treatment plan. For example, attending meetings or telephoning her sponsor might be strategies that your client uses for relapse prevention (p. 229). The 12-step groups in turn provide support for members' involvement in treatment programmes. NA also provides education about HIV and harm reduction strategies.

AA/NA offers your client an opportunity for reassurance that other people have survived the uncomfortable, initial side effects of quitting and have been able to maintain abstinence. This can help to increase your client's confidence in her own ability to abstain from alcohol or drugs. The group's encouragement can also reinforce her progress towards long-term abstinence.

Your client might also experience a sense of relief at meeting others who have had similar alcohol- or drug-related problems. She might have thought that she was the only person ever to go through these negative experiences. The meetings provide a supportive environment for your client to share these personal thoughts and feelings with others. Also fundamental to the 12-step approach is a spiritual outlook which can inspire in your client a new sense of purpose and hope.

If you intend to work with your client principally to support her involvement in AA, you might want to dedicate sessions to helping her work through the individual steps. The Twelve-Step Facilitation Therapy Manual from Project MATCH explains this approach in detail (Nowinski, Baker & Carroll, 1995).

Trouble shooting

You might need to dispel any myths that *your* client has about AA/NA. For instance, she might think that AA/NA is suitable only for people with very severe dependence or alcohol- or drug-related problems. Explain that AA/NA can be used to help anyone, regardless of how severe their alcohol- or drug-related problems have been.

Your client might consider that the 12 steps or their emphasis on spirituality are not relevant for her. Clients might also have different reactions to the message that alcohol dependence is a disease. For example, the idea that she is powerless over alcohol might undermine your client's confidence in her ability to change. Alternatively, by accepting that she is powerless over alcohol or drugs, your client might feel less shame and be more able to ask for help from others. Ultimately, however, it is important that you respect your client's decision about whether or not AA/NA is suitable for her. Bear in mind that the 12-step philosophy might not be effective for everybody.

SELF-HELP GROUPS FOR THE FAMILY

Based on the 12 steps of AA, Al-Anon Family Groups is a fellowship aimed at assisting families and friends of alcohol-dependent people. Regular meetings of Al-Anon offer opportunities for friendship and for sharing the experience of coping with alcohol dependence in the family with others who have had similar experiences. Al-Anon provides tips about how to minimise drink-related conflicts or over-involvement with the drinking problem. It also provides a programme for self-growth centred on the 12 steps. Al-Anon could be particularly helpful for other family members when your client is attending AA on a regular basis. It might also be a useful source of support for family members even when the drinker is not attending AA. If an Al-Anon group is not available in your area, the General Service Office will provide a free starter kit to assist people to start their own group.

Other 12-step family support groups include Al-Teen, a self-help group for teenagers who have an alcohol-dependent parent, and Nar-Anon, a self-help group for the family and friends of narcotic dependent people.

RESOURCES LIST

AA World Services Inc. (1975). *Living Sober*. New York: AA World Services Inc.
—A booklet with strategies for preventing relapse.

AA World Services Inc. (1989). *Twelve Steps and Twelve Traditions*. New York: AA World Services Inc.
—Explains each AA Step and Tradition.

AA World Services Inc. (2004). *Alcoholics Anonymous: The Big Book* (4th edn). New York: AA World Services Inc.
—Detailed description of the AA programme. Explains AA's perception of alcohol problems and presents personal stories of recovery through AA.

Connors, G., Tonigan, J. & Miller, W. (2001). A longitudinal model of intake symptomatology, AA participation and outcome: Retrospective study of the Project MATCH outpatient and aftercare samples. *Journal of Studies on Alcohol*, **62**(6), 817–825.
—Results of Project Match, indicating that AA activities may lead to increased self-efficacy to abstain from alcohol in a variety of drinking situations.

Edwards, G.E., Marshall, E.J. & Cook, C.C.H. (2003). *The Treatment of Drinking Problems: A Guide for the Helping Professions* (4th edn). Cambridge, UK: Cambridge University Press.
—Chapter 18 provides an excellent overview of AA.

Longabaugh, R., Wirtz, P.W., Zweben, A. & Stout, R.L. (1998). Network support for drinking, Alcoholics Anonymous and long-term matching effects. *Addiction*, **93**(9), 1313–1333.
—Results from Project MATCH, showing that clients whose social group is heavily involved in drinking have poorer outcomes from alcohol treatment and significantly benefit from participating in AA meetings.

McCrady, B.S. & Delaney, S.I. (1995). Self-help groups. In: R.K. Hester & W.R. Miller (eds), *Handbook of Alcoholism Treatment Approaches: Effective Alternatives* (2nd edn) (pp. 160–175). Boston: Allyn and Bacon.
—A guide to self-help groups, including a comprehensive account of the principles and practices of AA.

Moos, R.H. & Moos B.S. (2004). Long-term influence of duration and frequency of participation in Alcoholics Anonymous on individuals with alcohol use disorders. *Journal of Consulting & Clinical Psychology*, **72**(1), 81–90.
—This research paper shows that the duration of participation in AA may be more

important than the frequency of participation in predicting the reduction of alcohol-related problems and better social functioning.

NA World Service Office Inc. (2003). *Narcotics Anonymous—The Basic Text* (5th edn). Van Nuys, CA: World Service Office.
—Description of the NA programme, including personal stories of recovery through NA.

NA World Services Office Inc. (1992). *Just for Today: Daily Meditations for Recovering Addicts*. Van Nuys, CA: World Service Office.
—Provides daily meditations for recovery.

NA World Services Office Inc. (1993). *NA: It Works, How and Why?* Van Nuys, CA: World Service Office.
—Detailed description of the NA Steps and Traditions.

Nowinski, J., Baker, S. & Carroll, K. (1995). *Twelve Step Facilitation Therapy Manual: A Clinical Research Guide for Therapists Treating Individuals with Alcohol Abuse and Dependence* (Project MATCH Monograph Series, Volume 1). NIH Pub. No. 94-3722. Rockville, MD: National Institute on Alcohol Abuse and Alcoholism.
To order a copy, go to: www.niaaa.nih.gov/publications/match.htm
—A session-by-session manual aimed at supporting clients' active involvement in AA.

Peyrot, M. (1985). Narcotics Anonymous: Its history, structure, and approach. *International Journal of the Addictions*, **20**(10), 1509–1522.
—An overview of NA.

Robertson, D. (1979). *Talking Out of Alcoholism: The Self-help Process of Alcoholics Anonymous*. London: Croom Helm.
—A detailed introduction to AA.

WEBSITES FOR SELF-HELP GROUPS

www.alcoholics-anonymous.org
—Alcoholics Anonymous (World Services)—abstinence based, 12-step self-help groups available internationally. There are also local sites that list the times and places of meetings, such as: www.alcoholicsanonymous.org.au and http://www.alcoholics-anonymous.org.uk

http://www.al-anon-alateen.org/
—12-step self-help groups for families and adolescents.

www.moderation.org
—Moderation Management—a self-help group that has accepts a non-abstinence approach. They have online groups for those who live outside the USA.

http://www.na.org/
—Narcotics Anonymous (World Services). NA also has local sites.

www.smartrecovery.org
—Smart Recovery®—a non-profit self-help group to assist individuals to develop ways to manage their drug or alcohol dependence, based on cognitive-behavioural therapy. 'SMART' stands for 'Self Management And Recovery Training'.

THE TWELVE STEPS OF ALCOHOLICS ANONYMOUS

1. We admitted we were powerless over alcohol—that our lives had become unmanageable.

2. We came to believe that a Power greater than ourselves could restore us to sanity.

3. We made a decision to turn our will and our lives over to the care of God *as we understood Him*.

4. We made a searching and fearless moral inventory of ourselves.

5. We admitted to God, to ourselves, and to another human being the exact nature of our wrongs.

6. We were entirely ready to have God remove all these defects of character.

7. We humbly asked Him to remove our shortcomings.

8. We made a list of all persons we had harmed, and became willing to make amends to them all.

9. We made direct amends to such people wherever possible, except when to do so would injure them or others.

10. We continued to take a personal inventory and when we were wrong promptly admitted it.

11. We sought through prayer and meditation to improve our conscious contact with God *as we understood Him*, praying only for knowledge of His will for us and the power to carry that out.

12. Having had a spiritual awakening as the result of these steps, we tried to carry this message to alcoholics, and to practise these principles in all our affairs.

THE TWELVE STEPS OF NARCOTICS ANONYMOUS

1. We admitted we were powerless over our addiction—that our lives had become unmanageable.

2. We came to believe that a Power greater than ourselves could restore us to sanity.

3. We made a decision to turn our will and our lives over to the care of God *as we understood Him*.

4. We made a searching and fearless moral inventory of ourselves.

5. We admitted to God, to ourselves, and to another human being the exact nature of our wrongs.

6. We were entirely ready to have God remove all these defects of character.

7. We humbly asked Him to remove our shortcomings.

8. We made a list of all persons we had harmed, and became willing to make amends to them all.

9. We made direct amends to such people wherever possible, except when to do so would injure them or others.

10. We continued to take a personal inventory and when we were wrong promptly admitted it.

11. We sought through prayer and meditation to improve our conscious contact with God *as we understood Him*, praying only for knowledge of His will for us and the power to carry that out.

12. Having had a spiritual awakening as the result of these steps, we tried to carry this message to addicts, and to practise these principles in all our affairs.

16

Relapse Prevention Training

RECOMMENDED USE

Relapse prevention training should be part of any treatment programme aimed at modifying drug or alcohol use. Relapse prevention is equally relevant for those pursuing abstinence or moderation goals. Relapse prevention strategies are also easily adapted for clients with harm reduction goals who wish to abstain from needle-sharing or unsafe sexual practices. You can conduct relapse prevention training in either group or individual settings, although the skills training procedures incorporated in this approach are often facilitated by group learning. As previously mentioned (p. 10), it is not a good idea to include clients with different goals in the same group.

Relapse is so common that many practitioners see it as a natural part of the process of change rather than as a sign of failure. For example, within the first year after treatment for problem drinking, about 60 per cent of clients experience a relapse (Connors, Maisto & Donovan, 1996). Relapses provide a lot of information about what triggers your client's drinking or drug use and what strategies work or don't work for him. Therefore, relapse prevention is not only about helping your client to prevent relapses but also helping him to learn from his experiences of relapse.

Relapse prevention training draws on many of the skills from Part II of this book. For example, your client's plan for dealing with high-risk situations may involve problem solving, practising social skills, or challenging negative thinking. Relapse prevention training can also be effectively used in combination with pharmacotherapies (Chapter 14).

GOALS

The general goals of relapse prevention training are to ensure that your clients have:

- A variety of skills and the confidence to avoid lapses to alcohol or drug use.
- A set of strategies and beliefs that reduce the fear of failure and prevent such lapses turning into relapses.

KEY CONCEPTS

HIGH-RISK SITUATIONS

These are situations that your client identifies as those in which he is most likely to find it difficult to resist drinking or drug use. The research literature suggests that (re)lapses commonly occur in response to: (a) negative emotional states, such as anxiety or depression; (b) interpersonal conflicts and social isolation; (c) social pressure to use or drink; and (d) cravings and urges. However, the level of risk involved in these situations is likely to be higher if your client has inadequate coping skills, a high level of involvement in drinking or drug use, or a low self-efficacy. Of course, not all high-risk situations are negative—celebrations and special occasions might also pose a risk for your client!

LAPSES OR 'SLIPS'

In the context of relapse prevention training these terms are used to refer to an initial, relatively isolated use of drugs or alcohol after a period of abstinence, or alternatively, the first or an isolated instance of heavy use after a period of controlled substance use. These terms are used to distinguish between *some* use and a return to constant, heavy use.

RELAPSE

This term is generally reserved for a return to constant and/or heavy use of a substance.

METHOD

This section is based on the work of Marlatt and Gordon (1985) and in particular, draws on the relapse prevention strategies described by Saunders and Allsop (1989, 1991).

Allsop (1994, pers. commun.) has stated that relapse prevention training is about 'demystifying' relapses (i.e., it aims to help clients move away from the belief that staying abstinent is only about having a sufficient amount of 'willpower'). While a strong resolve to change is essential, successful relapse prevention is also about ensuring that your client has sufficient 'skill power' to recognise and effectively deal with triggers in the environment that can contribute to slips or relapses. These triggers occur in high-risk situations and can involve particular emotions, or be related to other aspects of the situation such as the presence of drinking or drug-using friends.

Relapse prevention training also attempts to change common beliefs about giving up addictive behaviours. It aims to reduce the overwhelming dread of 'failure' by emphasising that behaviour change is not an 'all or nothing' event. The goal is to help your client to see changing his substance use in the same way as giving up other fond habits by recognising that change is a process whereby learning from mistakes and lapses forms part of the progress toward reaching a final goal.

Finally, the maintenance of an initial change in addiction behaviour is largely influenced by lifestyle issues. Saunders and Allsop (1989) made a clear distinction between deciding to change or stop drug or alcohol use and deciding to change one's lifestyle, noting that the former is probably not possible without the latter. Therefore, relapse prevention training also involves examining lifestyle factors that can either hinder or support behaviour change.

Accordingly, this section divides relapse prevention training into the following areas which should be considered in the course of any programme:

(1) Enhancing the commitment to change.
(2) Identifying high-risk situations.
(3) Teaching coping and other useful skills.
(4) Other helpful hints to avoid temptation.
(5) Preparing for a lapse.
(6) Other lifestyle issues important to maintaining change.

BEFORE STARTING

You may wish to start by explaining the general rationale for relapse prevention training. In doing so cover the points that were discussed in the paragraphs above. We have also offered more details about the specific rationale for learning how to deal with a lapse in a separate section below, as this is often a more threatening notion for many clients.

ENHANCING A RESOLUTION FOR CHANGE

It is important to acknowledge that a high-quality resolution to change is an important aspect of maintaining abstinence or moderation. It will not matter very much how skilled or confident your client might become about coping with high-risk situations if he does not have a strong commitment to maintain behaviour change. Therefore, it might be important for your client to review both the negative reasons for changing substance-use patterns and the expected rewards of making such changes. If you haven't already done so, it might also be useful to get your client to write down his reasons for change so that they can be easily accessed as reminders and motivators when needed.

IDENTIFYING HIGH-RISK SITUATIONS

Identifying high-risk situations involves detailing the 'where, when, with whom, doing what and feeling what' of situations where your client feels most tempted to use drugs or alcohol. There are a variety of ways of identifying high-risk situations. One method is to measure your client's self-efficacy across a range of situations with a pencil and paper questionnaire (e.g., the *Situational Confidence Questionnaire*, Annis & Graham, 1988). We have listed some more pencil and paper tools in the *Resources List*.

Alternatively, high-risk situations can be identified from the self-monitoring forms of clients who are attempting to moderate their drinking (described in Chapter 12, *Behavioural Self-management*) or from discussion with clients about those situations which have caused difficulty in the past. Similarly, valuable information can also be gained by encouraging clients who are abstinent to self-monitor urges and cravings to drink or use drugs. An example of a day diary which can be used for monitoring urges and cravings is included at the end of this chapter.

As you gather this information, explore any patterns or common triggers across situations. Explore the strategies he has applied in his past attempts to cope with these situations and identify which strategies worked or didn't work. Your client's high-risk situations can then be graded from the least to the most threatening situations. This hierarchy should be used as a basis for exercises and home practice throughout the remaining sessions.

TEACHING COPING SKILLS

A Note on Avoidance

Particularly in the early stages of changing behaviour, advise your client to avoid high-risk situations whenever possible. Indeed there may be certain situations for some clients in which avoidance will often or always be the best solution. However, it is not always possible to avoid some potential high-risk situations. For example, it will be difficult to avoid ever feeling upset or to permanently avoid social occasions where alcohol is served. Therefore, other strategies also need to be addressed.

Teaching Problem-solving Skills

At this stage, if you have not already done so, you might choose to teach your client problem-solving strategies. Saunders and Allsop (1991) suggested that this approach has the advantage of providing your client with a general skill which he can apply to a variety of situations which challenge his resolve. The details of how to teach problem-solving skills are dealt with in Chapter 6 and will not be dealt with here. In brief, the basic tenets of problem solving include:

(1) Defining *exactly* what the problem is.
(2) Brainstorming options to deal with the problem.
(3) Choosing the best option(s) by examining the pros and cons of each potential solution.
(4) Generating a detailed action plan.
(5) Putting it into action—mentally rehearse, role-play and actually carry out the plan.
(6) Evaluating the results to see how well the selected solution worked and making adjustments if necessary.

Begin by working on easier high-risk situations first. Brainstorm a number of possible alternative ways of dealing with the high-risk situation without using drugs or alcohol. Then get your client to select his best solution and practise it either by thinking the solution through or by trying it out in a role-play (p. 12). It is useful to encourage your client to write down his possible options and the final selected solution so that these can also be referred to later if necessary.

Home practice exercises can include brainstorming and selecting solutions to other risky situations on the list, as well as carrying out the solution to situations that have been 'problem solved' during the session. Review practice exercises at the beginning of each session, affirming your client's successes and discussing any problems he has experienced. Ensure that easier situations are dealt with first, remembering that success breeds success. The aim is that your client should become confident about his ability to cope with known high-risk situations. It is also important that he becomes practised enough in using problem-solving strategies to be able to use them to cope with unexpected events that challenge his commitment to change (see below).

Other Skills

You might find that there are common themes among the types of relapse situations that have been identified by your client. For example, your client might be particularly prone to using drugs to help him cope with stress. Problem-solving techniques might offer a number of potential solutions, among them a need to learn relaxation skills (Chapter 11). You might then decide to focus some specific training in that area. Given that there is evidence to suggest that negative emotional states, interpersonal conflict and social pressure are very common precipitants of (re)lapse, you might want to focus on specific strategies to cope with these issues in detail—particularly in a group setting (where there is less flexibility to tailor to individual needs). Areas to address may include:

• *Coping with social pressure*: Almost all clients will at some time need to be able to refuse drinks or drugs offered to them by others. Therefore, you might wish to practise appropriate refusal skills (Chapter 7) using role-play. If social pressure is a very prominent high-risk situation, your client might need to rebuild his social network (see p. 230).

- *Coping with anxiety, depression or anger*: Your client might benefit from relaxation therapy to reduce his anxiety (Chapter 11) or the strategies outlined in Chapter 10, *Cognitive Therapy* for challenging negative thinking and dealing with strong emotions. Monti, Kadden, Rohsenow, Cooney and Abrams (2002) have also outlined anger management techniques in their treatment manual (*Resources List*). Of course, if your client has a dual diagnosis, you should consider referring him to a mental health specialist. Psychiatric medication may assist him to moderate intense, negative states such as depression and psychosocial therapy will also help him to overcome or manage his mental health symptoms (Chapter 20, *Dual Diagnosis*).

- *Coping with urges/craving*: It is particularly important to help your client cope with urges and cravings. Reassure him that feelings of craving are: (a) natural reactions following a change in drinking or drug use; (b) often a response to situations, people, and even moods which used to be part of drinking or drug taking; and (c) probably a good warning sign that he might be in a high-risk situation and should take care! Some clients might also have a fear of being overwhelmed by craving and/or expect that the craving will get more and more unbearably intense if it is not relieved by drinking or drug use. To allay such fears introduce your client to the analogy of an ocean wave and explain that, like a wave, craving builds to a peak but then subsides and fades. Also introduce the imagery of 'urge surfing', and suggest that it is possible to 'ride' out an urge, mastering rather than being swamped by it. Stress that the more often he successfully copes with a craving, the less frequent and/or intense the cravings will become.

As well as 'surfing the urge', your client will need a range of strategies for managing urges (e.g., he might postpone the decision to use or drink rather than acting on the urge immediately). He could then distract himself by doing some other rewarding activity, seeking support from others or recalling his reasons for wanting to change. Monti *et al.* (2002) provide more detailed guidelines on the range of strategies for managing urges (*Resources List*).

OTHER HELPFUL HINTS FOR AVOIDING TEMPTATION

Planning Ahead

You should also stress to your client that one of the most useful strategies for dealing with high-risk or other potentially difficult situations is to plan ahead (i.e., he should think about possible difficulties or pitfalls that might arise and plan strategies to cope with them in advance). Your client's plan should focus not only on what he needs to *do* in order to prevent relapse but also on how his *self-talk* increases or decreases his risk of relapse (Chapter 10, *Cognitive Therapy*).

Apparently Irrelevant Decisions

Often clients either fail to recognise or deliberately choose to ignore warning signs of an approaching high-risk situation. This aspect of relapse prevention training aims to highlight an awareness of such warning signs. It again emphasises that slips don't just happen 'out of the blue' but rather, that choices are always present. In fact, Saunders and Allsop (1991) have stressed that there is always *a strong element of personal responsibility* involved when a client resumes drinking or drug use.

It is useful to illustrate this point by describing an imaginary client and the chain of events leading to drinking or drug using. For example, an ex-user chooses to walk by a cafe known to be a meeting place for users. An old friend who is just leaving sees him and invites him back to her house for a meal. While he is at her house, some other people, who have just scored, drop by and the ex-user finds himself hitting up with the group.

Another more detailed example of a script is provided below. You can also create your own script that is relevant to your client's problems.

Ask your client if he believes that the imaginary drinker or drug user was 'unable to cope' or had actually made choices that led him to drink or use drugs! Get him to identify all the warning signs or decision points in the script. In the example script below, the various decision points are all marked by an asterisk. Encourage your client to use a problem-solving approach to generate alternative choices at each of the identified decision points. Ask your client how difficult he thinks the solution to the first event in the chain would be in comparison to an alternative solution at the last decision point before drinking or using drugs. This is a useful way of demonstrating the advantages of dealing with a potential slip by altering events early in the chain.

As a follow-up practice exercise, ask your client to describe a similar 'slippery slope' situation that he has experienced and examine it in the same way as above.

---

*John has just had a bad day at work, he skipped lunch and feels 'strung out'. In recent months, since he left treatment, he has been going swimming after work to relax. However, today he thinks that he is too tired to go swimming. *Just as he is about to leave work a friend and business associate (known to be a heavy drinker) phones and invites him to dinner with a group of his colleagues. *John decides to go straight from work and wait for the others at the club. *He has an important meeting early the next morning and does not want to overdrink. He feels quite confident about keeping within his four drink maximum. *He arrives early, thirsty from his walk, orders a pint of beer, gulps it down and without thinking orders another. *Friends arrive soon after, with a third round in hand. *John and his colleagues go in to dinner and his business associate immediately orders three bottles of wine among four people. *Already feeling lightheaded, John thinks 'I'll just sit on one or two glasses over dinner'. *The conversation gets lively and John's glass keeps getting refilled before it is empty.

PREPARING FOR A LAPSE

Rationale for Your Client

The next stage in relapse prevention training is concerned with responding to a 'slip', should it happen. Saunders and Allsop (1991) noted that some clients might feel that you are showing a lack of confidence in them or even condoning a return to (heavy) use by talking about lapse management. They therefore suggested that clients might be introduced to the analogy of the 'fire drill'. They explained that a 'fire drill' neither condones nor increases the likelihood of a fire, though it acknowledges that there is some risk it might happen. More importantly, the drill ensures that the harm can be minimised if a fire occurs. A 'relapse drill' therefore serves the same purpose by creating a contingency plan for preventing a slip from becoming a full-scale relapse.

The 'Relapse Drill'

Saunders and Allsop (1991) have suggested that you begin by getting your client to list the conditions (both situational and emotional) under which he would be most likely to continue to drink or use drugs after an initial slip in his resolve. For example, situational factors might involve the ready availability of the drug or alcohol. Very common emotional factors you might discuss would include feelings of guilt, a sense of failure, disappointment and self-blame. It is important that you acknowledge that lapses can produce these very powerful negative emotions for clients. Marlatt and Gordon (1985) have also referred to the 'abstinence violation effect'. This is the overwhelming feeling or belief that one slip inevitably leads to an uncontrollable and permanent return to use. You should strongly discourage your client from any belief that a slip is tantamount to total disaster or defeat. The emotional and situational conditions that might cause your client to keep on drinking or using should instead be seen as posing specific problems that could be resolved by using a problem-solving approach.

Brainstorm a number of different strategies that could be used to stop further drinking or drug use after an initial lapse. Weingardt and Marlatt (1998) suggested a series of steps that your client might take if a lapse occurs. We have briefly summarised their list of steps below, with the most crucial steps listed first:

(1) *Stop, look and listen*: The lapse is a signal for your client to take time-out and review his other strategies.
(2) *Stay calm*: Your client might feel guilt and self-blame. It is important for him to remember that the lapse is a mistake from which he can learn, and not a complete failure.
(3) *Renew his commitment*: It may be helpful for him to recall his reasons for wanting to cut down or quit and the benefits he will gain from maintaining the changes to his substance abuse.
(4) *Review the situation that led to the lapse*: Encourage your client to then consider

the context of the lapse, identifying the triggers (i.e., where, when, with whom, doing what and feeling what) and any obstacles to coping.

(5) *Make an immediate plan for recovery*: The quicker he takes action, the better. Discuss what action he could take. For example, he might get rid of the drugs or alcohol and the associated equipment, remove himself from the high-risk situation—either physically or mentally, and switch to an activity that distracts him from thoughts of using or drinking.

(6) *Use his support network*: Encourage your client also to quickly seek social support from family, friends, self-help groups and telephone counselling services.

(Adapted from Weingardt & Marlatt, 1998; pp. 343–344)

Help your client to generate *detailed* action plans for putting these strategies into operation. For example, one potential strategy for dealing with a slip might be to 'call someone'. However, as Saunders and Allsop (1991) have stressed, this response by itself lacks detail. Instead the client should decide on who to call, have their telephone number ready and be realistic about how that person might help. Where appropriate, 'relapse drills' could also be practised in session using role-play. The relapse drills should also be written down by your client and kept in a handy place for future reference.

If your client's goal is abstinence but his previous involvement with alcohol was so great that he is likely to lapse to drinking, you might educate him about the low-risk levels of drinking (see 'Guidelines for Sensible Drinking', p. 164) so that he could limit the potential for harm, if he does lapse. This strategy, however, is not suitable for all clients and it is advisable that you read the section on *Recommended Use* in Chapter 12, *Behavioural Self-management*.

Talking About the Bigger Picture of Lapses and Relapses

You should also further reinforce the notion that learning anything new involves making slips and mistakes. Encourage your client to see 'slips' as a natural part of the process of learning to change his behaviour. In this way you can also suggest that it is possible to learn from a slip by looking at what did or didn't work, using that information to devise better strategies to cope with similar situations in the future.

How Your Programme Responds to Lapses

Some programmes (usually residential) have a policy of discharging clients when they use alcohol or drugs. This can deter your client from telling you about a lapse or relapse. Discharging a client after they have used might also facilitate a full-blown relapse. You and your co-workers may want to consider alternative ways of addressing this problem, such as (a) allowing the client to stay in the programme after an incident of use, on the condition that he develops and follows a new relapse prevention plan; or (b) discharging the client with the promise that he can return after a short period provided that he follows a relapse prevention plan with the support of external counselling. In a therapeutic community, these alternative ways of working might need to be debriefed with the other residents in the programme.

OTHER LIFESTYLE ISSUES IMPORTANT TO MAINTAINING CHANGE

It is essential to remember that treatment does not happen in a vacuum. Lifestyle and other factors in the environment can be crucial determinants of the success of your client's attempt to change his behaviour. Clearly, also, it will be necessary to find new ways of achieving the positive effects that your client formerly derived from his substance use. Work with your client in identifying new, rewarding activities that could replace drinking or drug use. At the simplest level this might involve taking up new hobbies, joining clubs or taking up a sport or other physical exercise. However, on a more general level, you might consider linking him up with agencies that could help him to find a job or a new job, or help him to move to a new geographical location.

If your client's social group is heavily involved in drinking and supports your client's drinking, he is likely to find it hard to change his alcohol use (Longabaugh, Wirtz, Zweben & Stout, 1998). For these clients, and those who are socially isolated, building a new social network will be a vital part of treatment. We recommend that you:

- *Explore your client's social network.* Use diagrams such as the social atom (Chapter 19, *Working with Young People*) to map out the people in his life, including who is supportive and who might influence him to use or drink. Encourage your client to consider what kind of support he needs.
- Depending on his treatment goal, *encourage him to participate in self-help groups* such as AA, NA, or MM as these are a great source of social support and mutual understanding (Chapter 15, *Self-help Groups*).
- Where possible, *involve your client's family, friends or concerned others* in the treatment process (Chapter 13, *Involving Concerned Others*).
- *Help your client to enhance his communication skills.* For example, assertiveness (Chapter 8) and communication skills (Chapter 9) will help your client to form friendships, seek support and effectively resolve interpersonal conflict.
- *Assist your client to generate a list of pleasant social activities* that interest him. Invite him to start participating in one or two of these activities and debrief his experiences in future sessions. More ideas to help your client increase his pleasant activities are listed in the *Resources List*.

Trouble shooting

Needless to say, many relapses happen after treatment has ended. An appropriate plan for extended care (Chapter 17) will help your client to feel more comfortable about the possibility of returning to see you in the event of a relapse. It might be important to address feelings of 'failure' by reviewing once again the cyclical model of change according to which relapse is part of the learning process (see Figure 1, p. 33). In the context of this model you can reassure your client that all he has learnt will not be lost but can be drawn upon next time he decides to make a change.

A NOTE ON CUE EXPOSURE

Cue exposure is another promising approach that complements both relapse prevention and behavioural self-management (Chapter 12). This technique is based on the principle that people, places and events which repeatedly precede your client's substance use eventually become associated with his pleasant experiences of alcohol or drugs. These situations will then act as cues for your client to drink or use again. For example, cues for drinking commonly include seeing, smelling or tasting alcohol. In relapse prevention training, we would describe these cues as triggers to drinking.

As its name suggests, cue exposure is an intervention in which your client is repeatedly exposed to salient cues for drug or alcohol use without allowing him to drink or use. The aim is to weaken the strength of association between the cue and the substance use and thereby, prevent relapse. The types of cues will depend on whether the client's goal is abstinence or moderation. For example, a heavy drinker with a goal of either abstinence or moderation might have controlled exposure to the sight or smell of alcohol without drinking. If his goal is moderation, he might also consume a small amount of alcohol and then refrain from further drinking over a specified period of time.

Cue exposure is a specialist treatment intervention and should only be offered by suitably qualified professionals (Shand, Gates, Fawcett & Mattick, 2003). Expertise is required for the therapist to effectively control and monitor the client's exposure to the cues while also assisting him to apply coping skills in the presence of these cues.

RESOURCES LIST

Beck, A.T., Wright, F.D., Newman, C.F. & Liese, B.S. (2001). Cognitive Therapy of Substance Abuse. New York: Guilford Press.
—Chapter 10 of this book identifies different types of cravings and techniques for coping with cravings.

Dimeff, L.A. & Marlatt, G.A. (1995). Relapse prevention. In: R.K. Hester & W.R. Miller (eds), *Handbook of Alcoholism Treatment Approaches: Effective Alternatives* (2nd edn) (pp. 176–194). Boston: Allyn and Bacon.
—Provides session-by-session guidelines for a relapse prevention approach differing slightly from that presented in our chapter.

Connors, G.J., Maisto, S.A., & Donovan, D.M. (1996). Conceptualizations of relapse: A summary of psychological and psychobiological modes. *Addiction*, **91**(Supplement), S5–S13.
—An excellent summary article of the various models of relapse and their basic principles.

Copello, A., Orford, J., Hodgson, R., Tober, G., Barrett, C. & UKATT Research Team (2002). Social behaviour and network therapy: Basic principles and early experiences. *Addictive Behaviors*, **27**, 245–366.
—This paper outlines a promising new therapy approach aimed at assisting clients to build supportive social networks.

Cummings, C., Gordon, J.R. & Marlatt, G.A. (1980). Relapse: Prevention and prediction. In: W.R. Miller (ed.), *The Addictive Behaviours* (pp. 291–321). Oxford: Pergamon.
—Identifies the three most common relapse triggers as negative emotional states, interpersonal conflict and social pressure.

Gorski, T. (2000). *Relapse Prevention Counselling Workbook: Practical Exercises for Managing High-Risk Situations*. Independence, MO: Herald House.
—A relapse prevention approach that is of particular interest to those who work within a disease model formulation of addictive behaviours.

Gossop, M. (ed.) (1989). *Relapse and Addictive Behaviour*. London: Tavistock/Routledge.
—This book provides an overview of relapse across a variety of addictive behaviours from both clinical and research perspectives.

Kadden, R., Carroll, K., Donovan, D., Cooney, N., Monti, P., Abrams, D., Litt, M. & Hester, R. (1995). *Cognitive Behavioral Coping Skills Therapy Manual: A Clinical Research Guide for Therapists Treating Individuals with Alcohol Abuse and Dependence* (Project MATCH Monograph Series, Volume 3). NIH Pub. No. 94-3724. Rockville, MD: National Institute on Alcohol Abuse and Alcoholism.
To order a copy, go to: www.niaaa.nih.gov/publications/match.htm
—Includes sessions on coping with urges, lapses and seemingly irrelevant decisions.

Longabaugh, R., Wirtz, P.W., Zweben, A. & Stout, R.L. (1998). Network support for drinking, Alcoholics Anonymous and long-term matching effects. *Addiction*, **93**(9), 1313–1333.
—Results from Project MATCH, showing that clients whose social group is heavily involved in drinking are more likely to relapse and will benefit from AA involvement as a relapse-prevention strategy.

Marlatt, G.A. & Gordon, J. (eds) (1985). *Relapse Prevention: Maintenance Strategies in the Treatment of Addictive Behaviors*. New York: Guilford Press.
—One of the most comprehensive texts in the area of relapse prevention. Also provides a comprehensive theoretical and research overview of the area.

Monti, P.M., Kadden, R.M. Rohsenow, D.J., Cooney, N.L. & Abrams, D.B. (2002). *Treating Alcohol Dependence: A Coping Skills Training Guide* (2nd edn). New York: Guilford Press.
—Excellent and concise guidelines to skills training for relapse prevention. We have drawn particularly on the following sessions: Developing Social Support Networks (pp. 70–72), Managing Urges to Drink (pp. 96–99), Seemingly Irrelevant Decisions (pp. 113–115) and Planning for Emergencies (pp. 115–116). Other relevant sessions include Increasing Pleasant Activities (pp. 102–104), Anger Management (pp. 104–108) and Cue Exposure (pp. 132–150).

Shand, F., Gates, J., Fawcett, J. & Mattick, R.P. (2003). *Guidelines for the Treatment of Alcohol Problems* (pp. 116–117). Canberra: Australian Government Department of Health and Ageing.
—Evidence-based recommendations for the method of cue exposure.

Saunders, B. & Allsop, S. (1989). Relapse: A critique. In: M. Gossop (ed.), *Relapse and Addictive Behaviour*. London: Tavistock/Routledge.
—A critique of aspects of the relapse model presented by Marlatt and Gordon.

Saunders, B. & Allsop, S. (1991). Helping those who relapse. In: R. Davidson, S. Rollnick & I. MacEwan (eds), *Counselling Problem Drinkers*. London: Tavistock/Routledge.
—In combination with the reference above, this chapter outlines much of the relapse prevention approach described in this chapter.

Tanner, S. & Ball, J. (2000). *Beating the Blues: A Self-help Approach to Overcoming Depression*. Sydney: Doubleday.
—Includes a list of pleasant activities to help people plan new recreational options.

Wanigaratne, S., Wallace, W., Pullin, J., Keaney, F. & Farmern, R. (1990). *Relapse Prevention for Addictive Behaviours: A Manual for Therapists*. Oxford: Blackwell Scientific Publications.
—Provides a comprehensive session-by-session description of a treatment programme based on relapse prevention principles.

Weingardt, K.R. & Marlatt, G.A. (1998). Sustaining change. In: W.R. Miller & N. Heather (eds), *Treating Addictive Behaviors* (2nd edn) (pp. 337–351). New York: Plenum Press.
—A very practical chapter outlining research-based methods of relapse prevention training and giving more details on what to do if a lapse occurs.

ASSESSMENT TOOLS FOR IDENTIFYING HIGH-RISK SITUATIONS

Annis, H. & Graham, J. (1988). *Situational confidence questionnaire (SCQ) user's guide*. Toronto: Addiction Research Foundation.
—Assesses the self-efficacy of clients to cope with situations that involve resisting alcohol.

Annis, H.M., Turner, N.E. & Sklar, S.M. (1997). *Inventory of Drug Taking Situations— (IDTS)*. Toronto, ON, Canada: The Centre for Addiction and Mental Health (CAMH). Available for purchase from the Centre for Addiction and Mental Health, 33 Russell Street, Toronto, ON, Canada M5S 2S1 or at: http://www.camh.net/publications
—Assesses situations in which the client has consumed heavily or relapsed in the past. Companion to DTCQ (see below).

Annis, H.M., Turner, N.E. & Sklar, S.M. (1997) *The Drug-taking Confidence Questionnaire (DTCQ)*. Toronto, ON, Canada: The Centre for Addiction and Mental Health (CAMH). Available for purchase from the Centre for Addiction and Mental Health, 33 Russell Street, Toronto, ON, Canada M5S 2S1 or at: http://www.camh.net/publications
—Assesses self-efficacy across a range of high risk situations. There are two questionnaires—one for drugs and one for alcohol.

Barber, J.G. & Cooper, B.K. (1991). The Situation Confidence Questionnaire (Heroin). *International Journal of the Addictions*, **26**, 565–575.
—Assesses high-risk situations with opioid-dependent clients.

Litman, G.K., Stapelton, J., Oppenheim, A.N., Peleg, M. & Jackson, P. (1983). Situations related to alcoholism relapse. *British Journal of Addiction*, **78**, 381–389.
—The *Relapse Precipitants Inventory* identifies potential relapse situations and estimate an overall danger of relapse.

Litman, G.K., Stapleton, J., Oppenheim, A.N., Peleg, M. (1983). An instrument for measuring coping behaviours in hospitalized alcoholics: Implications for relapse prevention treatment. *British Journal of Addiction*, **78**(3), 269–276.
Available without charge at:
`http://eibdata.emcdda.eu.int/Treatment/Process/itcbi.htm`
—The Coping Behaviours Inventory (CBI) helps identify the client's coping skills.

Martin, G.W., Wilkinson, D.A. & Poulos, C.X. (1995). The Drug Avoidance Self-Efficacy Scale. *Journal of Substance Abuse*, **7**(2), 151–163.
—Designed to measure self-efficacy concerning the avoidance of substance use by polydrug users.

Sitharthan, T. & Kavanagh, D.J. (1990). Role of self-efficacy in predicting outcomes from a programme for controlled drinking. *Drug and Alcohol Dependence*, **27**, 87–94.
—A scale to assess your client's confidence in maintaining moderation across a range of situations.

Zywiak, W., Connors, G., Maisto, S., & Westerberg, V. (1996). Relapse research and the Reasons for Drinking Questionnaire: a factor analysis of Marlatt's relapse taxonomy. *Addiction*, **91**(Supplement), S121–130.
—The RFDQ can be used to identify triggers of relapse for individual clients.

URGES AND CRAVINGS DIARY

Day, date, time:	Where, with whom, doing what?	Rate strength of craving (0–100)	Thoughts and feelings associated with craving	Response to craving (thoughts and actions)	Rate strength of craving (0–100)
Mon 11/5 8.30pm	In a restaurant with friends	(80)	Happy and excited. I'd love to have a drink now	Thought about my reasons for not drinking; had mineral water instead	(20) Stayed sober and had fun Felt proud of myself

17

Extended Care

RECOMMENDED USE

Clients who have received your assistance in changing their drinking or drug use will require your support for some time after the formal programme has finished. Because relapse is very common among people who are trying to maintain abstinence or moderation, it is most important that you have a structured programme in place for extended care. Although relapse prevention techniques and referral to self-help groups are both important aspects of extended care, they are not enough. Donovan (1998) suggested that the value of extended care for your client is not so much in preventing relapses but in providing an opportunity to intervene when lapses or relapses occur, thereby helping your client to reduce the duration, severity and harm associated with these incidents of drinking or drug use.

Most clinics have some kind of follow-up but this often involves an informal approach that only attracts successful clients. *Take some time to assess the strengths and limitations of your own extended care arrangements.* You will need to look at both therapist- and client-initiated follow-up.

THERAPIST-INITIATED FOLLOW-UP

Therapist-initiated follow-up can serve several functions. It allows you to monitor your client's progress and discuss any problems she might have encountered. It is also an opportunity for you to reinforce her successes. When organised on a one-to-one basis, follow-up appointments allow you to work on strategies to cope with any new situations that might have arisen to challenge your client's resolve to maintain her behaviour change. You might also want to organise some extra 'booster sessions' to strengthen the skills that your client has learnt in treatment.

When extended care is organised on a group basis, there is the opportunity for clients to form important support networks and to learn from each other's mistakes and successes. However, you should also make time to review each individual client's experiences.

The following guidelines will help you to tighten the structure of your extended care plans:

(1) Your arrangement for continued contact with your client after the completion of therapy should be part of an overall package, *not an optional extra*. This will be the case regardless of the type of therapy your client has received. A structured follow-up plan is particularly important for clients leaving the relative security of residential programmes.

(2) Prepare your client for extended care while she is still in therapy. Stress that follow-up appointments are an important part of her therapy programme. Explain to her that clients *can benefit from these appointments, regardless of whether or not they have successfully maintained their goals*. You are not expecting her to relapse but if she does, the follow-up appointment will offer an opportunity for her to discuss this with you.

(3) *Do everything you can to ensure that your client keeps her appointments*. For example, you could provide her with a calendar indicating the appointment dates. You should also telephone her or write to her the week before, reminding her about the appointment.

(4) If your client misses an appointment, *reschedule the appointment for another time as soon as possible*. When she next comes to see you, use a motivational interviewing approach (Chapter 3) to explore her reasons for missing the appointment. She might, for example, have felt reluctant to see you because of a lapse or a relapse.

(5) Follow-up appointments can vary greatly in terms of frequency. You might want to have standard follow-ups at three, six and twelve months after therapy. Some clients will need more support and could benefit from more frequent, brief appointments or periodic phone calls in the early stages after you finish therapy. Your plan for extended care should be *both structured and flexible*.

(6) Your client might also benefit from services that bridge the gap between your programme and community living, such as transitional accommodation (e.g., half-way houses) and case management (Chapter 18).

CLIENT-INITIATED EXTENDED CARE

In addition to follow-up appointments, make arrangements with your client to contact you if she needs your help. As your client adjusts to life without drugs and without the support of ongoing treatment, she will encounter temptations, pressures and unexpected problems. She might need to contact you for assistance when these situations arise. The following guidelines will help you to organise a system that is convenient for you both:

(1) Your client might feel embarrassed to contact you if she has had a lapse in her

drinking or drug-using behaviour. Emphasise to her that the event of a lapse is a critical time for seeking help.

(2) There will also be times when you will not be available for contact. Help your client to brainstorm some ideas for getting assistance from other sources. *A plan of action should be in place for your client to use when her need arises.* For example, she could put the number for telephone counselling services near the phone for ready access or arrange for a sympathetic friend to be available (see p. 229). Another alternative for clients in group therapy is the 'buddy system'. This is where clients who have been in therapy together pair up and agree to telephone each other from time to time, to lend support.

RESOURCES LIST

Ahles, T., Schlundt, D., Prue, P., & Rychtarik, R. (1983). Impact of aftercare arrangements on the maintenance of treatment success of abusive drinkers. *Addictive Behaviors*, **8**, 53–58.
—Describes a highly structured approach to extended care for the treatment of alcohol problems.

Donovan, D. M. (1998). Continuing care: Promoting the maintenance of change. In: W.R. Miller & N. Heather (eds), *Treating Addictive Behaviors* (2nd edn), (pp. 317–336). New York: Plenum Press.
—Excellent review of the different types of extended care and the evidence supporting their use.

McAuliffe, W.E. & Ch'ien, J.M.N. (1986). Recovery training and self-help: A relapse prevention program for treated opiate addicts. *Journal of Substance Abuse Treatment*, **3**, 9–20.
—Provides clear evidence of the value of scheduled and structured extended care. Recommended reading on designing such an extended care programme.

Shand, F., Gates, J., Fawcett, J. & Mattick, R.P. (2003). *Guidelines for the Treatment of Alcohol Problems* (pp. 145–148). Canberra: Australian Government Department of Health and Ageing.
—Concise guidelines to the range of extended care options for clients of alcohol treatment programmes.

IV

Special Groups and Management Issues

18

Case Management

RECOMMENDED USE

Case management is an approach that looks at the broader needs of your client, including and beyond substance abuse treatment. Working jointly with your client, the case manager develops and facilitates a case plan. The plan aims to link your client with other services and community resources to ensure his identified needs are met in a coordinated and effective manner (Intagliata, 1982).

Case management is especially appropriate for clients with complex problems, special needs, or chronic alcohol or drug dependence. It has particular relevance for adolescent and ageing clients, and client sub-groups who have concerns about any of the following areas:

- the correctional system;
- disability or medical conditions;
- mental illness or brain injury;
- financial problems and/or unemployment;
- homelessness;
- pregnancy; and/or
- custody and parenting issues.

Case management may also be a key component of extended care (Chapter 17). For example, you might set up a case management plan to provide outreach support and to link your client back into his community (Donovan, 1998).

There are many models of case management. Some focus only on assessment and referral. Known as the 'brokerage model', this minimalist approach is the least effective type of case management. Alternative models involve direct support to help clients make and maintain effective contacts with other services. For the purposes of this chapter, we have drawn together the key components of these more supportive models, based on the research from substance abuse and mental health case management.

Excessive work loads reduce the effectiveness of case management. Depending on the complexities of your clients' needs, you should keep your case load to around 12–15 clients (Rapp, 1998).

GOALS

The goals of case management include any or all of the following:

- Building a supportive, trusting relationship with your client.
- Encouraging your client to stay in substance abuse treatment and comply with medications (if appropriate).
- Linking your client to relevant professional services in a coordinated way.
- Monitoring your client's use of services and helping him to overcome obstacles in accessing services.
- Linking your client with his community so that he can meet his basic needs, develop positive, lasting social contacts and get involved in activities that support an alcohol- and drug-free lifestyle.
- Providing a continuity of care and social support both during and after your client leaves treatment.
- Offering support to family and concerned others and helping your client rebuild positive personal relationships.
- Increasing your client's confidence to choose his own goals and to seek help independently.
- Addressing crises, lapses and other difficult situations as they arise.

METHOD

BEFORE STARTING

If you intend to take the role of case manager, you will need to build your knowledge of services and treatment programmes in the areas where your clients are likely to live. This should include the full range of drug and alcohol, medical, mental health and counselling services available to your clients. Get to know the government and non-government community services, such as public or low cost permanent and temporary housing, job search agencies, financial assistance, meal providers, child-care services and family support. Depending on your client sub-groups, you will also need to know about child protection agencies, adolescent services and the correctional system.

Familiarise yourself with community groups, such as self-help groups (Chapter 15), cultural groups, charities, drop-in centres and other outreach services. Find out about the range of options for alcohol- or drug-free recreation and social activities. Educational courses may also be important for clients, especially in literacy, numeracy, parenting and vocational skills.

It's a good idea to visit the agencies and see what they do. Establish your own links with contact people in the relevant services and get to know the formal and informal procedures of the service. For efficient referral, you will need to have knowledge of:

- *Criteria for admission*: Who is and who is not eligible for the service?
- *Method of referral*: What does the service need to know about the client and what does the client need to do in order to enter the programme?
- *Waiting lists*: Is the service in high demand and likely to have a waiting list? What other delays might be encountered in accessing the service?
- *Costs of the service* and any concessions available.
- *Nature of the service provided*: What are the goals and limitations of the service? How long will the service be offered?
- *Other issues of relevance to clients*: Is the client required to be abstinent? Can families be involved?

Build a contact list so that you can access up-to-date information quickly. You might also develop a collection of pamphlets and educational materials to give to your client.

Effective case management also draws on informal networks and naturally occurring community resources. Be prepared to liaise with landlords, neighbours, employers, teachers or local clubs, as well as your client's family, friends and concerned others (Chapter 13, *Involving Concerned Others*).

THE ROLE OF CASE MANAGER

Who Is a Case Manager?

If you are a case manager, your core role will involve assessing and linking your client to appropriate services and community agencies. You will also monitor, coordinate and advocate for your client's case plan and you might be required to provide practical assistance such as transportation, home visits, or being on-call for emergencies. Although counselling is not a core responsibility, case management can include brief counselling to assist the client in overcoming personal obstacles and in building skills that will support his case plan. It might also mean helping your client to learn basic living skills such as planning and preparing meals, organising household chores, managing money, planning excursions and community living.

The service where you work will define the limits of your role. In many agencies, the role of drug and alcohol therapist is a separate role from that of case manager. It is important to be aware of the distinction between these two roles. When the client already has a designated case manager, it is neither helpful nor appropriate for a therapist to replicate aspects of the case manager's role. Similarly, if there is a designated therapist, the case manager would avoid anything other than brief counselling and would encourage the client to discuss deeper issues with his therapist. The roles of case manager and therapist need to be clearly defined to avoid role confusion, unnecessary repetition of services or 'splitting' of professionals by troubled clients (see pp. 13–14). Clear role definition and delegation of responsibilities is achieved through case conferences and with the aid of professional supervision.

Sometimes, one worker will be required to carry out both roles. Since there are common tasks (e.g., assessment, referral and crisis intervention), it may seem economical to combine the two roles. However, by combining them, you may be losing some important distinctions between them. Therapy typically requires structured session times to allow your client the freedom to reflect on personal issues and explore new skills, whereas case management involves a more direct role in changing the circumstances of your client's external world. Also, these two roles are equally demanding and there are risks that one role will be neglected while the other takes precedence or that, in trying to do both, you will experience 'burnout'.

If you are combining the roles, reduce your overall case load. Allocate separate sessions for each task so that both you and your client are clear about the purpose of each meeting. Professional supervision is also necessary to help you balance your tasks and avoid the problems that sometimes arise in dual relationships (see Chapter 1, *General Counselling Skills* for further discussion of dual relationships).

The Case Management Relationship

Much of what is said in Chapter 1, *General Counselling Skills* is applicable to the case management relationship. The relationship is ideally built on respect, empathy and good listening skills. It is a collaborative relationship, where you and your client work together towards the client's self-defined goals. Social support and empowerment should be key aspects of the relationship.

It is not usually necessary for you to be available to your client 24 hours a day, seven days a week but it is important to link him with crisis and emergency services that he can access at any time. Nevertheless, case management may require some additional flexibility in your availability to clients. For example, with clients who are unlikely to come to your office because of ambivalence, disability, lifestyle or distance, you might need to do outreach or home visits.

Another key aspect of the case management relationship is the continuity of care over time. As the case plan evolves, your client should become both more positively connected with his community and more self-reliant. You can then gradually reduce your contact with your client to follow-up sessions. If you leave the job, make sure that you 'hand over' your client into the care of another case manager by having one or more three-way meetings until the client feels comfortable with the new case manager.

Case Conferences

Case conferences are structured meetings held between service providers to discuss and coordinate case planning. It is usual to have regular case conferences for on-going client care but impromptu meetings can also take place in response to crises or new information about a particular case. Inform your client that such meetings will occur and get his consent to exchange confidential information. Before the case conference, decide what it is that you want from the other professionals. Remember that they will also have goals in relation to your client and might also want to enlist your help. It may often be optimal for the client to participate in meetings about himself, allowing him to have a direct influence on the process. You and your client might also invite other supportive people such as close family members or concerned others.

ASSESSMENT

The general principles of case management assessment are the same as those discussed in Chapter 2. Assessment can occur over several sessions. There are two assessment approaches that are effective for case management in the drug and alcohol field: needs-based and strengths-based assessment. Although they spring from different theoretical models (the medical and solution-focused models respectively), you may be able to combine certain aspects of each approach to give a more holistic view of the factors affecting your client's situation.

Needs-based Assessment

In case management assessment, your client's *needs* are those conditions of life that prevent him from reaching his goals, particularly in relation to the drug or alcohol problem. You will already have some idea of your client's needs from the referring agent. In your first session, identify and address the most immediate areas of need. These will vary depending on whether the treatment programme is a residential or outpatient programme. Your client might need help to contact people, arrange accommodation, detoxification and other medical assistance, or to sort out the practical details of starting the programme.

Once your client's immediate needs have been addressed, the assessment focuses on longer term goals. You might assess your client's health and psychological well-being, education, employment, relationships and social support, risk-taking behaviour and legal issues. Guidelines for assessing these areas are provided in Chapters 2, *Assessment* and 20, *Dual Diagnosis*.

Be aware that an exclusive focus on the needs and problems of your client carries the risk of producing a 'problem-saturated' view of his circumstances. This can be experienced by clients as overwhelming or dis-empowering. It should be balanced with an equal focus on assessing your client's strengths.

Strengths-based Assessment

Assessment of your client's *strengths* helps to build his motivation, self-efficacy and independence. Despite his presenting problems, your client has strengths which he has drawn on in the past and which can be applied to help solve the problems he is currently facing. We have drawn on the work of Berg, Miller and de Yong (*Resources List*) to show how this 'solution-focused' method is relevant for drug and alcohol treatment clients. Two examples are 'miracle questions' and 'exception-finding questions'.

The miracle question focuses attention away from the feeling of being stuck with the problem. For example, ask your client:

'Suppose that one night there is a miracle and while you are sleeping, the problem we have been talking about is solved. How would you know? What would be different? What will you notice the next morning that will tell you that there has been a miracle? What will your partner notice?'

These questions will help your client to move to a point where he can identify what he wants and what it would be like to achieve it. If the client describes this as an absence of something (e.g., 'I wouldn't be addicted'), ask a question about the presence of something (e.g., 'What would you be doing instead?'). Then use your client's miracle image to explore the way forward. For example, ask him:

'What small step would bring you just a little bit closer to the miracle?'

This question emphasises small, positive steps rather than big goals. You can further unpack each step by asking what other things your client might do that would make this small step possible.

Exception-finding is another extremely useful example of solution-focused questioning. Exceptions are those moments in your client's life when the problem is not controlling him. They are found in your client's past and present experiences. For example, you might ask:

'Tell me about a time when you were able to resist the urge to use or drink, even for a short time?'
'You say that if a miracle occurs, you will be getting on better with your family. Are there times now or in the past when you felt you were getting on better with your family? What's different about those times?'
'How did you manage to feel okay this morning, when you were coping with these problems?'

The miracle and exceptions questions uncover solutions and skills that your client has already exercised in various areas of life. Through genuine curiosity, reflective listening, affirmations and summaries (as outlined in Chapter 1, *General Counselling*

Skills), help your client to amplify these solutions and fit them into the case management plan. This is particularly helpful for clients who feel discouraged or demoralised.

THE ACTION PLAN

From these assessments, you and your client will generate a list of case management goals. Once you have a list, you can decide on priorities. There are no hard and fast rules about what should be dealt with first (unless your client is at risk of self-harm). You should, however, take into account the need to stabilise your client's substance abuse so that he can work towards other goals. Some goals might be addressed simultaneously but be careful not to overload your client with too many appointments at once!

Your client's belief in his own ability to overcome problems will develop with his successful attainment of goals. Help your client to break demanding goals into short-term, achievable steps (Chapter 4, *Goal Setting*). Each step should involve some effort on the part of your client, so that he experiences the successes personally. Keep a record of what each of you will do towards a particular goal before your next meeting. When you meet again acknowledge successful work as well as exploring solutions to any obstacles that were encountered. This will provide the impetus for further planning and effort on the part of your client.

Sometimes your client will encounter insurmountable obstacles. Such obstacles could come from the difficulties and delays in accessing services. While acknowledging your client's sense of frustration, help him to accept that such delays are to be expected in every day life. In some situations, you might advocate on your client's behalf (see below). You or his therapist might also provide some basic communication skills training to help him advocate for himself (Chapter 9).

Trouble shooting

Sometimes you and your client will disagree about goals or the best course of action. For example, you might believe that the client will benefit from a particular service or intervention while the client is not ready to take that step. Provided there is no immediate risk of serious harm, respect your client's position. Motivational interviewing (Chapter 3) can be used to explore your client's concerns as well as giving him an opportunity to get further information about his choices.

LINKAGE WITH OTHER SERVICES

A key aspect of the case management role is to make connections with others on behalf of your client. This will involve communicating with other service providers in or outside your agency, as well as networking with community groups and concerned others. Graham and Timney (1995) distinguished two types of inter-agency contact in substance abuse case management programmes: *advocacy* and *coordination*. They defined them as follows.

Advocacy

Advocacy includes all those activities where the primary goal is to obtain something for your client, such as:

- accessing a service;
- getting practical help;
- enlisting someone's support in the treatment process; or
- finding out information about issues or services.

Coordination

Coordination refers to those activities where the primary goal is to give or receive information about the client, in order to:

- keep someone informed, such as the referring agency or the client's family;
- get information from another service about the client's progress;
- exchange information so that the link between the services runs smoothly;
- coordinate and define service roles for the client's case;
- develop a treatment plan;
- develop a plan for extended care;
- provide information for an agency to pass onto the client; or
- give testimony to the courts.

Obviously, some advocacy and coordination is done in your client's presence but a lot of this work is carried out between your meetings, over the phone, in face-to-face meetings with other agencies and via written letters or reports. Since advocacy and coordination involve disclosure of details about your client, you will need to obtain his consent about what will be disclosed.

Document each contact you have on behalf of your client. This only needs to be a short entry into a case file regarding who you spoke with, for what purpose and the outcome of the communication. Such documentation will help you to keep your client informed and monitor the progress of your action plan.

LIAISON WITH CONCERNED OTHERS

Depending on the service, the case management role might include liaison with and support for concerned others. For example, it is helpful to enlist at least one trusted person to support your client's involvement in his case plan. Such support might include social support (e.g., encouragement and recognition of your client's achievements) and practical support (e.g., helping your client to get to appointments).

It is very important to maintain your client's confidentiality when working with concerned others. It is sometimes easy to say too much to a concerned other, particularly during unscheduled phone contact. Pre-empt this problem by clarifying with your client how much information he is prepared for you to disclose to others, particularly those people who are his main sources of support.

Confidentiality is also best maintained by meeting with concerned others in the presence of your client. This approach has the added benefit of facilitating better communication between your client and his family or friends. For example, you and your client might meet with his family to help him move back home after a time away, or to negotiate agreements about how they will respond to relapse, difficult behaviour or sources of conflict. These issues are discussed in detail in Chapter 13, *Involving Concerned Others*.

Trouble shooting

It is not appropriate for you to do family therapy to resolve entrenched family problems or to provide individual counselling for your client's concerned others while you are still his case manager. If needed, refer your client's family or concerned other to an alternative service.

Other people can sometimes make it hard for your client to achieve his goals because of their own substance use or other difficult or violent behaviour. Although your client might recognise the destructive influence of such people, he may be uneasy about ending such relationships for various reasons. Use motivational interviewing (Chapter 3) to explore his ambivalence about the relationship. He might also benefit from assertiveness training (Chapter 8) and assistance in developing an alternative social network (Chapters 15, *Self-help Groups* and 16, *Relapse Prevention Training*).

RESOURCES LIST

We have drawn the following resources from both the substance abuse and mental health fields of case management.

Berg, I.K. & Miller, S.D. (1992). *Working with the Problem Drinker: A Solution-focused Approach*, New York: W.W. Norton.
    —A practical book on solution-focused counselling approaches to assist problem drinkers.

Brun, C. & Rapp, R.C. (2001). Strength-based case management: Individuals' perspectives on strengths and the case manager relationship. *Social Work*, **46**(3), 278–288.

—A comprehensive description of a strength-based approach for people with substance abuse problems.

Donovan, D. M. (1998). Continuing care: Promoting the maintenance of change. In: W.R. Miller & N. Heather (eds), *Treating Addictive Behaviors* (2nd edn), (pp. 317–336). New York: Plenum Press.
—This review includes a discussion of how case management can be effectively used in plans for extended care.

De Jong, P. & Miller, S.D. (1995). How to interview for client strengths. *Social Work*, **40**(6), 729–737.
—Describes how you can apply solution-focused counselling to drug and alcohol problems.

Godley, S.H., Godley, M.D., Pratt, A. & Wallace, J.L. (1994). Case management services for adolescent substance abusers: A program description. *Journal of Substance Abuse Treatment*, **11**(4), 309–317.
—Shows how to apply the key components of case management for younger clients.

Graham, K. & Timney, C.B. (1995). Continuity of care in addictions treatment: The role of advocacy and coordination in case management. *American Journal of Drug and Alcohol Abuse*, **21**(4), 433–452.
—Provides practical definitions of advocacy and coordination in the context of two case management programmes for clients with substance abuse.

Intagliata, J. (1982). Improving the quality of community care for the chronically mentally disabled: The role of case management. *Schizophrenia Bulletin*, **8**, 655–674.
—A definitive and influential article on the objectives and components of case management.

Rapp, C.A. (1998). The active ingredients of effective case management: A research synthesis. *Community Mental Health Journal*, **34**(4), 363–378.
—Another review article that uses the research to generate a list of the key components of effective case management.

Simpson, A., Miller, C. & Bowers, L. (2003). Case management models and the care programme approach: How to make the CPA effective and credible. *Journal of Psychiatric and Mental Health Nursing*, **10**, 427–483.
—This review article describes and compares the various models of case management and discusses the key components of effective case management.

19

Working With Young People

BASIC GUIDELINES

Although the techniques and strategies outlined in this book are relevant for clients of all ages, working with young people has some unique challenges. Engaging a 13-year-old in treatment will obviously be different from working with a 30 year old client! You will need to consider the developmental stage of adolescence and how this applies to your client. This might involve modifying your treatment approach to make it more interesting and meaningful for younger clients.

Young people rarely seek help for drug and alcohol problems without coercion or pressure from adults. The medical, legal, social and financial costs of substance abuse that prompt adults to seek help are often not apparent to the younger client. Your client might also be preoccupied with other major issues in her life and not yet ready or able to stop her substance abuse. Harm reduction is therefore a crucial aspect of working with young people.

As with older clients, you are likely to see a spectrum in the severity of substance abuse. As the severity of the problems increase, it is important to use a more multi-systemic approach with young clients. By multi-systemic, we mean that you not only intervene at an individual level but you also attempt to influence your client's broader social networks: family, peer, educational, vocational, recreational, community and other social systems. To do this successfully, you will need to work with other agencies and community services as well as your client's main sources of social support.

GOALS

Obviously the goals set out in other chapters are relevant for young people. Some additional goals that are relevant for younger clients include:

- engaging your client in treatment in a developmentally appropriate way;
- strengthening your client's support from family, peers and concerned others;
- reducing harmful and risky behaviours;
- reducing risk factors that facilitate your client's ongoing drug or alcohol use; and
- enhancing factors that provide potential protection against ongoing drug or alcohol use.

KEY CONCEPTS

ADOLESCENCE

'Adolescence' is *the transition out of childhood into adulthood* and generally refers to the years from puberty to late teens or early 20s. However, the terms 'young person' or 'youth' are applicable to people outside this range. For instance, you could have a client who is pre-pubertal. Alternatively, your 25-year-old client might still be resolving some issues of adolescence.

Research in western cultures has highlighted a number of defining changes or 'tasks' associated with adolescent development. With the physical changes of puberty, the young person will be increasingly aware of sexual feelings and changes to her body image. She will move from concrete to more abstract ways of thinking and begin to question what she has previously taken for granted. She might experience strong emotions and impulses which are not yet tempered by the experience of longer term consequences. Seeking to define herself as an adult, the young person is likely to experiment and take risks with new roles, values and behaviours. This might include experimentation with alcohol or drugs.

During adolescence, the young person's peers also become more influential as role models and as sources of support and acceptance. Your client might identify with a particular youth sub-culture, expressing this identification through her use of language, clothing, music and other activities. At the same time, there will be changes in her social roles and legal status. She is likely to experience new freedoms and responsibilities.

Of course, these summary comments reflect the experience of adolescence from within a western cultural perspective. It is crucial to note that the tasks and expected behaviours of adolescent development are very strongly influenced by culture and ethnicity. Many young people from non-western cultures who present with drug or alcohol problems are also struggling with tensions and clashes between the values of their family or culture of origin, and those of the dominant culture. Therefore, in your work with young people, it is important to be aware of cultural influences—including the influence of your own culture on your view of adolescence!

RISK AND PROTECTIVE FACTORS

Risk and protective factors are social, familial and developmental factors in your client's life that have contributed to, or have an ongoing influence on your client's use of alcohol or drugs. Factors contributing to, or exacerbating substance abuse are often called 'risk factors'. For example, sexual abuse is a risk factor because it is a trauma which often prompts young people to self-medicate with alcohol or drugs.

Factors that help your client to avoid or reduce substance abuse are often called 'protective factors'. Protective factors are not simply the opposite of risk factors. Rather, they are factors that increase your client's resilience so that she is more able to resist the influence of risk factors. A warm and consistent parental relationship, for example, will foster the social skills and self-confidence that the young person needs to cope with stress and resist peer pressure to use drugs or alcohol.

Risk and protective factors sometimes have a complex relationship with substance abuse. The substance abuse itself can bring your client further into contact with risk factors and may also undermine important protective factors. For example, your client's drug use might have caused her to associate with other drug users (thereby increasing her risk of using) and, at the same time, caused her to withdraw from other supportive social connections (thereby decreasing potentially protective influences).

EXPECTANCIES

Expectancies are beliefs, thoughts and memories that influence what a young person expects to happen if she uses or drinks. Your client's expectancies are uniquely shaped by her direct experiences of the effects and consequences of using substances, and, indirectly, by her observations of other people. These expectancies will influence her decisions about drinking or using drugs. For example, if your client's substance use leads to rewarding experiences such as physical or emotional pleasure, social acceptance, friendly interaction or relief from negative feelings, she will be more likely to use again.

METHOD

Since young people do not usually seek help voluntarily, your client is highly likely to have entered treatment because she was coerced or persuaded by adults. She might see you as just another authority figure. She might also find it hard to adjust to treatment that is designed for adult clients. Therefore, it is important to consider how you will engage your client in the treatment process.

Your client is more likely to trust you if you take a non-judgemental approach and show a genuine interest in her perspective. Work in a collaborative way by involving your client in all decisions related to her treatment, particularly when setting treatment goals. Engage her curiosity with open-ended questions and by fostering a shared interest in discovery. Be open and responsive to your client's sense of humour and fun. Encourage her self-efficacy by giving frequent and immediate positive feedback when you notice she is doing well.

Be flexible and ready to shift your focus if your client becomes defensive. For example, Howard (2004; pers. commun.) suggests the approach of skating in and out of crucial subjects, rather than rigidly persevering with what *you* think is important.

Your office might not be the best place to work with young clients. It might be better to go for a walk or choose some other location where she feels more comfortable. You can also make your treatment approach more youth-friendly by using metaphors, stories, pictures, cartoons, videos, music, therapeutic games, physical activities, role-play and the internet. Select materials and resources that are in tune with your client's interests, language and sub-culture. Some examples of youth-friendly internet sites are given in the *Resources List*.

Stay up-to-date with information about youth and community services and local avenues for recreation so that you can effectively link your client with protective social networks. For some clients, you might need to set up plans for coordinated care with juvenile justice, community and welfare services, mental health services or other professionals. Refer to Chapters 18, *Case Management* and 20, *Dual Diagnosis* for more information about how to work with other services.

Be aware of your legal and professional obligations regarding duty of care. For example, if your client is at risk of suicide or abuse, you may need to notify her guardian or other authorities. Inform your client about her rights to confidentiality and privacy, as well as your obligations regarding notification.

ASSESSMENT

A comprehensive assessment at the time of intake can be overwhelming—even for adults! It is advisable to break up your assessment over time. Introduce your client to the assessment process by explaining the types of questions you are going to ask, your reasons for asking, and what you intend to do with the information. Take a conversational approach and encourage her to talk about her concerns by using open-ended questions. Encourage her to ask any questions she has about the assessment as you go along.

Initially, you will need to explore your client's drug and alcohol use, main sources of social support and reasons for seeking help. It is also important to screen for any health or social issues that might require prompt intervention (e.g., homelessness, medical problems or suicide risk). As you continue to engage and work with your client, you can then assess those risk and protective factors that might influence her treatment outcome. This information will enable you and your client to develop relapse prevention plans based on reducing the influence of risk factors and enhancing protective factors.

Even if your client does not appear to be ready to change her substance abuse, she might have concerns about other areas of life where she is experiencing distress, unhappiness or dissatisfaction. Ask her what changes she would like to make and how these changes would be beneficial to her. Explore any connections between these preferred changes and her drug use or drinking. This is a key strategy because it invites your client to consider the broader impact of her substance use. For example, your client might express anger and frustration about being hassled by the courts and corrective services. If you then help her to consider the connections between her involvement in crime and her substance use, she might become a little more interested in changing her drug or alcohol use.

If your client is not yet ready to stop using drugs or alcohol, it is also crucial to consider harm reduction strategies that might help her to stay safe and well. Explore your client's awareness of risky behaviour. Use motivational interviewing (Chapter 3) to elicit and explore any concerns she might have about her own safety. You will need to consider, for example, her injecting practices and whether she uses drug cocktails, has unprotected sex or drives while intoxicated. Then invite your client to consider a range of options for reducing harm (see guidelines and resources in Chapter 4, *Goal Setting*). Drug refusal, assertiveness and communication skills will also be particularly relevant in helping her to negotiate safer sex or to refuse to share needles (Chapters 7, 8 and 9).

Some clients with severe polydrug abuse or dependence find it very difficult to avoid all risk-taking behaviour. In these cases, you might consider different goals for different drugs. For instance, your client might continue injecting drugs (as safely as possible) while quitting her use of pills as a way to reduce the risk of overdose. Your willingness to work with her on individualised goals is likely to help her stay engaged with the treatment process. You and your client might also consider using a substitution treatment such as buprenorphine or methadone as a way of reducing harm (Chapter 14, *Pharmacotherapies*).

Assessing Drug and Alcohol Use

Start your assessment by asking your client how she first started using alcohol or drugs and what caused her to keep using or drinking. Inquire into any periods of abstinence and how she achieved these. Explore in detail the situations in which she is currently most likely to use or drink by asking when? where? who with? and what is she feeling? on these occasions.

The guidelines for assessing drug and alcohol problems in Chapter 2, *Assessment* are applicable to younger clients. However, there are some differences between older and younger clients and some issues that are more pertinent for young people.

Young clients tend to be more experimental and opportunistic in their pattern of drinking and drug use than adults who report more routine patterns of use. This might make it harder to estimate quantities and frequencies of consumption. Suppose, for example, that your client is too young to legally access alcohol and she drinks by passing a bottle around with friends. In this situation, the number of standard drinks is impossible to measure! You can help your client to estimate the extent of her drug or alcohol use with other contextual information, such as how often and to what extent she gets drunk, how much money she spends or how many times a day she injects drugs.

Polydrug use is also more common among young clients. Therefore, ask your client about the whole range of substances. Young people are also more likely than adults to experiment with inhalants, such as aerosol cans and common household chemicals, because they are more easily obtained than other drugs. If your client uses inhalants, make sure she is informed about their potentially lethal effects.

Screening for Dual Diagnosis

Experiencing a mental health problem is a major risk factor for adolescent substance use. Often the disorders of adulthood begin to appear during adolescence (see Chapter 20, *Dual diagnosis* for diagnostic descriptions). However, some other disorders characteristically occur during the years of childhood and adolescence. In the descriptions below, we have highlighted some key symptoms that are sometimes related to these disorders. These are not full diagnostic descriptions. Instead, they describe behaviours that might indicate that your client could benefit from a mental health assessment.

Poor concentration, restlessness and impulsive behaviour could indicate that your client has an emotional or mental disturbance such as anxiety, depression, developmental delay or attention-deficit/hyperactivity disorder (ADHD). On the other hand, they might be normal behaviours for this adolescent! The behaviours might even indicate that your method of counselling is inappropriate for your client's age or developmental level. It is important to avoid jumping to conclusions that might result in your client being labelled with an inappropriate diagnosis. However, if the behaviours seem to occur in a consistent pattern, you might choose to refer her for further assessment. Regardless of their cause, poor concentration, restlessness and impulsivity impact on your client's ability to learn. You will need to adjust your style of counselling by breaking up information, using more youth-friendly methods of delivery and checking your client's understanding as you go along.

Aggressive and antisocial behaviour could indicate that your client has Conduct Disorder, particularly if she has an ongoing history of aggression, cruelty and law breaking (Chapter 20, *Dual Diagnosis*). However, many of these behaviours might also be linked to your client's drug or alcohol problem. You will need to negotiate with your client to set limits on her antisocial behaviour and monitor her behaviour over time.

Psychoses often first become evident in the late teen years. Signs that your client is having a psychotic episode might include delusions, hallucinations, inappropriate emotional responses or disorganised thinking and behaviour (Chapter 20, *Dual Diagnosis*). Psychosis is sometimes brought on by frequent use of methamphetamines or heavy use of cannabis.

Eating disorders can cause your client to feel intense fears about gaining weight and cause her to view her body in a distorted way. Symptoms of eating disorders include: not eating enough to maintain normal body weight and menstruation (as in Anorexia Nervosa); episodes of binge eating; and purging behaviour such as self-induced vomiting, overuse of laxatives or excessive exercise (as in Bulimia Nervosa).

Traumatic experiences such as sexual or physical abuse are frequently reported by young people with drug or alcohol problems. Trauma can lead to the use of substances as a form of self-medication, particularly if your client lacks alternative emotional coping skills and social support. Sadly, substance abuse can in turn increase her vulnerability to further victimisation. Chapter 20, *Dual Diagnosis* provides specific guidelines on how to screen for post-traumatic stress disorder (PTSD). Find out if your client is in any current danger from violence or abuse. She may need assistance to access safer accommodation or sexual assault counselling. Remember that you may also have a legal obligation to notify physical, sexual or other abuse.

Depression and suicide are important areas of assessment. Signs of depression or dysthymia are described in detail in Chapter 20, *Dual Diagnosis*. Young people are particularly vulnerable to thoughts about suicide. You should take seriously any indicators that your client has a high risk of suicide, such as a mental health disorder (e.g., depression or psychosis), past suicide attempts, a family history of suicide, recent losses or high levels of stress, an intense preoccupation with death or a strong wish to die, feelings of hopelessness or worthlessness, a plan involving a potentially lethal method or any indications of final preparations, such as giving away personal possessions or other gestures of goodbye. Broaching the subject of suicide with your client will not push her into an attempt and it may be a relief for your client to talk about it.

If there are signs that your client is at risk of attempting suicide, you should organise a referral to mental health services for further assessment as soon as possible. Your client might be ambivalent about this referral because it means adults are taking control. It is important to stand firm about the necessity of making a referral to ensure her safety but try to avoid being judgemental or taking a panicked approach. Use a motivational interviewing approach to help your client explore the pros and cons of seeking help (Chapter 3). Reflect back and build on any statements about her personal strengths or hopes for a solution. You might frame the referral as a way of giving her more time to sort out her feelings. Make sure that she has supportive people who can stay with her until her assessment interview at the mental health service.

REDUCING RISK AND ENHANCING PROTECTION

To build resilience, you and your client will need to consider risk and protective factors at individual, familial, social, recreational and educational levels. The following sections outline methods for assessing and intervening in a multi-systemic way.

Systems of Safety and Support

It is important for your client to feel connected with others through family, peers, school, employment and/or community. Social and interpersonal connectedness not only helps meet basic physical needs but also provides acceptance, affection, support, safety, guidance and meaning. However, your client might be socially disadvantaged in ways that cause her to feel alienated or marginalised. Find out whether she experiences socio-economic hardship, unemployment or homelessness. Has she experienced discrimination on the basis of her gender, sexuality, race, culture or psychiatric illness? Does she rely on sex work to support her drug use? Is her local community able to provide meaningful resources and support? Is she at risk of violence or abuse?

If your client is socially disadvantaged or has complex needs, it is advisable to link her up with helpful services and community resources to ensure that her identified needs are met in a coordinated and effective way. You may also need to work directly with other agencies for the purposes of coordinated care (p. 281). Your first priority should be to ensure that your client is living in safe circumstances and has access to reliable support.

Family and Concerned Others

The family is usually a major source of connectedness and support. Indeed, a strong, consistent and trustworthy bond with an adult role model, such as a parent or grandparent, is a very effective protective factor against substance abuse for a young person. Your client's family are often directly affected by her substance abuse, they may have facilitated or persuaded her to seek help, and they may provide an invaluable resource for supporting her in changing drug use behaviours.

However, not all family relationships are positive in their impact. Poor or inconsistent parenting, family conflict, a lack of bonding, or abuse by family members can significantly increase your client's risk of developing drug or alcohol problems. Substance abuse by parents or family members might also be a powerful influence that facilitates your client's continuing drug use. Familial substance abuse also increases the risks of victimisation and violence and your client may even have left her family to get away from their abusive behaviour.

In such cases, it will be important to help your client identify other people in her extended family or broader social network who are concerned, trustworthy and able to support her efforts towards change. She might even be able to draw on the support offered by other service providers (e.g., juvenile justice officer, teacher, coach or outreach worker).

One useful tool for assessing family and/or other support networks is the 'social atom', a technique from the field of psychodrama. Start by drawing two circles on a piece of a paper. Write your client's name in the middle. Then explain to your client that the inner circle represents people who are close to her and the outer circle represents other people in her life who are more distant. Ask her to write down all the important people in her life, showing where they go in the diagram. Include her family, friends, acquaintances and even pets!

Use open-ended questions and reflective listening to further explore her relationships with the people in her drawing. You might find some of the following questions to be useful:

• Who would your client go to for support or advice? What support would she hope to get?

- With whom does she feel close? What contributes to this closeness?
- With whom does she have conflict? What happens when there is conflict?
- What relationships have been cut off or lost (e.g., by divorce, death or conflict)?
- What relationships would she like to rebuild? How could she do this?
- How would she like to change her social picture?

It is particularly useful to explore what your client needs from her family or concerned others, and what she thinks they need from her. Help her to make a plan for contacting others to rebuild relationships and seek social support. Where appropriate, you may need to advocate on her behalf (p. 250). She might also need to develop skills that will enable her to effectively communicate with others (Chapters 8, *Assertiveness Skills* and 9, *Communication Skills*).

You and your client might also choose to directly involve her family or concerned others in the assessment and treatment process. This could be just to keep them informed about your client's treatment goals and progress. Alternatively, they might be more directly involved through a series of family meetings (Chapter 13, *Working with Concerned Others*).

Developing Personal Coping Skills

The strategies for skills training and cognitive therapy outlined in this book are all useful for young clients. However, their effectiveness will depend on delivering them in a way that engages your client. It is often helpful, for example, to use stories and metaphors as a way of exploring thoughts and behaviours. A metaphor is a way of framing treatment concepts in terms that are familiar and understandable to your client. For example, you could frame relapse prevention in terms of your client's favourite sport. Label relapse as the 'opponent' and continue the metaphor by exploring her 'ball skills' and her experiences of 'fumbling the ball' vs 'scoring a goal'. If the metaphor works, your client is likely to feel inspired to further expand these ideas in a creative way. Another strategy is to tell your client a story about a young person dealing with a difficult situation. Invite her to consider what the young person in the story is thinking or feeling and how these thoughts or feelings will influence what happens next. Ask her what advice she would give to help the young person in the story.

When you are talking with your client about her thoughts, feelings and behaviours, it is sometimes also useful to illustrate concepts in pictures. A simple example is the point rating scale (e.g., '1–5'), often used to measure cravings or other feelings such as anger. A scale is a useful way to show how feelings range in intensity. Invite your client to label the points on the scale, using her own words or colours. Further details about working with strong emotions are given in Chapter 10, *Cognitive Therapy*.

Trouble shooting

Your client might be inclined to test the limits and boundaries you set up. She might sometimes experience intense and changeable emotions and respond with behaviour that seems rebellious, inconsistent or uncooperative. Although such behaviour is challenging, avoid an overly judgemental response as this 'acting out' may simply reflect the adolescent search for self-identity, emotional expression or new social roles. When it occurs, deal with challenging behaviour in a firm, predictable and consistent way. In a calmer moment, you might then invite your client to reflect on the activating events, beliefs and consequences of her behaviour (see p. 131). For example, you and your client could explore the needs and motivations underlying her challenging behaviours and then consider alternative ways to meet these needs.

Inviting and Strengthening Alternative Expectancies

Your client's expectancies about the rewards of using drugs or drink can exert a strong influence and may undermine the effectiveness of refusal skills or other strategies. Assess your client's expectancies by asking what she thinks about when deciding to use or drink. Ask her what effect her substance use has on her moods, thoughts, behaviour, social life and sexual experiences.

You might be wondering why your client is more influenced by the rewarding effects of substance use than its unpleasant effects. Whereas the euphoric effects tend to occur not long after she starts using or drinking, the dysphoric effects might only start once she is heavily intoxicated or after she stops. Her memory of these effects might be influenced by substance-related amnesia or she might not link some longer term effects (e.g., depression) to the substance abuse.

One way of inviting her to explore other expectancies about her substance use is to enhance her awareness of its unpleasant effects. For example, help your client to piece together the whole experience of using or drinking by exploring an episode of use from when she starts using to some time after she has 'come down'. As you explore her experiences, reflect her comments about good things and not-so-good things related to her substance abuse (Chapter 3, *Motivational Interviewing*). Use open-ended questions to elaborate on any potential concerns she might have. For example:

'What's it like to wake up the next morning and not remember what happened?'
'What would you have used that money for, if you hadn't spend it on drugs.'

Summarise your client's responses to these questions, emphasising any statements she makes that show concern about the effects of substance use. You might use a decisional balance sheet as part of your summary (p. 61).

You and your client could also explore what other people have said about her substance abuse. It may be helpful to highlight when the concerns of others coincide with her own concerns. For example, she might disagree with her parent's perception that her drug use makes her uncontrollable but she might agree that their concerns are preventing her desired outcome of moving back home to live.

It is also very useful to help your client to build expectancies that favour alternative behaviours. For example, when you notice your client is coping well with stress, ask her how she is managing to do this without drugs or alcohol. Similarly, as your client develops new interests and recreational activities, spend some time talking about the 'highs' she gets from these new activities.

Enhancing Positive Peer Support

As your client matures, her peer group will become more influential as role models and sources of social acceptance. Her peers are very likely to influence her attitudes and behaviour with respect to drugs and alcohol. This influence is sometimes quite direct through persuasion or by the offering of drugs. Peers can also have an indirect influence through the normalisation of substance abuse in your client's sub-culture. In western cultures, for example, it is often considered normal for adolescents to drink heavily while socialising with friends, particularly once they reach the legal age for drinking alcohol. Your client might believe that all young people drink heavily.

Encourage your client to identify friends and acquaintances who are currently influential in her life and what kinds of influences they provide. You might wish to use a version of the 'social atom' (p. 260) just focusing on your client's friends and acquaintances, past and present. She could use different coloured pencils to circle each person, showing who uses substances, who doesn't use, who might pressure her to use and who might help her to avoid using.

Inquire about your client's feelings of satisfaction and dissatisfaction with particular relationships, as well as any feelings of loneliness. Open-ended questions will help you to explore her ideas and experiences of friendship. For example, you might ask her:

'What is a friend?'
'How do you know someone is your friend?'
'What do friends do for each other?'
'How does that fit with what you know about drug-using mates?'

Clients with more severe substance abuse problems are likely to mainly associate with other users and are less likely to have abstinent friends. Your client may want to make plans for building new friendships or renewing old ones with people who do not abuse substances. Her plans might need to include new avenues for social recreation (see 'Alternative pleasurable activities', below) or strategies for better communication (as outlined in Chapters 8, *Assertiveness Skills* and Chapter 9, *Communication Skills*).

The methods outlined in Chapters 7, *Refusal Skills* and 16, *Relapse Prevention Training* are also relevant when helping your client to deal with direct peer pressure to use drugs or alcohol. Initially, it may be less confrontational to talk about social pressure in general terms. For example, you might invite your client to tell you about her observations of peer pressure:

'When somebody doesn't want to use drugs, how do other people talk them into it?'

You could then brainstorm ideas about how to resist such social pressure. You may wish to draw on resources such as the *Adolescent Relapse Coping Questionnaire* (Myers, 1996) to generate further ideas. Encourage your client to make a detailed plan for refusal and rehearse it with her. It is important to explore how confident she is that she will really use these strategies. Allow time for her to express any doubts (e.g., 'It will make me look stupid', 'I would find it too hard', 'Everyone will think I'm uncool'). It can also be helpful to identify refusal and avoidance skills that she effectively practices in other situations and discuss how these strengths might be used in drug refusal situations. Encourage your client to debrief any real life experiences of social pressure as she encounters them.

Alternative Pleasurable Activities

Help your client to develop drug-free sources of fun, pleasure and social contact. These may be activities that your client gave up because of her substance abuse or new activities that she would like to try. Explore her interests and help her to draw up a list of potentially pleasurable activities, including both social and solitary pursuits. For more ideas on pleasant activities, you might want to consult Tanner and Ball (2000). Use a problem-solving approach to assist your client in planning one or two activities and review her experiences as she tries them out. You might also investigate the range of community-based recreational activities for young people in her local area.

Increasing Participation in Education and Employment

Participation in school or educational institutions has the potential to offer several protective factors by promoting your client's intellectual, vocational and social development and offering a range of recreational opportunities. However, your client's experiences of education might also include risk factors, such as academic failure, social rejection or victimisation. School can also be a significant source of contact with substance-abusing peers.

The substance abuse itself might have interferred with your client's education, because of poor concentration, truancy or conflict with school authorities. You can get some idea of your client's educational participation by asking about her school grades, her level of completed education and her impressions of school. Consider whether there is any need to refer your client for further assessment of her numeracy and literacy skills or for a neuropsychological assessment.

Talk with your client about the pros and cons of resuming her education, either through school or some other avenue. If your client is ready to consider further education, explore a range of goals and options for future action. Depending on your client's age, you might also explore your client's experiences of employment and her hopes for a future vocation. She may need assistance in getting further information about avenues for training and education.

Working in Groups

Most of the strategies outlined above can be used in a group therapy context. Group therapy is not only time and cost efficient but it also has many possible advantages for young people. It offers the opportunity for interactive learning through brain-storms, role-play (Chapter 1, *General Counselling Skills*) and therapeutic games. In a group setting, your clients are likely to:

- Learn more sociable behaviours through peer feedback.
- Share and learn from each other's experiences.
- Generate collective solutions to common problems.
- Try out new skills in a group context.
- Lead or educate others.

Be aware of the potentially less therapeutic peer influences in group settings. Be alert for:

- Subtle social reinforcement of relapse (e.g., joking or telling stories that condone substance abuse).
- Direct social pressure to use drugs or drink.
- Introduction to more harmful behaviours by more experienced or older clients.

You might pre-empt some of these negative attitudes and behaviours by inviting the group to brainstorm some behaviours that would make it hard for people in the group to stay focused on their goals. Encourage the whole group to establish some ground rules or strategies so that they can address these behaviours when they occur (see pp. 10–11).

When planning your group work, give consideration to individual differences. Consider how you will facilitate the group to respond to differences between clients in age, development, learning ability, gender and culture.

A NOTE ON EXTENDED CARE

Since adolescence is a transition phase, your client will experience developmental changes and face new challenges over time. Therefore, any changes that you and your client put into place will need to be monitored and adjusted to ensure that their protective influence is lasting. This can be achieved by having an effective plan for extended care (Chapter 17).

RESOURCES LIST

Baer, J.S. & Peterson, P.L. (2002) Motivational interviewing with adolescents and young adults. In: W.R. Miller & S. Rollnick (eds.), *Motivational Interviewing: Preparing People for Change* (2nd edn) (pp. 320–332). New York: Guilford Press.
—Discusses the relevance and effectiveness of using motivational interviewing with young people.

Brown, S.A. (1993). Drug effect expectancies and addictive behavior change. *Experimental and Clinical Psychopharmacology*, **1**(1-2-3-4), 55–67.
—An excellent paper outlining the research on 'expectancies' and providing clinical guidelines on expectancy-based interventions.

Smith, C.J., Nangle, D.W. & Hansen, D.J. (1993). Social-skills interventions with adolescents: Current issues and procedures. *Behavior Modification*, **17**(3), 314–338.
—Outlines key issues in skills training for young people including group therapy.

Dishion, T.J., McCord, J. & Poulin, F. (1999). When interventions harm: Peer groups and problem behavior. *American Psychologist*, **54**(9), 755–764.
—Explores and presents evidence for iatrogenic (or counter-productive) effects of group therapy with young people.

Dennis, M.L. (2002). Treatment research on adolescent drug and alcohol abuse: Despite progress, many challenges remain. *Connection, A Newsletter Linking the Producers of Drug Abuse Services Research*, pp. 1–2, 7.
Available at: http://www.academyhealth.org
—A brief summary of what we know from treatment research about adolescent substance use.

Dudley, M. & Waters, B. (1991). Adolescent suicide and suicidal behaviour. *Modern Medicine of Australia*, September, 90–95.
—A very good description of the risk factors for adolescent suicide and how to assess them.

Monti, P.M., Kadden, R.M. Rohsenow, D.J., Cooney, N.L. & Abrams, D.B. (2002). *Treating Alcohol Dependence: A Coping Skills Training Guide* (2nd edn) (pp. 70–72). New York: Guilford Press.
—This step-by-step approach to help your client develop a social support network can be adapted for young people.

Myers, M.G. & Brown, S.A. (1996). The Adolescent Relapse Coping Questionnaire: Psychometric validation. *Journal of Studies on Alcohol*, **57**, 40–46.
Available without charge at:
http://eibdata.emcdda.eu.int/Treatment/Needs/itarcq.htm
—The ARCQ is useful to relapse prevention planning, particularly in helping your client to generate strategies to resist social pressure.

Rhodes, J.E. & Jason, L.A. (1990). A social stress model of substance abuse. *Journal of Consulting and Clinical Psychology*, **58**(4), 395–401.
—Presents a model of risk and protective factors influencing the development of adolescent substance abuse.

Schulenberg, J.E. & Maggs, J.L. (2002). A developmental perspective on alcohol use and heavy drinking during adolescence and the transition to young adulthood. *Journal of Studies on Alcohol*, **63**(2) (Supplement 14), 54–70.

—A very comprehensive paper about the impact of risk and protective factors and the main theories of how these factors influence young people's alcohol use.

Tanner, S. & Ball, J. (2000). *Beating the Blues: A Self-help Approach to Overcoming Depression*. Sydney: Doubleday.
—Includes a list of pleasant activities which could be modified to include activities relevant for young people.

Tober, G. (1991) Motivational interviewing with young people. In: W.R. Miller & S. Rollnick (eds), *Motivational Interviewing: Preparing People to Change Addictive Behavior* (pp. 248–259). New York: Guilford Press.
—This chapter of the 1st edition of *Motivational Interviewing* provides an excellent example of some of the principles discussed in our chapter, such as personalised feedback and working with the young person's goals.

Winters, K.C., Latimer, W.W. & Stinchfield, R. (2002). Clinical issues in the assessment of adolescent alcohol and other drug use. *Behaviour Research and Therapy*, **40**, 1443–1456.
—Gives guidelines to many standardised screening and assessment instruments available for use with adolescents.

Inhalants, a booklet available from the National Drug and Alcohol Research Centre, University of New South Wales, Sydney NSW 2052, Australia. Copies can be ordered from Publications.resources at: `http://ndarc.med.unsw.edu.au/ndarc.nsf`.
—Examines the different types of inhalants available and the risks associated with their use.

HANDY LINKS

http://www.adf.org.au/drugstore/pdf/Harm Minimise Fact Sheet. pdg

Mainly focusing on the risks associated with intoxication, this fact sheet shows young people how to plan for safety at parties. Put together by Knox Community Health Service & the Australian Drug Foundation

http://www.freedoms.org.uk

A site for gay men. Click the 'Clued Up' link for information about drug-related harm reduction. Put together by Gay Men's Team, Health Promotion Service of Camden and Islington Community Health Services NHS Trust and the Healthy Gay Living Centre, UK

http://www.reachout.com.au

Fantastic graphics. Gives information on mental health and substance use including harm reduction, stories about young people and interactive activities. Put together by Inspire Foundation, Australia

http://www.somazone.com.au

Information on drugs, alcohol, sexual health and other health issues, stories about young people and an option to submit questions which will then be posted on the site with answers. Put together by young people for young people with help from the Australian Drug Foundation, ADF

http://www.talktofrank.com

Harm reduction advice for all types of drugs with interactive activities and an email/telephone advice service. Put together by an independent government-funded site, UK

http://www.thecoolspot.gov/life.asp

An interactive site with information about how to quit alcohol. Play a role-play game about resisting social pressure to drink. Put together by the Department of Health and Human Services, US

http://www.thesite.org.uk/info/drugs/

For young adults aged 16-25, in a magazine-style format. Features information about the effects of drugs, harm reduction advice, and interactive discussion boards. Put together by YouthNet UK

http://www.wrecked.co.uk

Quizzes about alcohol, aimed at harm reduction. Put together by the National Health Service, UK

20

Dual diagnosis

BASIC GUIDELINES

Many people with drug or alcohol problems also experience mental health problems, such as anxious or depressed mood states, disordered thinking patterns or brain injury. In drug and alcohol treatment practice, 'dual diagnosis' or 'co-morbidity' means that the client has a mental health disorder as well as the diagnosis of substance abuse or dependence. In some cases, there will be multiple diagnoses.

Historically, dual diagnosis has been a thorny issue for both drug and alcohol and mental health services. Both fields have struggled with the questions of which discipline should take primary responsibility for these clients and whether the mental disorder or the substance abuse problems should take priority in treatment. The complex needs and disturbed behaviour of some dual diagnosis clients also place a greater demand on services, skills and resources. As a result of these challenges, such clients can sometimes be shifted back and forth, unable to get adequate treatment for either of their diagnoses (Department of Health UK, 2002).

Dealing with the complex needs of a client with dual diagnosis can indeed seem daunting and, at times, frustrating. You may feel concerned that dealing with dual diagnosis is outside your role and that the workload will take your attention away from other clients. These are legitimate concerns. However, since a high percentage of drug and alcohol clients have a co-occurring mental disorder (35% according to Weaver et al., 2002), working with dual diagnosis clients will be a part of your role. Fortunately, the basic principles and strategies of drug and alcohol treatment are applicable to clients with dual diagnoses.

Although the diagnosis of mental disorders is a specialist activity, it is your responsibility as a drug and alcohol worker to screen for psychiatric symptoms and, where appropriate, to refer your client for mental health assessment and treatment. The presence of dual diagnosis may also influence the treatment process, particularly with respect to your client's risk of relapse.

GOALS

The goals related to working with dual diagnosis include:

- identifying clients who are at risk of mental health problems;
- taking action to help your client stabilise symptoms of mental disorder;
- reducing the impact of mental health symptoms on his risk of relapse;
- ensuring effective coordinated care between drug and alcohol and mental health services; and
- taking measures to secure the safety of your client.

KEY CONCEPTS

PRIMARY DIAGNOSIS

If the substance use precedes and contributes to the development of the mental disorder, the substance use disorder is known as the *primary* diagnosis. For example, the physiological and psycho-social effects of heavy alcohol use can lead to depression. When this is the case, your client's mental health might stabilise after a period of abstinence or reduced consumption.

SECONDARY DIAGNOSIS

If the substance abuse arises as a form of self-medication in response to pre-existing psychiatric symptoms, it is known as the *secondary diagnosis*. To reverse our previous example, depression can also lead to heavy use of alcohol ('drowning your sorrows'). In this case, the mental health disorder will continue after abstinence. It might even get worse for a while until your client, with assistance, develops other ways to deal with his depression.

DUAL PRIMARY DIAGNOSES

If the two diagnoses are not caused by each other but nevertheless co-occur, they are known as *dual primary diagnoses*. Even if the relationship between them is not causal, the two disorders are still likely to interact in a way that affects your client's functioning and influences his risk of relapse.

METHOD

This chapter sets out a series of practical steps for you to follow, illustrated in the flow chart in Figure 3. This flow chart might be useful as a guide when planning coordinated care for your clients. Obviously, procedures will vary across services and for individual clients.

The first step is to screen your client for mental health problems. We recommend that you include mental health screening in your routine assessment process.

If the screening indicates that your client might have a dual diagnosis, the next step is to make a referral to a mental health service or a mental health professional. The mental health service can provide a diagnostic assessment and a recommendation for appropriate treatment. If the diagnostic assessment confirms a dual diagnosis, talk with your client and the mental health service about treatment options.

Once your client is linked up with an appropriate mental health service, liaise with the mental health service provider in order to coordinate and clarify your respective roles. Protect your client's confidentiality by talking with him about the process and getting his consent before exchanging information.

WHEN TO SCREEN

Screening for mental health disorders begins at intake. Screening aims to identify whether your service is suitable for your client; any immediate needs for referral to mental health services; and any need for further monitoring and/or repeated screening.

Gate Keeping

Your service may have 'gate keeping' criteria that exclude clients with certain types of mental disorder—usually psychosis or severe mental disorders. Provided that your service's criteria for exclusion are clearly defined and justifiable, gate keeping is a valid way to ensure that clients are not admitted to services that can't meet their needs (Department of Health UK, 2002). If clients are excluded, make sure you refer them to other services or link them back to the mental health services they have already been using.

Depression and anxiety are not normally reasons for exclusion. Although these two conditions may make your client's treatment more complex, there are well-established ways of working with them. Personality disorders (see pp. 276–278) are more difficult to deal with as they are associated with disruptive and difficult behaviours. Such behaviour can impact on other clients and sometimes require a level of specialist expertise to manage properly. However, be aware that clients who are excluded from your service might also find it hard to access other services. Consider the possibility of admitting such clients and liaising with mental health services to arrange a plan for coordinated care, particularly in times of crises.

Need for Emergency Referral

Assess whether your client has immediate issues such as homelessness, is at risk of harm or has severe and debilitating symptoms that will interfere with his ability to

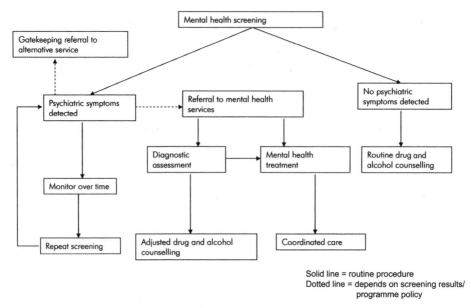

Figure 3: Dual diagnosis management flow chart

participate in treatment. Provide practical assistance and liaise with other services to help alleviate these problems.

Clients with a high risk of suicide should be linked with a mental health treatment service as soon as possible. When working with clients who have a risk of suicide, you should be familiar with your legal obligations to notify authorities and concerned others in order to ensure the safety of your client. You should also immediately inform and consult with your supervisor. Once your client has been linked with mental health services, organise a case consultation so that you can discuss how best to support your client's suicide prevention plan.

Monitoring Your Client's Symptoms

If symptoms are detected that do not require emergency attention, it is useful to monitor their course over a few weeks before deciding whether a referral is needed. Mental health symptoms are often affected by states of intoxication or withdrawal. For example, withdrawal from alcohol or benzodiazepines is often associated with symptoms of anxiety. Panic attacks, depression, sleep disturbance and irritability can also be part of the withdrawal process, depending on the substances your client has been using (see Chapter 2, *Assessment* for further discussion of withdrawal symptoms). By waiting three or four weeks after your client has withdrawn from heavy drinking or drug use, you will get a clearer picture about whether or not the symptoms are part of a pre-existing mental health problem. If the symptoms have persisted, refer your client for a diagnostic assessment.

Your client may experience feelings of loss as a result of giving up alcohol or drug use. He may feel grief, anger, sleeplessness, sadness, inadequacy, fear or anxiety. These normal reactions should be distinguished from serious psychiatric disturbance.

HOW TO SCREEN

Start by asking your client a few background questions about his emotional state. Has he had contact with mental health services or psychiatrists? If so, how often and how recently? Explore other counselling he has received and what services he has found to be helpful. Check whether he is currently on prescribed medication and what circumstances led to the prescription. Table 3, at the end of this chapter, gives brief descriptions of common psychiatric medications.

You may want to include a standardised checklist as a general method of screening for psychological distress. The *Symptom Check List* (SCL-90-R) (Derogatis, 1994) and its briefer version, the *Brief Symptom Inventory* (BSI) assess mental health symptoms that are relevant for people with alcohol and other drug problems. These scales are designed to be administered and interpreted by registered psychologists and they are copyright. The *General Health Questionnaire* (GHQ) (Goldberg & Williams, 1988) is another relevant checklist. Although it is less specific in its assessment of particular disorders than the SCL-90-R, it has the advantage that it can be administered and scored by a wider range of health workers. You can also screen specifically for anxiety, depression and your client's risk of suicide using the *Kessler 10 Symptom Scale* (K10) (Kessler *et al.*, 2002), a brief instrument designed for use by all counsellors regardless of professional backgrounds. Other assessment tools for dual diagnosis are listed in the *Resources List*.

You do not have to be an expert on mental health diagnosis to screen clients or work with mental health services. However, it is important to build an understanding of the most common mental health disorders and their effects on your client's experience and behaviour. Below are some brief descriptions of signs and symptoms that will help you to screen your clients for mental disorders. These descriptions are meant to be introductory rather than exhaustive, and it is advisable for you to expand your knowledge through further reading (*Resources List*).

Mood Disorders

Disorders of mood include dysthymia, major depression and bipolar disorders. Dysthymia is a state of depression occurring more days than not and lasting for two years or more. Major depressive episodes may span shorter periods of time (e.g., 2 weeks) and might occur just once or be recurrent. Symptoms of depression include persistent sadness, feelings of worthlessness, inappropriate guilt or loss of hope. Your client might be preoccupied with negative, fearful, self-defeating and/or suicidal thoughts. He might also feel lethargic, unable to concentrate and disinterested in previously pleasurable activities. There might also be disturbances in his sleep and/or appetite and, to others, it can seem as though he has either slowed down or is unusually agitated.

In bipolar disorder, periods of depression may alternate with abnormally elevated, grandiose and irritable mood states known as 'manic episodes'. During these episodes, your client's behaviour, thoughts and speech may be racing and 'pressured'. He will also find it hard to rest or sleep. He might seem easily distracted and likely to engage in impulsive sexual or financial behaviour with poor judgement. Both bipolar disorder and severe depression can also be associated with psychotic symptoms (see below).

Risk of Suicide

Always assess your client's risk of suicide. Clients who are particularly at risk of suicide include adolescents and those with traumatised backgrounds or signs of depression. Your client's drug and alcohol use may add to any suicide risk because it increases the likelihood of him behaving impulsively and means he may have ready access to a potentially lethal way of harming himself.

Don't ever shy away from asking your client directly about suicidal thoughts and intentions. Dealing openly and honestly with the issue will actually provide some emotional relief for most clients contemplating suicide. Ask your client whether he has thought about suicide recently, how often he has these thoughts, and whether he has a detailed plan for suicide. Ask your client if he has ever tried to kill himself in the past and if so, what happened.

You should make an emergency referral (see above), if your client has a current preoccupation with suicide and any of the following indicators of suicidal risk:

- symptoms of depression;
- past suicide attempts;
- feelings of hopelessness or worthlessness;
- a detailed and feasibly lethal plan;
- recent losses or stress;
- a family history of suicide;
- sudden recent changes in mood or personality (e.g., sudden cheeriness after a period of sadness or depression);
- giving away possessions or other gestures of goodbye; or
- social withdrawal.

We strongly recommend that all drug and alcohol counsellors are competently trained in detecting and managing suicide risk. If you have not yet received such training, talk with your supervisor about training opportunities.

Anxiety Disorders

If your client has an anxiety disorder, he will have anxious thoughts that are unrealistic, exaggerated or so persistent as to interfere with normal functioning.

He is likely to experience physical symptoms including restlessness, sleep difficulties, shortness of breath and heart pounding. Described below are some common anxiety disorders which can occur in isolation or in combination. You can use scales such as the K10 to screen for common anxiety symptoms.

Generalised anxiety disorder (GAD): This disorder involves a general and persistent feeling of anxiety and worry about all kinds of things.

Social phobia: If your client reports extreme anxiety about social interactions, making it hard for him to be in social situations, he may be suffering social phobia. He is likely to have a strong fear about being observed or evaluated by other people. These fears are obviously heightened in situations where he is expected to perform in front of other people (such as public speaking), but he is also likely to experience anxiety about ordinary social situations, such as eating in a restaurant or using a public toilet. His fears may be exacerbated if he has physical reactions of anxiety that others might notice (such as shaking or blushing). To briefly screen for social phobia, ask your client whether he has ever avoided doing things or going places because he was worried about what other people were thinking of him. Briefly explore whether such concerns have had any impact on his work and social relationships . Explore whether he has used alcohol or drugs to help him cope with these social anxieties.

Panic disorder: Panic disorder involves recurrent attacks of intense fear, thoughts of doom, and physical symptoms of anxiety (e.g., racing heart, palpitations, sweating). These are known as 'panic attacks' and are often also experienced by clients who have agoraphobia or post-traumatic stress disorder (PTSD). They can come 'out of the blue' or be triggered by stimulant intoxication or alcohol withdrawal.

Agoraphobia: Fear of going into places where escape might be difficult or where a panic attack might occur in the absence of help is known as agoraphobia. Since agoraphobia causes people to avoid many situations outside the home, you are less likely to see somebody with this disorder presenting voluntarily for drug and alcohol treatment.

Obsessive–compulsive disorder: Obsessions are distressing thoughts or impulses which constantly trouble your client. Compulsions are thoughts or rituals that your client feels driven to repeat in order to reduce high levels of anxiety. For example, a client might fear being contaminated and repeatedly wash his hands to the point of damaging his skin.

PTSD: Your client might have experienced an event or series of traumatic events involving threat to his life, serious injury, harm or extreme terror. This may have resulted in your client suffering traumatic symptoms such as: (a) mental intrusion (e.g., 'flashbacks', bad dreams, or constantly being reminded); (b) avoidance (e.g., feeling numb or dissociated, or avoiding activities, places and people that might evoke memories of the trauma); and (c) hyper-arousal (e.g., exaggerated fears for safety, extreme 'jumpiness', interrupted sleep patterns or outbursts of anger). He might use drugs or alcohol to block the intrusive symptoms or as an attempt to bolster his confidence in situations that he would otherwise avoid.

In your assessment, ask your client whether he has ever experienced a life-threatening or terrifying event, such as sexual or physical assault, military combat, armed robbery or a life-threatening accident. Ask him whether these events had any lasting effects. In your interview, avoid any in-depth exploration of the trauma or the events leading to it. Uncovering traumatic material can intensify symptoms of stress and increase the chances that your client will relapse (Chapter 2, *Assessment*, p. 27). Instead, advise him of the opportunity to arrange a referral to a trauma therapist if he decides to seek help.

Schizophrenia and Other Psychotic Disorders

Schizophrenia and other psychotic disorders may be evident from observing your client's behaviour or his psychiatric history. The term 'psychosis' refers to a group of symptoms including delusions, disordered thinking (jumbled or confused patterns of thought), hallucinations (e.g., hearing voices or strange perceptions) and disorganised behaviour. Your client might express strange beliefs such as the idea that he is being persecuted or is the target of special attention from people who do not know him. He is also likely to lack insight into the pathological nature of these symptoms, leading him to mistake them for reality.

Schizophrenia is an illness with a combination of the above psychotic symptoms (known as 'positive' symptoms), and other 'negative' symptoms. The most common negative symptoms are a flattening of your client's emotional expressions and a lack of response to social interaction. His responses to your questions might be unusually brief and lacking in content. The combination of positive and negative symptoms can disrupt your client's functioning in areas of employment, interpersonal relationships and self-care.

Psychotic disorders related to substance use may occur, such as 'alcoholic hallucinosis' and amphetamine-induced psychosis. Heavy use of cannabis can bring on temporary delusions and hallucinations. In some already vulnerable individuals, cannabis use may also predispose to psychotic symptoms (Hall & Solowij, 1998).

Personality Disorders

Personality disorders are patterns of experience and behaviour that are so at odds with what is accepted in the person's culture that they cause impairment and distress. The disorders influence the person's thinking, emotions, interpersonal functioning and self-control in all kinds of situations.

Personality disorders are hard to change and have the unfortunate reputation of being 'impossible to treat'. In fact, this is not accurate. While working with people who have personality disorders can be demanding, it can also lead to positive outcomes (Modesto-Lowe & Kranzler, 1999). A key principle, when dealing with disruptive or difficult behaviour, is to maintain firm boundaries and a consistent treatment approach. Boundaries are discussed in more detail in Chapter 1, *General Counselling Skills*.

There are a number of different personality disorders and it requires specialised training and experience to distinguish them. However, two types in particular are commonly recognised in the drug and alcohol treatment field: antisocial personality disorder and borderline personality disorder:

Antisocial personality disorder(ASPD): A client with ASPD is likely to show a pervasive disregard for, and violation of, the rights of others. He will also have a history of antisocial behaviours involving deceit, cruelty, law breaking, aggression, impulsiveness and/or irresponsibility. He will tend to deny or rationalise this behaviour and, in the extreme, may be incapable of feeling remorse towards his victims. Although ASPD is diagnosed after the age of 15 years, your client is likely to have had some of these behaviours during his childhood. A childhood pattern of aggression towards people and animals, destruction of property, deceitfulness and theft, and/or other serious rule breaking is known as *Conduct Disorder*.

If you believe that your client has ASPD or Conduct Disorder, be sure to also screen for a history of violence (see p. 283 for guidelines on dealing with aggression). As the disorder is otherwise largely defined by antisocial behaviours rather than the client's psychological state, a high proportion of clients in correctional services (especially drug users) are labelled with this diagnosis. In the case of youthful clients or older clients who started using illicit drugs in early adolescence, it can be hard to distinguish drug-related antisocial behaviour from antisocial personality disorder. Therefore, a diagnosis of ASPD should not necessarily be a barrier to alcohol and drug treatment.

Borderline personality disorder (BPD): The symptoms of BPD are not always easy to screen for, but are likely to become evident in ongoing contact with your client. A client with BPD is likely to have fears of abandonment, intense and changeable mood states, chronic feelings of emptiness and/or an unstable self-image. He is likely to have a pattern of instability in his interpersonal relationships. He might also have trouble with intense feelings of anger that are hard to contain or express in constructive ways. His substance abuse might be one of a few examples of impulsive self-destructive behaviour. He is also at risk of recurrent suicidal behaviour or threats, and acts of self-harm. When stressed, he may become paranoid or show signs of dissociating from reality. People with BPD often have histories of childhood or other traumas.

In your screening, ask your client if he has ever harmed himself or attempted suicide. Self-harm involves deliberate self-inflicted injury as a way of coping with intensely negative emotions. Sometimes clients will self-harm or threaten suicide in order to get a positive response from others. This can lead therapists to label the client as 'manipulative'. However, such labelling (or blaming) is not therapeutic. It is more therapeutic to encourage your client to use counselling to explore the underlying distress that has triggered the behaviour and to find more constructive ways of resolving it.

Although self-harm is not necessarily a suicidal behaviour and some suicidal threats are 'cries for help', people with BPD do have a very high risk of attempting suicide. Treat all threats of suicide seriously. Talk openly with your client about his risk and, if necessary, refer him to a mental health service or professional for the purpose of coordinated care. It is advisable that you consult with your supervisor to ensure that you have good professional support when dealing with potentially harmful client behaviours.

Pathological Gambling

Gambling becomes pathological when it is compulsive and uncontrolled even in the face of negative consequences. Your client might be preoccupied with thoughts about gambling and view it as a way of escaping life's troubles. He might gamble increasing amounts of money, either to win back his losses or to get the desired feeling of excitement. Although he might understate the extent of his problem, there is likely to be evidence of financial loss, criminal activity, loss of employment or problems with his relationships.

Ask your client whether he has ever lost money with gambling, how frequently this has occurred and what impact it had. Check out whether he has ever tried to cut down or stop gambling and whether this was easy or difficult. If your client seems to have a problem with gambling, invite him to consider the options for referral to a gambling counsellor and/or a financial counsellor.

Other Mental Disorders

Other types of psychiatric problems may also frequently co-occur with substance dependence. You might encounter clients who experience sexual dysfunction (see p. 27), attention-deficit/hyperactivity disorder (ADHD) or eating disorders. The latter two disorders are briefly discussed in Chapter 19, *Working with Young People*. One problem that is commonly reported by people with substance problems or mental health disorders is sleep disturbance. See the *Resources List* at the end of this chapter for further information on how to advise clients about overcoming sleep problems.

Cognitive impairment and brain injury can also co-occur with substance dependence, sometimes as a result of substance abuse, and other times as a pre-existing condition. The assessment of cognitive impairment is discussed in more detail in Chapter 2, where you will also find resources for screening neuropsychological function.

WORKING WITH MENTAL HEALTH SERVICES

How to Refer

For a thorough diagnostic assessment or mental health intervention, refer your client to mental health service providers, either within your own service or externally. Diagnostic specialists include psychiatrists, clinical psychologists and neuropsychologists. Some general medical practitioners and psychologists also provide assessments for anxiety and depression. If your client is in crisis and unable to attend an appointment, you might be able to arrange for the local mental health service to come and visit him.

Before making the referral, talk with your client. Ensure that he is fully informed about the reasons for making a referral and has given his consent for the exchange of information. Referrals can be verbal or written. If making a verbal referral, its a good idea to follow up with a written referral so that it is documented. In your referral, avoid making diagnostic judgements. Instead, give clear, brief descriptions of the following client details:

- the goal of the referral;
- the signs and symptoms observed by you or reported by your client;
- the name of any screening instrument used and the results;
- any previous history of treatment for mental disorder;
- your client's most recent drug and alcohol use;
- your client's goals regarding further use of drugs or alcohol; and
- what feedback you wish to receive.

Involuntary admission to psychiatric care can only be considered when the client's behaviour poses a risk of serious harm to self or others. Familiarise yourself with your state's mental health legislation regarding involuntary admission. Involuntary admissions require a formal assessment of risk by psychiatric professionals.

Types of Mental Health Treatment

Mental health treatment may involve psychological therapy, psychiatric medication or a combination of both, depending on the severity of your client's symptoms. You may choose to refer your client to a mental health specialist who provides therapy for a range of disorders. Alternatively, you could refer your client to a specialist programme, such as an anxiety treatment unit. Commonly used psychiatric medications are summarised in Table 3 (p. 288).

Therapy for anxiety will often involve systematic desensitisation, where your client is gradually exposed to thoughts, feelings and situations that trigger his anxiety. At the same time, the therapist will assist your client to develop skills for coping with these triggers, through cognitive therapy and skills training. Systematic desensitisation progresses at your client's own pace so that he gains a sense of confidence in overcoming his anxiety. Benzodiazepines are often prescribed for anxiety disorders. However, since their habit-forming properties make them less appropriate for clients with drug or alcohol problems, other medications (such as SSRI antidepressants, see p. 288) may be the preferred treatment (see Table 3, p. 288).

In therapy for depression, there is usually an emphasis on cognitive therapy, to assist your client to challenge his negative thoughts and to develop more positive ways of thinking. The therapist will also help your client to address situations in his life that are contributing to his distress and to resume activities that increase his experiences of pleasure and satisfaction. Medication for depression or anxiety is most appropriate when clients have moderate to severe symptoms.

Therapy for psychosis or bipolar disorder will often involve medication. Psychological therapy may also be useful in helping your client to recognise that his symptoms stem from his illness and in supporting him to keep taking his medication. The treatment might also involve behaviour therapy to assist your client with living skills, social skills and self-care.

You might also refer clients with personality disorders for mental health treatment, either at times of crisis or for ongoing therapy. For example, clients with BPD may be assisted in therapy to cope more effectively with intense emotional states, self-harming impulses, difficult social relationships and other challenging situations. Since many clients with BPD have a history of trauma, therapy might also focus on alleviating the symptoms of PTSD or depression. Clients with personality disorders also sometimes benefit from treatment with psychiatric medications to stabilise symptoms of irritability, depression or anxiety.

Residential care in a psychiatric unit may be an option for some clients, particularly if there is a high risk of suicide. Nowadays, most psychiatric units do not have long-term admissions. Your client is likely to be admitted during a time of crisis and remain in the unit until his symptoms are stabilised.

Hospital-based mental health teams may be available to provide case management and crisis interventions for outpatients with complex problems. Other services, such as brain injury services, may also offer outpatient case management programmes focusing on accommodation, financial matters, living skills and memory training. See Chapter 18 for further details about the case management approach.

Trouble shooting

Your client might express reservations about taking psychiatric medication as sometimes the side effects can be very unpleasant. Side effects typically subside over a few weeks in the case of antidepressants, but are likely to be an ongoing concern for people taking antipsychotics. Your client might also be concerned that prescribed medication compromises his goal to become drug-free. Allow time for your client to voice his worries and ambivalence. You and your client could review the potential benefits of taking the prescribed medication and weigh these against his experience of the effects of alcohol or illicit drugs. Also, you could encourage him to discuss any problems with side effects with his prescribing doctor. More guidance about helping clients to stay on medication is given in Chapter 14, *Pharmacotherapies*.

Make sure that your client is also aware of how his substance use might impact on the effects of the prescribed medication. Depending on the chemical mix, alcohol or other drugs might reduce the effectiveness of his prescribed drug, cause a toxic reaction, exacerbate unpleasant side effects or reduce his motivation to take his medication.

Coordinated Care

You will need a plan to ensure that your client will receive continuity of care over time and across services. Your plan should include consultation with the other services and, ideally, case conferences between service providers, clients and concerned others. Case conferences are discussed in detail in Chapter 18, *Case Management*. Always discuss with your client what information will be shared with the other service providers and obtain his consent for release of information. In cases where the client's needs are very complex and require linkage to a range of different services, it is advisable to have a case manager to coordinate your client's care (Chapter 18, *Case Management*).

Mental health services and drug and alcohol services have evolved separately and are not typically set up to deal with both diagnoses. If services are poorly coordinated, there may be redundant, uninformed, contradictory or incomplete approaches to assessment and treatment. Coordination between services should therefore involve more than just client-related contact. By building friendly networks, you might be able to achieve some of the following outcomes:

- clear admission criteria and referral networks for excluded clients;
- opportunities for telephone consultation between services;
- shared information about screening and assessment procedures to promote consistency and reduce repetition;
- exchange of information about respective treatment philosophies, goals and procedures;
- resolution of any barriers to coordinated care;
- communication of information about clinical issues; and
- a sense of goodwill between the services.

Trouble shooting

If your client has a high level of alcohol or drug dependence but refuses to undergo detoxification, the mental health service provider may see this as a barrier to referral. It raises the tricky dilemma about which problem should be treated first—the substance abuse or the mental health disorder? When your client is a pre-contemplater about his substance abuse, it might be better to start with the mental health intervention. Stabilising his mental health symptoms is a viable first step in engaging your client in substance abuse treatment (Carey, Purnine, Maisto, Carey & Simons, 2000). Obviously, the mental health service provider may have reservations about taking this approach. However, a plan for continuity of care in which your client agrees to revisit the drug and alcohol services after a period of mental health treatment could make this proposal more acceptable.

Sometimes, there may also be differences of opinion between the services about the best approach to take. The mental health service, for example, might insist that your client has a goal of abstinence in order to avoid the impact of substances on his symptoms and on the effectiveness of the prescribed medication. However, this might lead your client to be more guarded in his disclosure of current substance use.

The mental health team may also see their duty of care as proactive in ensuring that your client's symptoms are controlled through such procedures as home visits, pressure to resume treatment, increased dosage of medication, hospital admissions and, in the more extreme cases, calling the police to enforce an admission. This approach would tend to clash with the more collaborative approach we have outlined in this book, where our emphasis is on responding to your client's stage of readiness and encouraging him to take personal control over his treatment choices (see harm reduction goals, pp. 65–66). While these differences in philosophy can cause problems, they also provide a rationale for greater communication between the services.

ADJUSTED DRUG AND ALCOHOL COUNSELLING

A key principle when working with clients who have dual diagnoses is your ability to engage actively and meaningfully with your client (Saunders & Robinson, 2002). Your skills in empathic counselling (Chapter 1) and motivational interviewing (Chapter 3) are especially useful. Avoid confrontational approaches which can aggravate the symptoms of mental disorder. Be aware of your own attitudes about mental illness and any personal responses to your client's symptoms. To avoid over-labelling your client, use his language to describe the symptoms.

Drug or alcohol use may be valued by your client as a way of getting relief from psychological distress. If this is so, it is worth exploring whether he has adequate or appropriate medication to manage his symptoms. It may also be helpful to weigh the short-term relief of substance abuse against the long-term effects on his symptoms. Even when he is getting adequate medication, he may still choose to self-medicate. The pressure to self-medicate warrants a flexible approach to goal setting, guided by the principles of harm reduction. Consider, for example, how you would respond if your client decides to continue using cannabis but agrees to quit using cocaine and alcohol. If you choose not to work with these goals, there is a risk that your client will leave treatment. You might, alternatively, work out a plan based on your client's goals. Abstinence from cocaine and alcohol will enable your client to participate more effectively in interventions aimed at stabilising his mental disorder. Success in these interventions might, in turn, increase his readiness to change his cannabis use.

For most clients with either depression or anxiety, the main adjustments to your counselling will be a greater emphasis on the techniques of Chapters 10, *Cognitive Therapy* and 16, *Relapse Prevention Training*. For example, it is very important for your client to monitor the impact of his anxious or depressive self-talk on cravings, lapses or relapses. This impact can be reduced by helping your client to challenge negative ways of thinking and develop alternative coping responses. It is also important to consider past experiences of abstinence or freedom from symptoms, so that he can identify coping strategies that he already has. This helps to build his self-efficacy for change. Solution-focused questions can be helpful in eliciting past solutions (pp. 248–249).

Cognitive therapy is less effective with people who have cognitive impairment or psychosis. For these clients, it is better to focus on goal setting, problem solving, skills training and relapse prevention. Break the therapy up into simple steps, present information repeatedly, and use a variety of different materials that are both auditory and visual. Your client might benefit from using a notebook to assist his memory. Further discussion of treatment for clients with cognitive impairment is given in Chapter 21, *Putting It All Together*.

Dual diagnosis can isolate people and lead to social stigma. You and your client might explore the options of building social networks (p. 230), reuniting with concerned others (Chapter 13) or linking with other community networks. Be prepared to support him when he encounters setbacks, such as rejection by others or comparing himself unfavourably to people who do not struggle with additional mental health problems. Social support is sometimes available by participation in:

- self-help groups run by and for people with mental disorders (see the internet sites listed in the *Resources List*);
- living skills or drop-in centres providing social support and therapy;
- family support groups where concerned others can get information and support; and/or
- referral to a case management service (Chapter 18, *Case Management*).

Working with Difficult Behaviour

In your contact with clients who have a dual diagnosis you will sometimes encounter behaviour that makes your work difficult. This is particularly likely with clients who have bipolar disorder, brain injury, psychosis or personality disorders. You may have to deal with aggressive behaviour, repeated relapse and missed appointments, boundary testing and emotional splitting.

Aggressive behaviour: When working with people who have antisocial, aggressive or intimidating behaviour, be explicit about the rules of conduct for engaging with your service. Set clear guidelines for your client about any consequences of breaking these rules. If your client acts aggressively, keep a safe distance, avoid arguing or any escalation of conflict and use calm, non-aggressive body language.

Repeated relapse and missed appointments: Due to the disorganising effects of some mental disorders, your clients might need active support to maintain their engagement in treatment. Treatment progress might be interrupted by missed appointments, relapse and disturbed behaviour. You should actively follow up your client when he misses an appointment. You could also explore these behaviours in a way that links the client back to his achievements and restores a sense of continuity and progress. For example, you might ask 'What blocked you from using your skills?'

Boundary testing: It can be tempting to loosen the boundaries of your professional role in response to the emotional demands of your client. However, by maintaining good boundaries, you establish a reassuring consistency in the therapeutic relationship. Make a firm agreement about session times and durations, and keep to it. Draw up a list of support people for your client to talk with at times when you are not there. In this way, you will encourage your client to develop self-management strategies that he can apply between sessions. See Chapter 1, *General Counselling Skills* for further discussion of boundaries.

Emotional splitting: Sometimes an emotionally disturbed client will express hostile feelings about another service provider. You might be idealised as his favourite worker whereas the other worker is cast in a bad light. This is referred to in the literature as 'splitting'. Although your client's attitude may seem flattering, it is important to avoid openly criticising the other service provider. Such a response could contribute to a situation where workers become divided against each other and the client never has the opportunity to resolve his angry feelings. Take a neutral position and encourage your client to talk directly with the worker concerned. Obviously, if you have any indication that your client has been abused by another service provider, advise him about the proper avenues for complaint.

RESOURCES LIST

SCREENING AND DIAGNOSTIC INSTRUMENTS

Beck, A.T. & Steer, R.A. (1993). *Manual for the Beck Anxiety Inventory*. San Antonio, TX: The Psychological Corporation.
—Provides a validated measure of anxiety which is quick to administer. The inventory is available for purchase by qualified psychologists.

Beck, A.T., Steer, R.A., & Brown, G.K. (1996). *Manual for the Beck Depression Inventory-II*. San Antonio, TX: The Psychological Corporation.
—Provides a validated measure of depression which is quick to administer. The inventory is available for purchase by qualified psychologists.

Dawe, S., Loxton, N.J., Hides, L., Kavanagh, D.J. & Mattick, R.P. (2002). *Review of Diagnostic Screening Instruments for Alcohol and Other Drug Use and other Psychiatric Disorders* (2nd edn). Canberra: Australian Government Department of Health and Ageing.
Available at: http://www.health.gov.au/pubhlth/publicat/document/mono48.pdf
—A comprehensive resource providing detailed descriptions of screening and assessment tools for substance abuse and psychiatric disorders.

Derogatis, L.R. (1994) *Symptom Checklist-90-Revised: Administration, Scoring and Procedures Manual* (3rd edn). Minneapolis, MN: National Computer Systems, Inc.
—Screens for somatic, cognitive and phobic anxieties, obsessive–compulsive symptoms, interpersonal sensitivity, depression, hostility, paranoia and psychotic symptoms. The SCL-90 or its briefer version, the Brief Symptom Inventory (BSI), are available for purchase by qualified psychologists from Pearson Assessments at:
www.pearsonassessments.com

Goldberg, D. & Williams, P. (1988). *A User's Guide to the General Health Questionnaire.* Windsor, UK: NFER-NELSON.
—Screens for somatic symptoms, depression, anxiety and social functioning.

Kessler, R.C., Andrews, G., Colpe, L.J., Hiripi, E., Mroczek, D.K., Normand, S.-L.T., Walters, E.E. & Zaslavsky, A.M. (2002) Short screening scales to monitor population prevalences and trends in non-specific psychological distress. *Psychological Medicine,* **32**(6), 959–976.
—The K10 is a short instrument to measure anxiety, depression and risk of suicide. To access a free copy with scoring, go to www.crufad.com and click on Clinician Support and search for K10.

Lezak, M.D. (1995) *Neuropsychological Assessment* (3rd edn). New York: Oxford University Press.
—This classic text describes tests that can be used in screening for alcohol-related brain damage. More details are given in the *Resources List* of Chapter 2, *Assessment*.

Task Force on DSM-IV, American Psychiatric Association (2000) *Diagnostic and Statistical Manual of Mental Disorders DSM-IV-TR* (4th edn) (Text Revision). Washington, DC: American Psychiatric Association.
—Standardised guidelines for diagnostic assessment.

OTHER RESOURCES

Along with the readings below, you might wish to have a look at *Pillar to Post*, a video that features people with a dual diagnosis and a range of experts who describe the difficulties faced both by services and service users. Available from Mind in Croydon, 26 Pampisford Road, Purley, Surrey CR8 2NE or at:
www.mindincroydon.org.uk

Carey, K.B., Purnine, D.M., Maisto, S.A., Carey, M.P. & Simons, J.S. (2000). Treating substance abuse in the context of severe and persistent mental illness: Clinician's perspectives. *Journal of Substance Abuse Treatment,* **19**, 189–198.
—Provides recommendations for the treatment of clients with dual diagnoses, based on a focus group study with experienced clinicians.

Dawe, S. & McKetin, R. (2004). The psychiatric comorbidity of psychostimulant use. In: A. Baker, N.K. Lee & L. Jenner (eds), *Models of Intervention and Care for Psychostimulant Users* (2nd edn); National Drug Strategy Monograph Series Number 51) (pp. 154–168). Canberra: Australian Government Department of Health and Ageing.
—Discusses the relationship between the use of psychostimulants and psychiatric problems such as psychosis, including practical guidelines for screening.

Department of Health (2002) *Mental Health Policy: Implementation Guide. Dual Diagnosis: Good Practice Guide.* London: Department of Health.
Available from Department of Health Publications, PO Box 777, London SE1 6XH or at: www.dh.gov.uk
—A guide to drug and alcohol services on how to plan policies and procedures for working with dual diagnosis.

Edwards, G.E., Marshall, E.J. & Cook, C.C.H. (2003) *The Treatment of Drinking Problems: A Guide for the Helping Professions* (4th edn). Cambridge, UK: Cambridge University Press.
—A very readable and practical book with chapters on 'Drinking problems as cause of neuropsychiatric disorders' (pp. 94–109) and 'Alcohol problems and psychiatric co-morbidity' (pp. 110–132).

Hall, W. & Solowij, N. (1998) Adverse effects of cannabis. *The Lancet*, **352**, 1611–1616.
—Reviews the research on the health effects of cannabis, including mental health effects.

Kavanagh, D.J., Greenaway, L., Jenner, L., Saunders, J.B., White, A., Sorban, J. & Hamilton, G. (2000). Contrasting views and experiences of health professionals on the management of comorbid substance misuse and mental disorders. *Australian and New Zealand Journal of Psychiatry*, **34**, 279–289.
—Presents the results of a survey of professionals who worked with clients who had dual diagnoses and highlights commonly encountered problems and practical solutions.

Lishman, W.A. (1997). *Organic Psychiatry: The Psychological Consequences of Cerebral Disorder* (3rd edn). Oxford: Blackwell Scientific Publications.
—An excellent summary of cerebral dysfunction and clinical signs and symptoms thereof.

Modesto-Lowe, V. & Kranzler, H.R. (1999) Diagnosis and treatment of alcohol-dependent patients with comorbid psychiatric disorders. *Alcohol Health & Research World*, **23**, 144–149.
—A brief and informative guide to dual diagnosis and the types of treatments available.

Petrakis, I.L., Gonzalez, G., Rosenheck, R. & Krystal, J. (2002). Comorbidity of alcoholism and psychiatric disorders: An overview. *Alcohol Research and Health*, **26**(2), 81–89.
—A guide to treatment approaches for dual diagnosis, this article is particularly informative about prescribed medications. The article appears in an issue dedicated to dual diagnosis and its treatment (*Alcohol Research and Health*, **26**(2), 2002).

Preston, J.D., O'Neal, J.H. & Talaga, M.C. (2002). *Handbook of Clinical Psychopharmacology for Therapists*. Oakland, CA: New Harbinger Publications, Inc.
—A professionals' guide to psychiatric medications with explanations of how they work and how they are used to treat mental disorders.

Saunders, B. & Robinson, S. (2002). Co-occurring mental health and drug dependency disorders: work-force development challenges for the AOD field. *Drug and Alcohol Review*, **21**, 231–237.
—Examines the areas of dual diagnosis that need to be addressed by drug and alcohol counsellors.

Holmwood, C. (2003). *Comorbidity of Mental Disorders and Substance Use: A Brief Guide for the Primary Care Clinician*. Canberra: Commonwealth Department of Health and Aged Care.
—A very informative reference on how alcohol and drugs, and their combinations, affect mental health symptoms. The paper also gives guidelines to managing dual diagnosis, mainly from the perspective of primary health care providers. Available from Drug Strategy Branch, MDP 27, Commonwealth Department of Health and Ageing, GPO Box 9848, Canberra ACT 2601 or at:
http://www.health.gov.au/pubhlth/strateg/comorbidity

Linehan, M.M. (1993) *Cognitive-Behavioral Treatment of Borderline Personality Disorder*. New York: Guilford Press.

—An advanced text on the theory and methods of treatment for borderline personality disorder.

Rappee, R.M. (1998). Overcoming Shyness and Social Phobia: A Step-by-step Guide. Lanham, MD: Rowman & Littlefield.
—One example of the many evidence-based self-help books now available for depression and anxiety.

Tanner, S. & Ball, J. (2000). *Beating the Blues: A Self-help Approach to Overcoming Depression*. Sydney: Doubleday.
—Another self-help book aimed at overcoming depression.

Weaver, T., Hickman, M., Rutter, D., Ward, J., Stimson, G. & Renton, A. (2001). The prevalence and management of co-morbid substance misuse and mental illness: Results of a screening survey in substance misuse and mental health treatment populations. *Drug and Alcohol Review*, **20**, 407–416.
—Summarises the prevalence and types of dual diagnosis found among clients of drug and alcohol and mental health services.

Winkelman, J. & others (2001). *Improving Sleep: A Guide to Getting a Good Night's Rest*. Boston: Harvard Health Publications.
Available for purchase at:
http://www.health.harvard.edu/hhp/publication/view.do?name=IS
—A useful reference for therapist or client explaining the physiology of sleeping, identifying habits that promote or interfere with sleep, describing sleep disorders and discussing the use of therapies and medications to overcome sleep disorders. It also contains self-help material.

USEFUL INTERNET SITES

http://www.doubletroubleinrecovery.org/
—A 12-step fellowship for people with dual diagnosis.

http://www.growint.org.au
—A community mental health movement based on the 12-step approach.

http://www.healthinsite.gov.au/topics/Suicide_Prevention
—Provides resources and guidelines to help you screen for suicidal risk and implement prevention strategies, including youth-related resources.

Table 3: Commonly used psychiatric medications

Type of medication	Characteristics of treatment
Antidepressant re-uptake inhibitors are: *Selective Serotonin (SSRIs)* (e.g., Prozac (fluoxetine), Celapram (citalopram), Zoloft (sertraline), Luvox (fluvoxamine), Aropax, Paxtine (paroxetine)); *Serotonin and Norepinephrine (SNRIs)* (e.g., Effexor (venlafaxine), Remeron (mirtazapine)); and *Norepinephrine (NRIs)* (e.g., Edronax (reboxetine)).	Neurotransmitters such as serotonin and/or norepinephrine stay active for a longer time, causing a lift in mood and a reduction in depressive rumination. The prescription is usually for at least six months, followed by a gradual dosage reduction. Initial side-effects subside after a few weeks. Low risk of harm or overdose.
Other antidepressants include: *Tricyclic antidepressants (TCAs)* (e.g., Trofranil, Melipramine (imipramine)); and *Monoamine oxidase inhibitors (MOAIs)* (e.g., Nardil (phenelzine), Parnate (tranylcypromine)).	Not usually considered useful for drug and alcohol clients due to risks of harmful overdose, potential for abuse or toxic interactions with alcohol and other drugs.
Lithium carbonate is used to treat bipolar disorder.	Has mood stabilising effects. To avoid toxicity, the blood concentration of lithium is regularly monitored and the dosage adjusted over time.
Benzodiazepines are prescribed for anxiety and sleep disorders (e.g., Valium (diazepam), Xanax (alprazolam), Temaze or Normison (temazepam), and Stillnox (zolpidem)).	Used to depress the over-arousal of the central nervous system. Prescription is short-term with gradual withdrawal over several weeks. Risky for drug and alcohol clients due to potential for abuse, dependence and intoxication.
Other anxiolytics are *antidepressants* with anxiolytic effects (e.g., Zoloft) or Buspar (buspirone)).	Used as non-addictive alternatives to benzodiazepines. Both can take a few weeks to feel the full benefit.
Neuroleptic antipsychotics include Largactil (chlorpromazine), Mellaril (thioridazine), Serenace (haloperidol), or Stelazine (trifluoperazine).	Psychotic symptoms are reduced by blocking dopamine. May cause neurological side effects, such as abnormal movements. Treatment is long-term with regular monitoring and adjustment.
Atypical antipsychotics include Clozaril (clozapine), Risperdal (risperidone), Zyprexa (olanzapine).	Reduce both positive and negative symptoms of schizophrenia. Fewer neurological side effects but there are other uncomfortable side effects.

Note: The drugs are listed first by their brand name and then, in brackets, by their generic name.

V

Designing an Intervention

21

Putting It All Together

RECOMMENDED USE

As we have stressed throughout this book, the techniques that you include in your treatment plan should be chosen through *negotiation* with your client, and should reflect her unique *needs* and *preferences*. We also recommend that you frame any intervention within an empathic counselling style that supports your client's commitment to, and confidence in, change.

Recent research has not generally supported the popular idea that certain clients respond best to certain treatment interventions (Project MATCH Research Group, 1997). Nevertheless, it makes good clinical sense to tailor the intensity and components of the treatment to meet your client's treatment needs. This tailored approach to treatment should be based on careful screening and assessment (Chapters 2, *Assessment* and 5, *Brief and Early Interventions*) and might be influenced by your client's severity of dependence, motivation, previous treatment experiences, family and social network, skills deficits and strengths, and the presence of any complex problems such as dual diagnosis or an unstable lifestyle.

The length and intensity of your intervention will also be shaped to some extent by other factors such as the setting in which you work and, realistically, the time you have available. Below we outline a 'therapeutic skeleton' to use when planning your intervention (adapted from Shand, Gates, Fawcett & Mattick, 2003).

PRIMARY HEALTH CARE INTERVENTIONS

Primary health care settings provide an opportunity for brief interventions to address risky consumption or other alcohol- or drug-related risk taking. Depending on how much time you have available, such interventions would include:

- *For settings where there is no time available*: Provide pamphlets that set out guidelines for low-risk alcohol consumption (e.g., 'sensible drinking' guidelines) and information about reducing drug-related harm.

- *For settings where you have up to 30 minutes available*: Carry out screening and detection, give simple advice, provide information about how to reduce risk and offer a follow-up appointment.
- *For settings where you have more time available*: Carry out further assessment of the extent of your client's alcohol- or drug-related problems, give personalised feedback of negative health effects, discuss methods of limit setting and general self-management procedures, provide self-help material (if possible) and offer a follow-up appointment.

OUTPATIENT INTERVENTIONS

For some clients in drug and alcohol treatment settings, a relatively brief intervention over a few sessions (e.g., one to five sessions) will be all that is required, and might often be all that is wanted. These clients in general will probably have shorter histories of use, stable backgrounds and low levels of dependence and drug- or alcohol-related problems. With such a client your treatment should incorporate all of the following:

- An assessment of dependence and, if there is time, of other areas of her functioning, especially mental health status.
- Motivational interviewing if she appears to be unsure or ambivalent about changing her drug use or drinking behaviour.
- The negative health effects of excessive consumption described in a fashion that personalises them for your client.
- Introduction to methods of limit setting and self-management procedures.
- If resources allow, a self-help manual or pamphlet should be made available.
- Provision of information about harm reduction strategies if your client reports risk-taking behaviour or substance-related harm.
- The identification of high-risk situations and a brief explanation of relapse prevention strategies, including the identification of specific strategies to minimise the risk of relapse, such as drink- and drug refusal skills.
- The firm offer and arrangement of a follow-up visit and extended care sessions.

If your client has a more complicated drug or alcohol use history, you will need to consider a longer intervention. This form of intervention might occur for up to 15 or more sessions, and no precise guide can (or should) be made about the length of intervention required. However, your intervention should include the following:

- A comprehensive assessment covering readiness to change, pattern of drinking or drug use, level of dependence and need for supervised detoxification.
- Arrangements for detoxification, if your client is likely to experience physical withdrawal symptoms.
- Motivational interviewing and personalised feedback of substance-related health

effects, particularly if your client is unsure or ambivalent about changing her drug use or drinking behaviour.

- Referral for diagnostic assessment and/or intervention if mental health problems are detected.
- The development of a client-centred therapeutic relationship aimed to help your client explore methods of changing her substance use.
- The use of selected training in skills-based approaches according to your client's needs, to enhance problem solving, promote assertiveness, build communication skills, challenge negative thinking, develop emotional tolerance and promote relaxation.
- Training in methods of limit setting and self-management procedures, where appropriate.
- Provision of information about harm reduction strategies if your client reports risk-taking behaviour or substance-related harm.
- Pharmacotherapy if your client is medically stable and willing to comply with medication, supported by psychosocial therapy to help her stay on the medication.
- Relapse prevention training including specific strategies to minimise the risk of relapse, such as drink and drug refusal skills.
- Appropriate assistance and referral to help your client remedy other lifestyle problems, and in cases of complex needs, this should be coordinated through case management.
- A systematic plan for enhancing your client's social network including, where appropriate, an introduction to self-help groups (such as Alcoholics Anonymous), involvement of concerned others, social skills training or linking your client up with her local community and social groups.
- Scheduled extended care or booster sessions as an integral part of the intervention.

INPATIENT/RESIDENTIAL INTERVENTIONS

The guidelines set out for outpatient interventions are equally applicable to residential/inpatient settings. However, residential treatment is a less cost-effective option if your client could benefit equally well from a less intensive, less expensive intervention (Shand et al., 2003). There is, for example, no evidence that a residential treatment programme is needed for clients with mild to moderate levels of dependence and indeed some clients with low involvement in substance abuse may fare worse in a residential setting. However, residential care is beneficial if your client has a high level of physical dependence and one or more of the following:

- Need for detoxification to be monitored in a medical environment.
- Living in a home environment that is extremely conducive to drinking or drug use.
- Repeated relapses after non-residential care, with resulting alcohol- or drug-related harms.
- Serious mental health disorders that may affect her progress.

- Moderate to severe impaired cognitive functioning (such as alcohol-related brain injury) that might affect her capacity to cope with, or even attend a non-residential programme.
- Homelessness or living in a socially unstable environment.
- Severe deterioration or malnourishment.

For some of these circumstances, the residential care combines drug and alcohol rehabilitation with shelter and welfare services. If such circumstances are relevant for your client, these welfare services are necessary prerequisites to treatment. Ideally, such services should be coordinated through case management and continued after discharge. If your client has moderate to severe cognitive impairment, residential care offers the benefits of a daily structured intervention, particularly when it includes a clear daily routine, participation in memory training using diaries and other memory aids, practice in non-drinking social activities and repeated, simple messages about how to reduce drinking (Yohman, Schaeffer & Parson, 1988).

When an inpatient/residential intervention is desirable, your treatment should incorporate all of the procedures described in the section above with one further addition. In order to maintain abstinence or moderation, your client must be able to effectively apply skills learnt in treatment to her everyday environment. The opportunity to practise at home is one of the main advantages of outpatient treatment. Therefore, in the case of an inpatient or residential treatment programme, it is strongly recommended that there be a gradual 're-entry phase' following treatment, where you assist your client to return to her usual environment without relapsing.

CHOOSING THE RIGHT INTERVENTION

The process of choosing an intervention to meet your client's needs can be represented as a series of steps guided by careful screening and assessment. For example, the steps involved in screening and brief intervention are illustrated in Figure 4. Figure 5 shows the steps involved in planning more intensive interventions.

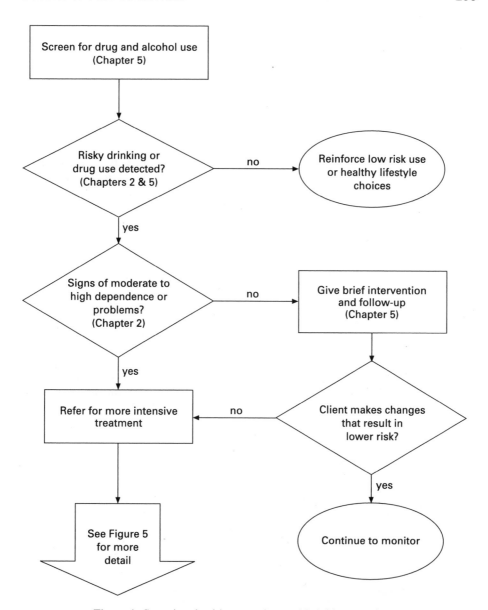

Figure 4: Steps involved in screening and brief intervention

Source: Shand, Gates, Fawcett & Mattick (2003). © Commonwealth of Australia. Adapted by permission of the Australian Government Department of Health and Ageing.

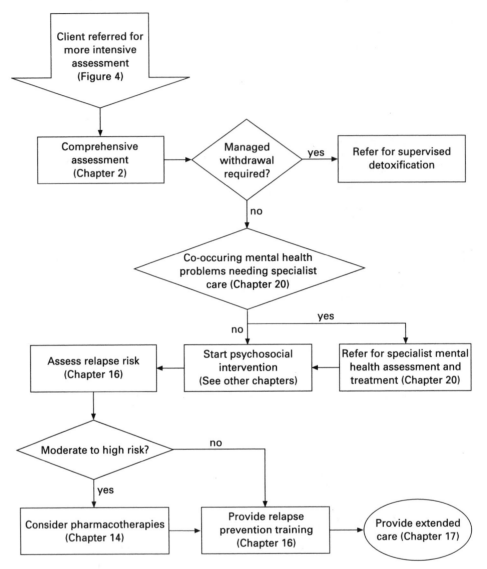

Figure 5: Steps involved in planning more intensive interventions

Source: Shand, Gates, Fawcett & Mattick (2003). © Commonwealth of Australia. Adapted by permission of the Australian Government Department of Health and Ageing.

RESOURCES LIST

The resources below provide examples of how the strategies described in this book have been combined in treatment programmes offered to clients with abstinence or moderation goals.

De Leon, G., Hawke, J., Jainchill, N., & Melnick, G. (2000). Therapeutic communities. Enhancing retention in treatment using 'Senior Professor' staff. *Journal of Substance Abuse Treatment*, **19**(4), 375–382.
—This article provides evidence that information sessions from experienced staff will help new clients to stay in residential treatment.

Gowing, L., Cooke, R., Biven, A. & Watts, D. (2002). *Towards Better Practice in Therapeutic Communities*. Bangalow, NSW: Australasian Therapeutic Communities Association.
Available from: `http://www.nada.org.au/downloads/TBPTC.pdf`
—Part of an ongoing project, this publication describes the key components of the therapeutic community (TC) approach and will be of interest if you are working in a TC setting.

McCrady, B.S., Dean, L., Dubreuill, E. & Swanson, S. (1985). The problem drinkers' project: A programmatic application of social-learning-based treatment. In: G.A. Marlatt & J. Gordon (eds), *Relapse Prevention: Maintenance Strategies in the Treatment of Addictive Behaviors* (pp. 417–471). New York: Guilford Press.
—Details a skills-training, cognitive-behavioural programme for clients with an abstinence goal.

Monti, P.M., Rohsenow, D.J., Colby, S.M. & Abrams, D.B. (1995). Coping and social skills training. In: R.K. Hester, & W.R. Miller (eds), *Handbook of Alcoholism Treatment Approaches: Effective Alternatives* (2nd edn) (pp. 221–241). Boston: Allyn and Bacon.
—Provides a detailed skills-training programme based on relapse-prevention principles.

Monti, P.M., Kadden, R.M. Rohsenow, D.J., Cooney, N.L. & Abrams, D.B. (2002). *Treating Alcohol Dependence: A Coping Skills Training Guide* (2nd edn). New York: Guilford Press.
—A session-by-session skills-based programme.

Shand, F., Gates, J., Fawcett, J. & Mattick, R.P. (2003). *Guidelines for the Treatment of Alcohol Problems* (pp. 169–176). Canberra: Australian Government Department of Health and Ageing.
—Describes how to design interventions for alcohol problems, depending on the severity and complexity of the presenting problems and the type of treatment setting.

Project MATCH Research Group (1997). Matching alcoholism treatments to client heterogeneity: Project MATCH post-treatment drinking outcomes. *Journal of Studies in Alcohol*, **58**(1), 7–29.
—The results from a major study testing whether clients can be effectively matched to motivational interviewing, cognitive-behavioural therapy or 12-step facilitation therapy on the basis of pre-treatment characteristics. Although the results did not generally support matching, they did indicate that the three types of manual-based intervention produce good outcomes. We have given references for these treatment manuals in the *Resources Lists* of the relevant chapters in our book.

Sanchez-Craig, M. (1996) *A Therapist's Manual for Secondary Prevention of Alcohol Problems*. Toronto: Addiction Research Foundation.
Available from the Centre for Addiction and Mental Health, 33 Russell Street, Toronto, ON, Canada M5S 2S1 or at:
`http://www.camh.net/publications/substance_use_addiction.html`
—This therapist's manual details treatment guidelines for clients with moderation or abstinence goals.

Wanigaratne, S., Wallace, W., Pullin, J., Keaney, F. & Farmern, R. (1990). *Relapse Prevention for Addictive Behaviours: A Manual for Therapists*. Oxford: Blackwell Scientific Publications.
—Provides a comprehensive session-by-session description of a treatment programme based on relapse prevention principles.

Yohman, J., Schaeffer, K., & Parson, O. (1988). Cognitive training in alcoholic men. *Journal of Consulting & Clinical Psychology*, **56**, 67–72.
—Describes treatment for clients with cognitive impairment.

22

Vignettes

In this chapter, we present five examples of how the techniques included in this book might be used to provide effective treatment for people with different drug-related problems. These vignettes are broadly based on the problems presented to therapists by real clients, but are not intended to represent actual people and, therefore, any such resemblance is purely coincidental.

CASE 1. SEVERE ALCOHOL DEPENDENCE WITH PSYCHIATRIC CONDITION: A CASE OF AN UNHAPPY DRINKER

ASSESSMENT

Background information: Roy was 39 years old. He had completed a high school education and then worked in the public service. At the time of seeking treatment, he was supervising a staff of three. He was also living in a de facto relationship with his partner, Tracey. Roy was referred by his local doctor because of physical signs of excessive drinking. He had memory problems and was facing the potential loss of his job.

Pattern and context of drinking: Roy began drinking at the age of 15 years and started regular consumption at 16. At that time, he lived in the country with his family and it was considered acceptable for him to drink alcohol. By the time he was 20 years old, he was drinking four to six large beers regularly through the week and on Friday and Saturday nights.

In his mid-twenties, he travelled to the city and joined the public service. In the company of male friends, he began to binge, drinking up to 15 or more large beers. Gradually, this pattern of heavier drinking became regular and he started drinking on the next day to recover from the effects of his hangover. He noticed that if he did not drink, he would feel shaky, sweaty and generally apprehensive after a heavy night. Over the years, as his drinking increased, Roy became tolerant to the effects of alcohol. Except on those occasions when he drank in a binge pattern, he rarely appeared to be drunk.

Roy would usually have a drink quite early in the morning. He would often get up before his partner, as she was a shift worker, and he was therefore able to drink without her knowledge. Whether or not he was able to consume alcohol at home, he would typically have had at least two beers by 10.00 a.m. in a tavern near his work. He would slip out on the pretext of buying some morning tea and consume the beers quite quickly, returning within 10 or 15 minutes. At lunchtime, he would usually consume four large beers which, he felt, helped him to get through the afternoon until his next opportunity to drink. After work, he would return to the tavern and have another five large beers. He then typically purchased some beer to take home with him. At home, in the evenings, it would not be unusual for him to drink another five beers before falling asleep on the couch. He followed this pattern throughout the working week and increased his consumption on the weekends. On some days, he would consume up to two dozen cans of beer, although this was a rare occurrence.

Level of dependence: If Roy did not have alcohol through the morning and day, he would experience tremor in his hands and body, excessive perspiration, nausea and a sense of apprehension and panic. The number of years over which he had experienced these symptoms, his morning drinking and his tolerance to large amounts of alcohol indicated that he was severely alcohol-dependent. This was confirmed by his SADQ-C score of 38. He was also showing signs of psychological dependence, including loss of control or inability to abstain, failed attempts to cut-down or stop and a persistent desire to drink.

Family background and social support: Roy's partner, Tracey, also drank heavily although not to the extent that he did. She occasionally objected to Roy's very excessive drinking, saying that she did not like to see him getting drunk. In the past few years, Roy had also developed an additional problem. He had become impotent as a consequence of his excessive alcohol consumption. Tracey wished to start a family and, while Roy was not against that idea, he had lost interest in sexual activity.

Vocational and financial background: Memory problems and lapses were causing Roy difficulties at work. He had recently been reprimanded on several occasions by his boss because he had failed to carry out routine tasks that were part of his duties. He thought that the escalation in his drinking had occurred approximately 10 years ago, when he realised that he was falling behind his peers at work in terms of promotion.

Alcohol-related health problems: Roy's increasing problems at home and work had prompted the visit to his family doctor. Roy's doctor noticed physical signs which immediately raised her concerns that Roy was drinking excessively. She noticed his dilated facial capillaries, bloodshot eyes, and a coating on his tongue. Roy also complained of diarrhoea and sleeping difficulties. These, taken together with Roy's complaints of memory problems and impotence, were interpreted by the doctor as evidence of excessive alcohol consumption. She gave Roy a medical examination and had some routine liver enzyme levels analysed. While Roy's liver was not enlarged, there were elevated levels of a number of liver enzymes, confirming the doctor's hunch that Roy was drinking excessively. On a follow-up visit, she discussed these issues with Roy and organised a referral to a drug and alcohol team.

Psychiatric disturbance: As well as having a drinking problem, Roy was also experiencing depression. In response to his feelings of failure resulting from his lack of promotion at work, Roy gradually became unhappy and lost self-esteem. Increasingly, he found that he was feeling sad and depressed on more days than not. This depression was not particularly severe but it was constant and had been present for approximately 8 years by the time that he spoke with his family doctor. Associated with his loss of self-esteem was a sense of hopelessness about the future. He also had difficulties with a lack of concentration, a symptom typically associated with depression but which, in Roy's case, was mainly due to heavy alcohol consumption.

Stage of change: Roy's concerns about the effects of his drinking on his work and family life increased his motivation to try to change his drinking patterns. At the time that he was assessed by the drug and alcohol team, he was at a stage of preparation for change. His therapist used motivational interviewing procedures to help Roy to describe his own concerns about his excessive drinking and to identify the benefits he thought he would gain from changing this behaviour.

GOAL SETTING

Roy and his therapist discussed the implications of his severe alcohol dependence, memory problems and abnormal liver function tests, and agreed that moderated drinking was not appropriate. They chose abstinence as the most appropriate treatment goal. Given that Roy had experienced marked withdrawal symptoms on those occasions when he went without alcohol, options for detoxification were discussed.

Since he had a good relationship with his family doctor, Roy could have been detoxified at home with supervision and the assistance of Tracey. However, Roy preferred the option of a residential detoxification facility where he could be monitored while withdrawing from alcohol.

STRATEGIES FOR ACTION

Detoxification: Roy received inpatient detoxification with sedative medication from the benzodiazepine group. While staying at the detoxification facility, he was introduced to AA. Roy had never been interested in religion and found that the ideas about surrendering power and the spiritual nature of the organisation led him to be uninterested in continuing with AA. He all but refused to participate in the meetings. He was discharged five days after admission, having successfully detoxified from alcohol.

Pharmacotherapy: Roy discussed with his therapist and his doctor the possibility of taking medication as a way of assisting him to return to work and reduce his cravings in the initial period after his detoxification. Roy was worried that he might forget to take the frequent doses required for acomprosate so his doctor suggested that he try naltrexone. Although Roy's liver enzymes were elevated by alcohol, his liver was not enlarged. His physician advised that, provided he stayed abstinent from alcohol and his liver function was monitored over time, naltrexone could be used safely. He experienced some headaches and nausea when he first started taking the medication. After talking about these side effects with his therapist, he found that he could alleviate the worst symptoms by planning regular meals and taking his medication with breakfast. He also used relaxation therapy to help with the headaches. These side effects diminished with time.

Couples therapy: Roy's partner Tracey wanted to come to therapy sessions with Roy so the therapist offered them couples therapy. They had four couples therapy meetings over three weeks, after which Roy came for individual therapy. The four couples therapy sessions focused on reducing conflict, improving the couple's communication and planning shared rewarding activities. Given their different working shifts, this meant planning ahead for weekends and other free days or evenings. Tracey was pleased that Roy had decided to attempt to change his drinking habits because she had been concerned for some time about his excessive alcohol consumption. She also saw this as a good opportunity for her to curb her own drinking. She talked with Roy and the therapist about how she might encourage Roy to continue his treatment without taking responsibility for policing his drinking or medication.

Skills training: After consultation with his therapist, Roy agreed that in addition to taking naltrexone, he would also benefit from learning skills to assist him to maintain abstinence in the long term. These skills were presented with an empathic counselling style, which conveyed a positive regard for Roy and an enthusiasm for the possibility that he would be able to make lasting changes to his lifestyle. In total, this outpatient intervention involved 12 sessions.

Roy was trained in drink refusal skills because many of his friends drank and it seemed unlikely that he would completely abandon his social network. He role-played and practised saying 'no' to offers of alcohol or pressure from others to drink. He also renewed contact with some of his old friends from whom he had been estranged because of his drinking.

Roy participated in relapse prevention training aimed at maintaining his abstinence. In particular, the therapist helped him to develop strategies to address high-risk situations such as disappointments and stress at work, and social situations that involved alcohol. Even after Roy had made a commitment to abstinence, the therapist continued to reinforce and help Roy to clarify his reasons for deciding to change.

Referral for dysthymia: Two weeks after detoxification, Roy's mood had lifted somewhat and his self-esteem improved as a result of his initial achievement of abstinence. However, continuing symptoms of dysthymia were considered to be sufficiently severe to warrant a referral for mental health assessment. Roy was referred to a clinical psychologist on the team. The psychologist concluded that Roy's symptoms were consistent with a diagnosis of dysthymia, a chronic but not severe depressive disorder. Roy continued to see the psychologist for cognitive therapy aimed at dealing with his dysthymia. Antidepressant medication was not considered necessary.

Extended care: Roy was successful in achieving and maintaining abstinence for a period of six months while he was taking naltrexone. Thereafter, he maintained further abstinence for six or seven months. During that time, his relationship with Tracey improved markedly as did his self-esteem and general mood. He was successfully treated for his chronic dysthymia. Although he remained somewhat disappointed in himself because of his failure to progress in his occupation, he was able to put this in perspective. He was generally happier in his work and home life, and found that he could perform his work duties more efficiently.

Roy lapsed on two occasions, the first of which was approximately 12 months after the initial detoxification. The second of these episodes resulted from Roy's decision that he had earned a drink to reward himself for his period of abstinence! He continued to drink heavily for a three-week period before Tracey contacted his therapist. Eventually Roy returned briefly to treatment, encouraged by the supportive and non-judgemental attitude of his therapist. Further motivational interviewing and relapse prevention training helped Roy to renew his commitment to abstain from alcohol.

CASE 2. MILD ALCOHOL DEPENDENCE: A CASE OF AN UNASSERTIVE PROBLEM DRINKER

ASSESSMENT

Background information: Kate was 32 years old. She had married Richard at 23 and had three children in the next four years. She had been working as a bank teller for several years after having her third child. Kate sought help after calling a telephone information service which referred her to a drug and alcohol agency.

Pattern and context of drinking: Kate had been drinking regularly since she was approximately 22 years old. Prior to that, she would only drink occasionally at parties and on special occasions. At age 22, Kate met Richard and they enjoyed going to restaurants and nightclubs. Approximately once or twice a week, Kate consumed between a half and a full bottle of wine. She did not often become drunk although she sometimes felt 'merry'.

After the birth of her third child, Kate's drinking gradually increased and she and Richard shared alcohol at most meals. Kate began having a glass of wine while she was cooking the dinner, before Richard arrived home. With time, she began to consume up to three or four glasses of wine regularly in the late afternoons. Occasionally, when feeling particularly stressed about the difficulties in her marital relationship, she would continue drinking with dinner and into the evening. On these occasions, she would consume up to 10 standard drinks. By the time she sought help, she was drinking this amount approximately three or four times a week.

Another situation in which Kate drank heavily was when she went out with friends. She had an active social life with co-workers and friends from her school days. On these social occasions, she typically drank at least a bottle of wine.

Level of dependence: Kate had developed some tolerance to the effects of alcohol but this was not particularly marked. She could easily go without drinking for a number of days without experiencing shaking, sweating or other withdrawal symptoms. She had tried to cut down on several occasions but found it particularly difficult when she was faced with stressful family situations or when socialising with moderate to heavy drinkers. Her SADQ-C score was 8, indicating a low level of alcohol dependence.

Family background and social support: Family difficulties that particularly exacerbated Kate's drinking related to her husband, Richard, and her mother-in-law, Patricia. Richard, whose job frequently required him to work late hours, tended to neglect home duties, leaving them to Kate, despite her own full-time job responsibilities. She was expected to arrive home early to care for the children, prepare the meals and clean the house.

Kate found it difficult to talk to Richard about the stresses that she was experiencing because of the obligations she felt both at work and at home. These stresses were complicated by Patricia's regular visits during which she tended to make snide remarks about Kate's drinking and about the children's behaviour. Patricia would imply that the children were not being sufficiently looked after or disciplined. Although Kate did not agree with her mother-in-law's view, she found it difficult to say so. Instead, she would drink more than usual after Patricia left in the late afternoon and before Richard arrived home. On these occasions, she would often drink three or four glasses of wine in quick succession in an attempt to cope with her frustration and pent-up anger.

Alcohol-related health problems: A medical examination showed that Kate had no alcohol-related physical problems. She had no psychiatric or marked psychological problems evident in her thinking or behaviour. She was, however, experiencing considerable difficulties because of a lack of assertiveness and an inability to communicate her needs and feelings to her husband and mother-in-law.

Stage of change: Kate appeared unsure about whether she had a problem and whether she needed to change her level of drinking. Because of her ambivalence, Kate's therapist employed a motivational interviewing approach. They talked about the good things and the less good things about her drinking, and the concerns that Kate had about her drinking and its effects on her family and children.

GOAL SETTING

As a result of the motivational interviewing, Kate decided that she wanted to change but was not interested in the goal of abstinence because she did not believe that she was an 'alcoholic'. She also said that there were social situations where she would like to be able to drink alcohol. She added that she enjoyed drinking but recognised that excessive drinking was causing problems. In light of her preference for moderation and her low alcohol dependence, Kate and her therapist opted for the goal of moderated drinking.

STRATEGIES FOR ACTION

Behavioural self-management: Kate and her therapist agreed to an initial two-week period of abstinence from alcohol which would allow her to focus on improving various aspects of her life. After this period of abstinence, Kate and her therapist set an upper limit on her drinking of two standard drinks per day with a maximum of four standard drinks. She was provided with a self-help manual and day diary sheets. Kate learned how to monitor her alcohol consumption, to set limits on her drinking, and to practise strategies that helped her to slow down her drinking and keep within her set limit.

Other skills training: Kate role-played and practised using drink refusal skills to deal with social pressure to drink excessively, especially when in the company of heavy-drinking friends.

Kate was taught how to use 'I-statements' to express her feelings openly and honestly to her husband, Richard. She began to feel more confident about making her needs known but found that she and Richard continued to disagree about household responsibilities.

Kate was also given assertiveness training to help her to deal more effectively with her mother-in-law's criticism. She role-played appropriate ways of telling Patricia that she did not like the comments about her children and that she disagreed with Patricia's views on discipline. Kate found this difficult initially and needed to practise. With time, she was able to assert herself in a way that prompted Patricia to stop saying things that caused her to become angry and frustrated.

Both during the period of abstinence and throughout the behavioural self-management training, Kate learnt to identify high-risk situations and devise strategies to cope with them based on the skills she was learning.

Referral for marital therapy: Marital difficulties continued because although Kate's husband was sympathetic about some of her needs, he still felt that the housework was her responsibility and could not see the potential impact of the difficulties in their relationship on Kate's drinking. There was not enough cooperation between Kate and Richard to involve him in a couples therapy approach to changing the drinking. Instead, Kate's therapist encouraged them to seek specialist marital counselling.

Extended care: Kate succeeded in moderating her drinking for approximately three months until a particularly upsetting visit from her mother-in-law. On that occasion, she did not use assertiveness skills but decided to drink excessively and consumed approximately 10 glasses of wine. After she had contacted her therapist, it was decided that regular, monthly sessions for extended care would be useful. If difficult situations arose, Kate telephoned her therapist to discuss them.

Gradually the need for such regular contact decreased as Kate became more confident about identifying and coping with high-risk situations. Four years later,

Kate had maintained her moderated drinking. She drank only on social occasions or with Richard at dinner and generally maintained her two standard drinks limit. On some occasions, she exceeded this limit but rarely drank beyond four standard drinks.

CASE 3. OPIOID DEPENDENCE: A CASE OF A SHY HEROIN USER

ASSESSMENT

Background information: John was a 24-year-old heroin user and occasional dealer. He came to the attention of health authorities after he overdosed on benzodiazepines and alcohol during a period when he could not obtain heroin. He was taken to the emergency section of a major hospital by friends after he had been unconscious for a number of hours. He was observed in hospital overnight and a drug and alcohol therapist attended his bedside. John agreed to a further assessment session.

Pattern and context of drug use: From the age of 12, John had used cannabis and alcohol. After leaving home at the age of 14 and travelling to the city, he began drinking regularly and smoking cannabis quite frequently. He also became involved in petty criminal activities including forgery and shoplifting. By the time he was 16 he had developed a regular heroin habit. He was not dependent at that time but was using three or four times a week, depending on how much money he had. Increasingly he spent time working as a male prostitute to support his developing heroin dependence. By the time he was 18, however, he had ceased this work and he became a courier for a drug dealer. The dealer provided John with heroin, as did some of John's customers as part payment of the delivery. Gradually, with time, he built up a habit of using approximately 1 gram of heroin a day. Usually he would inject before breakfast, around lunch time, in the early evening and late in the evening. By the time he was in his mid-20s he was using approximately 3 or 4 grams of heroin a day.

Level of dependence: John was quite tolerant to the effects of this amount of heroin. If he missed out on injecting for some reason he would soon develop opioid withdrawal symptoms. Even if he had not missed out on injecting, upon wakening before he injected he would find that his body ached and felt stiff, he would experience stomach cramps, notice his heart pounding, have hot flushes, feel miserable and depressed, would be tense and panicky and would have a strong craving to use opioids. He would typically inject within half an hour of waking up. These symptoms indicated that John was severely opioid-dependent.

Family background and social support: John's mother and father were both heavy drinkers and there had been frequent conflict in the family home. John was subject to frequent physical beatings from his father, who was always verbally abusive to him and to his mother. John ran away in his teenage years on four occasions before leaving home at the age of 14. When he left home he travelled to the city and lived in derelict housing with other adolescents slightly older than himself. At the time of assessment, John had been living in a de facto relationship with Jenny for the past six months. They shared rental accommodation with other heroin users in an inner city suburb.

Vocational and financial background: John had never had a full-time stable job and was currently receiving unemployment benefits. He had left school at the age of 14 years and not completed any certificate. Prior to that time he was often truant from school. He had left home soon after he finished with school. Apart from dealing, John had not recently been involved in other criminal activities and had no outstanding warrants or charges.

Drug-related health problems: At the time of his admission to hospital, John was malnourished. Blood tests showed that he was both Hepatitis B and C positive. John did not share needles with his friends or flatmates but did share with his partner, who generally used after him. He did not use condoms with Jenny but used them with occasional casual partners.

Psychiatric disturbance: John had been unhappy since he was quite young. He was also quite shy and reticent in social situations and tended to avoid them whenever he could, especially when he was 'straight'. When he did mix in a group he would try to use alcohol or more typically opioids to assist him to feel comfortable. If he did have to interact socially he would frequently feel tense and panicky, his heart would race and he would sweat, blush and feel very self-conscious. He was extremely concerned that people could see his anxiety and he worried about what they would think of him. These symptoms indicated that John was socially phobic.

Stage of change: John had been frightened by his recent overdose and was therefore prepared to contemplate changing his drug use. He was tired of the drug-using lifestyle but was not confident of his ability to resist the temptation to use. John's therapist used motivational interviewing strategies to help him to explore this ambivalence and John decided that he was prepared to attempt to change his drug use behaviour.

GOAL SETTING

John and his therapist discussed his options. The alternative of a drug-free intervention, either on an outpatient basis or in a residential therapeutic community, did not appeal to John. He recognised that his high tolerance and dependence on opioids made ongoing injecting likely, which would continue to expose him and others to the risk of infections and diseases. Therefore, he agreed, albeit initially somewhat reluctantly, to try a methadone maintenance programme.

STRATEGIES FOR ACTION

Methadone maintenance: Within four weeks, John had been stabilised and was taking 80 mg of methadone per day. At that time his social fears and phobias became more pronounced and he self-medicated with alcohol and benzodiazepines. He drank so much alcohol on one occasion that he was readmitted to hospital for emergency care.

Referral for treatment of social phobia: After a period of two months of daily attendance at the methadone maintenance clinic, a therapist decided that John required some psychiatric referral because of his social fear. He was referred to a psychiatrist who began treating him for social phobia. However, John did not attend a number of appointments and eventually dropped out of treatment.

Skills training: Over the next two years, methadone maintenance staff repeatedly detected that John was continuing to use illicit drugs on a regular basis. They referred him to a drug and alcohol therapist for further assistance. Problem-solving skills were considered essential to provide John with ways of coping with daily problems and challenges to his commitment to abstain from illicit drugs.

John's therapist helped to him to develop strategies for coping with social pressure to continue using drugs. Problem-solving and drug refusal skills were embedded in a relapse prevention approach where the need for lifestyle changes was emphasised. Gradually, John developed enough confidence to move out of his shared accommodation and was successful in obtaining work.

Extended care: With the change in environment, John developed a new relationship with a non-using partner. Having stabilised his lifestyle, John was again referred for treatment of his social phobia, this time with more successful results. He tried to withdraw from methadone completely on two occasions with the agreement of his prescribing doctor and dispensing staff. He reduced his methadone dose to 10 mg on each occasion. However, he could not cease completely, and remained on methadone after a 5-year period. John received regular counselling from the methadone maintenance programme staff.

CASE 4. POLYDRUG USE WITH ASSOCIATED PSYCHOLOGICAL DISORDERS: A CASE OF A SELF-MEDICATING SURVIVOR

ASSESSMENT

Background information: Dee was 23 years old. She had received two previous drug and alcohol treatments and had been detoxified once before. After a recent overdose, which was almost fatal, Dee returned to a residential drug and alcohol treatment agency to seek help.

Pattern and context of drug use: Since the age of 15, Dee had been using a variety of drugs including benzodiazepines, alcohol and, occasionally, heroin. She favoured benzodiazepines when she could get them. If she was unable to get benzodiazepine prescriptions from her frequent visits to various doctors, she would purchase them on the street. She had overdosed on seven separate occasions. Two of these overdoses resulted in serious medical emergencies in which she almost died from respiratory depression. At the time that she was assessed Dee was using benzodiazepines, alcohol and antidepressants, and she occasionally injected heroin. Her *OTI* results indicated that she was using an average of 25 tablets a day.

Level of dependence: Dee was moderately dependent on sedative medications. She had a tolerance to the effects of benzodiazepines and had experienced some withdrawal symptoms on those occasions when she had gone without these medications for a prolonged period.

Family background and social support: Dee described her early family life as chaotic and unhappy. Her family was regularly attended by welfare agency staff because of the neglect her mother showed towards Dee and her siblings. She had never known her father, and her mother was often absent. Over the years, Dee's mother had a number of different male partners, some of whom lived with the family for periods of time. At the time of this presentation to treatment, Dee was sharing accommodation with a female acquaintance but felt quite lonely and isolated.

Vocational and financial background: Dee had been unemployed since leaving school at the age of 15. She had no job skills. She was receiving social security benefits and occasionally did sex work to supplement her income.

Drug-related health problems: Dee was malnourished and had poor physical health. Blood tests showed that she was Hepatitis B positive. Her frequent overdoses indicated that continued drug use posed a serious threat to Dee's life. Dee was referred for neuropsychological assessment to assess whether the overdoses had resulted in cognitive dysfunction. The neuropsychological report did not indicate any significant cognitive impairment.

Psychiatric disturbance: Dee appeared to be both anxious and depressed and she also had very low self-esteem. This, coupled with her family background and her multiple suicide attempts, alerted the therapist to the possibility that she might have post-traumatic stress disorder as a result of being abused in the past. Using an empathic approach, the therapist asked about unwanted sexual contact and physical abuse. Dee disclosed that from the age of 11 until she left home at 15 years, she had been physically and sexually abused by two of her mother's partners. The therapist believed that these episodes had markedly contributed to Dee's mental health issues and drug use.

Stage of change: Dee felt quite desperate and was ready to take action to change her drug use. Unfortunately, her repeated experiences of relapse had led her to believe that she lacked the 'will power' to successfully maintain change. The therapist therefore focused on ways of building Dee's confidence in her own ability to make and sustain the change.

GOAL SETTING

Dee and her therapist discussed her previous attempts at quitting drug use. Their discussion highlighted some helpful aspects of past treatments and identified periods when she had successfully abstained from using pills. The therapist reframed past 'failures' as indicating Dee's need to learn additional skills to help her to confront challenges to abstinence.

STRATEGIES FOR ACTION

Detoxification: Dee and her therapist agreed that medicated detoxification was necessary to protect her from the risk of fits or seizures, resulting from her dependence on benzodiazepines.

Referral for child sexual abuse counselling: As a result of the supportive reaction of the therapist to Dee's disclosure, she was prepared to accept her therapist's referral for concurrent counselling to address issues related to the abuse. Her therapist felt that concurrent counselling was necessary because abstinence from drugs might have triggered flashbacks related to the abuse, which in turn might precipitate relapse.

Inpatient group programmes: Dee and her therapist agreed that cognitive strategies would be particularly useful because Dee tended to use drugs in a solitary fashion as a means of coping with negative thoughts and feelings. A group teaching cognitive therapy and relapse prevention skills was provided as part of the inpatient programme. Dee also agreed to participate in a relaxation training group during her period of inpatient therapy. The group taught progressive muscle and meditative procedures and required a commitment to regular practice. For Dee, relapse prevention training underscored her new awareness that preventing relapse required skills and planning as well as a strong resolve to abstain.

As part of the inpatient programme, Dee was encouraged to try NA. She found the social support and encouragement invaluable and used some of the individual therapy sessions to focus on the 12 steps. She made new friends at the meetings and continued her involvement with NA after leaving the residential programme.

Extended care: The residential programme had a firm commitment to assist clients in coping with the stress of returning to their home environment. In Dee's case, the agency arranged temporary accommodation at a half-way house run by the drug and alcohol team. She stayed in this half-way house for two months during which she was assisted in obtaining entry into a job-training programme.

Dee relapsed to drug use repeatedly over the next two years. However, she stayed in touch with the extended care programme of the drug and alcohol agency, her sexual abuse counsellor and the NA meetings and she therefore received further help through these difficult periods.

CASE 5: POLYDRUG USE AND LEGAL PROBLEMS: A CASE OF A YOUNG PERSON ON PROBATION

ASSESSMENT

Background information: Sixteen-year-old Alex was referred to a drug and alcohol outpatient counselling programme as part of his conditions of probation. He was referred by Fiona, his Juvenile Justice Officer.

Pattern and context of drug use: Alex started smoking cannabis at age 13 with friends from school. He began to truant and spent his time at a friend's house, smoking pot. His use of the drug increased to whenever he could get it. At the time of assessment, he was smoking pot daily. Alex's friends were mostly drug users and he was recently encouraged to try heroin. After trying it a couple of times, he enjoyed the feeling of oblivion and had since used three more times. He injected the drug with friends and although he did not share needles, he did share other injecting equipment. He had also experimented with other drugs (e.g., pills, speed) and got drunk about once a week.

Level of dependence: Alex has never tried to change his cannabis use. He did not have any signs of dependence on alcohol or heroin but he showed some signs of dependence on cannabis, such as an increased tolerance, difficulty sleeping without cannabis and having given up other interests in favour of using cannabis.

Family background and social support: Alex entered the country as a refugee with his mother, father and younger brother when he was five years old. His father had witnessed much extreme violence in his community and the family was forced to leave their home. Alex's father did not believe that the children witnessed or remembered any violent events.

Alex had stolen from his parents several times and was aggressive when confronted about this. He and his father had several major arguments about his behaviour and his poor school performance. After major arguments, Alex would 'take off' and stay with friends for days at a time.

Alex's parents were both very concerned about their son but at a loss about how to help him. The father and son had a tense relationship but Alex also admired his father and wanted his acceptance.

Educational background: Alex experienced learning difficulties throughout his school years. He felt unable to discuss these problems with his parents, especially because his father expected him to get high grades. Although Alex said he hated school, he did enjoy playing school sport and his father confirmed that he was a talented sportsman. Alex was recently suspended from school for increasingly aggressive behaviour and truancy.

Legal problems: Alex had a history of minor shoplifting offences. Recently, however, he was charged with breaking and entering and stealing electrical goods, which he later sold. When the police searched his room they found a small amount of heroin. He was arrested and subsequently placed on a 12-month probation supervised by Juvenile Justice with conditions to attend drug and alcohol counselling.

Peers: Since early adolescence, Alex has associated with an increasingly delinquent group of peers. Fiona and Alex's father both mentioned that he was 'easily led'.

Stage of change: Alex was not happy about being coerced to see a drug and alcohol counsellor. At the start of therapy, he was particularly adamant that he would continue to use drugs and alcohol and that there was nothing wrong with it.

GOAL SETTING

Since Alex was a pre-contemplator, the drug and alcohol counsellor decided to offer him a brief intervention. The initial goals were for Alex to attend five weekly sessions and not to be stoned when he came to sessions. Alex attended four of the five scheduled sessions and appeared to be unaffected by drugs for all sessions except the second session. On that occasion, the therapist asked him whether he was stoned and he admitted that he'd had a joint before coming. The therapist postponed the session and arranged to meet with him later on that week.

STRATEGIES FOR ACTION

Case plan: Fiona, Alex's Juvenile Justice Officer, initially organised a case conference with Alex, his parents, and the drug and alcohol counsellor. Since Alex had a good rapport with Fiona, it was agreed that she would take the role of case manager. Over time, she explored a range of options with Alex and his family. The case plan included:

- A referral for Alex to have a psycho-educational assessment. This resulted in a diagnosis of dyslexia. Fiona discussed the implications of this diagnosis with Alex and his parents and arranged a subsequent referral for him to have appropriate literacy training.
- Linking Alex with the local community sports team and asking Alex's father to go with him.
- Exploring the possibility of an apprenticeship for Alex.
- A referral for Alex's family to a refugee trauma counselling service, initially to provide supportive counselling but also with a view to improving Alex's relationship with his father.

Although Alex's family attended sessions at the trauma counselling service, Alex refused to accompany them. He also dropped out of the literacy training. However, he enjoyed joining the local community sports team and regularly trained and participated in sporting matches. His father went with him and watched while he played.

Family meetings: Fiona met with Alex and his parents for three meetings. It was stressed that these meetings were not to take the place of family therapy but to provide an opportunity for (a) working out ways for Alex's parents to help him build a new lifestyle and (b) negotiating an agreement about Alex's behaviour at home. An early outcome was that Alex's father agreed to provide transport for Alex to attend sports training and matches. The family also discussed how they could resolve conflict by using non-aggressive communication skills.

Motivational interviewing: As Alex was a pre-contemplator with respect to his drug use, the drug and alcohol counsellor initially focused on his legal problems and his desire for a better relationship with his father. After identifying some goals to improve these areas of his life, Alex was more willing to explore how his drug use might influence his ability to achieve these goals.

Harm reduction advice: The drug and alcohol counsellor also offered Alex brief advice regarding the effects of cannabis and information about how to cut down his consumption, education about the risks of shared injecting equipment and information about safer injecting practices.

Peer network: Fiona and the drug and alcohol counsellor worked in a coordinated way to help Alex build a more supportive and positive peer network. With Fiona, he drew a map of his friends and acquaintances and talked about the meaning of friendship. After some time considering the impact of offending on his lifestyle and freedom, Alex identified some former friends who were still friendly towards him but whom he had cut off because of his drug use and criminal activities. He made detailed plans to re-establish these friendships, particularly with one of his former friends who shared his interest in sport.

The drug and alcohol counsellor talked with Alex about drug refusal skills. Although Alex stated that he could turn down drugs any time he wanted to, he did agree to explore some different scenarios about peer pressure to use drugs. The counsellor read several short stories about young people and after each story, they discussed what type of refusal would be effective for that scenario.

Relapse prevention: Although Alex initially did not intend to change his drug use, the drug and alcohol counsellor nevertheless monitored his drug use and explored the situations in which he was most likely to use. Her non-judgemental style of counselling made it more comfortable for Alex to explore and distinguish between situations 'when pot is more attractive' and 'when he could take it or leave it'.

Case management: Alex came close to breaching his court order on two occasions. At these times, he missed sessions with Fiona without notice. On the first occasion, Fiona contacted him by telephone and reminded him that he would have to return to the court if he did not abide by his probation conditions. He resumed sessions with Fiona. However, some months later, after an angry argument with his father, he left home for two nights and missed his sessions again. There were also signs that he had increased his drug use and had been injecting and his parents were concerned that he was spending more time with his drug-using friends. Fiona arranged a case conference and renegotiated the case plan to help Alex fulfill his probation conditions.

The agreement included:

- Alex to resume drug and alcohol counselling for two more sessions.
- Alex to attend two family sessions with the refugee counselling service to help talk through and perhaps resolve the conflict with his father.
- Alex's father accepted that his son might not return to school and agreed to work with Fiona in trying to find an apprenticeship for Alex.

Extended care: As it turned out, Alex attended three more drug and alcohol counselling sessions! In his last two sessions, he explored the impact of cannabis use on his fitness. As he had increased his training with the local sports team, he had become more sensitive to the detrimental impact of smoking pot on his breathing capacity and energy levels. The drug and alcohol counsellor used motivational interviewing to elicit, explore and elaborate Alex's concerns about his fitness.

Alex attended two sessions of family therapy at the refugee trauma counselling service. The sessions focused on his relationship with his father. They resolved some differences during the therapy and developed a plan to further negotiate disagreements by using communication skills that would reduce their conflict.

Alex's involvement in sport led to the offer of an apprenticeship from the father of one of Alex's team mates. He completed his conditions of probation and at the end of the 12-month period, he was still involved in sport and had started his apprenticeship. Although he continued to get drunk on weekends, he stopped using heroin and cut down his cannabis use to once every three or four months on social occasions.

Index

A-B-C model of negative thinking 131
abstinence from alcohol 21, 211
  cognitive dysfunction 31, 67
  cue exposure 231
  pre-moderation 68, 159, 305
  short-term targets 64, 69
abstinence from drug use 69–70
  see also drug-free lifestyle goal
abstinence-violation effect 228
abstinence vs. moderation goals 66–69, 155,
    156, 159, 162, 301, 304–305
  see also goal setting
acamprosate 193, 200–201
action plan 96, 98, 100, 225, 229, 239, 249
active listening 125
addiction *see* dependence
adolescence 254, 265
  see also young people, working with
advice to cut down 80, 84, 292
advocacy 250
affirming, counselling skill 9
aggressive behaviour
  vs. assertiveness 108, 111–114
  responding to client's 171, 283
agoraphobia 275
alcohol
  assessment of current use 21–22, 82–83,
    257–258
  damage to physical health 29, 66–67
  dual diagnosis 270, 275, 276
  effect on cognitive function 31–32, 67, 278
  level of dependence 22–25
  levels of risk in drinking 81, 94

  pharmacotherapies for treating
    dependence 198–202
  treatment goals 66–69
  withdrawal from 23
alcohol-free days 159, 164
  see also drinking guidelines
alcohol-related brain injury *see* cognitive
    dysfunction; memory loss
Alcoholics Anonymous 14, 68, 130, 293
  twelve steps of 218
  see also self-help groups
ambivalence 46
  about taking medication 196–197, 280
  brief and early interventions 86
  motivational interviewing 45, 46, 47,
    53–54, 58, 304, 307
  reflecting 7–8, 9
  stages of change 32
amphetamines 22, 30, 276
  see also psychostimulants, withdrawal
    from
anger 116, 161, 226
  see also assertiveness
Antabuse *see* disulfiram
anxiety
  and substance use 222
  screening for 30, 258–259, 274–276, 278
  test-related 30
  treatment of 31, 129, 131, 144, 145, 226,
    271, 279, 282–283, 288, 308, 310
  withdrawal symptom 23
  see also post-traumatic stress disorder;
    relaxation training; social phobia

apparently irrelevant decisions 227
assertiveness 108
assertiveness training 107–119, 161, 305
  goals 107
  key concepts 108
  recommended use 107
  rights 108, 111, 119
assessment 19–43
  brain injury and cognitive impairment
    30–31
  dependence 22–25, 85–86
  estimating levels of consumption 21–22,
    83, 257–258
  involving concerned others 26, 172–173,
    181, 230, 260–261
  lifestyle and social stability 25–28
  mental health disorders 30, 258–259,
    271–278
  motivation 20–21, 256–257
  needs-based 247
  pattern of drinking or drug use 21–22,
    257–258
  physical health problems 29–30, 82–83,
    84, 85
  risk-taking behaviour 27–28, 257
  sexual abuse 27, 258–259, 275–276
  sexual problems 27, 176, 278
  social support 26, 230, 259–261
  stages of change 31–33, 85
  standardised questionnaires 20, 83, 224,
    273
  strengths-based 19, 25, 248–249
assessment tools
  Addiction Severity Index (ASI) 25
  Adolescent Relapse Coping Questionnaire
    264
  Alcohol Problems Questionnaire (APQ)
    25
  Alcohol Use Disorders Identification Test
    (AUDIT) 83–86, 92
  Brief Drinker Profile (BDP) 20, 25
  Brief Symptom Inventory (BSI) 273
  Comprehensive Drinker Profile (CDP) 20
  Drug Abuse Screening Test (DAST) 83,
    93
  General Health Questionnaire (GHQ) 273
  Kessler 10 Symptom Scale (K10) 273
  Maudsley Addiction Profile (MAP) 20
  Mini-Mental State Examination 31
  One-Week Retrospective Diary 83
  Opiate Treatment Index (OTI) 20, 25
  Severity of Alcohol Dependence
    Questionnaire (SADQ-C) 24, 56, 67,
    38–39
  Severity of Dependence Scale (SDS) 24, 43
  Severity of Opiate Dependence
    Questionnaire (SODQ) 24, 41–42
  Short form Alcohol Dependence Data
    Questionnaire (SADD) 24, 40, 67
  Situational Confidence Questionnaire 224
  Symptom Check List (SCL-90-R) 273
  Time Followback Method (TLFB) 22
attention-deficit/hyperactivity disorder
    (ADHD) 258
automatic thoughts 130, 131–133

behavioural self-management 71, 85,
    155–168, 293, 305
  drinking limits 63–64, 158–160
  goals 156
  key concepts 156–157
  rationale 157
  recommended use 155–156
beliefs 110, 132–133
  see also automatic thoughts
benzodiazepines 23, 24, 30, 83, 84, 279, 288,
    309–310
  see also pills, risk taking
binge drinking 21, 158–159, 299–300
  see also drinking guidelines
bipolar disorder 273–274
blackouts 31, 262
blood alcohol concentration (BAC)
    159–160, 167, 168
boundaries 13, 262, 276, 283–284
brainstorming 97–98
  examples of application 10, 57, 96,
    100–102, 105, 132, 174, 177, 225, 228,
    239, 265
brief and early intervention 79–94, 295,
    310–314
  for drug use 87
  goals 80
  in drug and alcohol settings 86–87, 292
  in primary health care settings 84–86,
    291–292

key concepts 80–81
recommended use 67, 79–80
screening and detection 82–83
buprenorphine 193, 202–204
burnout 246

Campral *see* acamprosate
cannabis 22, 23, 24, 28, 30, 79, 83, 258, 276, 282, 310–314
case conferences 247
case management 65, 243–252, 281, 283, 293, 294, 310–314
  assessment 247–249
  goals 244
  liaison with concerned others 250–251
  other services 224–245, 249–250
  recommended use 243–244
  the role of case manager 13, 15, 245–246
change talk 47, 53, 86
child care 4, 25, 110, 244
cocaine 22, 282
  see also psychostimulants, withdrawal from
coercion 7, 21, 27, 31, 45, 69, 253, 255, 256–257, 310–314
  see also court mandated clients; involuntary admission
cognitive therapy 71, 129–141, 195–196, 261–262, 282–283
  goals 129–130
  key concepts 130
  rationale 130
  recommended use 129
cognitive dysfunction
  abstinence as preferred option for 67
  assessment of 30–31
  treatment for clients with 129, 280, 283, 294
communication skills 112, 121–127, 179, 182, 187, 230
  goals 121
  key concepts 122
  rationale 122
  recommended use 121
compliments 10, 113, 115
conduct disorder 258, 277

confidence, building client's 3, 9, 19, 21, 54, 103, 104, 113, 130, 134, 213, 215, 222, 244, 255
  see also self-efficacy; self-esteem
confidentiality 13, 15, 16, 20, 83, 181, 247, 251, 256, 271
conflict 96, 111, 117, 124, 161, 173, 222
  helping couples to resolve 170, 172, 173, 175, 178, 215
  helping families to resolve 181, 183–184, 185–186, 187
  in group therapy 11
  see also time-out
confrontation, alternatives to 4, 7, 11, 46, 50–51, 263–264, 282
conversation skills 123–124
coordinated care 249–250, 281–282, 312–314
coping skills 26, 222, 224–226, 261–262
counselling skills 3–18, 47–48
  goals 3
  ideal therapist 4
couples therapy 171–178, 302
  assessment for 172–173
  goals 171–172
  responsibility for substance use 172, 177, 178
  supporting medication 177
  when partner presents alone 178–179
court mandated clients 82
cravings
  ways of coping with 71, 213, 226
  during therapy 105–106
  high-risk situation 26, 222
  pharmacotherapies to reduce 193, 199, 202, 204
  self-monitoring 97, 166, 195, 207, 214, 224, 235, 261
  self-talk as a trigger for 130, 131, 282
  symptom of dependence 23
criticism 112–115, 117
cue exposure 231
culture 5, 169, 254, 310–314

day diary 69, 158, 160, 166, 224, 235
decisional balance sheet (also known as decision matrix) 57, 61, 262
dependence 23
  assessment of 22–25, 83, 86, 292

dependence level as a guide to
  brief intervention 79–80, 86, 292, 295
  case management 243
  goal setting 67, 69–70, 193
  inpatient/residential care 293
  intensive treatment 85, 292, 295
  pharmacotherapies 69–70, 193
  self-help groups 211
depression 273–274
  and substance use 222, 270
  screening for 30, 258–259, 274, 278
  treatment of 129, 131, 133, 226, 271, 279,
    282–283, 288, 302–303
  withdrawal symptom 23
  see also suicide, risk of
detoxification
  dependence 22–23
  intervention 64, 85, 247, 292, 293, 296
developmental delay 258
disease model 212, 215
disulfiram 193, 201–202
domestic or family violence 10, 25–26, 64,
    169, 171, 173, 175, 179, 259, 260
drink and drug refusal skills 26, 71, 103–106,
    160, 225–226, 257, 262, 263–264, 293,
    313
  goals 103
  rationale 103–104
  recommended use 103
drink driving 27, 28, 66, 179, 257
drinking guidelines
  BAC 167, 168
  levels of risk 81, 82, 94
  limit setting 85, 158–160, 173, 292, 293
  sensible 80–81, 84, 155, 156, 158, 164, 291
drug-free lifestyle goal 69, 212
drug use
  abstinence from 69
  assessment of 22, 82–83, 257–258
  cognitive dysfunction 30–31
  dependence 22–25
  health effects 29–30, 87, 193
  see also risk-taking behaviour
DSM-IV 23–24
dual diagnosis 258–259, 269–288
  adjusted drug and alcohol counselling
    282–284
  basic guidelines 269
  goals for working with 270

influence on goal setting 64, 67
key concepts 270
management flowchart 270–271, 272
screening for 27, 28, 30, 65, 258–259,
    271–278, 293, 296
types of mental health treatment 278–282,
    288
dual relationships 14–16, 181, 245–246
dysthymia 273, 301, 301, 302–303
  see also depression

eating disorders 258, 278
ecstasy see MDMA
education 264–265
elaborating, counselling skill 8
emotions
  dealing with 108–109, 132–133, 133–135,
    161, 226
  as a high-risk situation 109, 222, 228
empathy 4, 5, 11, 19, 50, 56, 58, 87, 126, 174,
    178, 246, 282, 291
  defined as a skill 6–7, 46
  defined as a value 5
engaging your clients 3, 4–5, 19–20, 181,
    255–256, 261, 282, 283
ethical dilemmas 16
ethical practice 12–16
expectancies 255, 262–263
extended care 4–5, 12, 32, 162, 243, 250,
    237–239, 292, 293, 294
  for young people 265
  in response to lapses or relapses 230–231,
    238–239
  recommended use 237
  re-entry phase, after inpatient care 294,
    310

family meetings 179–188, 312
  goals 180
  rationale 182
  when the young person does not seek help
    188
family or concerned others
  assessment of 25–26, 172–173, 181,
    259–261, 291
  case management involving 244, 247,
    250–251

involvement in goal setting 68, 169–170,
  172, 182–183
involvement in therapy 26, 169–192, 195,
  201–202, 229, 230, 253, 260–261
own drinking or drug problems 172–173,
  179, 260, 306
self-help groups 215–216, 283
specialist therapy for 26, 169, 179
see also couples therapy; domestic or
  family violence; family meetings
fire drill analogy *see* relapse drill
foetal alcohol syndrome 29
follow-up
  after an intervention 16, 80, 84, 85, 246,
    292
  missed appointments 5, 11, 195, 283, 313
  see also extended care
'FRAMES' 58

gambling 278
gender xvii, 5, 10, 214
generalised anxiety disorder 275
goal setting 19, 21, 29, 31, 32, 63–75, 155
  for alcohol 66–69
  for opioids, other drugs 69–71
  harm reduction 65–66, 70–71
  lifestyle 64–65
  negotiating 63–64, 249, 255, 257, 282
  support of concerned others for 68,
    169–170, 172, 182–183
  see also abstinence; abstinence vs.
    moderation; drug-free lifestyle; harm
    reduction; moderation;
    pharmacotherapies
good and less good things 48–51
  see also motivational interviewing
group therapy 10–12, 95, 103, 105–106, 107,
  121, 125, 126, 129, 143, 156, 171, 221,
  225, 239
  iatrogenic effects 11, 265
  motivational interviewing 57–58
  working with young people 265
Guidelines for the Treatment of Alcohol
  Problems xiv, xv

harm reduction 54–55, 70–71, 103, 155, 193,
  214
  brief and early interventions 82, 87

clients with dual diagnosis 282
goal setting 65–66, 70–71
with young people 253, 257, 268
hepatitis 28, 29, 69, 70–71, 193, 199
high-risk situation 222
  identifying 26, 47, 86, 160, 177, 184–185,
    223, 224, 292
  planning for 87, 97, 160–161, 169–170,
    186–187, 224–227
HIV 28, 29, 56, 64, 69, 70–71, 193, 214

inhalants 257–258
injecting drug use
  assessment of 22, 28, 257
  risks associated with 28, 29–30, 31, 193
  safer practices 65–66, 70, 257
  see also harm reduction
inpatient/residential programmes xv,
  229–230, 293–294
interests and hobbies *see* pleasurable
  activities
internet, use in therapy 256, 268
intoxication during therapy 11, 21, 312
I-statements 122
  applications 112, 124, 171, 176, 179, 182,
    187
involuntary admission 279
involving concerned others 169–192
  basic guidelines 169
  key concepts 170–171
  see also couples therapy; family or
    concerned others

lapse 222
  programme response to 229–230
  reducing harm 66, 155
  use in relapse prevention 173, 177, 183,
    183–184, 186–187, 223, 229, 228–229
legal problems 27
length of treatment xvi–xvii, 291–292,
  295–296
  assertiveness skills training 107
  behavioural self-management 156
  brief interventions 79, 84, 86
  cognitive therapy 129
  pharmacotherapies 194, 198
  relaxation training 145

lifestyle treatment goals 64–65, 223, 230,
    293, 293–294
liver function 29

MATCH, Project 59, 73, 99, 106, 117,
    126–127, 135–136, 189, 215, 216, 217,
    232, 291, 297
MDMA (Ecstasy) 28, 30
mean corpuscular volume (MCV) 29
mental health services 272, 278–282, 296
memory loss 30–31
    see also blackouts; cognitive dysfunction
menu or range of strategies 32, 54, 58, 71–72
metaphors or stories, used in therapy 256,
    261
methadone maintenance 193, 194, 202,
    203–204, 211, 307–308
methamphetamine 258
    see also psychostimulants
moderation 67, 69, 80, 155, 165, 231
    see also abstinence vs. moderation goals;
        behavioural self-management; brief and
        early interventions; goal setting
Moderation Management, 211
mood disorders 273–274
    see also bipolar disorder; depression;
        dysthymia
motivational interviewing 45–62
    counselling applications of 4, 21, 32, 63,
        80, 86, 151, 152, 238, 249, 251, 282, 292,
        292–293
    counselling with pharmacotherapies
        195–197, 203
    counselling with young people 257, 259,
        262
    goals 45–46
    key concepts 46–47
    recommended use 45
    see also stages of change

naltrexone 193, 198–200, 301–302
Narcotics Anonymous 310
    twelve steps of 219
    see also self-help groups
negative thinking
    becoming aware of 131
    challenging 132–133, 139

non-assertiveness 108, 109, 110–111
    see also aggressive behaviour; passive
        under-assertion
non-residential programmes see outpatient
    programmes
non-verbal communication 104, 112, 116,
    124, 125, 176
notification 16, 20, 27, 256, 259, 272

obsessive–compulsive disorder 275
open-ended questions 8
    applications 4, 22, 47, 48–50, 123, 185,
        197, 255, 260–261, 262, 263
opioids 194
    assessment 20, 22
    brief intervention for 82–83, 87
    goal setting 69–71
    pharmacotherapies for 193–194, 202–204
    withdrawal from 23
outpatient programmes xv, 292–293
outreach 243, 245, 246
overdose 27, 31, 70, 200, 202, 203, 278, 306,
    308

panic disorder 275
partner or spouse see couples therapy;
    family or concerned others
passive under-assertion 108, 110–111,
    111–114
    see also assertiveness training
peer group 253, 255, 254, 259, 263–264, 265
    see also social networks; young people
personalising health effects 55–57
    assessment 19, 24–25, 29
    clinical applications 85, 86, 87, 157, 196,
        292, 292–293
    with results in the normal range 57
personality disorders 271, 276–277, 283
    antisocial personality disorder (ASPD)
        277
    borderline personality disorder (BPD)
        277–278
pharmacotherapies 29, 71, 156, 193–208,
    293, 296
    as a harm reduction strategy 66, 69–70,
        193, 257
    goals 194

helping your client stay on medication
    177, 195–197
for treating alcohol dependence 197–202
for treating opioid dependence 202–204
key concepts 194
monitoring the medication 195, 207
rationale 195
recommended use 193
pills, risk-taking 27, 28
pleasurable activities 27, 123, 161–162, 230,
    263, 264
polydrug use 22, 69, 257, 257–258, 282
positive interactions, promoting 170,
    175–177, 192
positive specific requests 122, 125, 175, 182
post-traumatic stress disorder 258–259,
    275–276, 309
pregnancy 29, 80, 83
primary health care settings 32, 45, 81,
    84–86, 291–292
problem-solving skills training 95–102
    applications of 135, 151, 161, 175, 178,
        185, 202, 224–225, 227, 228, 264, 283,
        293
    goals 95
    rationale 95–96
    recommended use 95
protective factors 254–255, 259–265
providing information 54–55
psychiatric medication 279–280, 288
psychoses 258, 271, 276, 283
psychostimulants, withdrawal from 23

Quality Assurance Project xiii–xiv, xv

readiness for change
    and resistance 7, 50–51
    assessment of 85, 292
    signs of 53
    treatment responses to 3, 31, 45, 47–48,
        80, 87, 253, 257, 281–282, 282
    see also stages of change
referrals, making 85–86, 245, 271–272,
    278–279
reflective listening, counselling skill 6–7
    applications 13–14, 47, 53, 56, 58, 125,
        134, 182, 196–197, 248–249, 260–261
reframing, counselling skill 8–9

in motivational interviewing 46, 51, 57, 58
involving concerned others 170–171, 174,
    182–183
relapse
    beliefs about 196, 228
    definition 222
    part of a learning process 33, 183, 221,
        229, 283
    responding to 229–230, 230–231, 237, 238,
        283, 293
    triggers for 22, 96, 108, 121, 144, 269, 270,
        276, 282
    see also relapse prevention training
relapse prevention training 221–236
    applications 4, 32, 72, 86, 103, 122, 133,
        134, 174, 193, 198, 203, 204, 261,
        263–264, 283, 292, 293, 296
    assessment for 21, 26, 47, 256, 296
    goals 221–222
    group applications 10, 12, 211, 214, 221
    harm-reduction and 66, 70, 155, 221
    key concepts 222
    recommended use 221
    with concerned others 170, 172, 173, 174,
        177–178, 180, 183, 186, 186–187, 188
    with moderation goals 160–162
    see also high-risk situation; lapse; relapse
relapse drill 177, 183, 228–229
relaxation response 144
relaxation training 143–154
    applications 10, 71, 134, 161, 197, 204, 293
    goals 143
    key concepts 144
    isometric 146–147, 150–151
    meditative 146, 149–150
    progressive muscle 146, 148–149
    rationale 144–145
    recommended use 143
requests, dealing with 116
residential programmes see inpatient/
    residential programmes
resistance 4, 7, 46–47, 53, 186
    rolling with 7–8, 50–51, 57–58, 86
    see also counselling skills; motivational
        interviewing
resources list
    assertiveness skills 117–118
    assessment 34–37
    behavioural self-management 162–163

resources list (*cont.*)
brief and early interventions 88–91
case management 251–252
cognitive therapy 135–136
communication skills training 126–127
drink and drug refusal skills 106
dual diagnosis 285–287
extended care 239
general counselling skills 16–18
goal setting 72–74
how to use this book xvii
involving concerned others 188–191
motivational interviewing 58–60
pharmacotherapies 206
problem solving skills 99
putting it all together 297–298
relapse-prevention training 231–234
relaxation training 151–152
self-help groups 216–217
working with young people 266–267
Revia *see* naltrexone
risk factors 254–255, 259–265
risk-taking behaviour
assessment of 22, 27–28, 82, 257
goal setting 64, 65, 70–71, 257
intervention for 54–55, 55–56, 79, 87, 193, 203
see also harm reduction
risk in drinking alcohol, levels of 94
see also drinking guidelines
role-play 12
assertiveness training 107, 111–112, 114, 117
communication skills training 121, 123, 124, 125
couples therapy 174, 176, 177
drink and drug refusal skills 103, 104, 105, 160, 225–226
problem solving 98–99, 100, 225
relapse prevention training 229
working with young people 256, 265
rolling with resistance, counselling skill 7–8

safe sex 71
sensible drinking guidelines 164
see also drinking guidelines

schizophrenia 276
see also psychoses
screening
for dual diagnosis 258–259, 271–278
for drug problems 83
for risky drinking 83
see also brief and early interventions
seizures, in response to withdrawal 23
self-disclosure
by counsellor to client 13, 14
by young person to family 186
self-efficacy 47, 87, 224
supporting 54, 58, 87, 248, 255, 282–283
self-esteem 7, 46, 64, 52–53, 71, 109, 129
see also confidence, building client's
self-help resources 85, 157
assertiveness 118
behavioural self-management 90–91, 142
brief interventions 90–91, 142
families 191
harm reduction 73–74, 90–91
sexual intimacy 190
young people 68
self-help groups 209–219
goals 212
internet sites 217, 287
key concepts 212–213
linking with therapy 214–215
rationale 213–214
recommended use 211–212
social support and 68, 71, 211,214, 229, 230, 283, 293
to assist family members 178, 215–216
see also Alcoholics Anonymous; Moderation Management; Narcotics Anonymous; Smart Recovery
self-monitoring
behavioural self-management 156–157, 158, 159, 160, 162, 166
high-risk situations 160, 224
use of medication 195, 207
tension 146, 153
thoughts 131, 133, 135, 140–141
urges and cravings 224, 235
self-motivational statements *see* change talk
self-reward 155, 161
self-talk 130, 131, 174, 177
see also automatic thoughts; beliefs

sex differences in alcohol guidelines 158–159, 160, 164
sexual abuse 10, 16, 27, 254–255, 258–259, 275–276, 309, 310
sexual problems 27, 176, 278
shared rewarding activities 170, 172, 175–176, 187
side effects
    helping your client to cope with 196–197, 280
    of acamprosate 200
    of methadone and buprenorphine 203
    of naltrexone 199
    of psychiatric medications 288
situational confidence questionnaires 26, 224, 233–234
sleep disturbance 23, 273, 273–274, 275, 278
Smart Recovery 211
    see also self-help groups
splitting 13–14, 284
social atom 260
    applications 26, 230, 260–261, 263
social networks
    assessment of 25–26, 230, 259–261, 291
    building 198, 211, 213–214, 214, 225–226, 230, 253, 256, 261, 263, 264, 283, 293, 313
    influence on goal setting 68
    support from other clients, 10, 12, 237–238, 239
social phobia 275, 307, 308
social pressure
    high-risk situation 222, 265
    interventions 103, 114, 160, 225–226, 263–264
    see also drink and drug refusal skills
solution focused questions 9, 184, 248–249, 282–283
sponsors, self-help groups 213, 214
stages of change 31–33, 48, 84, 87
    action 32
    contemplative 32, 45, 54, 80
    maintenance 32
    precontemplative 31–32, 45, 50–51, 54–55, 80, 85, 28, 312
    preparation 32
    relapse 32, 33
    see also readiness for change
standard drinks 80–81, 164

estimating 21–22, 83, 166
setting limits 63, 94, 156, 158, 158–159, 164, 167, 168
    see also drinking guidelines
stress management see relaxation training
substitution therapy 194
    see also pharmacotherapies, for treating opioid dependence
Subutex see buprenorphine
suicide, risk of 30, 259, 272, 274, 277, 279
    see also notification
summarising, counselling skill 9
    applications 47, 48, 50, 53, 53–54, 57, 57–58, 180, 182, 262
supervision, professional 12, 14, 16, 246, 272, 274, 277–278

tension 144, 145–146, 153
therapeutic community xv, 69, 230
thinking errors 131, 132, 137–139
    see also automatic thoughts; beliefs
time-out
    from drinking 68, 159
    from interpersonal conflict 170, 174–175, 178, 184, 187
tolerance 23, 57
twelve
    steps 212, 218, 219
    traditions 212
    see also self-help groups

validating
    client's feelings 134
    communication skill 125–126, 175, 182
vocation 25, 230, 264–265

withdrawal symptoms
    assessment 18
    goal setting 67, 292, 293, 296
    pharmacotherapies and 197, 199, 202, 202–203, 204
    to distinguish from dual diagnosis 272, 275
workplace interventions 81

X-Y-Z statements 124

young people, working with 253–268
  assessment 256–259
  basic guidelines 253

goals 253–254
key concepts 254–255
reducing risk and enhancing protection
  259–265
see also family meeting; family or
  concerned others